COMMUNICATION WORKS

THIRD EDITION

COMMUNICATION WORKS

Teri Kwal Gamble, Ph.D.
Michael Gamble, Ph.D.

McGraw-Hill Publishing Company

New York   St. Louis   San Francisco   Auckland   Bogotá   Caracas   Hamburg
Lisbon   London   Madrid   Mexico   Milan   Montreal   New Delhi   Oklahoma City   Paris
San Juan   São Paulo   Singapore   Sydney   Tokyo   Toronto

COMMUNICATION WORKS

Copyright © 1990, 1987, 1984 by McGraw-Hill, Inc. All rights reserved. Printed in the
United States of America. Except as permitted under the United States Copyright Act of
1976, no part of this publication may be reproduced or distributed in any form or by any
means, or stored in a database or retrieval system, without the prior written permission of
the publisher.

4 5 6 7 8 9 0   DOH DOH   9 5 4 3 2 1

ISBN   0-07-022783-7

Library of Congress Cataloging-in-Publication Data

Gamble, Teri Kwal.
    Communication works / Teri Kwal Gamble, Michael Gamble.—3rd ed.
      p.   cm.
    Includes bibliographical references.
    ISBN 0-07-022783-7
    1. Oral communication.   I. Gamble, Michael.   II. Title.
P95.G32   1990
302.2'242—dc20   89-13217

This book was set in Century Expanded by Monotype Composition Company.
The editors were Hilary Jackson and Jeannine Ciliotta;
the designer was Wanda Siedlecka;
the production supervisor was Birgit Garlasco.
R. R. Donnelley & Sons Company was printer and binder.

For Matthew Jon and Lindsay Michele

Contents

PART II
COMMUNICATING INTERPERSONALLY 169

7

Understanding Relationships 171

8

Person to Person: Handling Emotions and
Expressing Feelings in Relationships 189

9

Interviewing: From Both Sides of the Desk 227

PART III
COMMUNICATING IN THE SMALL GROUP 251

10

The Role of the Group in Problem Solving 253

11

Group Networks, Membership, and Leadership   275

12

Handling Group Conflict: How to Disagree without Becoming Disagreeable   297

PART IV
COMMUNICATING TO THE PUBLIC   315

13

The Speaker and the Audience   317

14

The Occasion and the Subject   337

15

Developing Your Speech: Gathering Support for Your Ideas 357

16

Designing Your Presentation: The Organizer in You   379

17

Meeting Your Public: The Speechmaker Speaks 403

18

Informative Speaking 425

19

Persuasive Speaking 443

Preface

The third edition of *Communication Works* reflects the intent of the two earlier editions. Theme and point of view are basically the same. We followed the same approach that contributed to the success of the earlier editions, and pursued the same two major goals: (1) to motivate students to want to learn about interpersonal, small-group, and public communication, and (2) to provide materials that would encourage students to internalize and practice key communication principles. Experience has shown us that after reading this book, completing the Skill Builders (exercises), and "living" the course, students develop a clear understanding of communication and handle themselves better in interpersonal, small-group, and public communication situations. As before, we strove to ensure that the text's content, exercises, readings, and probe questions would work together systematically to precipitate active participation both inside and outside of the classroom. We tested the materials incorporated in the book on a variety of student groups; the materials were used to motivate and challenge students of all ages from the traditional 18-year-old to the more mature adult returning to college.

We made a special effort to produce a book students would enjoy reading. How information is presented can affect the student's interest level, and thus we aimed to achieve clarity of language, student participation, and a graphically alive format. Because we still believe that individuals learn better if they are actively involved, we again provided a wide selection of Skill Builders—in-class and out-of-class learning experiences—designed to help students look at communication, assess its effects, and gain the insights and practice they need to improve their communication behavior. Of course, we do not expect anyone to use all the Skill Builders in a single semester. Instead, you may pick and choose from them to fit the needs of your class, as well as the time available. Each Skill Builder you do use will focus student attention on a specific aspect of communication, and research shows that students find that Skill Builders help make the study of communication active, experiential, exciting, and rewarding.

We retained several attractive pedagogical features from the previous two editions. Each chapter of *Communication Works* begins *with a preview of behavioral objectives*. The preview outlines exactly what students should be able to do after completing the chapter; in effect, objectives illuminate and specify goals and help prepare the readers for the concepts that will be introduced. Included at the end of each chapter is a *summary* of the chapter content and the relevant skills that were stressed. In addition, students are periodically expected to complete self-assessment scales designed to aid them in measuring skill mastery. To further encourage interest, *Communication Works* offers a wide array of *career-oriented examples and applications* as well as marginal queries. The marginal queries are there to arouse curiosity and prompt students to ask and/or try to answer questions.

Parts I through V offer a number of other special features.

Part I. The chapters on the essentials of communication in Part I offer a unified approach to the study of communication. Models, self-concept, perception, listening, language, and nonverbal communication are explored with respect to how they affect one's ability to relate in interpersonal, small-group, and public communication settings. *Communication Works* also examines how the media affect the development of self-image and perceptual capabilities and whether males and females see themselves in different ways.

Part II. Interpersonal communication is the topic of Part II, which begins with a chapter on understanding relationships. Chapter 8 provides a unique view of how feelings and emotions affect and are affected by relationships. This section includes a special segment on male and female display rules and a thorough discussion of assertiveness. Chapter 9 examines types of interviews, with particular emphasis on the employment interview; it also provides practical guidelines for functioning as either interviewee or interviewer. In addition, this chapter contains suggestions for in-class role-playing and gives students a number of exercises to complete in preparation for a career search.

Part III. Part III focuses on small-group communication and provides ample group experiences for in-class use. This part examines in detail the steps involved in problem solving; reviews the roles people play in groups; provides a career-oriented discussion of leadership; looks at how cooperation and competition, defensiveness and supportiveness, and conflict affect the climate of a work group; and compares how "groupthink" and "freethink" alter a group's ability to function effectively.

Part IV. The chapters on speechmaking in Part IV provide students with a straightforward format—in effect, a speechmaking map—for preparing in-class and on-the-job presentations. Exercises, speechmaking checklists, tryout sheets, and evaluation forms are included to help students as they research and develop their own speeches.

Epilogue.   The last chapter, the Epilogue, provides techniques for continuing to improve communication in interpersonal, small-group, and public settings on the job, in school, at home, or with friends. *Communication Works* is still the only text that contains suggestions and strategies for developing communication skills *after* the course has ended.

As an additional resource for instructors, we have prepared a comprehensive instructor's manual. It includes, for each chapter of the text, test questions and answers, student self-assessment scales, and additional Skill Builders. The test questions will also be provided in computerized versions for Apple and IBM.

Several changes in the new edition clarify some important issues discussed in the first two editions and add to the text's usefulness. Among the most significant additions and revisions are the following:

1. Chapter 2, "Self-Concept," contains additional information on the Pygmalion effect and a new section on whether males and females perceive themselves in different ways.

2. We have expanded on our discussion of first impressions in Chapter 3, "Perception."

3. Chapter 4, "Language and Meaning," includes new sections on meaning and culture and meaning and power.

4. Chapter 5, "Nonverbal Communication," includes additional information on facial cues and touch in particular.

5. Our chapter on listening (Chapter 6) now follows rather than precedes the discussion of nonverbal communication to reflect the fact that we listen to both verbal and nonverbal messages. In addition, we have expanded our consideration of listening deficiencies.

6. Material on deception and relationship development has been added to Chapter 7, "Understanding Relationships." We have also included a consideration of judgments of vulnerability and their impact.

7. Chapter 8, "Person to Person," contains additional information on sex roles and the expression of emotion.

8. We have enlarged the scope of Chapter 9, "Interviewing," to include a consideration of a variety of interview types.

9. Part III, "Communicating in the Small Group," contains a section on questions for decision making (Chapter 10).

10. The chapters in Part IV, "Communicating to the Public," have

been restyled to facilitate understanding, with particular attention to the chapters on speech organization and informative speaking.

11. New material reflecting new insights and emphases has been added throughout the text to enhance its meaningfulness to students.

The improvements reflect the experiences of students and the suggestions of our colleagues; they truly are the result of a team effort. Consequently, the efforts made by our editors, evaluators, and students merit special attention. Specifically, we would like to thank Roth Wilkofsky, our original acquiring editor, Hilary Jackson, our acquiring editor, Kathleen Domineg and Brian Henry, our manuscript editors, whose sensitivity to changing emphases and needs kept us on track; the book's designer, who saw to it that the visual design of the work supported the content; and the following reviewers, who willingly shared with us the insights and experiences that enabled us to create this work: Allan Broadhurst, Cape Cod Community College; Jerald Carstens, University of Wisconsin–River Falls; Sharon Condon, University of Kansas; Elizabeth Coughlin, Northern Virginia Community College; David Edgecombe, Marian College; Susan Holton, Bridgewater State College; Michael L. Lewis, Abilene Christian University; Don Wallace, Brewton-Parker College; and Samuel P. Wallace, University of Dayton.

Finally, of course, we would like to thank our children, Matthew and Lindsay; their love, patience, and communication instincts made it all worthwhile—again.

TERI KWAL GAMBLE
MICHAEL GAMBLE

AN INTRODUCTION TO THE ESSENTIALS OF COMMUNICATION

Communication: The Starting Line

Whether clear or garbled, tumultuous or silent, deliberate or fatally inadvertent, communication is the ground of meeting. . . . It is, in short, the essential human connection.

Ashley Montagu and Floyd Matson

CHAPTER PREVIEW

When you finish this chapter, you should be able to:

Define communication

Assess your own effectiveness as a communicator

List and explain the essential elements of communication

Provide examples of representative communication models

Create and explain an original model of communication

Describe the characteristics of communication

Identify and provide examples of Watzlawick's communication axioms

Explain how you can improve your own communication effectiveness

---

A college student. A corporate vice president. A teenager. An octogenarian. A man and woman in love. Parents. Children. Friends. Enemies. Decision makers. Speakers. You. All these people share at least one thing—the need to communicate. This book *is* about *you*, your need to communicate, and how communication can help you relate more effectively to others. Whether or not you possess or develop the ability to communicate effectively to others is not only essential for your success, it is essential for the success of the organization you will work for, the groups you will become part of, and the people you will come to know. In today's world, job-specific talent, technical expertise, and graduation from a prestigious school do not carry with them any guarantees for goal attainment or upward mobility. Instead, the one common factor shared by people who are able to ascend both the professional and personal ladders of success is superior communication skills. These people are promoted more rapidly, have happier marriages and relationships, and in general view their lives as being richer and more fulfilling. That is why this book can be of value to you. The topics we cover in it will help you as you go about your usual business of making friends, informing and persuading others, solving problems, falling in or out of love, and making personal and professional relationships work.

We all depend on our communication skills to help us meet our needs, attain happiness, and find personal fulfillment. From birth to death, the many types of communication are an integral part of your life. Whatever your sex, your occupation, and your goals, communication of one form or another plays a major role. The challenge, however, is to communicate as effectively as possible—to build your communication skills so that communication works for you and not against you.

Whether you are 18 or 80, female or male, married or single, employed or unemployed, it is never too late to learn skills that will enrich and improve the quality of your life. Effective interpersonal, small-group, and public communication skills are not inborn. You have to develop them, and this development is a process that will continue throughout your life. That is why this book is designed to provide you with a program for lifelong learning. If you want to improve your ability to relate to people in your social life, your job, or your academic life, now is the time to start to make communication work.

WHO IS THE COMMUNICATOR?
HOW GOOD A COMMUNICATOR ARE YOU?

Communicators are people who enter into relationships with other people. Without communication we would be unable to function. During the course of a single day we interact with others to share information and beliefs, exchange ideas and feelings, make plans, and solve problems. Sometimes this is done interpersonally, sometimes in a small group, and sometimes in a public forum. However communication occurs, it is essential in helping us initiate, develop, control, and sustain our contacts with others.

We are all *interpersonal* (one-to-one), *small-group* (one-to-a-few), and *public* (one-to-many) *communicators*. Every time we knowingly or unknowingly send a verbal or nonverbal message to a friend, lover, relative, stranger, audience, acquaintance, supervisor, employee, co-worker, or group of people, communication takes place.[1] In effect, *communication* is the deliberate or accidental transfer of meaning. Thus each facet of our lives from birth to death is dependent on and affected by our communication skills.

Communication is a very significant part of your life. From the day you are born, your ability to communicate is the largest single factor influencing the kinds of relationships you share with others and what happens to you as you make your way in the world. However, simply communicating frequently or having many, many person-to-person contacts each day does not mean that you are as effective a communicator as you can be. Although we frequently neglect to consider the problems that plague our communicative relationships, these issues are at the heart of contemporary literature and art. The following examples illustrate the importance of communication.

Communication is basic to all relationships with others throughout our lives. It is vital in social as well as educational settings. (Kathy Sloane)

Notice
STATE OF LOUISIANA
DAVID C. TREEN
GOVERNOR
Proclamation

WHEREAS, November 21, 1981, has been declared Worldwide "Hello Day"; and

WHEREAS, we are asking everyone, regardless of what language or nationality, who wants to make it a special day to say "hello" to ten people they have never spoken to before; and

WHEREAS, the purpose is to foster friendship, warmth and good relations among mankind.

NOW, THEREFORE, I, DAVID C. TREEN, Governor of the State of Louisiana, do hereby proclaim November 21, 1981 as

"HELLO DAY"

in the State of Louisiana.

(SEAL)

IN WITNESS WHEREOF, I have hereunto set my hand officially and caused to be affixed the Great Seal of the State of Louisiana, at the Capitol, in the City of Baton Rouge, on this the 24th day of February, A.D., 1981.

DAVID C. TREEN
Governor of Louisiana

ATTEST BY THE GOVERNOR:
Jim Brown
Secretary of State
ST–44–Nov. 18–1

How would a "hello day" affect your work relationships?

☐

It's a mark of real leadership to take the lead in getting to know people. . . . It's always a big person who walks up to you and offers his/her hand and says hello.

David J. Schwartz, *The Magic of Thinking Big*

☐

"Why didn't you talk to me the first time I approached you?"
"I didn't know what to say."
"You have trouble talking to people?"
"I got out of practice."

Bernard Slade, *Tribute*

☐

"I want him to know how to holler and put up an argument, I want a little guts to show. . . . I want him to know the subtle, sneaky reason why he was born a human being and not a chair."

Herb Gardner, *A Thousand Clowns*

Contacts!

Make a list of each communication contact you experience (each person with whom you communicate) during the next 24 hours. (Note: The contact need not be initiated by you.) Indicate the nature of your communication (the subject or message), the context or environment in which it occurred (classroom, office, home, etc.), the type of interaction experienced (interpersonal, small-group, or public), and the outcome (what happened as a result of the interaction). Finally—and this is important—as an assessment of your communication effectiveness, rate each communication contact on a scale of 1 to 5, with 1 representing "extremely ineffective" and 5 representing "extremely effective," and give your rationale for each rating. Now, how would you replay each contact if given the opportunity?

□

The worst sin towards our fellow creatures is not to hate them, but to be indifferent to them; that's the essence of inhumanity.

Bernard Shaw

□

"I don't talk to many people—except to say like: give me a beer, or where's the john, or what time does the feature go on, or keep your hands to yourself, buddy. You know—things like that. . . . But every once in a while I like to talk to somebody, really talk; like to get to know somebody, know all about him."

Edward Albee, *The Zoo Story*

□

I . . . have never been the same person alone that I am with people.

Philip Roth

Communication is the greatest single factor affecting a person's health and relationships to others.

Virginia Satir, The New Peoplemaking

When we lack sensitivity and fail to consider the feelings of others, our relationships suffer. We can all improve our communication skills. There is no such thing as being *too* effective at establishing, maintaining, and controlling personal and public contacts with others. In the Skill Builder on page 7, you evaluated your own proficiency during a variety of interpersonal, small-group, or public communication experiences. Now let's consider steps that you can take to improve or enhance your ability to relate to others in a variety of communication settings. First, use the accompanying

When has insensitivity caused problems for you or others on the job? At home?

scale of 0 to 100 to rate your own overall effectiveness as a communicator. Next, on the same scale rate the communication skills of your best friend, an older relative, a fellow student, a boss or instructor, or a boyfriend, girlfriend, or spouse.

Totally
ineffective   0, 10, 20, 30, 40, 50, 60, 70, 80, 90, 100   Totally
                                                                              effective

According to the evaluation you have just completed, whose communication skills do you consider better than yours? Why? Whose communication skills do you consider equal to yours? Why? Whose communication skills do you consider inferior to yours? Why? Now set a goal that indicates the extent to which you would like this course to improve your communication effectiveness rating. In order to realize this improvement, there are probably a number of skills you should work to maintain, a number of skills you should work to master, and a number of ineffective behaviors you should work to eliminate. For you to function effectively in interpersonal, small-group, or public communication, you will need to acquire certain skills and perceptions:

1. The ability to understand and communicate with *yourself*
2. The ability to know how and why you and those with whom you relate see things the way you do
3. A capacity to listen and then process the information you receive
4. A sensitivity to the "silent" messages that you and others send
5. Knowledge of how words affect you and those with whom you relate
6. An understanding of how relationships develop
7. An understanding of how feelings and emotions affect relationships
8. An understanding of how to prepare for an interview
9. The ability to handle conflict by learning how to *disagree* without being *disagreeable*
10. An understanding of the behaviors that contribute to successful group decision making
11. An understanding of how beliefs, values, and attitudes affect the formulation and reception of messages and the development of speaker-audience relationships
12. The desire to apply all these skills to each communication experience

As we continue exploring and investigating what it means to experience effective interpersonal, small-group, and public communication you will realize that the objectives just provided describe, in brief, the method and purpose of this book.

ELEMENTS OF COMMUNICATION

All communication encounters have certain common elements that together help define the communication process. The better you understand these elements, the easier it will be for you to develop your own communication abilities. Let's begin by examining the essentials of communication, those components present during every interpersonal, small-group, and public communication contact.

People

Obviously, every human communication contact of any kind involves people. Interpersonal, small-group, and public communication encounters take place between and among all types of "senders" and "receivers." *Senders* and *receivers*, respectively, are simply persons who give out and take in messages. Although it is easy to picture an interpersonal, small-group, or public communication experience as beginning with a sender and ending with a receiver, it is important to understand that during communication the sending role does not belong exclusively to one person and the receiving role to another. Instead, the sending and receiving processes are constantly being reversed; thus, when we communicate with one or more individuals, we simultaneously send and receive.

In *That's Not What I Meant*, Deborah Tannen writes, "Communication is a continuous stream in which everything is simultaneously a reaction and an instigation, an instigation and a reaction." Why do you think this is so? Provide examples based on situations you have experienced and/or observed.

If we were just senders, we would simply emit signals without ever stopping to consider whom, if anyone, we were affecting. If we were just receivers, we would be no more than receptacles for signals from others, never having an opportunity to let anyone know how we were being affected. Fortunately this is not how effective communication works. The verbal and nonverbal messages we send out are often determined in part by the verbal and nonverbal messages received from others.

SKILL BUILDER

Receiver-Source-Receiver-Source

Choose a partner and role-play one of the following situations: a quarrel between lovers, a conversation between two strangers waiting for a bus during a storm, a teacher-student controversy over a grade, a discussion between friends about the rising cost of tuition. After enacting your scene, explain how what one person did and said influenced what the other person did and said.

Messages

During every interpersonal, small-group, or public communication encounter we all send and receive both verbal and nonverbal messages. What you talk about, the words you use to express your thoughts and feelings, the sounds you make, the way you sit and gesture, your facial expressions, and perhaps even your touch or your smell all communicate information. In effect, the message is the content of a communicative act. Some messages we send are private (a kiss accompanied by an "I love you"), and others are public and directed at hundreds or thousands of people. Some messages we send purposefully ("I want you to realize . . ."), and others we send accidentally ("I had no idea you were watching . . ."). Everything a sender or receiver does or says is a potential message as long as someone is there to interpret the behavior; consequently, everything a sender or receiver does or says has potential message value. When you smile, frown, shout, whisper, or turn away, you are communicating and your communication is having some effect.

Channels

Inventory each message you receive during a 2-minute period, and note the channel through which the message came.

We send and receive messages with and through all our senses; equally, messages may be sent and received through both verbal and nonverbal modes. Thus in effect we are multichannel communicators. We receive sound messages (you hear noises from the street), sight messages (you see how someone looks), taste messages (you savor the flavor of a particular food), smell messages (you smell the cologne of a friend), and touch messages (you feel the roughness of a fabric). Which channel are you most attuned to? Why? To what extent do you rely on one or more channels while excluding or disregarding others? Effective communicators are adept channel switchers. They recognize that communication is a multichannel experience.

Noise

From a communication perspective, *noise* is anything that interferes with or distorts our ability to send or receive messages. Thus, although we are accustomed to thinking of noise as some particular sound or group of sounds, the aware communicator realizes that noise can also be created by physical discomfort, psychological makeup, intellectual ability, or the environment. Thus noise includes distractions such as a loud siren, a disturbing odor, or a hot room as well as personal factors such as prejudices, day-dreaming, or feelings of inadequacy.

The "Noise Noose"

In what ways might each of the following elements function as noise and thus interfere with effective interpersonal, small-group, or public communication?

1. A black eye
2. Chewing gum
3. A cold, damp room
4. A personal bias
5. An inappropriate word choice
6. A stomachache
7. Sunglasses
8. Shyness
9. Television
10. The habit of not smiling

Context

Communication always takes place in some *context* or setting. Sometimes the context is so natural that we hardly notice it. At other times, however, the context makes such an impression on us that it exerts considerable control over our behavior. Consider the extent to which your present environment influences the way you act toward others or determines the nature of the communication encounter you share with them. Consider the extent to which certain environments might cause you to alter or modify your posture, manner of speaking, or attire. Take into account the fact that sometimes conditions of place and time (context) affect our communications without our consciously realizing it.

Feedback

Whenever we communicate with one or more persons, we also receive information in return. The verbal and nonverbal cues that we perceive in reaction to our communication function as *feedback*. Feedback tells us how we are "coming across." A smile, a frown, a chuckle, a sarcastic remark, a muttered thought, or simply silence can cause us to change, modify, continue, or end a transaction. Feedback that encourages us to continue behaving as we are is *positive feedback*, and it enhances our behavior in progress. In contrast, *negative feedback* serves to extinguish a behavior and is a corrective

What positive and negative feedback messages have you recently given to others? What positive and negative feedback messages have you received?

Contact in Context

Compare and contrast the types of communication that would be most apt to occur in each of the following contexts. Include a description of the nature of each interaction, the probable attire of each interactant, and his or her demeanor.

1. The first few minutes of a party
2. A business meeting
3. Your home at mealtime
4. A funeral home
5. A college classroom
6. A political rally
7. A football stadium

rather than a reinforcing function. Thus, negative feedback can help to eliminate unwanted, ineffective behaviors. Note that *positive* and *negative* should not be interpreted as meaning "good" or "bad" but simply reflect the way these responses affect behavior.

Both positive and negative feedback can emanate from internal or external sources. Internal feedback is feedback you give yourself as you monitor your own behavior or performance during a transaction. External feedback is feedback from others who are involved in the communication event. To be an effective communicator, you must be sensitive to both types of feedback. You must pay attention to your own reactions and the reactions of others.

Effect

As people communicate, they are each changed in some way by the interaction, which in turn influences what follows. In other words, communication can be viewed as an exchange of mutual influences. This means that communication experience always has some *effect* on you and on the person or people with whom you are interacting. An effect can be emotional, physical, cognitive, or any combination of the three. An interpersonal, small-group, or public communication contact can elicit feelings of joy, anger, or sadness (emotional); communication can cause you to fight, argue, become apathetic, or evade an issue (physical); or it can lead to new insights, increased knowledge, the formulation or reconsideration of opinions, silence, or confusion (cognitive). The result of a communication encounter can also be any combination of the three effects just mentioned. Since effects are not always visible or immediately observable, there is obviously more to a communication reaction than meets the eye or the ear!

A LOOK AT SOME COMMUNICATION MODELS

Now that we have examined the basic components of communication— people, messages, channels, noise, context, feedback, and effect—we are ready to see how they can be joined together in a picture, or model, of the communication process. Through communication we share meaning with others by sending and receiving sometimes intentional and sometimes unintentional messages. In other words, communication includes every element that could affect two or more individuals as they knowingly or unknowingly relate to one another.

At this point we can say that communication occurs whenever one person assigns significance or meaning to the behavior of another person. And equally at this point you can ask, "So what? Will knowing this enable me to understand or establish better and more satisfying relationships with my friends, my spouse, my employer, my parents?" The answer is yes! If you understand the processes that permit people to contact and influence each other, if you understand the forces that can impede or foster the development of effective communication contacts of every kind, then you stand a better chance of experiencing them yourself. Communication models can help explain the process by which we initiate and maintain our communicative relationships with others. You will find these models useful tools in discovering how communication operates and in examining your own communication encounters.

Figure 1-1 is a model adapted from the work of communication researcher Gerald R. Miller.[2] It illustrates how a *source-encoder* (a person) sends out a message to a receiver-decoder (another person) about some *referent* (an object, act, situation, experience, or idea). The source-encoder's message is made up of at least three elements: *verbal stimuli* (words), *physical stimuli* (such as gestures, facial expressions, and movements), and *vocal stimuli* (such as rate, loudness and pitch of voice, and emphasis). The receiver-decoder who receives the message that has been consciously or unconsciously sent by the source-encoder responds to it in some way (positive or negative feedback). Both the source's message and the receiver's response are affected by the context and by each person's communication skills, attitudes, and past experiences. The message sent differs from the message received because of noise (remember our definition), even though noise is not shown as an element in this particular model.

As an illustration, let's analyze the following husband-wife dialogue with reference to the model.

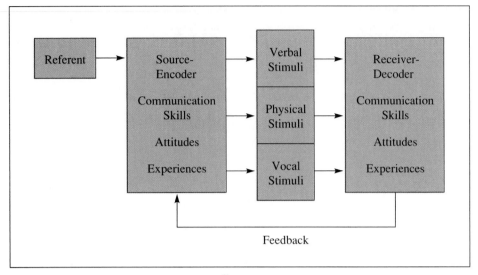

Context

FIGURE 1-1
Communication model (Gerald R. Miller)
Reprinted from Gerald R. Miller, Speech Communication: A Behavioral Approach. *© Bobbs-Merrill Educational Publishing.*

SHE: What's the matter with you? You're late again. We'll never get to the Adams' on time.

HE: I tried my best.

SHE: (Sarcastically) Sure, you tried your best. You always try your best, don't you? (Shaking her finger) I'm not going to put up with this much longer.

HE: (Raising his voice) You don't say! I happen to have been tied up at the office.

SHE: My job is every bit as demanding as yours, you know.

HE: (Lowering his voice) Okay. Okay. I know you work hard too. I don't question that. Listen, I really did get stuck in a conference. (Puts his hand on her shoulder.) Let's not blow this up. Come on. I'll tell you about it on the way to Bill and Ellen's.

What message is the wife (the initial source-encoder) sending to her husband (the receiver-decoder)? She is letting him know with her words, her voice, and her physical actions that she is upset and angry. Her husband responds in kind, using words, vocal cues, and gestures in an effort to explain his behavior. Both individuals are affected by the nature of the situation (they are late for an appointment), by their attitudes (how they feel about what is occurring), and by their past experiences.

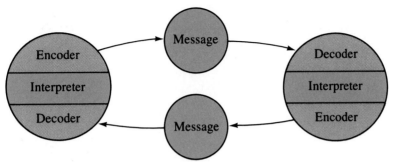

FIGURE 1-2
Communication
model (Wilbur
Schramm)
Reprinted from Wilbur Schramm, The Process and Effects of Mass Communication. © 1954 *The University of Illinois Press.*

Next, consider a model developed by communication expert Wilbur Schramm (Figure 1-2).[3] This model shows us more explicitly that human communication is a circle rather than a one-way event. Here each party to the communication process is perceived as both an encoder and a decoder. In addition, each party acts as an interpreter, understanding the messages he or she receives in a somewhat different way. This is because we are each affected by a field of experience or psychological frame of reference (a form of noise) that we carry with us wherever we go.

Consider this brief dialogue:

WIFE: Hey kids, don't bother Dad now. He's really tired. I'll play with you.
HUSBAND: Don't isolate me from my own children! You always need to have all their attention.
WIFE: I'm not trying to do that. I just know what it's like to have a really trying day and feel that I have to close my eyes to get back to myself.
HUSBAND: I sure must be wound up.
WIFE: I understand.

Here we see how one's psychological frame of reference can influence the meaning given to a message received. In addition, we come to realize that neither party to the communicative encounter functions solely as a sender or a receiver of messages. Rather, each sends and receives messages simultaneously. The wife receives the message that her husband is exhausted and sends a message that the kids should let him rest. The husband receives a message that his wife is trying to "alienate" him from the children and sends a message expressing his concern. By listening to her husband's message, the wife is able to determine how he has interpreted *her* message and is thus able to avoid a serious misunderstanding.

The model in Figure 1-3 combines the strengths of the first two models. Here communication is a circle, and the sending and receiving responsibilities are shared by the communicators. A message or messages may be sent through one or more channels, and the interaction occurs in and is affected by a definite context. Note that noise can enter the interaction

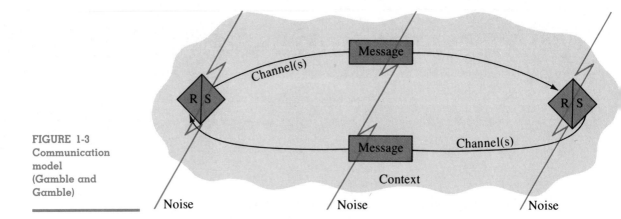

FIGURE 1-3
Communication
model
(Gamble and
Gamble)

process at any point and can affect either the sending or the receiving abilities of the interactants. Furthermore, noise can be caused by the context, can be present in the channel, or can pop up in the message itself.

Frank Dance, a noted communication theorist, has created a more abstract model to depict the dynamic nature of the communication process (see Figure 1-4).[4] Dance's spiral, or helix, represents the way communication evolves or progresses in an individual from birth to the present moment. This model also emphasizes the fact that every individual's present behavior is affected by his or her past experience and, likewise, present behavior

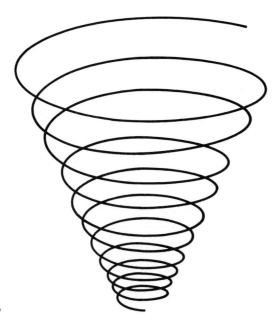

FIGURE 1-4
Communication helix
(Frank Dance)
Reprinted from Frank
E. X. Dance, Human
Communication Theory:
Original Essays. © 1967
Frank E. X. Dance.

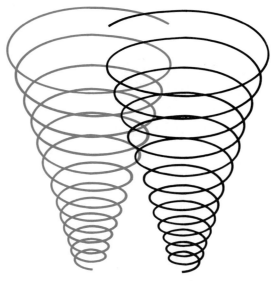

FIGURE 1-5
The meeting of
helixes

will have an impact on his or her future actions. Thus Dance's helix indicates that communication is additive or accumulative; it has no clearly observable beginning and no clearly observable end.

We can picture two communication spirals as meeting in a number of different ways, as shown by Figure 1-5. The point where the spirals touch is the point of contact; each time a contact occurs, messages are sent and received by the interactants. Some helical spirals touch each other only

SKILL BUILDER

Modeling

Draw or build something that represents your understanding of communication. You can focus on any or all components of the processes we have examined thus far. Your model can be a lifelike or an abstract representation. Be ready to present your model (representation) to the class. Specifically, be sure to offer

1. A description of what your model suggests are the essential elements of the communication process (whether pictured or inferred)
2. An explanation of what your model says about the communication process
3. A slogan that sums up your perception of the state of human communication

FIGURE 1-6
A model of
communication in
relationships

What insights into
interpersonal, small-
group, and public
communication are
provided by your
model?

once during a lifetime, whereas others crisscross or intertwine in a pattern
that indicates an enduring relationship. Furthermore, the spirals (interactants) may sometimes develop in similar ways (grow together) and sometimes in different ways (grow apart) (see Figure 1-6).

Now that we have examined a number of communication models, let us
explore the basic characteristics of communication.

CHARACTERISTICS OF COMMUNICATION: A CLOSER LOOK

Besides having specific ingredients, or elements, in common, all interpersonal, small-group, and public communication experiences also share certain
general characteristics.

Communication Is a Dynamic Process

When we call communication a *dynamic* process, we mean that all its
elements constantly interact and affect each other.[5] Since all people are
interconnected, whatever happens to one person determines in part what
happens to others.

Like the human interactors who compose them, interpersonal, small-group, and public communication relationships constantly evolve from and affect one another. Nothing about communication is static. Everything is accumulative. We communicate as long as we are alive, and thus every interaction that we engage in is part of a series of connected happenings. In other words, all our present communication experiences may be thought of as points of arrival from past encounters and as points of departure for future ones—as Dance's helixes illustrate so well.

Can you think of an interpersonal, small-group, or public communication encounter you had that affected a later encounter?

Communication Is Unrepeatable and Irreversible

Every human contact you experience is unique. It has never happened before, and it will never happen in just that way again. An old adage says that "you can never step into the same river twice," because the experience changes both you and the river forever. Similarly, a communication encounter affects and changes the interactors so that the encounter can never happen in exactly the same way again. Thus communication is both unrepeatable and irreversible. We can neither "take back" something we have said nor "erase" the effects of something we have done. And although we may be greatly influenced by our past, we can never reclaim it. In the words of the old Chinese proverb, "Even the emperor cannot buy back one single day."

Can you describe a work-related or personal situation in which the irreversible nature of communication caused difficulties for you?

FUNCTIONS OF COMMUNICATION: WHAT CAN IT DO FOR YOU?

Every communication experience serves one or more functions. For example, communication can help us discover who we are, aid us in establishing meaningful relationships, or prompt us to examine and try to change either our own attitudes and behaviors or the attitudes and behaviors of others.

Self—Other Understanding

One key function of communication is *self-other understanding*. When you get to know another person, you also get to know yourself, and when you get to know yourself, you learn how others affect you. In other words, we depend on communication to develop self-awareness. Communication theorist Thomas Hora put it this way: "To understand himself man needs to be understood by another. To be understood by another he needs to understand the other."

We need feedback from others all the time, and others are constantly in need of feedback from us. Interpersonal, small-group, and public communications offer us numerous opportunities for self-other discovery.

Through communication encounters we are able to learn why we are trusting or untrusting, whether we can make our thoughts and feelings clear, under what conditions we have the power to influence others, and whether we can effectively make decisions and resolve conflicts and problems.

Establish Meaningful Relationships

In order to build a relationship we cannot be overly concerned with ourselves but must consider the needs and wants of others. It is through effective interpersonal, small-group, and public communication contacts that our basic social needs are met.

Communication offers each of us the chance to satisfy what psychologist William Schutz calls our "needs for inclusion, control, and affection." The *need for inclusion* is our need to be with others, our need for social contact. We like to feel that others accept and value us, and we want to feel like a full partner in a relationship. The *need for control* is our need to feel that we are capable and responsible, that we are able to deal with and manage our environment. We like to feel that we can influence others. The *need for affection* is our need to express and receive love. Since communication allows each of these needs to be met, if we are able to communicate meaningfully with others, we are less likely to feel unwanted, unloved, or incapable. (For a more in-depth discussion of these needs, see Chapter 12.)

A person who is unable to communicate with others may feel isolated, unwanted, and incapable of controlling life circumstances. (Jim Anderson/Woodfin Camp & Associates)

Examine and Change Attitudes and Behaviors

During interpersonal, small-group, and public communication interactions, individuals have ample opportunities to influence each other subtly or overtly. We spend much time trying to persuade one another to think as "we" think, do what "we" do, like what "we" like. Sometimes our efforts meet with success, and sometimes they do not. In any case, our persuasion experiences afford each of us the chance to influence another so that we may try to realize our goals.

COMMUNICATION: ENCOUNTERING FIVE AXIOMS

Now that we have looked at the elements, characteristics, and functions of communication, it will be useful to turn our attention to five basic axioms of communication (see Figure 1-7). These communication principles have been described in a classic study by Paul Watzlawick, Janet Beavin, and Don Jackson.[6] Each axiom has functional implications and is essential to our understanding of the communication process.

Axiom One: You Cannot Not Communicate

It is not uncommon for individuals to believe that we communicate only because we want to communicate and that all communication is purposeful, intentional, and consciously motivated. Obviously, this is often true, but just as often we communicate without the awareness of doing so—and at times even without wanting to!

SKILL BUILDER

Can You Send an Unmessage?

1. Describe a situation in which you tried to avoid communicating with someone. In your description, identify the person you didn't want to communicate with, give your reasons, and describe the strategies you used to try to avoid communicating and the results of your efforts.

2. Describe a situation in which someone tried to avoid communicating with you. Again, identify the person involved, give your perception of her or his reasons for not wanting to relate to you, describe the strategies used to try to avoid communicating, and describe the results.

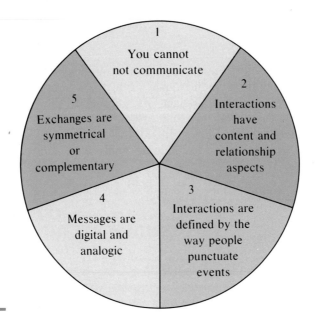

FIGURE 1-7
The five axioms of
communication

Whenever we are involved in an interactional situation, we must respond in some way. Even if we do not choose to respond verbally, even if we maintain absolute silence and attempt not to move a muscle, our lack of response *is itself* a response and therefore has message value, influences others, and hence communicates. In other words, we can never voluntarily stop behaving—because behavior has no opposite!

Watzlawick, Beavin, and Jackson have identified four basic strategies that we usually employ when trying not to communicate—when we want to avoid making contact with someone. First, we try to *reject* communication by making it clear to the other person that we are not interested in conversing. By doing this, however, not only do we not avoid communicating, but instead we probably create a strained, embarrassing, and socially uncomfortable condition. (Furthermore, as a result of this action a relationship now does exist between us and the person we want to avoid.) Second, we may decide to *accept* communication. In this strategy we operate according to the law of least effort, giving in reluctantly and agreeing to make conversation in the hope that the person will go away quickly. Third, we may attempt to *disqualify* our communication.[7] That is, we communicate in a way that invalidates our own messages or the messages sent to us by the other person. We contradict ourselves, switch subjects, or utter incomplete sentences or non sequiturs in the hope that the other person will give up. Fourth, we may simply pretend we would like to talk but that, because we are tired, nervous, sick, drunk, mourning, deaf, or otherwise incapacitated, we simply cannot communicate at the moment. In other words, we use some *symptom* as a form of communication. To repeat, no matter how hard we try, we cannot not communicate, because all behavior is communication and therefore has message value.

Axiom Two: Every Interaction Has a Content and a Relationship Dimension

The *content* of a communication is its information or data level and describes the behavior expected as a response. In contrast, the *relationship level* of a communication indicates how the exchange is to be interpreted, and it signals what one individual thinks of the other. For example, "Close the door" is a directive whose content asks the receiver to perform a certain action. However, the statement "Close the door" can be delivered in many ways—as a command, a plea, a request, a come-on, or a turnoff. Each manner of delivery says something about the relationship between the source, or sender, and the receiver. In this way we constantly give others clues about how we see ourselves in relationship to them.

Watzlawick, Beavin, and Jackson have also identified three types of responses that we use to indicate our reactions to each other. First, we can *confirm* other people's self-definitions, or self-concepts, and treat them as they believe they ought to be treated. For example, if your friend believes herself to be competent and smart and if those around her reward her by asking for advice or seeking her help, her self-concept is being confirmed.

Second, we can *reject* the other people's self-definitions by simply refusing to accept their beliefs about themselves. If your friend imagines himself to be a leader but no one else treats him as if he had leadership potential, he may be forced to revise his picture of himself.

Third, we can *disconfirm* other people's self-definitions. While confirmation says, "I accept you as you see yourself. Your self-assessment is correct," and rejection says, "I do not accept you as you see yourself. Your self-assessment is wrong," disconfirmation says simply, "You do not exist. You are a nonentity." Disconfirmation implies that we do not care enough to let other people know how we feel, and we always treat people the same way no matter what they say or do. In other words, we do not offer individuals *any clues whatever* to indicate that we believe they are or are not performing well. In effect, we totally ignore these people. The psychologist William James noted that consistent disconfirmation is perhaps the cruelest psychological punishment that a human being can experience: "No more fiendish punishment could be devised . . . than that we should be turned loose in a society and remain absolutely unnoticed."

SKILL BUILDER

Confirm, Reject, Disconfirm

1. Working with a partner, improvise three scenes: (a) in one a person confirms another person's self-image, (b) in one a person rejects the other person's self-image, and (c) in one a person disconfirms the other person's self-image. Note the verbal and nonverbal behaviors that aid in confirming, rejecting, or disconfirming the person.
2. Describe a communication experience during which you were (a) confirmed, (b) rejected, and (c) disconfirmed by another person. How did you respond in each?
3. Describe a communication experience during which you (a) confirmed, (b) rejected, and (c) disconfirmed another person. How did he or she respond in each situation?

Axiom Three: Every Interaction Is Defined by How the Interactants Punctuate Events

Think of a recent argument you had that you believe was started by the other person. Describe the situation, and identify the person's stimulus behavior (the starting point). Now, put yourself in the other person's place. How might he or she have answered this same question?

Even though we understand that communication is continuous, we often act as if there were an identifiable starting point or a traceable cause for a particular elicited response. In many communication interactions it is extremely difficult to determine what is stimulus and what is response. For instance, it is quite as feasible for a father to believe he reads or daydreams to escape his child's screaming as it is for the child to believe she screams because her father is reading or daydreaming and won't play with her. The father sees behavior as progressing from screaming to retreating, whereas the child sees it as progressing from retreating to screaming. In other words, what is stimulus for one is response for the other. We all divide up, or punctuate, a particular experience somewhat differently because each of us "sees" it differently. Thus, whenever you suggest that a certain communication began because of a particular stimulus, you are forgetting that communication has no clearly distinguishable starting point or endpoint. Try to remember that communication is circular—a continuous, ongoing series of events.

Axiom Four: Messages Are Digital and Analogic

When we talk to others we send out two kinds of messages: (1) discrete, digital, verbal symbols (words) and (2) continuous, analogic, nonverbal cues.

According to Watzlawick, Beavin, and Jackson, the content of a message is more likely to be communicated through the digital system, whereas the relationship level of the message is more likely to be carried through the analogic system. Although words are under our control and for the most part are uttered intentionally, many of the nonverbal cues that we send are not. Thus Watzlawick, Beavin, and Jackson write that "it is easy to profess something verbally, but difficult to carry a lie into the realm of the analogic." This means that while you may lie with words, the nonverbal signals you emit are likely to give you away.

Axiom Five: Communication Exchanges Are Either Symmetrical or Complementary

The terms *symmetrical* and *complementary* do not refer to good (normal) or bad (abnormal) communication exchanges but simply represent the two basic categories into which all communication interactions are divided. Each type of interaction serves important functions, and both will be present in a healthy relationship.

During a communication encounter, if the behavior of one person is mirrored by the behavior of the other person, Watzlawick, Beavin, and Jackson would say that a *symmetrical interaction* has occurred. Thus, if you act in a dominating fashion and the person you are relating to acts the same way, or if you act happy and the other person also acts happy, or if you express anger and the other person likewise expresses anger, for the moment the two of you share a symmetrical relationship.

In contrast, if the behavior of one interactant precipitates a different behavior in the other, Watzlawick, Beavin, and Jackson would say that a *complementary interaction* exists. In a complementary relationship you and your partner engage in opposite behaviors, with your behavior serving to elicit the other person's behavior or vice versa. Thus, if you behave in an outgoing manner, your partner might adopt a quiet mood; if you are aggressive, he or she might become submissive; if you become the "leader," your partner might become the "follower."

Neither the symmetrical nor the complementary relationship is trouble-free. Parties to a symmetrical relationship are apt to experience what is termed *symmetrical escalation*. Since they believe they are "equal," each also believes she or he has a right to assert control. When this happens, the interactants may feel compelled to engage in a battle to show how "equal" they really are. Since it is not uncommon for individuals sharing a symmetrical relationship to find themselves in a status struggle with each other, the main danger of this type of interaction is a runaway sense of competitiveness.

In contrast, the problem that surfaces in many complementary relationships is *rigid complementarity*. This occurs when one party to an

How could the attitude expressed here affect the employer-employee relationship?

"Treat people as equals and the first thing you know they believe they are."

Drawing by Mulligan; © 1982 The New Yorker Magazine, Inc.

interaction begins to feel that control is automatically his or hers and as a result the relationship becomes rigid or fixed. Control no longer alternates between the interactants, and as a result both persons lose a degree of freedom in choosing how they will behave. Thus a teacher who never pictures herself as a learner, a father who cannot perceive that his child has reached adulthood, and a leader who can never permit herself to act as a follower have all become locked into self-perpetuating, unrealistic, unchanging, and unhealthy patterns of behavior.

In this excerpt from "When Did I Become the Mother and the Mother Become the Child?" Erma Bombeck describes the switch in power that can occur in the parent-child relationship.

When will the baby catch up with the mother?
When indeed.
Does it begin one night when you are asleep and your mother is having a restless night and you go into her room and tuck the blanket around her bare arms?

Does it appear one afternoon when, in a moment of irritation, you snap, "How can I give you a home permanent if you won't sit still? If you don't care how you look, I do!" (My God, is that an echo?)

Or did it come the rainy afternoon when you were driving home from the store and you slammed on your brakes and your arms sprang protectively between her and the windshield and your eyes met with a knowing, sad look?

The transition comes slowly, as it began between her and her mother. The changing of power. The transferring of responsibility. The passing down of duty. Suddenly you are spewing out the familiar phrases learned at the knee of your mother.

How do you imagine you would feel if some years from now, while riding with your daughter in her car, she slammed on the brakes and at the same time instinctively placed her arm between the windshield and your body? Do you think you would be ready for the shift in power? Or would you say, "My God! So soon."

The five axioms of communication that we have just explained should provide you with the background knowledge you will need as you prepare to focus on increasing the effectiveness of your communication experiences.

HOW TO IMPROVE YOUR EFFECTIVENESS AS A COMMUNICATOR: ARE YOU READY?

The major purpose of this book is to help you gain an understanding of communication and to assist you in developing your interpersonal, small-group, and public communication skills. To achieve these goals you will need to accomplish the following tasks.

Understand How Each of the Topics in This Book Influences Your Own Communication Effectiveness

Each section of this book contains information that clarifies and illuminates the communication experience. The chapters in Part I explore how self-concept, perception, listening, language, and nonverbal communication all affect our ability to relate to others in a variety of settings. In Part II we focus more directly on communicating interpersonally. We examine the nature of relationships and explore a very special type of interpersonal communication, the interview. The chapters in Part III investigate the role of the group in problem solving; networks, group membership, leadership, and intragroup-intergroup conflict are also examined. In Part IV you will meet both the speaker and the audience, and you will have an opportunity to examine how best to prepare for the speechmaker's challenge. Finally, in the Epilogue we have created a learning "package" for you to use and carry with you all through life.

Become Actively Involved in the Study of Communication

The materials contained in this book will benefit you only if you make a commitment to try out and experience the principles discussed. Each Chapter Preview contains targets (behavioral objectives) that specify what you should have learned after completing your study of the chapter materials. Use these previews to clarify your own communication objectives as you make your way through the book. Next, a plethora of exercises (Skill Builders), probe questions, and assessment scales are included to help you become aware of what you must know and do to become a more effective communicator. They will give you an opportunity to apply your new knowledge to actual communication experiences. If you use them as directed, you will increase your opportunities to grow because you will be actively testing your own learning and diagnosing your own needs for self-improvement. Growth takes time, and lasting change does not just happen. Mistakes should be viewed as occasions for learning, and new learnings must be continually practiced. Only in this way can ineffective patterns of behavior be "unfrozen" and new, effective patterns made a part of your communication repertoire.

Believe in Yourself

Above all else, you must believe that you are worth the time and effort needed to develop your communication skills. You must also believe that developing these skills will immeasurably improve the quality of your life. We think you are worth it. And we know communication works! Do you?

SUMMARY

Communication is the deliberate or accidental transference of meaning. Human communication takes place interpersonally (one-to-one), in small groups, and in public forums. The essential elements of communication are people, messages, channels, noise, a context, feedback, and some effect or result. Communication theorists have devised a number of models to show how these elements are related and interact.

All communication acts share two general characteristics: (1) Since communication is a dynamic process, each interaction is part of a series of interconnected communication events. (2) Every communication experience is unique, unrepeatable, and irreversible. Communication has a number of essential functions in our lives. It promotes self-other understanding, helps us establish meaningful relationships, and enables us to examine and attempt to change the attitudes and behavior of others.

Researchers Watzlawick, Beavin, and Jackson have developed five basic axioms which further clarify the communication process: (1) You cannot not communicate. (2) Every interaction has both a content and a relationship dimension. (3) Every interaction is defined by the way the interactants punctuate events. (4) Messages are digital and analogic (verbal and nonverbal). (5) Communication exchanges are either symmetrical or complementary.

Developing communication skills is a lifelong process. This book explains the strategies you can use to assess your own communication abilities, improve the effectiveness of your communication relationships, and enhance the quality of your life.

SUGGESTIONS FOR FURTHER READING

Dance, Frank E. X. "Toward a Theory of Human Communication." In *Human Communication Theory: Original Essays*, edited by Frank E. X. Dance. New York: Holt, Rinehart and Winston, 1967. Dance's helical spiral is described.

Gallwey, Timothy W. *Inner Tennis*. New York: Random House, 1976. This book goes far beyond tennis; a self-mastery guide.

Holtzman, Paul D., and Donald Ecroyd. *Communication Concepts and Models*. Skokie, Ill.: National Textbook Company, 1976. This work offers an understandable and thorough treatment of communication models.

Knapp, Mark L. *Social Intercourse: From Greeting to Goodbye*. This work offers a theoretical overview of dimensions of interpersonal communication.

Miller, Gerald R. *Speech Communication: A Behavioral Approach*. Indianapolis: Bobbs-Merrill, 1966. Discusses the Miller model of communication.

Miller, Gerald, and Mark Steinberg. *Between People*. Chicago: Science Research Associates, 1975. Examines the forces that affect person-to-person communication.

Schramm, Wilbur. "How Communication Works." In *The Process and Effects of Mass Communication*, edited by Wilbur Schramm. Urbana, Ill.: University of Illinois Press, 1954. Contains a description of Schramm's model of communication.

Watzlawick, Paul H., Janet Beavin, and Don D. Jackson. *Pragmatics of Human Communication: A Study of Interactional Patterns, Pathologies and Paradoxes*. New York: Norton, 1967. This comprehensive work offers an analysis of the systemic nature of communication and the pathologies that can hamper healthy relationships.

NOTES

1. See, for example, E. T. Klemmer and F. W. Snyder, "Measurement of Time Spent Communicating," *Journal of Communication*, Vol. 22 (1972), pp. 142–158. These authors reported that people spend 50 to 80 percent of their workdays communicating.

2. Gerald R. Miller, *Speech Communication: A Behavioral Approach* (Indianapolis: Bobbs-Merrill, 1966), pp. 72–74.

3. Wilbur Schramm, "How Communication Works," in *The Process and Effects of Mass Communication*, edited by Wilbur Schramm (Urbana, Ill.: University of Illinois Press, 1954), pp. 3–10.

4. Frank E. X. Dance, "Toward a Theory of Human Communication," in *Human Communication Theory: Original Essays*, edited by Frank E. X. Dance (New York: Holt, Rinehart and Winston, 1967).

5. See, for example, Alan E. Ivey and James C. Hurse, "Communication as Adaptation," *Journal of Com-*

munication, Vol. 21 (1971), pp. 199–207. Ivey and Hurse reaffirm that communication is adaptive like biological evolution—not an end in itself, but a process.

6. Paul H. Watzlawick, Janet Beavin, and Don D. Jackson, *Pragmatics of Human Communication: A Study of Interaction Patterns, Pathologies and Paradoxes* (New York: Norton, 1967).

7. For additional information on disqualification, see Janet Beavin Bavelas, "Situations That Lead to Disqualification," *Human Communication Research*, Vol. 9 (1983), pp. 130–145.

2

Self-Concept: Who Are You and How Do You Know?

Even the simplest clown manages by gesture and incident to explore
the mythology of the self. . . . In him, in his ludicrous contradictions
of dignity and embarrassment, of pomp and rags, of assurance and
collapse, of sentiment and sadness, of innocence and guile, we
learn to see ourselves.

Samuel Howard Miller

CHAPTER PREVIEW

When you finish this chapter, you should be able to:

Define *self-concept*, describe the part role-taking plays in the development of self-concept, and identify dimensions of yourself that you had not recognized before

Identify how popular culture helps shape your self-concept

Define *self-fulfilling prophecy* and explain how a self-fulfilling prophecy can influence behavior

Identify factors that contribute to the development of an unrealistic self-concept

Compare and contrast your own assets and liabilities

Identify the purposes and functions of the Johari Window and self-disclosure and provide examples of the types of information contained in the open, blind, hidden, and unknown areas of the self

Describe how you see yourself and how you think others see you

T he lights in the circus arena suddenly are dimmed. Accompanied by a drumroll and fanfare, an incredibly small car drives into the center ring. A spotlight highlights the red, blue, green, yellow, and orange colors that decorate the tiny automobile. Cymbals crash as the car's door opens and a small clown with a bright, happy face tumbles out. As the elflike figure gets up only to stumble again and again, a larger clown suddenly jumps out of the car. This clown wears a mask of anger and fury and begins to chase the "vulnerable" little clown around the center ring. Suddenly, a third clown timidly and nervously crawls out of the car. Following this clown is a fourth, large, rotund, smiling clown, who rolls about the ring like a Slinky. These antics continue until approximately 15 to 20 different clowns have emerged from the single car. Each clown has a distinctive "face," or mask, that depicts a particular attitude or emotion. One looks perpetually happy; another looks perpetually sad; one looks chronically silly; another looks eternally angry; one looks jealous; another appears to be in love; one has eyes that dance; another has a nose that trails on the floor. Finally, the empty clown car backfires a few times and begins to chase the clowns out of the arena as the cheering crowd roars with laughter.

MEET YOUR SELF-CONCEPT: A DEFINITION

Spectators in the circus arena see what they would call "a clown," but how many clowns do the spectators really see? In other words, how many faces or masks are associated with the word *clown?* One? Two? Ten? An infinite number? Student clowns at the Ringling Brothers Clown College in Florida pride themselves on their ability to create original clown masks. The number of clown faces that can be designed is infinite. Just as each person who creates such a face is unique, so each mask created is unique. Thus, the question we must consider is, Which face really represents the concept of *clown?* The answer must be that *all* the faces are representations of the word *clown,* for each expresses a different facet, or view, of what a clown is.

Let us consider one other aspect of the clown before we move on. Who are these people who live behind clown masks or faces? What kind of people are they? Presumably a person who performs as a clown takes on that role and behaves in a specified, planned, and rehearsed manner only while the circus performance is in progress. And those of us in the audience assume that a role is being played by each clown-person—that this is not the real person.[1]

Do you ever wear a special face, or "mask," in your own life? Obviously you do not normally walk around wearing a painted-on clown face any more than the circus performers do, yet you may find that you in fact wear a variety of masks during the course of a single day. For example, does your face look the same when you are happy as it does when you are sad? How do you know? And how does your face look when you are really furious?

Actually, we wear many different masks throughout our lives. We wear happy and sad masks, peaceful and angry masks, bored and excited masks, sorry and vengeful masks. Besides the masks we wear to display our innumerable feelings, we also wear those which are associated with the roles we play—student, brother, spouse, sister, boss, or whatever. As the psychologist William James observed: "A man has as many social selves as there are individuals who recognize him and carry an image of him in their mind." We wear so many faces that the question ultimately becomes, Who am I, really?

No matter what your age or position, it is important that you spend some time considering who you are and what you intend to do with the rest of your life. It is important that you use each available opportunity to find out about yourself. In this chapter you will be given the chance to explore some aspects of the question, Who am I? Your answer will be extremely significant, since who you think you are to a large extent

What types of masks might people in business wear?

Part of knowing who we are is knowing we are not someone else.

Arthur Miller, Incident at Vichy

"Might I point out, sir, that that one goes particularly well with your tie?"

Drawing by Gahan Wilson; © 1982 The New Yorker Magazine, Inc.

determines what you choose to do, how you choose to act, whom you choose to communicate with, and even whether you choose to communicate at all. Unquestionably, you are the center of your communication system. But who are you, anyway? Jolene Tennis, a muscular dystrophy victim, movingly described her unique sense of self:

> My wheelchair is my life. My wheelchair is my legs, and it gets me wherever I want to go. I have climbed Mt. Ranier, and I have gone across swinging foot bridges, and I have crossed streams. My wheelchair to me is me. It is part of me. I can tell when somebody touches it with two fingers because it is part of my skin. I know I live in an able-bodied world, but I don't think of myself as disabled. I've never been any other way than the way I am now. I've always been in a wheelchair, and that's normal. When David and I decided to get married, I'm not even sure David realized people in wheelchairs got married. I showed David that there were a lot of things to do other than physical things, and that you could have fun. Freedom is being able to do what you have to do when you have to do it. I moved away from home when I was two months short of eighteen. I couldn't live at home anymore. I wasn't being allowed to change there, I guess. Being alive is changing. Being able to change. That's what being alive is to me.
>
> I love the sound of water. I can move freely when I am in the water. I can move my body from one place to another and I don't have anything doing it for me. Not anybody or any wheelchair. I don't think about the passage of time any more. I'm happy now.

From a videotaped speech by Jolene Tennis, aired on a Muscular Dystrophy Telethon.

A positive sense of self can help an individual lead a full life and overcome physical disabilities. (Michael Weibrot & Family)

If someone were to ask you separately 10 times "Who are you?" and if each time you had to supply a different answer, what types of responses do you think you would offer? To what extent could your responses be grouped into categories? For example, would you see yourself in reference to your feelings (happy, sad)? Your attitudes (optimistic, insecure)? Your physical attributes (tall, short)? Your intellectual attributes (capable, slow)? Your occupation (student, salesperson)? Your role relationships with others (brother, father, sister, mother, son, boss, employee)? Chances are, your responses would fall into these groupings. But more important, what would your answers tell you about your self-concept?

Your *self-concept* is everything that you think and feel about yourself. It is the entire collection of attitudes and beliefs you hold about who and what you are. This theory or picture you have of yourself is fairly stable and difficult to change. For example, have you ever tried to alter your parents' or your friends' opinions about *them*selves? Did you have much luck? Our opinions about ourselves grow more and more resistant to change as we become older and "wiser."

How did your self-concept develop? To a large extent it is shaped by your environment and by those around you, including your parents, relatives, teachers, supervisors, friends, and co-workers. If people who are important to you have "sent you messages" that have made you feel accepted, valued, worthwhile, lovable, and significant, you have probably developed a *positive self-concept*. On the other hand, if those who are important to you have made you feel left out, small, worthless, unloved, or insignificant, you have probably developed a *negative self-concept*. It is not difficult to see how people we value influence the picture we have of ourselves and help determine the ways we behave. The nineteenth-century poet Walt Whitman recognized this.

> There was a child went forth every day,
> And the first object he look'd upon, that object he became,
> And that object became part of him for the day or a certain part of the day,
> Or for many years or stretching cycles of years.

Self-concept, besides being your own theory of who and what you are, is the mental *picture* you have of yourself. This mental image is easily translated into the faces, or masks, that you wear, the roles you play, and the ways you behave. To see this illustrated graphically, examine the pictures on page 36. The top panel presents the self-image of a man who thinks of himself as a lowly cockroach. He developed this image because he felt that he was performing a dull job in an impersonal work environment. However, when invited to attend a conference, he alters this perception and as a result changes his demeanor and adopts an "executive appearance." The middle panel shows how our man viewed various colleagues who attended the conference. One is as proud as a peacock, and another is as

How do your employer and friends picture you?

According to Virginia Satir in *The New Peoplemaking*:

"*Every person has a feeling of worth, positive or negative;* the question is, Which is it?

Every person communicates; the question is, How, and what happens as a result?

Every person follows rules; the question is, What kind, and how well do they work for her, or him?

Every person is linked to society; the question is, In what way, and what are the results?"

Now, how do you answer each of these questions for you? Your parents? Your friends? The person(s) you work for?

Adapted from *Psychology Today*, August 1972, p. 5.

close-mouthed as a clam; one is ill-tempered like a ram; one is loyal like a dog; one is unforgetful like an elephant; one is a dangerous wolf; and still another is a stubborn mule. Finally, in the bottom panel we see what happens to our man once the meeting is over: He retreats into "roachhood" once more. He reemerges at lunch to play the "knight in shining armor" for his secretary. However, once lunch is finished, he goes back to what he perceives as mindless busywork. To put it politely, he views himself as a donkey. Yet our man has not completely submerged his "better" self. When he is called on to make a decision, he once again changes his self-image and this time pictures himself as a "captain of industry."

We know that if you feel you have little worth, you probably expect to be taken advantage of, stepped on, or otherwise demeaned by others. When you expect the worst, you usually get the worst. Similarly, if you feel you have significant worth, you probably expect to be treated fairly, supported, and otherwise held in esteem by others. When you expect to succeed, you usually find success.

We can conclude that the nature of the self at any given moment is a composite of all the factors that interact in a particular environment. Thus, how you look at yourself is affected by how you look at people, how people actually look at you, and how *you* imagine or perceive that people look at you. In effect, we might say that self-concept is derived from experience and projected into future behavior.

WILL THE REAL SELF-ESTEEM STAND UP?

By Anne Taylor Fleming

Los Angeles, Nov. 8—The California Task Force to Promote Self-Esteem and Personal and Social Responsibility: it seemed a parody, an idea born in a hot tub. Even many natives laughed when the task force was created a little over two years ago, though the laughter was checked a little by the realization that they were footing the bill—$735,000—for a three-year exploration into the state of self-esteem of the state's citizenry.

Nonnative Californians were even more amused, most notably the cartoonist Gary Trudeau, who lampooned the new task force in his "Doonesbury" comic strip. But eager applicants were undaunted; more than 300 applied to fill 21 appointive slots on the 25-member commission, the largest number ever to apply to any state task force or commission. The chosen—all unpaid volunteers—include a Christian-school principal from Redding at the top of the state and a turban-wearing Sikh yoga teacher from Del Mar near the bottom. Four more members were named by state officials.

First the members had to agree on a definition of self-esteem. That took more than a year. After considerable discussion, they settled on this: "Appreciating my own worth and importance, and having the character to be accountable for myself and to act responsibly toward others."

Then they had to go about finding out who in the state had self-esteem and why, who didn't and why. Over the past months they have met in daylong forums around the state and listened to everybody: street-gang members and single mothers, counselors and community leaders. They were seeking to find out, as their mandate says, "whether healthy self-esteem relates to the development of personal responsibility and social problems (like crime and alcoholism and violence) and how healthy self-esteem is nurtured, harmed or reduced, and rehabilitated."

So popular has this search become that there are now mini-self-esteem task forces in 42 California counties, including Los Angeles County, which puts out its own chatty little newsletter, The Self-Esteemer. This is clearly an idea whose time has come in California. . . .

Underneath the snickering generated by the task force and the buoyant reach of its own stated goals lies the garrulously tortured soul of its creator: Assemblyman John Vasconcellos of San Jose. There would be no Self-Esteem Task Force without him. It is his baby, born of his own struggle to find self-esteem. . . .

. . . And he is still often in pain, he said, still fighting his own lack of self-esteem, which he defines as "the felt appreciation of my own innate, instinctual being."

That appreciation can be elusive. "I'm not all healed yet," he said in an interview in San Francisco, a rueful smile momentarily

lighting up his face. "I wish I were. It started so far back. I'm much more comfortable with my body and my own being, but I'm still a little self-conscious and shy. I came from a very traditional Catholic family. My father was very buttoned down, locked away. I did everything right. I got good grades, ran for class president. I've been running for office since the eighth grade, when I lost by one vote—my own. I just didn't think I should vote for myself."

John Vasconcellos sees the task force as the ultimate self-help program. "I know some people are still frightened by this," he said, "so they deride it as New Age. But after all, 60 to 80 million Americans have already been in some kind of counseling."

The other point of the task force, he emphasized, is to save money: "I've seen the cost of prisons—$17,000 a year to lock somebody up—and dropouts and drugs. We're doing too little too late. We have to get at the root cause; self-esteem informs everything. . . .

New York Times, November 9, 1988.

ROLE TAKING AND SELF-EXPLORATION: CATEGORIZING THE SELF

We vary the masks we wear and the roles we perform a number of times each day. The language we use, the attitudes we display, and the appearances we present constantly change. In effect, we become different selves as we move from one set of conditions to another. The more we attempt to be ourselves, the more selves we find there are to be. We should recognize that conditions and circumstances affect the nature of the self. In every situation, how we see ourselves and how we think about ourselves in relation to others directs and modifies our behavior. Our self-concept and

A Day in My Life

1. List the names of all the people with whom you interacted on a particular day this week. For each, identify the environment in which you communicated.

2. Next, choose an animal, object, or color to represent your image of yourself during each interaction; also select an animal, object, or color to represent your image of the individual with whom you spoke.

3. Finally, graph your perceptions on a chart like the following by entering each of your responses in an appropriate box. (For example, you might see yourself as a puppy, but person 1 sees you as a gorilla.)

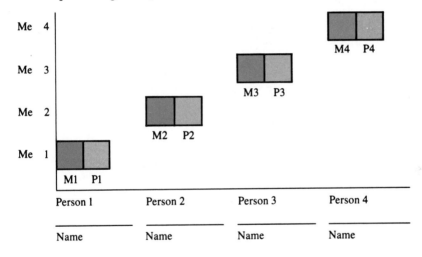

4. Demonstrate your understanding by responding to these questions: What does your chart tell you about the nature of your self-image? To what extent does your view of yourself change as you move from person to person? What factors can you point to in yourself, the individual with whom you were interacting, or the environment that help account for the changes?

demeanor are affected by our perceptions of others and how we think they will respond to us. Thus the roles we choose to play are in part a result of the values held by the members of our society.

Clues to self-understanding come to you continually as you interact with others and your environment. And if you are to understand yourself

Are you who you think you are, who someone else thinks you are, or who you think someone else thinks you are? Why?

well, you need to be open to information that other people give you about yourself. Just as we tend to categorize ourselves and others, so others also tend to categorize themselves and us. For better or worse, the categorization process is a basic part of interpersonal communication. We classify people according to their roles, their status and material possessions, their personality traits, their physical and vocal qualities, and their skills and accomplishments. Which of these categories are most important to you? Which do you think are most important to the people who are significant in your life? How do others help shape your image of yourself? How do they serve to enhance or belittle your own sense of self?

POPULAR CULTURE AND YOU: THROUGH THE ELECTRONIC LOOKING GLASS

Thus far we have established that your self-image is composed of information and feelings drawn from past experiences and from your interactions with others. There are at least two other important sources that affect your opinion of who you are: television and film. We are all influenced by television and film characters and their life styles to a greater extent than we may realize. Subtly but effectively, these two media shape our views of ourselves and our relationship to our world. The following poem, although geared to the fantasies of childhood, nevertheless reflects a major concern of our culture.

JIMMY JET AND HIS TV SET

Shel Silverstein

I'll tell you the story of Jimmy Jet—
And you know what I tell you is true.
He loved to watch his TV set
Almost as much as you.

He watched all day, he watched all night
Till he grew pale and lean,
From "The Early Show" to "The Late Late Show"
And all the shows between.

He watched till his eyes were frozen wide,
And his bottom grew into his chair.
And his chin turned into a tuning dial,
And antennae grew out of his hair.

And his brains turned into TV tubes,
And his face to a TV screen.

Television and film have a profound effect on the way we perceive ourselves. For many children, the TV set acts like a looking glass. They see themselves as the characters on the screen. (Susan Woog Wagner/Photo Researchers)

And two knobs saying "VERT." and "HORIZ."
Grew where his ears had been.

And he grew a plug that looked like a tail
So we plugged in Little Jim.
And now instead of him watching TV
We all sit around and watch him.

Let's consider some actual ways that media affect the picture you have of yourself. Through the media we come face to face with standards of living few of us can emulate or expect to achieve. Thus, our evaluations of ourselves as providers—or even whether we view ourselves as successful—can be seriously colored by what we see. Television and film can also affect the ways in which parents and children perceive themselves and each other. After all, both parents and children are exposed to a steady diet of media counterparts who are either so "perfect" that even their mistakes become the raw material of a closer relationship or so absurd that their foibles can only constitute charming comedy. Finally, the visual media can fill a need to have a bigger, better, smarter, prettier, stronger personal image. When we were younger, it was easy and fun to "try on" television and film images. For example, you could put on a cape or mask and become Batman, Wonder Woman, Spiderman, Flash Gordon, Superman, or the Bionic Woman. As we mature, however, the emulation process becomes a bit more subtle. Today, we attempt to become like popular idols or heroes

If you could trade places with any television or film star or character, who would you be? What does this person, real or fictional, "do" for you? Do you have a more positive image of this chosen character than you have of yourself? Why? Would you like to be more like the media image or would you like the image to be more like you?

by imitating the fashion trends they set, by adopting their speech mannerisms, and by copying their movements and gestures. Thus, we communicate part of the picture we have, or would like to have, of ourselves through the way we dress, move, speak, and arrange ourselves. When you put on a certain outfit, comb your hair in a new style, walk or speak in a particular way, or choose to wear a certain artifact, you are telling other people something about who you think you are, who you would like to resemble, and how you would like to be treated.

Programs and films offered by the media can support us or deflate us. They can cause us to feel good, adequate, or inferior.

THE SELF-FULFILLING PROPHECY: MEETING POSITIVE AND NEGATIVE PYGMALIONS

Take some time to consider the following excerpt from *The People Yes* by the poet Carl Sandburg:

> Drove up a newcomer in a covered wagon. "What kind of folks live around here?" "Well, stranger, what kind of folks was there in the country you come from?" "Well, they was mostly a lowdown, lying, gossiping, backbiting lot of people." "Well, I guess, stranger, that's about the kind of folks you'll find around here." And the dusty grey stranger had just about blended into the dusty grey cottonwoods in a clump on the horizon when another newcomer drove up. "What kind of folks live around here?" "Well, stranger, what kind of folks was there in the country you come from?" "Well, they was mostly a decent, hardworking, law abiding, friendly lot of people." "Well, I guess stranger, that's about the kind of people you'll find around here." And the second wagon moved off and blended with the dusty grey. . . .

In the preceding passage the speaker understands the significance of a self-fulfilling prophecy. A *self-fulfilling prophecy* occurs when your expectations of an event help create the very conditions that will permit that event to happen. In other words, your predictions can cause you and others to behave in ways that will increase the likelihood of an unlikely occurrence. For example, have you ever had to perform a task that others told you would be dull and uninteresting? Was it? Why? If it was dull, did it occur to you that you might have acted in a way that caused the prediction to come true?

Perhaps the most widely known example of the self-fulfilling prophecy is the "Pygmalion effect." The term comes to us from a Greek myth in which Pygmalion, a sculptor, falls in love with a beautiful ivory statue of his own creation. The goddess Aphrodite, moved by Pygmalion's obsession with the statue, comes to his rescue and brings it to life. George Bernard Shaw adapted the story to a more modern setting, and Shaw's rendition in turn served as the basis for the stage and film musical *My Fair Lady*. In this version, Henry Higgins (Pygmalion) transforms a flower girl, Liza Doolittle, into a fine upper-class lady. The play illustrates the principle that we "live up to" labels. We, like Liza Doolittle, act like the sort of person others perceive us to be. In *My Fair Lady*, Liza herself understood this when she noted:

> ". . . you see, really and truly, apart from the things anyone can pick up [elegant dress, the proper way of speaking, and so on], the difference between a lady and a flower girl is not how she behaves, but how she's treated. I shall always be a flower girl to Professor Higgins because he always treats me as a flower girl, and always will: but I know I can be a lady to you, because you always treat me as a lady, and always will."

A real-life example of the startling effects of self-fulfilling prophecies is the classroom experiment described by psychologist Robert Rosenthal.[2] A number of teachers were notified that certain of their students were expected to "bloom," or do exceptionally well, during the course of the school year. What the teachers did not know was that there was no real basis for this determination. The experimenters had simply selected the names of the "late bloomers" at random. Do you believe the selected students bloomed? If you said yes, you are quite right. Those students did perform at a higher level than would otherwise have been expected and did improve their IQ scores. Why? First because the expectations of the instructors apparently influenced the way *they* treated the late bloomers. The instructors gave these students extra positive verbal and nonverbal reinforcement, waited patiently for them to respond if they hesitated, and did not react negatively when they offered faulty answers. In turn it seems the way the teachers treated the students had a marked impact on the way the students perceived *themselves* and their own abilities. The late bloomers were simply responding to the prophecy that had been made about them by fulfilling it.

It should be recognized that the self-fulfilling prophecy has many important implications for one's education as well as one's personal life. Have you ever joined a group of people you were convinced would not like you? What happened? Very likely you were proved right. What you probably did was to act in a way that encouraged them to dislike you. Far too frequently we make assumptions about how others will behave and then act as if they had already behaved that way. For example, if you view yourself as a failure in school or in a particular subject, it is likely that you will begin to act the part. Poor study habits, lack of participation in class, and poor grades will help to reinforce your feelings. In this way a growing negative image can mushroom into a vicious, all-consuming spiral.

J. Sterling Livingston, president of the Sterling Institute, a management consulting firm, believes that the Pygmalion effect is also found at

Identify people who have functioned as positive and/or negative Pygmalions in your own life. Then complete these sentence starters:

I work best for people who . . .

I work least for people who . . .

the root of many business problems. Apparently, although some managers treat employees in ways that precipitate superior performance, many others unconsciously treat workers in ways that precipitate inferior performance. Again, high expectations tend to result in increased productivity, whereas low expectations result in decreased productivity. Thus, subordinates more often than not confirm the expectations of their superiors. For this reason managers have the potential to function as both *positive* and *negative* Pgymalions for those who work under them. In other words, the Pgymalion effect can hinder as well as help.

A variation of the Pygmalion effect is the Galatea effect. The Galatea effect relates to the expectations we have for ourselves rather than the expectations others have for us; in other words, the Galatea effect is self-expectation. Just as we generally live up to the expectations others have for us, we also tend to realize the expectations we have for ourselves. That is, we react to the internal messages we continuously send to ourselves, not only to the external messages others send to us. Our feelings about our own competence and ability can exert an influence on our behavior in much the same way that our performance can be influenced by others' high or low expectations for us. At any point in our lives we can begin to acquire higher self-worth. It is important to recognize that we can change and grow each day we exist. Thus how we and others answer the question, Who are you? affects how we behave.

> Biologists have determined that technically speaking, the bumblebee cannot fly. Fortunately, the bumblebee doesn't believe a word of it. Remember, people rise no higher than their expectation level.

DO MALES AND FEMALES SEE THEMSELVES IN DIFFERENT WAYS?

Do you believe you would feel differently about yourself if you were of the opposite sex? Why or why not? If you answered yes, is it because you believe that others would treat you differently? Would they encourage you to exhibit some behaviors or traits while at the same time discouraging you from exhibiting others?

Research tells us that others do treat us differently because of our sex. For example, we dress babies in different colors and styles, and we even tend to give them different toys to play with. For the most part, our prevalent male/female conceptions are reinforced in the television shows we view, the films we watch, and the books we read. Unfortunately, studies reveal that women tend to develop a less positive view of themselves than men do. Why? In our society men are expected to exhibit the following personality characteristics to a greater degree than are women: aggressiveness, arrogance, assertiveness, autocratic style, conceit, confidence, cynicism, deliberateness, dominance, enterprising spirit, forcefulness, foresightedness, frankness, handsomeness, hardheadedness, industriousness, ingeniousness, inventiveness, masculinity, opportunism, outspokenness, self-confidence, sharp-wittedness, shrewdness, sternness, strongness, toughness, and vindictiveness. In contrast, women are more apt to be perceived to possess the following traits than are men: appreciativeness, considerateness, contentment, cooperativeness, dependence, emotionality, excitability, fearfulness, femininity, fickleness, forgiving nature, friendliness, frivolity, helpfulness, joviality, modesty, praise giving, sensitivity, sentimentality, sincerity, submissiveness, sympathy, talkativeness, timidity, warmth, and the tendency to worry. What is noteworthy for the development of our self-worth is that the male characteristics are valued more highly overall than are the female characteristics. Rewards are given out accordingly. Hence, more men rise to positions of leadership than do women. But this is changing, and education and the media are beginning to help accomplish these changes. Whereas women used to be underrepresented in television programming, their numbers are on the rise; whereas men were typically depicted in professional roles, women are now joining them and are permitted to have similar occupations. A little more than 15 years ago researcher Ann Beuf reported a particularly revealing observation. When asked what he would want to be when he grew up if he were a young girl, a young boy said, "Oh, if I were a girl, I'd have to grow up to be nothing."[3] It is doubtful whether females or males would answer that way today.

What we know today is that both men and women can change their self-concepts. And each of us can function in such a way as to make that change a positive one.

THE SELF-CONCEPT IS NOT THE SELF: DEVELOPING SELF-AWARENESS

The self-concept represents who you *think* you are, not necessarily who you are. In general, we are not usually very objective about our self-concepts. Sometimes your image of yourself may be more favorable than

SKILL BUILDER

Growing Up Male/Female

Conduct brief interviews with five males and females from each of these age groups: 5 to 8, 9 to 12, 13 to 16, and 17 to 20 years old. Ask the interviewees what they want to be when they grow up. Compare and contrast their responses. To what extent, if any, do you see a trend emerging? To what extent do the younger or older respondents offer gender-related answers? Explain.

DON'T BE AFRAID TO FAIL

You've failed
many times,
although you may not
remember.
You fell down
the first time
you tried to walk.
You almost drowned
the first time
you tried to
swim, didn't you?
Did you hit the
ball the first time
you swung a bat?
Heavy hitters,
the ones who hit the
most home runs,
also strike
out a lot.
R. H. Macy

failed seven
times before his
store in New York
caught on.
English novelist
John Creasey got
753 rejection slips
before he published
564 Books.
Babe Ruth struck out
1,330 times
but he also hit
714 home runs.
Don't worry about
failure.
Worry about the
chances you miss
when you don't
even try.

United Technologies Corporation.

No one can make you
feel inferior without
your consent.

Eleanor Roosevelt

If men define situa-
tions as real, they
are real in their con-
sequences.

W. I. Thomas

---

the one others have of you. For instance, you might view yourself as an extremely talented writer, but others might consider you a hack. There are many reasons why we are able to maintain a picture of ourselves that others may regard as unrealistic or ridiculous. For one thing, we might be so worried about our presentation of self that we fail to pay attention to feedback from others about how they see us. Or others might send us distorted information about ourselves in an attempt not to hurt our feelings. Or we might be basing our self-view on outdated, obsolete information that allows us to cling to the memories of the past rather than facing the realities of the present.

Just as there are times when we view ourselves more favorably than we should, there are times when we view ourselves more harshly than we ought. For example, a person might be convinced of her "ugliness" despite the insistence of others that she is attractive. Why? Because this young woman might be acting on the basis of *obsolete data*. Perhaps as a child she was gawky or fat, and even though she is now graceful and slender, those past traits still pursue her. *Distorted feedback* can also nourish a negative self-image. Individuals who are strongly influenced by an overly critical parent, friend, teacher, or employer can develop a self-view that is far harsher than the view others hold. Another reason people often "cheat" themselves of a favorable self-concept is the *social customs of our society*. In the United States, at least, it is far more acceptable for individuals to downplay, underrate, and criticize themselves than it is for them to praise or boast about themselves or openly display their self-appreciation. To put it simply, far too many people are taught SPS—self-praise stinks.

Walt Whitman in the poem "Song of Myself" writes, "I celebrate myself and sing myself." To what extent are you able to celebrate yourself? Do you possess a predominantly positive or negative self-concept? Take some time now to inventory what you perceive to be your own assets and liabilities. The practice of honestly reviewing your own strong and weak points can help to reshape your image of yourself.

JOINING TOGETHER: THE JOHARI WINDOW AND SELF-DISCLOSURE

We need to realize that self-understanding is the basis for our self-concept. To understand yourself, you must understand your own way of looking at the world. To understand others, you must understand how they look at the world.

Some of your answers to the Skill Builder on page 48 may illustrate one of the ideas of the psychiatrist Eric Berne. Berne believes that we sometimes pattern our transactions in such a way that we repeatedly reenact the same script with a different set of players. In other words, it is not uncommon for us to attempt to "stage" a drama with casts of characters drawn from different points in our life cycle. This repetition urge can become a problem for you if it leads you to fail rather than to succeed. Take some time and examine the extent to which your three separate sets of responses in the preceding Skill Builder demonstrated flexibility rather than rigidity. Attempt to determine to what degree you have eliminated or extinguished behaviors you did not like. In addition, try to understand what each of your responses says about your past, present, and future needs.

At one time or another we all wish we knew ourselves or others better. The concept of self-awareness, so basic to all functions and forms of communication, may also be explored through a psychological testing feature known as the Johari Window. Joseph Luft and Harrington Ingham devised an illustration of a paned window to help us examine both how we view ourselves and how others view us.[4] Before proceeding further let's look at the window (see Figure 2-1).

The first square, "window pane" I, represents information about yourself that is known to you and to another. At times your name, age,

Yesterday, Today, and Tomorrow

1. Your instructor will divide you into small groups.

2. Each group can use the incomplete sentences listed below as conversation starters. During the first round you should reveal how you would have responded to each incomplete statement as a very young child (between 5 and 8 years old). During the second round you should indicate how you would have responded to the conversation starters during your older childhood and adolescent years. Finally, during the third round you should disclose how you would respond to these statements today.

   a. Other people want me to . . .
   b. The best way to measure personal success is . . .
   c. When I do what I really want to do, I . . .
   d. I get frustrated when . . .
   e. I want to be a . . .
   f. I have fun when . . .
   g. Marriage for me is . . .
   h. People who are "in charge" should be . . .
   i. I miss . . .
   j. What I really like about myself is . . .
   k. When I am with people who do a lot of talking, I . . .
   l. Sometimes I feel like . . .
   m. A decade from now, I . . .

3. What do the responses tell you about yourself and your peers during these three life stages? Were there discernible consistencies? Were there changes? Why?

religious affiliation, and food preferences might all be found in this pane. The size and contents of the quadrant vary from relationship to relationship, depending on the degree of closeness you share with another individual. Do you allow some people to know more about you than others? Why?

Pane II, the blind area, contains information about you that others, but not you, are aware of. Some people have a very large blind area and are oblivious to either the faults or the virtues they possess. At times, some individuals may feel compelled to seek outside help or therapy to reduce the size of their "blind panes." Do you know something about a friend that he or she does not know? Do you feel free to reveal this information to that friend? Why? What effect do you think your revelation would have on your friend's self-image?

Pane III represents your hidden area. It contains information you

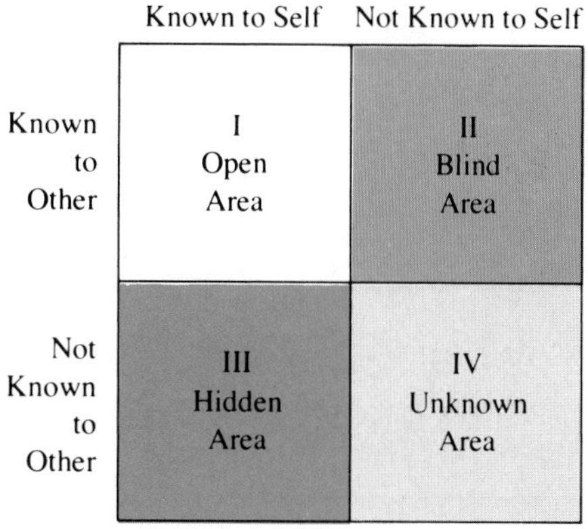

Known to Self   Not Known to Self

Known to Other	I Open Area	II Blind Area
Not Known to Other	III Hidden Area	IV Unknown Area

FIGURE 2-1
The Johari Window
Reprinted from Group
Process: An Introduction
to Group Dynamics *by
Joseph Luft, by
permission of Mayfield
Publishing Company.
Copyright © 1963, 1970
Joseph Luft.*

know about yourself but do not wish others to find out for fear they will reject you. John Powell, author of *Why Am I Afraid to Tell You Who I Am?* expresses the rejection fear this way: "If I tell you who I am, you may not like who I am, and it is all that I have." Sometimes it takes a great deal of effort to avoid becoming known, and at one time or another each of us feels a need to have individuals important to us know us well and accept us for what we are. When we move information from quadrant III to quadrant I we engage in this self-disclosure process. *Self-disclosure* occurs when we purposefully reveal to another individual personal information that the person would not otherwise know. By self-disclosure we show others that we trust them and care enough about them to reveal to them intimate information we would not willingly share with everyone. Often, our attempts at self-disclosure will be reciprocated, and this sharing of hidden parts is essential if meaningful and lasting relationships are to develop.[5] None of this is to suggest that the hidden area should not be allowed to exist within each of us. It is up to you to decide when it is appropriate for you to share your innermost thoughts, feelings, and intentions with others; it is also up to you to decide when complete openness is not in your best interest.

Pane IV is the unknown area in your makeup. It contains information about which neither you nor others are aware. Eventually education and life experiences may help to bring some of the mysteries contained in this pane to the surface. Only then will its disclosures be available for examination. Have you ever done something that surprised both you and people close to you? Did you and a friend ever exclaim together, "Wow! I didn't know I/you could do that!"

People commonly develop an interpersonal style that is a consistent and preferred way of behaving interpersonally. Figure 2-2 illustrates representative styles. *Style A* is characteristic of people who adopt a fairly impersonal approach to interpersonal relationships. Dominated by their

Can you identify some of the things you are hesitant to let others know about yourself? Why are these aspects of you easier to hold back than express? (Or are they?)

Which style appears to be most characteristic of you and the people you interact with?

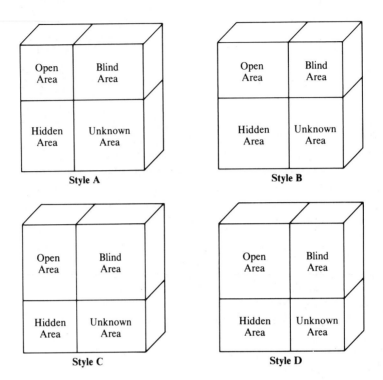

FIGURE 2-2

unknown areas, these individuals usually withdraw from contacts, avoid personal disclosures or involvements, and thus project an image that is rigid, aloof, and/or uncommunicative. In *style B*, the hidden area, or façade, is the dominant window. Here we find individuals who desire relationships but also greatly fear exposure and generally mistrust others. Once others become aware of the façade, they are likely to lose trust in this individual. *Style C* is dominated by the blind area, and people who illustrate this style are overly confident of their own opinions and painfully unaware of how they affect others or are perceived by others. Those who communicate with such individuals often feel that their ideas or insights are of little concern, and thus they are apt to develop resentments and hostility. In *style D* behavior, the open area, or area of free activity, is dominant, and relationships involve feelings of candor, openness, and sensitivity to others' needs and insights.

Communication of any depth or significance is sure to be lacking if the individuals involved have little open area common to them. In any relationship you hope to sustain, your goal should be to increase the size of the open area while decreasing the size of the hidden, blind, and unknown areas of your makeup. The open area becomes larger whenever information is moved from any of the remaining quadrants into it, as when you disclose

Symbolizing the Self

Bring four objects to class. The first object should reveal something about the way you see yourself, something you believe everyone recognizes about you. In other words, it should represent an aspect of your open area. The second object should reveal something about you that up until this point you believe resided in your hidden area. The object you select could symbolize an attitude, feeling, desire, or fear that you had hoped to keep from others but are now willing to move into the open pane. The third object you bring to class should represent how you believe another person sees you. For example, do you believe a particular friend or relative sees you as you see yourself? How do you think your perceptions are similar? How are they different? Finally, after selecting these three objects, ask someone to choose an object that represents his or her perception of you. Bring this object to class. Be prepared to discuss how your perceptions of yourself and the other person's perception of you conflict or coincide. For example, did the object selected by the other person help you move information from the blind area to the open area? To what extent has each phase of the experience altered the appearance of your Johari Window?

any of your hidden perceptions to others or when others reveal any hidden perceptions they may have about you. We know that as human beings we are constantly thinking about others and what they think about us. The question is whether we are able and willing to share what we are thinking.

HOW TO MAKE YOUR SELF-IMAGE WORK FOR YOU: IMPROVING AWARENESS OF SELF AND OTHERS

Throughout this chapter we have stressed that we all carry figurative pictures of ourselves and others with us wherever we go. Together these pictures form a mental "collage." Contained within the collage are past, present, and future images of us alone or interacting with people. If you closely examine your various images, you probably will be able to discern that how you look in each is related to when the picture was taken, the environment you were in, and the people you were communicating with. Even though each picture reveals a somewhat different you because you change and grow from moment to moment, situation to situation, and year to year, you may tend to forget that your self-image also can change. Keeping "self-pictures" updated and current is indeed a challenge. Sharpening a fuzzy image, refocusing an old image, and developing a new image are processes that can help you discard worn-out or inaccurate perceptions of yourself and others. The following guidelines can be used to further improve the self-other "picture-taking" skills you have gained while working your way through this chapter.

Continue Taking Pictures

You can further your self-awareness by continuing to take the time to examine your self-image and your relationship to others. Developing a clear sense of who you are is one of the most worthwhile goals you can set for yourself. Be willing to watch yourself in action. Periodically examine your own self-perceptions—and *self-misconceptions*. Consider how you feel about yourself, how you think you look, and to what extent you approve of your values and behaviors. Study the composite picture that emerges as a result of your reflections. How close are you to becoming the person you would like to be? In what ways would you like to alter your various self-portraits? We hope you will take the time and have the courage and open-mindedness required to engage in productive and worthwhile self-examinations.

Encourage Others to Take Pictures of You

As we have seen, how others perceive you may be very different from how you perceive yourself. Obtaining information from others can help you assess how realistic your self-concept is. Others who come to know you may observe strengths you have overlooked, traits you undervalue, or weaknesses you choose to ignore. However, you do not have to accept all the pictures other individuals take of you. No one can prevent you from adhering to your original beliefs and rejecting the opinions of others. Looking at others' pictures of you does mean, however, that you are at least opening yourself to the possibility of change by attempting to see yourself as others see you. Receiving messages from others can help you acquire insight into who others think you are and how they think you are coming across.

Refocus, Refocus, Refocus

Carl Sandburg wrote, "Life is like an onion; you peel off one layer at a time." As you move from yesterday through today and into tomorrow, your self is in constant transition. Try not to let your view of your self today prevent you from adapting to meet the demands of changing circumstances and conditions. Continually formulating new answers to the question, Who am I? will allow you to discover the vibrant, flexible, and dynamic qualities of your self. Self-discovery is an unending, ongoing way of reacting to life.

SUMMARY

Self-concept is the entire collection of attitudes and beliefs you hold about who and what you are. It is the mental picture you have of yourself. It can be positive or negative, accurate or inaccurate. Your self-concept influences all aspects of your communicative behavior—with whom, where, why, and how you choose to communicate.

You are not born with a self-concept. Rather, your self-concept is shaped by your environment and by those around you, including your parents, your relatives, instructors, supervisors, friends, and coworkers. In addition, television and film can subtly shape your opinion of who you are.

Conditions and circumstances affect the nature of the self. Sometimes it seems that we become different "selves" as we move from situation to situation; our demeanor is affected by our perceptions of others and how we imagine they perceive us.

The development of a self-concept can also be affected by what is known as a self-fulfilling prophecy. A self-fulfilling prophecy occurs when your expectations of an event help create the very conditions that permit the event to occur. Here again, the media as well as people help determine which self-fulfilling prophecies we make.

You can change and improve your self-concept by developing greater self-awareness and self-understanding. One device that can be used to achieve this is the Johari Window, which can help you identify the open, blind, hidden, and unknown areas of your self.

SUGGESTIONS FOR FURTHER READING

Branden, Nathaniel. *The Psychology of Self-Esteem.* New York: Bantam, 1969. The author examines our need for self-esteem and discusses the conditions necessary for mental well-being.

Campbell, Colin. "Our Many Versions of the Self: An Interview with Brewster Smith," *Psychology Today*, February 1976, pp. 13–33. Dr. Smith, a psychologist, discusses the myriad ways in which the self may be viewed.

Gergen, Kenneth J. *The Concept of Self.* New York: Holt, Rinehart and Winston, 1971. In this scholarly work Gergen examines how self-concept develops and how it influences behavior.

Goffman, Erving. *The Presentation of Self in Everyday Life.* Garden City, N.Y.: Doubleday, 1959. A valuable reference in which Goffman explores the honest and dishonest ways in which we reveal who we are to others and ourselves. The concept of "mask" is explained.

Jourard, Sidney M. *The Transparent Self.* New York: Van Nostrand, 1971. An interesting, in-depth look at the self and the nature of the self-disclosure process.

Luft, Joseph. *Group Processes: An Introduction to Group Dynamics*, 2d ed. Palo Alto, Calif.: Mayfield Publishing Company, 1970. Provides a clear, well-written explication of the Johari Window and how it can be used to analyze our relationships.

Powell, John. *Why Am I Afraid to Tell You Who I Am?* Chicago: Argus Communications, 1969. A basic introduction to the defenses people construct in an effort to avoid becoming known.

Rosenthal, Robert, and Lenore Jacobson. *Pygmalion in the Classroom.* New York: Holt, Rinehart and Winston, 1968. Reports on the role self-fulfilling prophecies play in education, research, and everyday life.

Schutz, William C. *The Interpersonal Underworld.* Palo Alto, Calif.: Science and Behavior Books,

1966. Contains a discussion of the needs that must be satisfied through human interaction.

Tuchman, Gaye, Arlene Kaplan Daniels, and James Benet, eds. *Hearth and Home: Images of Women in the Mass Media*. New York: Oxford University Press, 1978. This work contains articles that explore and describe the ways women are portrayed in the media.

Villard, Kenneth L., and Leland J. Whipple. *Beginnings in Relational Communication*. New York: Wiley, 1976. Explores the dynamic nature of human interaction.

NOTES

1. For an explanation of the differences between role-taking and role-playing see Robert L. Kelley, W. J. Osborne, and Clyde Hendrick, "Role-Taking and Role-Playing in Human Communication," *Human Communication Research*, Vol. 1 (1974), pp. 62–74.

2. Robert Rosenthal and Lenore Jacobson, *Pygmalion in the Classroom* (New York: Holt, Rinehart and Winston, 1968).

3. Ann Beuf, "Doctor, Lawyer, Household Drudge," *Journal of Communication*, Vol. 24 (1974), pp. 142–145.

4. Joseph Luft, *Group Processes: An Introduction to Group Dynamics*, 2d ed. (Palo Alto, Calif.: Mayfield Publishing Company, 1970).

5. For example, as reported by Morgan Worthy, Albert L. Gay, and Guy M. Kahn, self-disclosure seems to be reciprocal and regarded as a reward in interpersonal relationships. See their article "Self Disclosure as an Exchange Process," *Journal of Personality and Social Psychology*, Vol. 13 (1969), pp. 59–63.

3

Perception: I Am More Than a Camera

If, to people, crickets appear to hear with their legs, it is possible
that to crickets, people appear to walk on their ears.

Anonymous

CHAPTER PREVIEW

After you finish this chapter, you should be able to:

Explain why a person is "more than a camera"

Demonstrate how an individual's angle of vision, or perspective,
affects perception

Identify how we limit what we perceive

Demonstrate how an individual's sensory capabilities
affect perception

Define *perception*

Explain the figure-ground principle

Describe the ways in which past experience can influence perception

Distinguish between an *open orientation* and a *closed orientation*

Compare and contrast *selective exposure* and *selective perception*

Define *closure*

Explain how first impressions affect perception

Define *stereotyping*

Explain how the media perpetuate stereotypes

Identify common stereotypes that you and others hold

Define and provide examples of *allness*

Explain what is meant by *blindering*

Distinguish between facts and inferences

Identify ways to increase the accuracy of your perceptions

Picture this. The setting is a football stadium. Larry, Joan, and George are seated next to each other watching the game. Suddenly, a long pass is thrown by the quarterback, caught, and run into the end zone for a touchdown. Larry screams, "Did you see that pass!" Joan comments, "What do you mean? The receiver saved the day." And George notes, "Forget it. If it weren't for the sensational block by 38 there wouldn't have been a play."

Why is it that when we look at the same event, we do not all see the same thing? Do we see things as they are? Do we see things as we want them to be? Or do we see things as we are? How do our sensory capabilities affect perception? How do our experiences affect perception? In this chapter we will attempt to answer these questions as we explore how we perceive the world around us and why we are, in effect, "more than a camera."

WHAT IS PERCEPTION? THE "I" AND THE EYES

In many ways we each live in or inhabit different worlds. We each view reality from a different angle, perspective, or vantage point. Our physical location, our interests, our personal desires, our attitudes, our values, our personal experiences, our bodily conditions, and our psychological states all interact to influence our judgments or perceptions.

Now, how do you absorb information from the world around you? Do you look and listen? Do you touch, taste, and smell your environment and those who interact in it? Certainly! Your senses function as perceptual "antennae" and gather information for you all the time. However, it is impossible for you to internalize or process all the stimuli or data available to you. Without realizing it, you take steps to limit what you perceive. You can see this for yourself if you try the following test:

1. During the next 60 seconds, attempt to internalize everything that exists in the room you now inhabit. Make an effort to react to each sound, sight, smell, touch, and taste stimulus that is present in your environment.
2. Were you able to focus simultaneously on each stimulus, or did you find yourself skipping from one stimulus or sense experience to another stimulus and back again?

If your answer to the last question was yes—and it most probably was—you are aware that you simply cannot effectively handle, or process, all the sensory experiences that compete for your attention. In many respects, we humans are like television sets. We simply are limited in the number of "shows" we can present. Information theorists tell us that the eye can process about 5 million pieces, or "bits," of data per second; they also tell us that the brain can utilize only some 500 bits per second. We therefore are forced to identify or *select* those stimuli we will attend to or experience. By doing this we create a more limited but more coherent and meaningful picture of our world.

Not only are perceptual processes highly selective, they also are personally based. For this reason, different people will experience the same cues in very different ways. Communication expert William Haney emphasized this when he noted that we never really come into direct contact with reality.[1] Instead, everything you experience is "manufactured" by your nervous system. The kind of "sense" we make out of the people and situations in our world depends somewhat on the world outside but more on what kind of perceivers we are. In other words, everything that is seen, heard, tasted, felt, or smelled depends on *who* is doing the experiencing. Thus your perceptions of a stimulus are shaped by your loves and hatreds, your desires, your physical capabilities, the quality of your senses, the organizational processes you employ, and how you interpret and evaluate your past experiences. We could say, then, that your perception of a stimulus and the stimulus itself are not even one and the same thing. The stimulus is "out there," whereas your perception of it is unique, personal, and inside you.

But what is perception? Certainly, as we now realize, perception includes more than just the eye alone, more than just the ear alone, more than just the nose alone, more than just the skin alone, and more than just the tongue alone. Perception is the "I" behind the senses—the I behind the eye, as it were. Keeping this in mind, we can define *perception* as the process of selecting, organizing, and interpreting sensory data in a way that enables us to make sense of our world. The remaining sections of this chapter elaborate on this definition.

THE "I" OF THE BEHOLDER: THROUGH A GLASS DARKLY

We have said that perception provides each of us with a unique view of the world—a view sometimes related to, but not necessarily identical with, that held by others. Since we can never actually become one with the world out there, we are forced to use our senses to help create a personal picture of the people and objects that surround us. How do we make sense out of our world? How do we process the stimuli that compete for our attention? To be sure, during the perception process we are active, not passive, participants. We do not simply relax and absorb stimuli available to us the way a sponge absorbs liquid. We select, we organize, and we evaluate the multitude of stimuli that bombard us so that what we focus on becomes the *figure* and the rest of what we see becomes the *ground*.[2]

To further clarify the figure-ground concept, look at Figure 3-1. What do you see? At first glance you probably see a vase, or you may see two people facing each other. When stimuli compete for your attention, you can focus on only one because it is simply impossible to perceive something in two ways at once. Although you may be able to switch your focus rapidly, you will still perceive only one stimulus at any given time.

In addition, when we are confronted with more input than we can handle, we sometimes need to eliminate or reduce the number of stimuli

FIGURE 3-1
Figure and ground

"Do you enjoy being a Margarita?"

New Yorker, October 17, 1988, p. 32.

impinging on our awareness. We cannot "catch" or process each idea or each sensory stimulus in our world or environment. Again, we must select.

What other variables affect us during the perceptual process? In other words, what additional forces interact to guide us in making our perceptual selections?

Are Your Past Experiences Following You? The Creation of Perceptual Sets

If you took a third-grade boy to one of your college classes, do you think he would perceive the class experience in the same way you do? If you asked him to take notes, would his notes be identical to yours? Of course

FIGURE 3-2
A test for perceptual
sets

Exchange notes from
the same class with
someone in your sec-
tion. Can you read
the other person's
notes? Would you be
able to study from
them? What has this
student included that
you omitted? What
did you include that
he or she did not?
Why?

not. How would they differ? Would you mind if the notes were taken in
crayon? Would you mind if your script were replaced with a large scribble
and supplemented with doodles? Although doodling is not unknown among
college note takers, the child's notes would probably be far inferior to the
notes you take. Why? First, you have learned to take notes. Second, you
have some familiarity with the material being presented. And third, your
intellectual capabilities are probably superior to the child's. The sum total
of all the differences we have been describing can be summed up as *past
experience*. (Remember, however, that age alone does not determine the
part played by past experience. Even among people of the same age, past
experiences differ and hence affect the way stimuli are perceived.)

Past experiences also provide us with expectations, or "perceptual
sets," that affect how we process our world.[3] In order to better understand
the concept of *perceptual set*, quickly read the statements written in the
triangles in Figure 3-2. Now examine the words more carefully. During
your first reading, did you miss anything that you now perceive? Many fail
to see the second *the* or *a* in the statements the first time they read them.
Did you? Why? We are so accustomed to seeing words in familiar groups,
or clusters, that often we simply fail to perceive a number of single words
when we see them in such phrases. Faster, more accomplished readers
make this mistake more readily than do slower, less skillful ones. In their
attempt to perceive the overall meaning fast readers simply skip what they
perceive as unessential words. Based on this, how do you imagine first-
and second-graders would respond to the triangle experience? The authors
showed these triangles to a group of such students and found that, for the
most part, since they still read individual words rather than word groups,
many noticed the repetition immediately. They were not "set" to perceive
the phrases.

Obviously, the *educational experiences* we have had are also an
important part of our total past experience. The amount and kind of
education affect the way we process and perceive information. For instance,
you may find that your views of television and other media have also
changed since you were in grade school and that they will change again as
you acquire additional education. (Young children, for example, view
television commercials as a kind of absolute truth.) At times, however,

education can serve as a barrier rather than as a facilitator and aid to common sense. The humorous essay by the columnist Russell Baker reprinted here pokes fun at the ridiculously exaggerated perceptions obviously fostered by widely differing types of educational backgrounds.

OPINION: AN ANALYSIS OF MISS MUFFET

Russell Baker

Little Miss Muffet, as everyone knows, sat on a tuffet eating her curds and whey when along came a spider who sat down beside her and frightened Miss Muffet away. While everyone knows it, the significance of the event had never been analyzed until a conference of thinkers recently brought their special insights to bear upon it. Following are excerpts from the transcript of their discussion:

SOCIOLOGIST: Miss Muffet is nutritionally underprivileged, as evidenced by the subminimal diet of curds and whey upon which she is forced to subsist, while the spider's cultural disadvantage is evidenced by such phenomena as legs exceeding standard norms, odd mating habits and so forth.

In this instance, spider expectations lead the culturally disadvantaged to assert demands to share the tuffet with the nutritionally underprivileged. Due to a communications failure, Miss Muffet assumes without evidence that the spider will not be satisfied to share her tuffet, but will also insist on eating her curds and whey. . . .

MILITARIST: Second-strike capability, sir! That's what was lacking. If Miss Muffet had developed a second-strike capability instead of squandering her resources on curds and whey, no spider on earth would have dared launch a first strike capable of carrying him right to the heart of her tuffet. I am confident that Miss Muffet had adequate notice from experts that she could not afford both curds and whey and at the same time support an early-spider-warning system. . . .

BOOK REVIEWER: Written on several levels, this searing, sensitive exploration of the arachnid heart illuminates the agony and splendor of Jewish family life with a candor that is at once breath-taking in its simplicity and soul-shattering in its implied ambiguity. Some will doubtless be shocked to see such subjects as tuffets and whey discussed without flinching, but hereafter writers too timid to call a tuffet a tuffet will no longer . . .

EDITORIALIST: Why has the Government not seen fit to tell the public all it knows about the so-called curds-and-whey affair? It is not enough to suggest that this was merely a random incident involving a lonely spider and a young diner. . . .

PSYCHIATRIST: Little Miss Muffet is, of course, neither little, nor a miss. These are obviously the self she has created in her own fantasies to escape the reality that she is a . . . divorcee whose superego makes it impossible for her to sustain a normal relationship with any man, symbolized by the spider. . . .

FLOWER CHILD: This beautiful kid is on a bad trip. Like . . .

STUDENT: Little Miss Muffet, tuffets, curds, whey and spiders are what's wrong with education today. They're all irrelevant. Tuffets are irrelevant. Curds are irrelevant. Whey is irrelevant.

CHILD: This is about a little girl who gets scared by a spider.

(The child was sent home when the conference broke for lunch. It was agreed that the child was too immature to add anything to the sum of human understanding and should not return until he had grown up.)

© 1969 by The New York Times Company. Reprinted by permission.

Except for the child, each individual in the preceding passage had exhibited a perceptual set, a readiness to process a stimulus in a predetermined or conditioned way. This set encouraged each one to interpret the nursery rhyme's meaning as she or he wanted to. As is apparent, perceptual sets are the result of unique experiences. The lessons life has taught you necessarily differ from those life has taught others. As a result we each perceive the same stimulus differently. This helps explain why a boss and an employee, a teacher and a student, a parent and a child, or two friends can have widely differing opinions and interpretations about a job, a company, an institution, or a situation. For instance, the boss or the person with more power may be situated at the top "looking down," and the employee or person with less power may be situated at or near the bottom "looking up." One's position in an organization affects how one perceives that organization. The role we play or the position we hold helps us internalize perceptual sets that in turn cause us to react to people, places, and situations in particular ways.

> How might varied educational backgrounds create tensions on the job?

Are You "Open" or "Closed"? The Role of Selective Exposure

A key factor in how we view our world is the extent to which we open ourselves to experiences. Despite the numerous sensory stimuli that compete for our attention, we tend to select only those experiences which reaffirm existing attitudes, beliefs, and values. We likewise tend to ignore or diminish the significance of those experiences which are incongruent or dissonant with our existing attitudes, beliefs, and values. Just as children sometimes place their hands over their ears to avoid hearing what a parent is saying, so we can select what we will perceive by deciding whether to expose ourselves to a variety of types and sources of information. When driving through poverty-striken areas, for example, people often roll up

We all tend to ignore what we don't want to see. This selective exposure affects the way we perceive and deal with the world. (Emilio A. Mercado/The Picture Cube)

their automobile windows. They tell themselves they are doing this for self-protection, but rolling up the windows is also a means of *self-deception* that helps them avoid contact with some of the depressing sights and sounds of their society.

A 1959 study gave support to the premise of *selective exposure*. Researchers Wilbur Schramm and Richard Carter determined that after a massive television campaign by a Republican senatorial candidate, Republicans were twice as likely to have seen a portion of the campaign as were Democrats.[4] Likewise, during the 1972 presidential campaign, researcher Dorothy Bartlett discovered that twice as many Republicans as Democrats failed to open an envelope with the return-address slogan "Voters for McGovern." Similar results were obtained among Democrats who received a letter with the return-address slogan "Voters for Nixon."[5] In each instance voters chose to expose themselves to only that information with which they already agreed. How difficult is it for you to expose yourself to certain ideas, places, or experiences? Why?

Are You a Distorter?
The Role of Selective Perception and Closure

A concept related to selective exposure is *selective perception*. We see what we want to see and hear what we want to hear. Through the process of selective perception, the same message or stimulus may be interpreted in different ways by different people. But why do we distort stimuli until they conform to what we want or expect?

Each individual's perception of an event is influenced by his or her existing attitudes. Thus, out of the swirling mass of information available to us, we interpret and digest the information that confirms our own beliefs, expectations, or convictions, and we reject the information that contradicts our beliefs and convictions. Try viewing the same news broadcast with someone whose political views differ sharply from your own. How similar do you imagine your interpretations of the delivered information will be? Why?

Our selective processes allow us to add information, delete information, or change information so that we can avoid dealing with certain information. Time and time again past experiences, expectations, needs, and wants join forces and help determine our present perceptions. They are aided in this effort by our desire for *closure*—that is, our desire to perceive a completed (and secure) world. Examine Figure 3-3 and identify each item you see.

Can you cite instances when you chose not to expose yourself to a particular stimulus or idea? Are there some subjects you would prefer not to know about? Are there some people whom you would just as soon avoid?

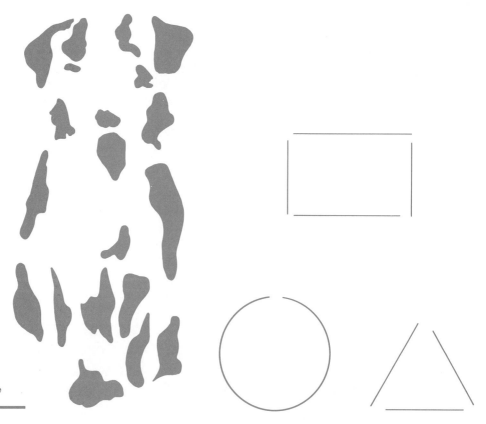

FIGURE 3-3
A test for closure

You probably see a dog rather than a collection of inkblots and a rectangle, a triangle, and a circle rather than some lines and an arc. We tend to complete familiar figures in our mind. We fill in the forms based on our previous experiences and our needs. In just the same way we complete stimuli until they make sense to us: We fill in gaps.

What significance does this tendency to fill in missing information have for your everyday perceptions and interpersonal communication? How often do you feel a need to fill in "people gaps"? How often do you make sense out of the actions of people by "completing" them as you would like to see them? It is important to realize that your perceptions of an individual are a key determinant of the type of relationship you will share with that individual.

PERCEIVING OTHERS: WHAT ARE YOU, PLEASE?

On what basis do you form first impressions or make initial judgments about the people you meet? What makes you decide if you like or dislike someone? Is it his economic status? Is it the job she holds? Perceiving others and the roles they play is an essential part of the communication process. (Can you imagine walking into a bank and not being able to determine to whom you should give your money!) In this section we will explore how we form first impressions of others and why we sometimes stereotype others. We will attempt to determine why we often feel it necessary to "freeze" people and "squeeze" people until they fit into or conform to our expectations for them.

First Impressions: Making Them or Breaking Them

"You must make a good first impression" is advice frequently given to individuals as they start a new job, embark on an interview, or prepare to participate in some other communication encounter. How important is the first impression? Let's find out by analyzing the responses you obtained in the Skill Builder on page 66 (adapted from an experiment conducted by Solomon Asch). People usually attribute positive qualities to person A, selecting a descriptive word with very positive connotations. In contrast, person B is often perceived as possessing negative qualities, and for this reason the word chosen to describe B also has negative connotations. Why? Because the first list begins with positive traits and the second begins with negative traits. Otherwise, each list is precisely the same. As we see, first impressions can dramatically affect perception. In addition, the first impression, or "primacy effect," as it is sometimes termed, can even alter the

What's On First?

1. Read the following ordered list of individual A's character traits to another person:
   a. Intelligent
   b. Industrious
   c. Impulsive
   d. Critical
   e. Stubborn
   f. Envious

   Ask that person to choose one word to represent his or her impression of individual A.

2. Next, read this ordered list of individual B's character traits to another person and repeat the exercise as indicated in item 1.
   a. Envious
   b. Stubborn
   c. Critical
   d. Impulsive
   e. Industrious
   f. Intelligent

   As before, ask the person to choose one word to represent her or his impression of individual B.

result of communication efforts. Trial lawyers, for example, depend to some degree on the primacy effect when selecting persons to serve on a jury. The first impression that potential jurors make on the lawyer will often determine whether the attorney accepts them or uses a preemptory challenge. Eventually, this decision may have an important impact on the outcome of the case and the future of the defendant.

Even if first impressions are wrong, we tend to hold on to them. Doing this can cause a number of different problems. For example, if the opinion you have of someone is erroneous, you can sustain your inaccurate perception by clinging to it and reshaping the conflicting information available to you until it conforms to the image you hold. Thus, we may never come to experience the real person—only our faulty conception of him or her. Yet it is this faulty conception that will influence the way we respond to that person. Suppose, for instance, you meet a new friend, John, at work. You tell an old friend about him. Your old friend tells you: "Yeah. I know that guy. Worked with him two years ago. He's nothing but trouble. Always looking to use people. He'll bleed you of your ideas, pass them off as his own, and leave you far behind as he makes his way to the top. Did it to me. And he'll do it to you. Watch and see." The danger here is that this evaluation may be unfair, biased, or simply wrong. The new guy might have changed during the past two years, or your friend's initial assessment of him might have been all wet. But sadly, your friend's words will probably influence the way you interact with John, and whether they are there or not, you will probably find reasons to substantiate your first impression.

You simply may not be able to overcome a basic stumbling block to accurate perception—not keeping an open mind.

In a communication interaction the receivers' psychological states can also affect their first impressions of senders. Sometimes receivers use cues provided by the senders, mix them with their own preconceptions, and create a perception based partly on myth or fiction. Another factor that affects how we perceive others is our tendency to divide people into groups—to stereotype them. Let's explore this concept next.

Stereotyping: Have I Got a Niche for You!

A *stereotype* is a generalization about people, places, or events that is held by many members of a society. For example, when we go into a physician's waiting room for the first time, we carry with us a general idea, or stereotype, about how to behave in that particular environment. In other words, we have developed an ability to identify and generalize about the actions we feel are appropriate to display in a physician's office. To be sure, we would not expect to find flashing colored lights or people dancing to loud music while waiting to be examined! (Our stereotype does not allow for this.)

What are some of the more common stereotypic impressions held by people you know?

It would be difficult for us to operate without stereotypes. If, for example, you had formed no picture of how a salesperson, mechanic, waiter, or politician functions in our society, you would find it somewhat difficult to get along in daily life. Knowing what categories people and things fit into helps us decide how to deal with them: Somehow, knowing whether a stranger is a corporate president, a lawyer, or a teacher helps us decide how to behave in his or her presence. When we stereotype people, we simply judge them on the basis of what we know about the category to which we feel they belong. We assume the individual possesses characteristics similar to those we attribute to others in the group, and we simplify our task by overlooking any discrepancies that may exist. By implication, when we stereotype we say, "Those who belong in the same niche all have the same traits. Those who belong in the same niche are alike."

The media help us to create and maintain stereotypes. Television news programs, for one, help us identify people, places, ideas, and things by providing us with "standard" images of them. In his book *News from Nowhere*, Edward Jay Epstein explains that television news camera operators and correspondents are told to pepper their stories with pictures that have universal meaning. "Hence, stories tend to fit into a limited repertory of images, which explains why so often shabbily dressed children symbolically stand for poverty [and] . . . fire symbolically stands for destruction."[6] If you look closely, you will also notice that producers of television news shows try to select images that illustrate "the human experience." Inflation is portrayed as the housewife shopping in a supermarket; jobless statistics are depicted by an unshaven man walking into the unemployment office. In television news, as in newspapers and magazines, emotionally charged stereotypical images are often chosen to supplement and illustrate factual data that would otherwise seem complicated or uninteresting.

Unfortunately, stereotyping is rarely a positive force in interpersonal relations or in the various institutions that make up our society. Ralph Ellison, a black man and the author of *Invisible Man*, noted this when he wrote the following:

> I am an invisible man. No, I am not a spook like those who haunted Edgar Allan Poe. . . . I am a man of substance, of flesh and bone, fiber and liquid . . . and I might be said to possess a mind. I am invisible, understand, simply because people refuse to see me. Like the bodiless heads you see sometimes in circus side shows, it is as though I have been surrounded by mirrors of hard, distorting glass. When they approach me they see only my surroundings, or figments of their imagination—indeed, everything and anything except me.

The practice of stereotyping can be extremely harmful. At one time or another almost every one of us has formed fixed impressions of a racial group, an ethnic group, a religious group, people who hold a particular job, or people who occupy a certain economic level of society.[7] When we stereotype, we take our attitudes toward a group of people and project them onto one particular group member. What should be emphasized instead is that we are *all* individuals. Whenever we interact with another person, we must realize that we are communicating with a person, not with a stereotype. Furthermore, we need to understand that our stereotype of any group is necessarily based on incomplete information and that although stereotypes may be partly true, they are never completely true. Clearly, then, when we stereotype, categorize, or pigeonhole others, we are really stereotyping or categorizing aspects of ourselves!

In the long run, although stereotyping simplifies and gives a sense of order and stability to our lives, it can have very limiting and debilitating effects. Far too frequently we fail to recognize the variations and differences in apparently similar individuals. We overlook differences and emphasize similarities. We enjoy classifying and categorizing and find differentiating too difficult. Yet to improve our perceptual capabilities, we must make an effort to see the differences as well as the similarities among people. To paraphrase communicologist Irving J. Lee, the more we are able to discriminate *among* individuals, the less we will actively discriminate *against* individuals.

Other Barriers to Perception: "Don't Fence Me In!"

We have seen that a number of barriers limit and impede our perceptual accuracy. Many of these barriers are a result of our past experiences.

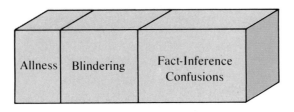

FIGURE 3-4
Barriers to perception

However, theorists have identified at least three additional factors that can function as perceptual blocks. These are allness, blindering, and fact-inference confusions (see Figure 3-4). Let us consider each of these forces.

Allness: "Is That All There Is?"   Have you ever noticed how some radio and television commentators speak with great finality? Several have based their careers at least partially on a parentlike image—that is, they seem to have all the answers about everything happening in the world. Is it possible for a commentator—or for any of us, for that matter—to know, much less tell about, all there is to know concerning a topic? Of course not. Knowledge of everything about anything is certainly an impossibility. In his book *Science and Sanity*, Alfred Korzybski coined the term *allness* to refer to the erroneous belief that any one person could possibly know all there is to know about everything. Even if we are wise and do not assume that our favorite newscaster (or even our favorite friend) is telling us all there is to know about a topic, we often persist in believing that she or he is telling us all that is *important* about that topic.

Did you ever have someone "fill you in" on the content of a class you missed? Did you assume that the person was delivering all the important information to you? Did a later exam prove you wrong? The allness fallacy is aptly illustrated in John Godfrey Saxe's poem reprinted here.

THE PARABLE OF THE BLIND MEN AND THE ELEPHANT

It was six men of Indostan
   To learning much inclined
Who went to see the Elephant
   (Though all of them were blind),
That each by observation
   Might satisfy his mind.

The First approached the Elephant,
   And happening to fall
Against his broad and sturdy side,
   At once began to bawl:
"God bless me! but the Elephant
   Is very like a wall."

The Second, feeling of the tusk
Cried, "Ho! what have we here
So very round and smooth and sharp?
  To me 'tis very clear
This wonder of an Elephant
  Is very like a spear."

The Third approached the animal
  And, happening to take
The squirming trunk within his hands
  Thus boldly up he spoke:
"I see," quoth he, "the Elephant
  Is very like a snake!"

The Fourth reached out an eager hand,
  And felt about the knee:
"What most this wondrous beast is like
  Is very plain," quoth he;
" 'Tis clear enough the Elephant
  Is very like a tree!"

The Fifth, who chanced to touch the ear,
  Said: "E'en the blindest man
Can tell what this resembles most;
  Deny the fact who can
This marvel of an Elephant
  Is very like a fan!"

The Sixth no sooner had begun
  About the beast to grope
Then seizing on the swinging tail
  That fell within his scope:
"I see," quoth he, "the Elephant
  Is very like a rope!"

And so these men of Indostan
  Disputed loud and long,
Each in his own opinion
  Exceeding stiff and strong.
Though each was partly in the right,
  They all were in the wrong!

Have you ever considered why the United States almost always appears in the center in maps of the world? Is there any sensible geographical rationale for this? Could it be an example of allness on the part of mapmakers and those who use the maps?

Each person in the poem assumed that he knew *all there was to know* about the elephant. Because we sometimes succumb to the allness mis-evaluation, our perceptions of others and of the world around us can be as limited as those of the six blind men. Remaining open to new ideas and experiences is important for lifelong learning. We fall victim to allness when we close ourselves to new or different information.

How can we avoid allness? We can begin by recognizing that because we focus on only a portion of a stimulus or an event we necessarily neglect other aspects of that stimulus or event. Another safeguard is to refrain from thinking of ourselves as the center of the world. The allness attitude can impede the development of effective relationships. To counter this possibility, try to mentally end your assessment with the words *et cetera* ("and others"). Because you could never know everything there was to know about anything, the words remind you that you do not pretend to "know it all."

Blindering: A Person Is Not a Horse   The concept of *blindering* as a factor in perception can best be illustrated by the following exercise. Attempt to draw four straight lines that connect each of the dots in Figure 3-5. Do this without lifting your pencil or pen from the page or retracing over a line.

Did you find the exercise difficult or impossible to accomplish? Most people do. Why? The problem imposed only one restriction—that you connect the dots with four straight lines without lifting your pen from the page or backtracking over a line. Most of us, however, add another restriction: After examining the dots, we insist that the figure to be formed is a square. Actually, no such form or restriction exists, and once you realize this the solution becomes clear. (The answer appears on page 483.) In effect, the word or image of a square blindered you in your attempts to solve the problem. (Just as we put blinders on a horse to cut down on the number of visual stimuli it receives, so we also put blinders on ourselves.)

Blinders may aid a horse, but they can drastically hinder a human. Blindering is a habit that forces us to see only certain things or to see things only in certain ways. For example, much time was wasted and many lives were lost because the word *malaria* was contracted from the Italian words *mala* and *aria*, meaning "bad air." As communication specialist William Haney notes, this could have perpetuated the faulty assumption that the dread disease was carried by the bad air around swamps instead

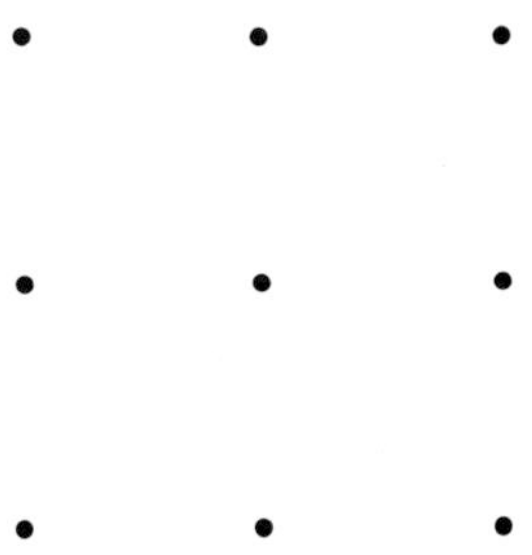

FIGURE 3-5
A test for blindering

of by mosquitoes. This is how blindering can lead to undesirable solutions or actions. It can also impede or slow down needed actions or decisions.

Observation or Inference: Which Is Which? Another factor that affects our perception and evaluation of people and events in our world is our inability to distinguish what we have *inferred* from what we have *observed*. For example, if you plan to leave your home to drive to a friend's house about a mile away, you probably make some inferences: that when you put the key into the ignition, your automobile will start; that you will not have a flat tire; and that no construction will block your approach to the friend's home. Likewise, when a traffic light turns green, you usually infer that it is safe to cross the street. (The authors found it difficult to walk across many streets in London because the custom there is for the pedestrian to enter the crosswalk and infer that all traffic will stop!)

It is important to distinguish facts from inferences. A *fact* is something that you know to be true, based on observation. You see a woman walking down the street carrying a briefcase. The statement "That woman is carrying a briefcase" is a fact. Our woman with the briefcase also has a frown on her face. We may state, "That woman is unhappy." This second statement, however, is an *inference*, since the truth of it cannot be verified by observation. In the old crime series *Dragnet*, Jack Webb would often tell witnesses, "All I want is the facts. Just the facts." Facts are not always easy to come by, and sometimes we falsely believe we have facts when we actually have inferences. Failing to recognize this distinction can be embarrassing or dangerous.

Sharpen your understanding of facts and inferences by reading the following newspaper story:

> He laughed because he thought that they could not hit him; he didn't imagine that they were practicing how to miss him.
>
> *Bertolt Brecht*

NORWICH, N.Y. (AP) They had arrested him for drunken driving, but he insisted he was sober.

Police said his eyes were glassy, his speech thick and his walk unsure.

Roswell Woods was given the usual tests. He was asked to blow up a balloon as a test. He couldn't do it.

He was taken to court. He pleaded not guilty and asked for an attorney.

Before a jury, the 47-year-old veteran heard himself accused. His attorney, Glen F. Carter, asked Woods to stand. He did.

"It has been testified that your eyes were glassy," the attorney said gently.

The accused pointed to his glass eye, placed there after he had lost an eye in battle.

"It has been testified that your speech was thick," the lawyer continued.

The defendant, speaking with difficulty, said he had partial paralysis of the throat. He said it resulted from one of the 27 injuries received in the line of duty in the South Pacific.

"Well, gee, frankly, Mr. Danforth, you being my boss, and asking me to lunch and all, I thought you would pick up the tab."

Drawing by Stan Hunt; © 1979 The New Yorker Magazine, Inc.

"It is also testified," Carter went on, "that you failed to pick up a coin from off the floor."

He brought out that Woods had been injured in both legs and had undergone an operation in which part of a bone in one leg was used to replace the shattered bone in the other. Woods was unable to stoop, he said.

"And now, the blowing-up of the balloon," the attorney said. "You couldn't blow it up, could you?"

The defendant replied: "I lost one of my lungs in the war. I can't exhale very well."

The jury returned its verdict quickly: "Not guilty."

© *The Associated Press*

Acting as if an assumption is a certainty can be risky. When we confuse facts and inferences we are likely to jump to conclusions. Now, test your own ability to distinguish facts and inferences by completing the Skill Builder "The Detective." How did you do? (Check your answers against those in the answer key on page 483.) This test is not designed to discourage you from making inferences. Of necessity we live our lives on an inferential level. It is designed, however, to discourage you from making inferences without being aware of doing so. It is also designed to help you stop operating as if your inferences were facts.

Are you aware of the inferences you make? As general semanticist S. I. Hayakawa notes, the real question is not whether we make inferences

The Detective

Read the story below. Assume that the information contained in it is true and accurate. On a sheet of paper, answer the questions that follow the story in order. Do not go back to change any of your answers. After you read a statement, simply indicate whether you think the statement is definitely true by writing *T*, definitely false by writing *F*, or questionable by writing a question mark. (Note: A question mark indicates that you think the statement could be true or false, but, on the basis of information contained in the story, you cannot be certain.)

A tired executive had just turned off the lights in the store when an individual approached and demanded money. The owner opened the safe. The contents of the safe were emptied, and the person ran away. The alarm was triggered, notifying the police of the occurrence.

1. An individual appeared after the owner had turned off the store's lights.
2. The robber was a man.
3. The person who appeared did not demand money.
4. The man who opened the safe was the owner.
5. The owner emptied the safe and ran away.
6. Someone opened the safe.
7. After the individual who demanded the money emptied the safe, he sped away.
8. Although the safe contained money, the story does not reveal how much.
9. The robber opened the safe.
10. The robber did not take the money.
11. In this story, only three persons are referred to.

but whether we are cognizant of the inferences we make. One of the key characteristics of a mature relationship is that neither party to it jumps to conclusions or acts on inferences as if they were facts.

The following list summarizes some of the essential differences between facts and inferences:

FACTS	INFERENCES
1. May be made only after observation or experience	1. May be made at any time
2. Are limited to what has been observed	2. Extend beyond observation
3. Can be offered by the observer only	3. Can be offered by anyone
4. May refer to the past or to the present	4. May refer to any time—past, present, or future
5. Approach certainty	5. Represent varying degrees of probability

HOW TO INCREASE THE ACCURACY OF YOUR PERCEPTIONS

Although our effectiveness as communicators is determined in part by our perceptual abilities, we rarely consider ways to increase our perceptual accuracy. Let's examine some suggestions for improving perceptual skills.

Realize That Your Perceptual Processes Are Personally Based

As we have mentioned, your perception of a person, thing, or event is different from the actual person, thing, or event. The object of your perception is "out there," but your perception is not "out there." Instead, your perception is a composite, or mixture, of what exists "out there" and what exists in you. You are the major actor in the perception process; you are its "star." Thus, what you perceive is determined by the physical limitations of your past experiences, needs, fears, desires, and interests. By becoming aware of your role in perception, by recognizing that you have biases, by acknowledging that you do not have a corner on the "truth market," you can increase the probability that your perceptions will provide you with accurate information about the world around you and the people who are a part of it.

A good communicator listens carefully to others, processes information fairly and objectively, and is willing to revise and update perceptions of the world. (Jim Pickerell/Stock Boston)

Take Your Time

Effective communicators are not in a hurry; rather, they take the time they need to process information fairly and objectively. When we act too quickly, we often make careless decisions that display poor judgment. In our haste, we overlook important clues, make inappropriate or unjustified inferences, and jump to conclusions. To combat this, we need to take our time to be sure we have assessed a situation correctly. Delaying a response instead of acting impulsively gives us an opportunity to check or verify our perceptions.

Remember, quick, impulsive reactions contribute to faulty perceptions and make us act on inferences as if they were facts. Accurate interpretation of our perceptions does not occur instantaneously.

Try to Be More Open

Frequently we act like robots that have been programmed to look at the world in a set way. But a person is neither a robot nor a computer. We can take steps to become more observant and broaden our expectations. We need to become willing to expect the unexpected and to expand the size of our perceptual "window." This will happen if we recognize that our reality is subjective, incomplete, and unique. Thus, if we want to cultivate a fuller, more valid perception of our world, we must be willing to review, revise, and update our view of the world.

As we work to internalize the premise of change, we should recognize that if we remove our self-imposed blinders, we will also remove some of the self-imposed restrictions that limit our ability to perceive accurately the individuals with whom we relate, the situations in which we become involved, and the problems we would like to solve. If we want our perceptions to be valid, we must make a commitment to search out alternatives in an effort to acquire as much information as possible. Furthermore, we cannot expect our perceptions to be accurate or useful if we are unwilling to change them by adding to them, discarding them, or readjusting them as needed. Remember, the more valid your perceptions, the better your chances of communicating effectively with others.

SUMMARY

Perception is the process of selecting, organizing, and interpreting sensory data in a way that enables us to make sense of our world. Perceptions are personally based. They are affected by the perspective we adopt, our sensory capabilities, and our past experiences. The accuracy of our perceptions is strongly influenced by perceptual sets (the readiness to process stimuli in predetermined ways), selective exposure (the tendency to close ourselves to new experiences), and selective perception (the inclination to distort our perceptions of stimuli to make them conform to our need for internal consistency or closure).

How we perceive another person is a key determinant of the kind of relationship we will share with that person. Thus perceiving others and the roles they play is an essential part of the communication process. A number of factors can prevent accurate perceptions. We frequently evaluate others on the basis of first impressions, and we tend to stereotype people, to divide them into groups and place them in niches. Stereotyping can be especially harmful by promoting prejudice, since it encourages us to emphasize similarities and deemphasize differences. Other barriers to perceptual accuracy are allness (the habit of thinking we know it all), blindering (the tendency to obscure solutions to problems by adding unnecessary restrictions), and fact-inference confusions (the inability to distinguish observations from assumptions).

It is important that you work to increase the validity of your perceptions. As a first step, you need to recognize the role you play in the perceptual process.

SUGGESTIONS FOR FURTHER READING

Allport, Gordon W. *The Nature of Prejudice.* Garden City, N.Y.: Doubleday, 1958. A classic work. A comprehensive treatment of the nature of prejudice and specific stereotypes.

Bartlett, Dorothy L., Pamela B. Drew, Eleanor Fable, and William A. Watts. "Selective Exposure to a Presidential Campaign Appeal," *Public Opinion Quarterly*, Vol. 38 (1974), pp. 264–270. Discusses the factors that influence the type of information individuals will expose themselves to during a campaign.

Berman, Sanford I. *Why Do We Jump to Conclusions?* San Francisco: International Society for General Semantics, 1969. A simple yet effective analysis of how we can avoid jumping to conclusions.

Cook, Mark. *Interpersonal Perception*, Baltimore: Penguin, 1971. Discusses the variables that affect perceptual capabilities.

Crouse, Timothy. *The Boys on the Bus.* New York: Ballantine, 1973. A definitive look at the prism through which reporters view events.

Epstein, Edward J. *News from Nowhere.* New York: Vintage, 1974. A detailed examination of the evening news programs of major networks. Epstein attempts to determine whether television mirrors or creates reality.

Haney, William V. *Communication and Organizational Behavior.* Homewood, Ill.: Irwin, 1973. A comprehensive look at the misevaluations we are prone to make and how we can avoid them.

Hastrof, Albert, and Hadley Cantril. "They Saw a Game: A Case Study," *Journal of Abnormal and Social Psychology*, Vol. 49 (1954), pp. 129–134. Describes how football fans perceive their home team and the opposition.

Hastrof, Albert, David Schneider, and Judith Polefka. *Person Perception.* Reading, Mass.: Addison-Wesley, 1970. A thorough survey of research in the field.

Milgrim, Stanley. "Confessions of a News Addict," *The New York Times*, August 7, 1977. A readable detailing of one person's news views.

Schramm, Wilbur, and Richard F. Carter. "Effectiveness of a Political Telethon," *Public Opinion Quarterly*, Vol. 23 (1959), pp. 121–126. An analysis and discussion of voter exposure preferences.

Tagiuri, Renato. "Person Perception." In *The Handbook of Social Psychology*, 2d ed., edited by G. Lindzey and E. Aronson. Reading, Mass.: Addison-Wesley, 1969. A classic article, scholarly and thorough.

Wilmot, William. *Dyadic Communication.* Reading, Mass.: Addison-Wesley, 1975. A clear discussion of the perceptual process.

NOTES

1. William V. Haney, *Communication and Organizational Behavior* (Homewood, Ill.: Irwin, 1973), p. 55.
2. E. Rubin, "Figure and Ground," in *Readings in Perception*, edited by D. Beardslee and M. Werthheimer (Princeton, N.J.: Van Nostrand), pp. 194–203.
3. See, for example, Hadley Cantril, "Perception and Interpersonal Relations," *American Journal of Psychiatry*, Vol. 114 (1957), pp. 119–126.
4. Wilbur Schramm and Richard F. Carter, "Effectiveness of a Political Telethon," *Public Opinion Quarterly*, Vol. 23 (1959), pp. 121–126.
5. Dorothy L. Bartlett, Pamela B. Drew, Eleanor Fable, and William A. Watts, "Selective Exposure to a Presidential Campaign Appeal," *Public Opinion Quarterly*, Vol. 38 (1974), pp. 264–270.
6. Edward Jay Epstein, *News from Nowhere* (New York: Vintage, 1974), p. 262.
7. See, for example, Gordon W. Allport, *The Nature of Prejudice* (Garden City, N.Y.: Doubleday, 1958).

4

Language and Meaning: Helping Minds Meet

Whatever we call a thing, whatever we say it is, it is not. For whatever we say is words, and words are words and not things. The words are maps, and the map is not the territory.

Harry L. Weinberg, "Some Limitations of Language"

CHAPTER PREVIEW

After finishing this chapter, you should be able to:

Define *language*

Describe and explain the Triangle of Meaning; identify a *word barrier*

Discuss the relationship between words and meaning

Explain how time, place, and experience affect meaning

Identify the differences between connotative and denotative meaning

Provide examples of bypassing

Distinguish between intensional and extensional orientation

Identify when the use of a sublanguage is appropriate and when it is inappropriate

Provide examples of the ways *word shading* can modify meaning

Identify factors that contribute to your own effective or ineffective use of language

H ave you ever considered the type of person you would be if you were unable to use words to express yourself? Going even further, have you ever considered the kind of person you would be if you were unable to make a sound? How would it feel to have certain ideas and not be able to communicate them? Like so many other things of importance, the value of speaking is frequently appreciated only when it is threatened, lost, or taken away. We depend on language to help us communicate meaning to others, and meaning is what communication is all about. If we understand how language works, we will be able to use words to help us share meaning with others.

LANGUAGE: WHAT'S THAT?

Language is a unified system of symbols that permits a sharing of meaning. A *symbol* stands for, or represents, something else. *Words* are symbols, and thus words represent things. Notice that we have said "represent" and "stand for" rather than "are." This is a very important distinction. Words *stand for or represent* things but *are not* things. Words are spoken sounds or the written representations of sounds that we have agreed will stand for something else. Thus by mutual consent we can make anything stand for anything.

The process of communication involves using words to help create meanings and expectations. However, important as words are in representing and describing objects and ideas, the meaning of a verbal message is not stamped on the face of the words we use. Meanings are in people, not in words. What is important to realize is that you have your meaning and other people have theirs. Even a common word such as *cat* can bring to mind meanings ranging from a fluffy angora to a sleek leopard. Your goal in communicating with another person is to have your meanings overlap so that you can each make sense out of the other's messages and understand each other. Thus, in order to communicate you translate the meaning you want to express into language so that the other person will respond to it by forming a meaning similar to yours. Although the use of language is obviously intended to aid effective communication, far too often language serves as an obstacle to communication.

THE TRIANGLE OF MEANING: WORDS, THINGS, AND THOUGHTS

Language can fulfill its potential only if we use it correctly; to do this, we must understand a number of things. The Triangle of Meaning, developed

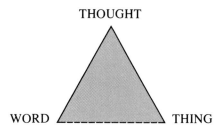

THOUGHT

WORD   THING

FIGURE 4-1
The Triangle of
Meaning

by communication theorists C. K. Ogden and I. A. Richards, helps explain how language works.[1] (See Figure 4-1.)

The dotted line connecting WORD (a symbol) and THING (a referent, or stimulus) indicates that the word is not the thing and that there is no *direct* relationship or connection between the two. Thus when you use words, you must constantly remind yourself that the only relationships between the words you use and the things they represent are those which exist in people's minds (including, of course, your own). Frequently, even the existence of an image (a physical object of some type) does not establish meaning. A few years back, a public service commercial depicting a rat and a child living in a tenement was shown on television. The child was seen beckoning to the rat as she repeated, "Here Kitty, Kitty! Here Kitty, Kitty!" Although this example may appear somewhat bizarre to you, its meaning is really quite clear: It is quite possible for two of us to look at the same object but give it different meanings. No one else will respond to a stimulus (word or thing) exactly as you do, because the meaning of anything is inside each of us who experiences it.[2] If you are to be a successful communicator, you should understand the relationships that exist between words and people's thoughts and reactions.

Word Barriers

In talking to others we often assume too quickly that they understand what we mean. There are, however, many reasons why we may not be understood as we want to be and why the words we use can create barriers. In Lewis Carroll's *Alice in Wonderland*, Humpty Dumpty and Alice have the following conversation:

> "I don't know what you mean by 'glory,' " Alice said.
> Humpty Dumpty smiled contemptuously, "Of course you don't—till I tell you. I meant, 'There's a nice knock-down argument for you!' "
> "But 'glory' doesn't mean 'A nice knock-down argument,' " Alice objected.
> "When I use a word," Humpty Dumpty said in a rather scornful tone, "it means just what I choose it to mean—neither more nor less."

We can make words mean whatever we want them to mean. Nothing stops us—except our desire to share meaning with others.

Words, like eyeglasses, blur everything that they do not make more clear.

Joseph Jourbert

How have words "blurred" your relationships?

MEASURING DENOTATIVE AND CONNOTATIVE MEANING

Sometimes we forget that we may experience a problem in communication if we consider only our own meaning for a word. (*We* know what we mean.) The crucial question is, What does our word bring to mind for those with whom we are communicating?

Meaning and Time

A definition is not attached to a word forever. Words evolve new meanings from era to era, from generation to generation, and sometimes even from year to year. When we use a word that referred to a particular object at one time, we should attempt to determine if it still means the same thing now. "Old" words often acquire vivid new meanings every decade or so. Remember this when speaking with others who are older or younger than you.

SKILL BUILDER

The Word-Time Capsule

1.   Write the following words on a sheet of paper:

pot	pad
gay	grass
high	speed
freak	gross
trip	hip
swing	dust
straight	joint
rock	stoned

2.   On a separate sheet of paper, write your definition of each of the words.

3.   Show the list, without definitions, to your parents, older relatives, or older friends and ask them to write *their* definitions for the words. Compare your meaning for each term with the meaning given by others you questioned. Why do you suppose their meanings differed from yours and each other's?

4.   Pretend it is now the year 2020. Create new meanings for each of the words listed.

Meaning and Place

Not only do words change meaning with the times, they also change meaning from one region of the country to another. For example, what would you envision having if you were to stop for a "soda"? For an "egg cream"? For a "Danish"? For some "pop"? What each word brings to mind probably depends on what region of the country you grew up in. In some parts of the United States a soda is a soft drink, but in others it refers to a concoction of ice cream and a soft drink. In some sections of the country an egg cream refers to a seltzer, syrup, and milk mixture, but elsewhere it conjures up images of an egg mixed with cream. To people in certain parts of the United States a Danish is any kind of breakfast pastry; in other regions people expect to be served a particular *kind* of breakfast pastry. In still other places the waiter might think that you were ordering a foreign specialty—or even a foreigner! As a further example of the effects of regional differences on communication, consider the accompanying piece by William Safire.

Meaning and Culture

Of course, different cultures and subcultures have different languages; hence, language usage among these cultures varies. If a concept is important to a particular culture, there will be a large number of terms to describe

---

TRAFFIC TALK

William Safire

A person whose curiosity causes him to slow traffic is called a *rubbernecker* in Texas, a *gonker* in Detroit and a *lookie-Lou* in L.A. Such obstructive gaping is called *gaper's block* in Denver.

How do traffic-casters refer to stalled cars? By converting adjectives to nouns: A disabled vehicle is called a *disable* in Texas and a *stall* in Baltimore. In Minneapolis, stalls and disables along the icy roadways are called *snowbirds*.

At interchanges, where freeways merge, the traffic-casters have a field day reporting trouble. In Dallas, beware *the Mixmaster;* in Denver, motorists dread *the Mousetrap;* in Detroit, the most jammable interchange is called *the Malfunction Junction.*

Rhyme and alliteration attract the troubadors of traffic trouble. In Detroit on days when roadways are icy, listeners are warned of *bunch and crunch;* after dry spells in Texas, when oil on the road is suddenly mixed with rain, the danger spoken of is *slip and slide.*

it. For example, in our culture, the word *money* is very important and we have many different words to describe it: *wealth, capital, assets, backing, resources,* and *finance* are just a few. Similarly, Eskimos have a number of different words for *snow* because they need to be able to make fine verbal distinctions when speaking of it. Thus, for Eskimos, *gana* refers to falling snow, and *akilukah* to fluffy fallen snow. As we see, the world we experience helps shape the language we speak, and the language we speak helps sustain our perception of reality and our view of our world. This idea is contained in the Sapir-Whorf hypothesis, which expresses the belief that the labels we use help shape the way we think, our world view, and our behavior. In other words, according to the Sapir-Whorf hypothesis, people from different cultures perceive stimuli and communicate differently, at least in part because of their language differences. For this reason you should not assume that the words you use and the words people from other cultures use mean the same thing to each of you, nor should you assume that you even see the same reality when viewing the same stimulus. Quite simply, our language and our perception are intertwined.

Meaning and Gender

Compile a list of language differences you believe exist between men and women. Why do you think each exists?

Sometimes the sex of communicators affects not only the meaning we give to their utterances but also the very structure of those utterances. Women, for example, use more tentative phrases or qualifiers in their speech than men do. Phrases like "I guess," "I think," and "I wonder if" abound in the speech patterns of women but not in those of men. This pattern is also passed on to the very young through their favorite cartoon characters. Just as their real-life counterparts are prone to do, female cartoon characters use verbs which indicate lack of certainty ("I suppose") and words judged to be more polite than do males.[3] The question is, Is art mirroring life or vice versa? Are our cartoons helping to perpetuate stereotypes? Women also tend to turn statements into questions more than men do. Women typically ask something like: "Don't you think it would be better to send them that report first?" Men, in contrast, typically respond with a more definitive "Yes, it would be better to send them that report first." According to language and gender researcher Robin Lakoff, women fail to lay claim to their statements as frequently as men do. In addition, women use more "tag" questions than men do. A *tag* is midway between an outright statement and a yes-no question. For instance, women often make queries like these: "Joan is here, isn't she?" "It's hot in here, isn't it?" By seeking verbal confirmation for their perceptions, women build a reputation for tentativeness. Similarly, women use more disclaimers than men do, prefacing their remarks with statements like "This probably isn't important, but . . ." Such practices weaken the messages sent to others.

Meaning and Power

Both males and females have the potential to influence the way others perceive them by communicating in ways that make them appear to be more confident, more forceful, and thus more in control of a situation.

Powertalkers, in contrast to those who announce their powerlessness through their language, make definite statements such as "Let's go out to dinner tonight" rather than uttering weaker hedges such as "I think we should go out to dinner tonight." In other words, powertalkers direct the action; they assume control.

Powertalkers also use fewer hesitations in their speech. Instead of making statements filled with nonfluencies such as "I wish you wouldn't, uh, keep me waiting so long," powertalkers enhance their sense of self-worth by projecting their opinions with more confidence. They eliminate fillers such as "er," "um," "you know," "like," and "well" that serve as verbal hiccups and make them appear weak.

Powertalkers use fewer unnecessary intensifiers than do more submissive talkers. "I'm not very interested in going" is a less forceful statement than is "I'm not interested in going." Rather than strengthening a position, intensifiers actually can serve to deflate it.

As we see, powerful talk is talk that comes directly to the point. It also does not contain disclaimers ("I probably shouldn't mention this, but . . .") or tag questions (see the preceding discussion of tag questions). If you succeed in speaking powertalk, your credibility and your ability to influence others will increase. Changing the power balance may be as simple as changing the words you use.

> Cite an instance when speaking "powerlessly" caused you to appear uncertain or confused. What happened as a result? How might you replay that situation now?

> To a great extent, power is just a matter of how you express yourself.
>
> *Jeffrey Eisen, Ph.D.*
> *Powertalk!*

Meaning and Experience

The meanings we assign to words are based on our past experiences with the words and with the things they represent. Take the word *cancer*, for example. If you were dealing with three different people in a hospital—a surgeon, a patient, and a statistician—how do you imagine each would react to this word? The surgeon might think about operating procedures, diagnostic techniques, or how to tell a patient that he or she has the disease. The patient might think about the odds for recovery against death and might well experience fear. The statistician might see cancer as an important factor in human life-expectancy tables.

Unlike "denotative" (or "dictionary") meanings, which are objective, abstract, and general in nature, "connotative" (or "personal") meanings are subjective and emotional in nature. Thus, your own experiences influence the meanings you assign to words; that is, your connotative meanings for a word vary according to your own feelings for the object or concept you are considering.

> If you cry "Forward" you must be sure to make clear the direction in which to go. Don't you see that if you fail to do that and simply call out the word to a monk and a revolutionary, they will go in precisely opposite directions.
>
> *Anton Chekhov*

ON LANGUAGE, YOUTHSPEAK

By Richard Bernstein

If you think *PC* stands for *personal computer*, what do you think *non-PC* means? Anything that is not a PC? Students these days, while familiar with high technology, are using the term *PC* as an abbreviation for *politically correct; non-PC* for its opposite. The term has a leftist connotation and, more likely than not, is used by those who believe the university works hand in glove with the capitalist establishment.

As always, the schools and colleges are producing a lot of slang. Some are invented words; some have been absorbed from street language, rap music, ethnic jargon; others are twists on the special vocabulary of an earlier generation. . . .

Every student generation, of course, wants to make its mark with its own words. In the 1960's, when I was a student, we used to say *cool it* to encourage calmness when all hell breaks loose. The expression has changed slightly; the word is now *chill* (another usage derived from street talk), usually spoken as a command.

Chill also seems to have replaced *to stand somebody up*, or *to fail to turn up for a date*. "She chilled on me," the young man said, after waiting disconsolately for several hours. (On the other hand, the word *chillin'*, with origins in rap music, means *first rate, terrific*, as in, "The concert was chillin'.") *Chill* seems a useful and even instructive term. It puts the ice on humiliation, muffles it in the com-fort of jargon, helps the sufferer to feign a bit of indifference. Much of the student lexicon has this euphemistic quality, since students, being of a tender age, are a vulnerable lot.

Connie C. Eble, an associate professor of English at the University of North Carolina at Chapel Hill, who has been collecting student slang for several years—keeping her burgeoning collection on 3 x 5 cards in green file drawers in her office—has a long list of these expressions. Her favorite, she says, is "talking to Ralph on the big white phone."

Ralph, Professor Eble explains, is onomatopoeic, mimicking the sound of regurgitation. *The big white phone* is a metaphor for the toilet bowl, and the expression means to *throw up*; "pray to the porcelain goddess" is a common alternative. . . .

Students have a host of words to refer to other students who study a great deal or who have the sort of seriousness of purpose that, when combined with a pronounced lack of social graces, produces what used to be called "grinds" or "nerds." The new insults are *dweeb*, *geek*, *goober* and *wonk*. And *corn dog*, *goob-a-tron* and *groover*.

A variation on this theme is *granola*, which refers to someone who dresses and acts as students did in the 1960's, perhaps somebody who wears sandals and beads and who says "nerd" instead of "goober." A *buzz crusher* is someone who puts a damper on things, a kill-joy. *Bite* moose is a way of telling somebody to get lost, to go to hell. . . .

On the subject of sex, Professor Eble's students have a rich vocabulary describing various forms of behavior that they either indulge in, or wish they did. There is often a defensive quality to this extreme irreverence—a preemptive unwillingness to care too deeply. *To box tonsils*, for example, means *to kiss passionately*, as does *to play tonsil hockey*. The sex act is *parallel parking* or the *horizontal bop*.

Sleep, on the other hand, is not something that students spend a great deal of time doing, and their words for it seem to reflect this. A *rack monster* is a bed; "to get some rack" is "to get some sleep." A *power nap* is a deep sleep induced by extreme exhaustion.

More than any other group, it would seem, students constantly use words in entirely new ways. Take *random*. When something makes no sense and you are resigned to its utter nonsensicalness, "it is random, really random, totally random." "This really random guy" would not be a flattering way of describing a new acquaintance. And *radical* is no longer the make-the-world-over-in-our-own-image word used ad nauseam during the 60's. *Radical*—often shortened to *rad*—means *great, wonderful, remarkable*.

In the old days, we used to say "awesome" to express an approving wonderment, while *radical*, of course, was associated with things revolutionary. *Far out*, for *astonishing* or *wondrous*, was another common term of 20 years ago that seems to have completely disappeared. It just goes to show how much things haven't really changed; the words may be different, but student preoccupations remain the same. . . .

Still, for someone of my generation, it's difficult to think of *radical* as synonymous with *awesome*, just as *far out* is not an allusion to something a great distance away. Perhaps by giving the word *radical* its new twist, students are telling us they aren't so radical anymore. If I objected to this apparent apathy, I would probably be called a *dweeb*, maybe a *granola*. Certainly I would be told to *bite moose*—or should that just be *chill*?

New York Times Magazine, December 11, 1988, Section C.

As we mentioned earlier, if we do not make an attempt to analyze how people's backgrounds influence them in assigning meaning, we may have trouble communicating with them. For most of us, words have more than a single meaning. In fact, commonly used words frequently have more than 20 different definitions. We know that a "strike" in bowling is different from a "strike" in baseball. We know that "to strike" a match is not the same as "striking up" the band. For this reason, we must pay careful attention to the "context" of a message. Unfortunately, we frequently forget that words are rarely used in one and only one sense, and we assume when we speak to others that words are used in only the way we intend them to be understood. Like us, our receivers may assume that we intended our words the way "they" happen to interpret them. Let's explore what happens when this occurs.

BYPASSING, AND BYPASSING THE BYPASS

Sometimes people think they understand each other when in fact they are really missing each other's meaning. This pattern of miscommunication is termed *bypassing* because the interactors' meanings simply *pass by* one another. We can identify two main kinds of bypassing.[4] One type occurs when people use different words or phrases to represent the same thing but are unaware that they are both talking about the same thing. For example, two politicians once argued vehemently over welfare policies. One stated that the city's welfare program should be totally overhauled, whereas the other believed that the program's concept should be kept intact but that minor changes should be made. Far too much time passed before one politician realized that what he termed an "overhaul" was equivalent to what the second politician considered "minor changes." How many times have you argued unnecessarily because you were unaware that the other person was using a different word or words to mean the same thing you were expressing?

Think of some instances when bypassing has caused problems for you.

The more common type of bypassing occurs when people use the same word or phrase but give it different meanings. In such cases, people appear to be in agreement when they substantially disagree. Sometimes this type of bypass is relatively harmless: A young man from England was astonished that he got slapped when he told an American acquaintance that he would "knock her up" before he returned to Britain. (It was only after he explained that to him "knock you up" meant "come and see you" that the young woman apologized.) At other times such bypassing can be less innocuous. Semanticists tell a tall but otherwise useful story about a motorist who was driving on a parkway outside New York City when his engine stalled. He managed to flag down another driver, who, after hearing his story, consented to push the stalled car to get it started. "My car has an automatic transmission," the first man explained, "so you'll have to get up to 30 or 35 miles an hour to get me moving." The other driver nodded in understanding, and the stalled motorist then climbed into his own car and waited for the other car to line up behind his. After much more waiting, he turned around—to see the other driver coming at him at 30 miles per hour!

Developing an awareness that bypassing can occur when you communicate is a first step in preventing it from interfering with or needlessly complicating your relationships. If you believe it is possible for your listener to misunderstand you, then be willing to take the time needed to ensure that your meanings for words overlap. Try never to be caught saying, "It never occurred to me that you would think I meant—" or, "I was certain you'd understand." To avoid bypassing, you must be "person-minded" instead of "word-minded." Remind yourself that your words may generate unpredictable or unexpected reactions in others. Trying to anticipate these reactions will help you forestall communication problems.

WORD-THING CONFUSIONS: "LABEL MADNESS"

Sometimes we forget that it is people, not words, who make meanings. When this happens, we pay far too much attention to labels and far too little attention to realities. We can approach this phase of our study of meaning by considering this problem of labels and how strongly they can influence us. For example, what type of behavior would you exhibit around vats labeled "Gasoline Drums"? You would probably be careful not to light any matches, and if you smoked, you would be certain not to toss away any cigarette butts. Would you change your behavior if the labels on the containers read "Empty Gasoline Drums"? Chances are, you might relax a bit and give less thought to the possibility of starting a fire. (Despite the label, however, empty drums are actually more dangerous because they contain explosive gasoline vapor.)

Which detergent would you be more likely to buy—the one with the label, or the one without? People tend to be influenced by labels, even if the products are identical and the brand-name product costs more. (Left, Barbara Alper/Stock Boston; right, Ellis Herwig/Stock Boston)

SKILL BUILDER

"Sticks and Stones . . ."

Pretend that you are a district court judge and are faced with the following case. Simon Maynard Kigler would like to change his name to 1048. That is, Simon would like to be called One Zero Four Eight, or "One Zero" for short. It is your task to decide whether to grant Simon this requested name change. Justify your decision with specific reasons.

Each of us has learned to see the world not as it is, but through the distorting glass of our words. It is through words that we are made human, and it is through words that we are dehumanized.

*Ashley Montagu,
"The Language of
Self-Deception"*

After studying such incidents, linguistic researcher Benjamin Lee Whorf suggested that the way people define or label a situation has a dramatic impact on their behavior. As we discussed earlier in this chapter, according to Whorf, coformulator of the Sapir-Whorf hypothesis, the words we use help mold our perceptions of reality and the world around us.[5] In other words, Whorf believes that our words actually *determine* the reality we are able to perceive. Thus, a person from a tropical country who rarely if ever has experienced snow and who simply calls snow "snow" probably "sees" only one thing ("snow") when confronted with different kinds of frozen moisture falling from the sky. In contrast, skiers, who depend on snow, seek out snow, and diligently follow snow reports, are able to label and distinguish approximately six different types.

How important are labels in our culture? The skill builder above may help answer this question. A real-life judge faced with a similar case ruled that the individual could not change his name because a number was totalitarian and an offense to human dignity. What does a number signify? Would *we* change if our names were changed?[6] In *Romeo and Juliet*, Shakespeare offered some thoughts on the significance of names when he had Juliet, of the Capulet family, say these words to Romeo, a Montague:

> 'Tis but thy name that is my enemy;
> Thou art thyself, though not a Montague.
> What's Montague? It is nor hand, nor foot,
> Nor arm, nor face, nor any other part
> Belonging to a man. O! be some other name;
> What's in a name? that which we call a rose
> By any other name would smell as sweet;
> So Romeo would, were he not Romeo call'd. . . .

Are most people blinded by labels? A storekeeper who wanted to know attempted to answer this question by conducting the following test. The storekeeper had just received an order of identical handkerchiefs. He arbitrarily divided the order in half and placed one half on a table and labeled it "Genuine Irish Linen Handkerchiefs—2 for $3." He placed the other half of the order on another counter and labeled it "Noserags—2 for 25¢." What do you think happened? Right! The storekeeper's customers reacted negatively to the "noserag" label and bought the "Genuine Irish Linen Handkerchiefs" instead. It seems nobody likes to buy "noserags"— even if they are "Genuine Irish Linen"! Would you?

In his book *Influence*, Robert B. Cialdini provides an example that illustrates *intensional orientation* in action.[7] A friend of his who had recently opened an Indian jewelry store in Arizona, in an effort to move some turquoise jewelry she had been having trouble selling, scribbled the following note to her head salesclerk: "Everything in this display case, price × ½." The owner then left for a business trip. When she returned to her jewelry store a few days later, she was not surprised to find that every piece had been sold, but she was surprised to discover that because the employee had read the "½" in her scribbled message as a "2," the entire supply of turquoise jewelry had sold out at twice the original price. The store's customers had displayed intensional orientation. In their mind, expensive meant good, and items' higher prices made them believe that the worth of the items had increased too. In other words, a dramatic increase in price had led the buyers to see the turquoise pieces as more valuable and desirable. But the customers were reacting to a label—the price. And labels don't always tell us all we have to know. The label-happy customers had failed to inspect the territory. Remember, if you react to a label without examining what the label represents, you are displaying an intensional orientation. Individuals who are intensionally oriented are easily fooled by words and labels. In contrast, when you take the time to look beyond a label, when you inspect the thing itself, you display an *extensional orientation*. Individuals who are extensionally oriented are disposed to reality rather than to fantasy.

Frequently, our reactions to a person or event are totally changed by words, or by even a single word. We simply confuse words with things. If we are not aware of our responses, we can very easily be manipulated or "conned" by language. Take some time to analyze how your reactions may change as the labels in each of the following word sets change:

1.	coffin	casket	slumber chamber
2.	girl	woman	broad
3.	backward	developing	underdeveloped
4.	the corpse	the deceased	the loved one
5.	cheat	evade	find loopholes
6.	janitor	custodian	sanitary engineer
7.	kill	waste	annihilate
8.	war	police action	defensive maneuvers
9.	toilet	bathroom	rest room

10.	senior citizens	aged	old people
11.	air strike	bombing raid	protective reaction
12.	broke	poor	disadvantaged
13.	bill collector	debt chaser	adjuster
14.	love child	illegitimate child	bastard
15.	an illegal	an alien	an undocumented resident

IMPROVING ORAL LANGUAGE ABILITIES: A CALL FOR COMMON SENSE AND CLARITY

Whenever we communicate, we consciously or unconsciously select the level of language we will use. Normally, the words we select depend on the person we are communicating with and where we are communicating. It is important to recognize that different styles of behavior are required in different circumstances.

A Call for Common Sense

It should be apparent that just as particular styles of apparel and behavior are appropriate for certain situations, so certain styles of language are appropriate at certain times and in certain places. Although we may use slang (a style of language used by special groups but not considered "proper" by society at large) when conversing with our friends, slang would be inappropriate and unwise when speaking to an instructor or when delivering a speech to the town council. You have the capability to adapt the language you use as you move from one situation to another, but first you need to be aware of the conditions and circumstances that can affect your language usage. Jonathan Swift said it long ago when he noted that style is simply "proper words in proper places." Thus it all boils down to deciding what is meant by "proper." What you think is proper may not always coincide with what someone else thinks is proper.

A Call for Clarity

In day-to-day communication, for any one of several reasons we far too frequently use language that our cocommunicators cannot easily understand. It doesn't matter how accurately a selected word or phrase expresses *our* ideas if, when the receivers hear it, they cannot comprehend it. If you want to be understood, you must make every attempt to select words with meaning for your listeners. If you can accomplish this, you will have taken a giant step toward achieving understanding.

First, as a communicator you want to be sure to use words geared to the *educational level* of your listeners. The following example, adapted

What's Taboo to You?

1. Would you feel comfortable using obscenities with any of the following people? Why or why not?

Your grandparents   A maître d'
Your best friend   Your team coach
The president of your school   Your instructor
Your state senator   Your physician
Your employer

2. How would your answers to the preceding question change if you were in each of the following environments?

A fancy restaurant   A department store
A truck-stop diner   The school cafeteria
Your living room   A sports stadium
Your den   An auditorium
A classroom

3. How would your answers change if each individual listed in question 1 were a man? A woman? To what extent, if any, did your responses vary? Why?

from Stewart Chase's *The Power of Words*, aptly illustrates the problems that can arise from a lack of consideration for the receiver's educational background.

A plumber with a limited command of English was aware that hydrochloric acid opened clogged drain pipes quickly and effectively. However, he thought he had better check with the National Bureau of Standards in Washington, D.C., to determine if hydrochloric acid was safe to use in pipes, so he wrote the bureau a letter. A scientist at the bureau wrote back, stating: "The efficacy of hydrochloric acid is indisputable, but the corrosive residue is incompatible with metallic surfaces."

The plumber wrote a second letter, thanking the bureau for the quick reply and for giving him the okay to use hydrochloric acid.

The plumber's second letter bothered the scientist and he showed it to his boss. The boss decided to write another letter to the plumber. The boss's letter read: "We cannot assume responsibility for the production of toxic and noxious residue which hydrochloric acid can produce; we suggest that you use an alternative procedure."

This left the plumber somewhat confused. He dashed off a letter to the bureau telling them that he was glad they agreed with him. "The acid was working just fine."

When this letter arrived, the boss sent it to the "top administrator" at the bureau. The top administrator solved the problem by writing a short note to the plumber: "Don't use hydrochloric acid. It eats the hell out of pipes!"

Another good rule to follow if you hope to achieve clarity is to keep *jargon usage* to a minimum unless your receiver is schooled in the jargon. In other words, "speak the same language" as your listener. Most of us who live in the United States share a common language, but many of us also frequently use one or more sublanguages. A *sublanguage* is simply a special language used by members of a particular subculture. We all belong to several subcultures—a national group, an occupational group, an educational group, and perhaps an ethnic or religious group. Having a common sublanguage helps members of the group attain a sense of identity. (For example, when some blacks address their acquaintances as "Brother" or "Sister" in greeting each other in the street, they are affirming their subcultural membership.) However, since all sublanguages are intended to enable communication only within a particular group, a sublanguage is probably not readily understood by outsiders to that group. As an example, consider this brief dialogue between two doctors.

> DOCTOR 1: How's that patient you were telling me about?
> DOCTOR 2: Well, she's improving. But now she's suffering from cephalagia complicated by agrypnia.

In analyzing this interchange you would probably not immediately guess that *cephalagia* is the medical term for headache and that *agrypnia* refers to insomnia. Thus, people schooled in the technical language of a particular group should constantly guard against what may be termed an innate temptation to impress others rather than to communicate. In short, we must always ask ourselves "Who am I talking to?" if we want our receiver to understand us.

All that we've said notwithstanding, using readily understandable language need not keep you from aiming for accuracy. Never abandon your efforts to find the exact words that represent the ideas you want to communicate. Remember that a clear message is neither ambiguous nor confusing. Your precise meaning will be shared with other people only if your words tell them precisely what you mean. Thus, be concrete rather than vague in the words you select to represent your thoughts. For example, if you were trying to convey how a man sounded when he spoke, you could state: "He said," "He yelled," "He cried," "He purred," "He chuckled," "He growled," "He boomed," or "He sang." Each description would leave your listener with a somewhat different impression and feeling. Your words would shape the meaning you convey to others. As you increase your sensitivity to language, your awareness of the subtle shades of meaning that can be achieved with words will grow.

HOW TO MAKE WORDS WORK FOR YOU: A GUIDE TO FURTHER SKILL DEVELOPMENT

Throughout this chapter we have stressed that the mastery of certain language skills will improve your ability to communicate effectively with others. Use the following guidelines to ensure that your words work for rather than against you.

Identify How Word Labels Affect Your Behavior

We can state one of the most fundamental precepts of language usage simply and directly: *Words are not things*. Always remember that words are nothing more than symbols. No connection *necessarily* exists between a symbol and what people have agreed that symbol represents. In other words, symbols and their representations are independent of each other. All of us at times respond as if words and things were one and the same, for example, when we make statements resembling the following: "A bathroom is a bathroom. It's certainly not a water closet." "Pigs are called 'pigs' because they wallow in mud and grime." Think of how often you buy products such as Intimate, Brute, Bold, Caress, Secret, or Gleem because of what the label seems to promise. How many times have you turned against a person because he or she is called "liberal," "conservative," "feminist," "chauvinist," "intellectual," or "brainless"? Examine your behavior with others. Make certain you react to *people*, not to the categories within which you or others have placed them.

Too frequently we let words trigger our responses, shape our ideas, affect our attitudes, and direct our behavior, because we assume that words have magical or mystical powers that they do not have. We foolishly transfer qualities implied by labels to the things that labels represent. Becoming conscious of how labels affect you is the first step in changing your attitudes toward them. Don't permit labels to blind you, mislead you, fool you, or imprison you.

Identify How the Words You Use Reflect Your Feelings and Attitudes

It is important to recognize that few of the words you select to describe things are neutral. S. I. Hayakawa, author of *Language in Thought and Action*, noted this when he wrote the following:

We are a little too dignified, perhaps, to growl like dogs, but we do the next best thing and substitute series of words, such as "You dirty double crosser!" "The filthy scum!" Similarly, if we are pleasurably agitated, we may, instead of purring or wagging the tail, say things like "She's the sweetest girl in all the world."

Count the number of times you use "purr words" or "snarl words" each day. What do they reveal about your likes and dislikes? How do your words give you away?

We all use "snarl words" and "purr words." These words do not describe the persons or things we are talking about; rather, they describe our personal feelings for and attitudes toward the objects of our orientation. When we make statements like "He's a great American," "She's a dirty politician," "He's a bore," "She's a radical," "He's a Wall Street slicky," "She's a greedy conservative," "He's a male chauvinist pig," or "She's a crazy feminist," we should not delude ourselves into thinking that we are talking about anything but our own preferences. We are neither making reports nor describing conditions that necessarily exist. Instead, we are expressing our attitudes *about something.* Under such circumstances, if others are to determine what we mean by our descriptions, they are compelled to follow up and ask why.

It is also important to realize that a word that does not function as a snarl word or purr word for you may function that way for someone else, even if you did not intend your words to be given such an interpretation. What does matter is the response of the person with whom you are interacting. Therefore, become conscious of the ways others react to words you use. Listen to people around you and attempt to read their responses to your words. Which words that incite them would not incite you? Which words do they find unacceptable or offensive? Why?

We all have our own meanings for words. When engaging in communication, however, we have to be concerned with how others will react to the words we use. We have to consider the possible meanings they may have for our words. In order to accomplish this, you must make an honest effort to get to know the people with whom you interact. Become familiar with how their background could cause them to respond to certain words or phrases with hostility, anger, approval, or joy. Remember, your ability to communicate effectively with someone else can be positively or adversely affected by the words you use.

Identify How Experience Can Affect Meaning

Since we give meaning based on our experience and since no two people have had exactly the same set of experiences, it follows that no two people will have exactly the same meanings for the same word. This aspect of language should be neither lauded nor cursed; it should simply be remembered.

Remember that word meanings can change as the people who use words change. The fact that you might wear a sport jacket and slacks or a skirt and sweater if invited to a "casual" party does not mean that everyone else invited to the party would interpret "casual" in the same way. One person might wear jeans and a sport shirt, another shorts and a T-shirt. Likewise, because you feel that the word *freak* has only positive connotations does not exclude the possibility that another person might believe it has only negative connotations. The meanings people attribute to symbols are affected by their backgrounds, ages, educational levels, and professions. Forgetting this can cause misunderstandings and lead to communication difficulties.

Be guided by the fact that words in themselves have no meaning; remember that meaning resides in the minds of the communicators. Try to identify how the life experiences of people with whom you communicate can cause them to respond to words in ways in which you would not respond. Remember, the responses of the people are neither right nor wrong, only different. Do not take your—or anyone's—language for granted. Do not conclude that everyone thinks as you think and means what you mean. You know what a word means from your own frame of reference, but do you know what it means to someone with a different frame of reference? Have the patience to find out.

Be Sure That Meaning Is Shared

Since intended meanings are not necessarily the same as perceived meanings, you may need to ask the individuals with whom you are speaking such questions as "What do you think about what I've just said?" or "What do my words mean to you?" Their answers can serve two important purposes: They help you determine whether you have been understood, and they permit the other people to become involved in the encounter by expressing their interpretations of your message. If differences in the assignment of meaning surface during this feedback process, you will be immediately able to clarify your meanings by substituting different symbols or by relating your thoughts more closely to the background, state of knowledge, and experiences of your receivers.

Keeping each of these guidelines in mind as you interact with others should help to improve your communication skills. If you recognize that every time you communicate with others you run the risk of being misunderstood, then you will be more likely to become sensitive to the ways in which your words affect those with whom you relate. As John Condon, author of *Semantics and Communication*, advises, "Learning to use language intelligently begins by learning not to be used by language."

SUMMARY

Language is a unified system of symbols that permits a sharing of meaning. Language allows minds to meet, merge, and mesh. When we "make sense" out of people's messages, we learn to understand people.

There is no direct relationship between words and things, as Ogden and Richards's Triangle of Meaning demonstrates. Words don't "mean"; people give meaning to words. A principal barrier to communication is the fact that different people give different meanings to the same words. Words change across time, from place to place, and according to individual experience.

Among the communication problems that result from changes in word meaning are (1) bypassing (when people think they understand each other but in fact do not) and (2) mistaking the label for the thing itself (displaying an intensional rather than an extensional orientation).

There are two strategies we can use to improve our oral language abilities. First, we can use common sense to recognize that certain styles of language are appropriate at certain times and in certain places. Second, we can seek to make ourselves as clear as possible by selecting words with meaning for our listeners, taking account of their educational level and the sublanguages they understand.

SUGGESTIONS FOR FURTHER READING

Chase, Stuart. *The Power of Words*. New York: Harcourt Brace Jovanovich, 1953. A very readable description of some of the semantic problems that plague us.

Condon, John C. *Semantics and Communication*, 2d ed. New York: Macmillan, 1975. Contains a good discussion of barriers to verbal interaction.

Haney, William V. *Communication and Organizational Behavior*, 3d ed. Homewood, Ill.: Irwin, 1973. A clear discussion of the misevaluations that impede communication effectiveness.

Hayakawa, S. I. *Language in Thought and Action*. New York: Harcourt Brace Jovanovich, 1964. A comprehensive study of general semantics containing useful exercises.

Hayakawa, S. I. *The Use and Misuse of Language*. Greenwich, Conn.: Fawcett, 1962. A collection of essays treating common language problems.

Newman, Edwin. *A Civil Tongue*. Indianapolis: Bobbs-Merrill, 1976. Contains wonderful examples of semantic "atrocities."

Ogden, C. K., and I. A. Richards. *The Meaning of Meaning*. New York: Harcourt Brace Jovanovich, 1930. A classic work. Scholarly discussion of the nature of meaning.

Osgood, Charles, George Suci, and Percy Tannenbaum. *The Measurement of Meaning*. Urbana: University of Illinois Press, 1957. A scholarly discussion of how words mean.

Pearson, Judy Cornelia. *Gender and Communication*. Dubuque, Iowa: William C. Brown, 1985. A scholarly compilation about how gender affects communication.

Whorf, Benjamin Lee. "Science and Linguistics." In *Language, Thought and Reality: Selected Writings of Benjamin Lee Whorf*, edited by John B. Carroll. Cambridge, Mass.: M.I.T. Press, 1966. Explores how thinking and language are related to each other.

NOTES

1. C. K. Ogden and I. A. Richards, *The Meaning of Meaning* (New York: Harcourt Brace Jovanovich, 1930).
2. Charles F. Vich and Ray V. Wood, "Similarity of Past Experience and the Communication of Meaning," *Speech Monographs*, Vol. 36 (1969), pp. 159–162.
3. A. Mulac, J. Bradac, and S. Mann, "Male/Female Language Differences and Attributional Consequences in Children's Television," *Human Communication Research*, Vol. 11 (1985), pp. 481–506.
4. See William V. Haney, *Communication and Organizational Behavior*, 3d ed. (Homewood, Ill.: Irwin, 1973), pp. 247–248.
5. Benjamin Lee Whorf, "Science and Linguistics," in *Language, Thought and Reality: Selected Writings of Benjamin Lee Whorf*, edited by John B. Carroll (Cambridge, Mass.: M.I.T. Press, 1966).
6. For a discussion on names and the way they affect us, see Mary Marcus, "The Power of a Name," *Psychology Today* (October 1976), pp. 75–76, 108.
7. For a more complete discussion of this incident, see Robert B. Cialdini, *Influence* (New York: Quill, 1984), pp. 15–27.

5

Nonverbal Communication: Silent Language Speaks

What you are speaks so loudly that I cannot hear what you say.

Ralph Waldo Emerson

CHAPTER PREVIEW

After finishing this chapter, you should be able to:

Define *nonverbal communication*

Explain why nonverbal cues can be ambiguous

Define *kinesics*

Explain why the face is an important source of information

Demonstrate how the face is used to send emotionally charged messages

Explain the meaning of *microfacial expression*

Provide examples of the kinds of messages communicated by postural cues

Distinguish between mesomorphic, endomorphic, and ectomorphic body types

Explain how dress style can affect communication

Define *paralanguage*; explain how pitch, volume, rate, and pause affect communication

Define *proxemics*

Distinguish between intimate distance, personal distance, social distance, and public distance

Explain why territoriality is an important concept in communication

Describe how color can be used to communicate

Explain the types of messages communicated by touch

Assess your own effectiveness as a nonverbal communicator

A rthur Conan Doyle's most famous character, the detective Sherlock Holmes, frequently used to tell his cohort Dr. Watson, "You see, but you do not *observe*." The meaning of this statement is contained in a bit of pithy Holmesian advice:

> By a man's finger nails, by his coat-sleeve, by his boots, by his trouser-knees, by the callosites on his forefinger and thumb, by his shirt-cuffs— by each of these things a man's calling is plainly revealed. That all united should fail to enlighten the competent inquirer in any case is almost inconceivable.

Sherlock Holmes was of course a fictional creation able to solve the most perplexing crimes because he noticed the minute details that elude most people. His method can be profitably applied to real-life situations and specifically to our study of communication.

CAN YOU HEAR WHAT I'M NOT SAYING?

The founder of psychoanalysis, Sigmund Freud, once wrote: "He that has eyes to see and ears to hear may convince himself that no mortal can keep a secret. If his lips are silent, he chatters with his finger tips; betrayal oozes out of him at every pore." Many a time, our creative problem-solving abilities are challenged as we seek to make sense out of human communication situations. The following is one such mystery that challenged the thinking capabilities of many human minds.

In turn-of-the-century Berlin Herr Von Osten purchased a horse, which he named Hans. Von Osten trained Hans, not to jump, stand on his hind legs, or even dance, but to count by tapping his front hoof. To his master's astonishment the horse learned to count very quickly, and in a short time he also learned to add, multiply, divide, and subtract.

Von Osten exhibited Hans at fairs and carnivals, and the crowds loved it when the horse would correctly count the number of people in the audience, identify the number of persons wearing eyeglasses, or count the number of individuals wearing hats. In addition, Hans thrilled observers by telling time and announcing the date—all by tapping his hoof. Von Osten also decided to teach his horse the alphabet: An *A* was one hoof tap, a *B* two taps, and so on. Once he learned this, Hans was able to reply to oral and written questions alike, and his proficiency earned him the title "Clever Hans."

Naturally, some who heard about the feats of "Clever Hans" were skeptical and reasoned that no horse could do these things and so there must be some trickery involved. A committee was charged with the task of deciding whether there was any deceit involved in Hans's performances. On the committee were professors of psychology and physiology, the head of the Berlin Zoo, a circus director, veterinarians, and cavalry officers. Van Osten was not permitted to be present when the committee tested the horse, but despite the absence of his trainer, Hans was able to supply correct answers for all the questions put to him. The committee decided there was no trickery involved.

Some skeptics, however, were still not satisfied, so a second investigation was conducted by a new committee. This time, however, the procedures were changed. Von Osten was asked to whisper a number into Hans's left ear, then another experimenter named Pfungst whispered a number into Hans's right ear. Hans was then instructed to add the two numbers—an answer none of the observers, Von Osten, or Pfungst knew. Hans couldn't do it. It seems that Hans could only answer a question if someone in his visual field knew the answer.

Why do you think Hans had to see someone who knew the answer? Apparently, when the horse was asked a question that all the observers had heard, the observers assumed an *expectant posture* and increased their body tension. When Hans tapped the correct number of hoofbeats, the observers would relax and slightly move their heads—cues Hans used in order to know when to stop tapping. Thus somehow the horse had the ability to respond to the almost imperceptible movements of people around him. Much as you are able to sense when someone wants you to stop talking or when it is time to leave a party, Hans was able to interpret the nonverbal messages of his onlookers.

Whether we are aware of it, we all communicate nonverbally. Theorists Albert Mehrabian, Mark Knapp, and Ray Birdwhistell agree that in a normal two-person conversation the verbal channel carries less than 35 percent of a message's social meaning; this means that more than 65 percent of the meaning is communicated nonverbally.[1] (See Figure 5-1.) By analyzing

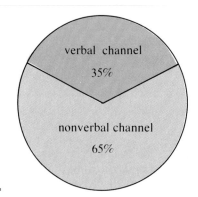

FIGURE 5-1
The communication
of social meaning

nonverbal cues we can enhance our understanding of what is really being said when people talk. The nonverbal level can also help us define the nature of each relationship we share with someone else. With practice, we can learn to use the nonverbal mode to provide us with "ways of knowing" that would not otherwise be available to us.[2] The goal of this chapter is to help you increase your awareness of nonverbal stimuli and expand your ability to use the cues you perceive. Doing so will help you immeasurably in becoming a more effective communicator.

CHARACTERISTICS OF NONVERBAL COMMUNICATION: CUES AND CONTEXTS

What is nonverbal communication? How do you recognize it? How can you become a nonverbal cue "detective"? The term *nonverbal communication* designates all the kinds of human responses not expressed in words. This includes a wide range of behaviors. Bernard Gunther in his book *Sense Relaxation below Your Mind* has identified some of the factors we should be concerned with when analyzing human communication—your messages and others':

Shaking hands
Your posture
Facial expressions
Your appearance
Voice tone
Hair style
Your clothes
The expression in your eyes
Your smile
How close you stand to others

How you listen
Your confidence
Your breathing
The way you move
The way you stand
How you touch other people

These aspects of you affect your relationship with other people, often without you and them realizing it. . . .

The body talks, its message is how you really are, not how you think you are. . . .

. . . Many in our culture reach forward from the neck because they are anxious to get a-head. Others hold their necks tight; afraid to lose their head. Body language is literal.

Gunther is correct when he observes that we communicate with our bodies and appearance. However, nonverbal content is even more extensive than he indicates. We also communicate by sending messages through the environment we create and live in. If, for example, someone entered and walked through your house or apartment at this very moment, what kinds of assumptions would they be able to make about you and your family? The spaces we inhabit broadcast information about us to others, even when we are not in them. For instance, are you sloppy or tidy? Do you like roominess, or do you crave the security of cozy places? How you dress your environment and how you dress yourself provide clues about your role, status, age, and goals. Your voice also carries information about you to others.

Nonverbal communication is perpetual and, frequently, involuntary. As Paul Watzlawick, author of *Pragmatics of Human Communication*, points out, "no matter how hard one may try, one cannot not communicate." You cannot stop sending nonverbal messages; you cannot stop behaving. As long as one person is observing the actions of another, it is impossible not to communicate. Even if one partner in a conversation suddenly leaves the room, he or she is communicating personal attitudes. If you stuck your head in a paper bag or sat in class while completely encased in a sack, you would still be communicating with those around you. You are communicating nonverbally right now. If, at this very moment, someone were to photograph you, what could others surmise by examining the photograph? How are you sitting? Where are you sitting? How are you dressed? What would your facial expression reveal about your reaction to this chapter? Would different people interpret the photograph in the same way? Why?

Like verbal communication, nonverbal communication is ambiguous. Like words, nonverbal messages may not mean what we think they do. Thus, we have to be careful about misinterpreting them. Don't be surprised if you find that the real reason a person glanced at a clock, left a meeting early, or arrived late to class is quite different from what you assumed. It

For the next two minutes, face another person and try not to communicate anything to him or her. What happened? Did you look at each other? Look away? Giggle? Smile? Shift positions? Pick your fingers? What specific behaviors did your partner display?

is simply not possible to develop a list of nonverbal behaviors and attach a single meaning to each. All nonverbal communication must be evaluated or interpreted *within the context in which it occurs*. You cannot "read" a person "like a book," nor can others always "read" you. Still, you should realize that those you interact with will attribute meaning to your behavior and make important judgments and decisions based on their observations.

As you say "I am really glad to be here," try to do everything you can to indicate the opposite. What devices did you use? Voice tone? Posture? Facial expressions?

Furthermore, verbal and nonverbal messages can—and often do—contradict one another. When we sometimes say one thing but do another, we send a "mixed," or incongruent, message. As you become aware of the nonverbal cues you and others send, you will begin to recognize contradictory messages that impede communication effectiveness. Wherever you detect an incongruity between *verbal* (word-level) messages, you would probably benefit by paying greater attention to the *nonverbal* messages. Researchers in communication believe that nonverbal cues are more difficult to fake than verbal ones, hence the importance of examining the nonverbal dimension. If we are going to rely on the nonverbal mode, then we must understand it.

"IF YOU COULD READ MY . . ."

In order to arrive at a better understanding of communication and develop skills that will permit us to both send and receive cues more accurately, we will examine the following areas:

Body language (kinesics)
Physique and dress style
Voice (paralanguage)
Space, distance, color, and time (proxemic and environmental factors)
Touch

The types of messages that fall within these categories do not occur in isolation; they interact, sometimes supporting and sometimes contradicting one another. We will first examine these areas separately and then, during the skills section of this chapter, bring them together so that you can reassemble the nonverbal "puzzle" and increase your overall communication effectiveness.

Body Language

The study of body communication has received much attention. *Kinesics*—body motion, or "body language," as it is popularly called—typically includes gestures, body movements, facial expressions, eye behavior, and posture.

Thus, hand movement, a surprised stare, drooping shoulders, a knowing smile, and a tilt of the head are all part of kinesics.

Facial Expressions.   To a large extent, we can send messages with our facial muscles. Why is the face so important? First, it is our main channel for communicating our own emotions and for analyzing the feelings and sentiments of others. This is one reason why motion picture and television directors employ so many close-ups. Television is often referred to as "the medium of talking heads." It is the face that is relied on to reinforce or contradict what is being communicated through dialogue. Likewise, in your personal relations your face and the faces of those around you broadcast inner feelings and emotions. How well do you read faces? Research has shown that many individuals are able to decipher facial cues with great accuracy, whereas others do not display such proficiency. Your ability to read someone's face increases when you know that person, understand the context of the interaction, or are able to compare and contrast the individual's facial expressions with others you have seen him or her make.

Of all the nonverbal channels, the face is the single most important broadcaster of emotions. You may be able to hide your hands, and you may choose to keep silent, but you cannot hide your face without making people feel you are attempting to deceive them. Since we cannot "put the face away," we take great pains to control the expressions we reveal to others.

How do we do this? To control our facial behavior, we can intensify, deintensify, neutralize, or attempt to mask a felt emotion. When we *intensify* a felt emotion, we exaggerate our facial responses to meet what we believe to be the expectations of others who are watching us. Remember the time you pretended you loved a gift you received so as not to disappoint the giver, when in reality you couldn't stand it? When we *deintensify* a felt emotion, we deemphasize our facial behaviors so that others will judge our reactions to be more appropriate. Remember the time you were very angry with a professor but restrained yourself because you feared the professor's response if you let your anger show, the way you would with a good friend? When we *neutralize* a felt emotion, we avoid displaying any emotion. Sometimes this neutralization is an attempt to display inner strength, as when we are saddened by the death of a relative but want to appear brave. In our culture men more frequently neutralize the emotions of fear and sadness than do women. This emotion suppression, or *internalization*, may account for the fact that men are more frequent sufferers of ulcers than are women. Finally, when we *mask* a felt emotion, we replace one emotion with another to which we believe others will respond more favorably. Thus, we sometimes conceal feelings of jealousy, disappointment, or rage. George Orwell spoke of the need for face masking in his novel *1984:* "It was terribly dangerous to let your thoughts wander when you were in any public place or within range of a telescreen. The smallest thing could give you away. A

Did you know that the 80 muscles in the face can create more than 7,000 expressions?

Have you ever been guilty of "face-crime"? Were you punished? Should you have been? Why or why not?

How can you use facial cues to determine if others, including your boss, co-workers, and friends, are being honest with you?

nervous tic, an unconscious look of anxiety, a habit of muttering to yourself—anything that carried with it the suggestion of abnormality, of having something to hide. In any case, to wear an improper expression on your face (to look incredulous when a victory was announced, for example), was itself a punishable offense. There was even a word for it in Newspeak: *facecrime*, it was called."

Certainly, controlling our facial expressions is a formidable task. Let's examine why.

Facially, we may at any time—without realizing it—be communicating multiple emotions rather than one. Researchers Paul Ekman and Wallace Friesen call these facial movements "affect blends."[3] The presence or absence of certain affect blends may help explain why we feel comfortable around some people and uncomfortable around others. It seems that some expressions appear on a person's face for only fractions of a second. Thus, what began as a smile may ever so briefly become a grimace and then may

SKILL BUILDER

When people assume expressions of anger, fear, or sadness, the heart rate increases. According to psychologist Robert Levenson, this is because emotions are often associated with the need to behave in a certain way on very short notice. For example, anger and fear are associated with either fighting or fleeing, and both activities start the heart pumping.

Facial Broadcast

1. Choose a partner. Each of you in turn will select at random one of these emotions: happiness, sadness, anger, surprise.

2. Turn away from your partner and formulate a facial expression that you believe portrays the selected emotion. Turn back to your partner, who is to guess the emotion you are portraying. Reverse roles and repeat the exercise. What is it about your partner's face that causes you to select one feeling rather than another? What did your partner's eyes tell you? Mouth? Nose? Repeat this step a number of times, alternating roles. Your goal during each round is to analyze how various facial features and their positions help broadcast emotions.

3. Now challenge yourselves by adding the following emotions to the list:

shame	love
despair	sorrow
humiliation	rage
disgust	astonishment
coyness	nervousness

   To what extent were the second set of emotions more difficult for the "performer"? For the "observer"? How accurate were your observations?

What message is this person's face conveying? What can you tell about his emotions and thoughts? (Joel Gordon)

be retransformed into a smile. The change in emotion may last no more than one-eighth to one-fifth of a second. Researchers call these fleeting emotional displays "microfacial, or micromomentary expressions."[4] They discovered their presence by employing slow-motion film techniques. What escaped the naked eye at the normal speed of 24 frames per second became visible when the film was slowed to 4 frames per second. Micromomentary expressions are believed to reveal actual emotional states and usually occur when an individual is consciously or unconsciously attempting to conceal or disguise an emotion or feeling. Although microexpressions may be little more than a twitch of the mouth or an eyebrow, they can indicate to observers that the messages senders are trying to transmit are not the messages they are thinking. If you have not done so already, you are probably beginning to realize the importance of observing the facial expressions of others. But what should you watch for? Read on.

For purposes of analysis, a person's face can be divided into three general areas: (1) the eyebrows and forehead, (2) the eyes, and (3) the mouth. Let us focus on each separately. If you raise your eyebrows, what emotion do you show? Surprise is probably the most common response. Fear, however, may also be expressed by raised eyebrows, and when we experience fear, the duration of the movement will probably be more sustained. The brows help express other emotions as well. Right now, move your brows into as many different configurations as you can. With each movement analyze your emotional response. What do the brows communicate?

The forehead also helps communicate your physical and emotional state. A furrowed brow suggests tension, worry, or deep thought. A sweating forehead suggests nervousness or great effort.

The last of the three areas is the eyes. Ralph Waldo Emerson displayed wisdom when he said, "The eyes of men converse at least as much as their tongues." What do your eyes reveal to others? Various eye movements are associated with emotional expressions: A downward glance suggests modesty; staring suggests coldness; wide eyes suggest wonder, naiveté, honesty, or fright; and excessive blinking suggests nervousness and insecurity. Researchers have also shown that as we begin to take an interest in something, our blinking rate decreases and our pupils dilate. As an example, consider this:

> Anthropologist Edward T. Hall says PLO leader Yasir Arafat wears dark glasses to take advantage of the pupil response—to keep others from reading his reactions by watching the pupils of his eyes dilate.
>
> Hall is an authority on face-to-face contact between persons of different cultures. In an interview on understanding Arab culture, he says a University of Chicago psychologist discovered the role pupils play as sensitive indicators. Hall says Eckhard Hess found pupils dilate when you are interested in something but tend to contract if something is said that you dislike.
>
> " . . . The Arabs have known about the pupil response for hundreds if not thousands of years," Hall says. "Since people can't control the response of their eyes, which is a dead giveaway, many Arabs, like Arafat, wear dark glasses, even indoors."
>
> © 1979 *United Press International*

Like pupil response, eye-gaze direction also has provided us with interesting insights. For example, have you considered in what direction people look when they are not looking directly at you? What might such directional gazes signify? Richard Bandler and John Grinder, two of the founders of Neuro Linguistic Programming, have developed a number of interesting theories. They suggest that people look in one direction when they try to *remember* something and in another direction when they try to *invent* something. To test their hypotheses, try this with a partner: Face each other. One person asks the other the following series of questions, and the person asked each question needs only to think of a response. When asking the questions, watch for any consistency in the direction your partner looked while thinking of a response.

"Perhaps the witness would care to reconsider his answer to the last question?
Drawing by Stevenson; © 1979 The New Yorker Magazine, Inc.

Questions That Evoke Visually Remembered Images
What color are the carpets in your car?
What color are your mother's eyes?
What color is your instructor's hair?

Questions That Evoke Visually Invented Images
How would you look from my point of view?
How would you look in purple and green hair?
What would your home look like after it had been ravaged by fire?

Questions That Evoke Auditorily Remembered Images
Can you hear your favorite music?
Can you hear music you dislike?
What are the first four notes of Beethoven's Fifth Symphony?

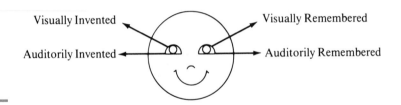

FIGURE 5-2
Gaze direction
according to
character of item
considered

Questions That Evoke Auditorily Invented Images
How would your dog sound singing "Mary Had a Little Lamb"?
What would King Kong sound like tiptoeing through the tulips?

Bandler and Grinder suggest that the right-handed person will look in the suggested directions in Figure 5-2. Do your experiences confirm the findings of Bandler and Grinder? Could a lawyer or negotiator ask questions and then use these findings to assess if the person answering invented the reply or actually remembered? Could a CIA agent use the technique to determine if a paid informant was really telling the truth? The answer is yes. The agent, for example, could inquire about where hostages were being held: "What does the house look like? Did you see Islamic Jihad members there?" If the informant looked up and to his or her right, he or she might have been creating images of the future rather than actually remembering what he or she had seen; in other words, the informant might well have been lying. Try this experiment yourself. Whatever your conclusions, it is important to maintain eye contact with others to recognize not only when others are not looking at you but also where they are looking, because each cue provides you with potential information about people's unconscious processes and how they internally access data.

Another eye cue that helps tell the world what is on a person's mind is the eye blink. In her article "In the Blink of an Eye," Shawna Vogel notes the following:

> Someone should have told Richard Nixon that his eyelids were giving him away. On August 22, 1973, during his first nationally televised press conference since the Senate's Watergate investigation began six months earlier, the president maintained a calm, controlled tone of voice. But in answering such pointed questions as, "Is there any limitation on the president, short of impeachment, to compel the production of evidence?" Nixon's eyes became a blur. In an average minute he blinked 30 to 40 times. Unimpeachable adults blink only about 10 to 20 times a minute, and even that may be excessive; studies on infants show that the physical need to blink comes just once every two minutes.
>
> (*Discover* Magazine, February 1989)

The fact is, the eyes have much to tell us.

How long we look or gaze at another person or thing also communicates a message. In our culture it is deemed acceptable to stare at animals and inanimate objects, such as paintings or sculptures, but rude to stare at people. (Julius Fast, author of the popular book *Body Language*, suggests that we stare at individuals we believe to be "nonpersons.") Instead of staring at others we are supposed to demonstrate "civil inattention," the practice of avoiding sustained eye contact and letting our eyes rest only momentarily on people (in other words, the practice of "keeping our eyes to ourselves"). Although it is permissible to look at someone we do not know for one or two seconds, after that we are expected to "move our eyes along." Notice your own eye behavior the next time you walk down a street. Your eyes will probably wander from face to face. However, if you and a stranger happen to make eye contact while approaching one another from opposite directions, at least one of you will redirect his or her gaze before you actually get too close. If we look at people for a long time, it may make them fidgety and uncomfortable or may seem to imply we are challenging them. Have your eyes innocently rested on other people only to have them demand, "What are you staring at? You want to start something?" Despite the code of civil inattention, in any gathering the first thing most people do is eye one another.

Eye contact is important in communication because it gives us certain types of information. First, it gives us feedback on how we are coming across to others in interpersonal and public situations. Eye contact can indicate that the communication channel is open. It is much easier to avoid talking or listening to people if we have not made eye contact with them. (According to researchers Michael Argyle and Janet Dean, eye contact almost makes interaction an obligation![5]) Eye contact between people can also offer clues to the kind of relationship they share. For one thing, it can signal our need for inclusion or affiliation. Persons who have high affiliative needs will frequently return the glances of others. There is a high degree of eye contact between people who like each other. We also increase eye contact when communicating with others if the physical distance between us is increased.

What is communicated if eye contact is missing? A lack of eye contact can cause others to think that we are trying to hide something or that we do not like them. It can also suggest that two people are in competition with each other. Others may interpret its absence as signifying either boredom or simply a desire to end an interaction. How do you rate your own eye contact? When are you a looker and when a nonlooker?

Like the eyes, the lower facial area also has much to communicate. Some people smile with just their mouth and lips. For others, like Bette Midler, the smile appears to consume the entire face. As a child, were you ever told to "wipe that smile off your face"? Why? Besides happiness, what can a smile communicate? How does your face look when you are not

Experiment with how the presence or absence of eye contact affects your interactions with others by operating under each of these conditions when talking to others:
1. Keep your eyes on the floor.
2. Keep glancing around.
3. Stare at the other person's face.
4. Look at the other person's waist.
5. Maintain a comfortable eye contact.
Be prepared to report your findings to the class.

Even though women smile more than men in general, young children think that the smile of a male is friendlier than the smile of a female. Do you agree? Explain.

smiling? When it is at rest? Some faces display neutral expressions, and others evidence frowns, snarls, or habitual smiles—that is, the corners of the mouth seem to normally turn up. (One of your authors had a student in class who grinned constantly. He could have been told that he failed the course, and still he would have appeared to grin!) What about when you choose to smile? How do people react to your smile? People often find that others will respond by returning a smile to those who smile at them but will look away or avoid stopping to speak to a person whose lips are pursed in a frown. To what extent do your experiences confirm this? Both men and women smile more often when seeking approval, but in general, women smile more frequently than men do. Women tend to smile even when given negative messages. Why do you think this is so?

So far we have described the many options available when expressing our emotions through facial expressions. As you watch television actors, comics, and performers work, examine closely how they use facial expressions. Facial cues communicate large portions of the messages you send to others. In fact, researcher Albert Mehrabian has concluded that while verbal and vocal cues are used extensively to help transmit meaning, the face is relied on to a greater extent than is either of these.

Posture.   How many times have you heard the following admonitions?

"Hey, stand up straight!"
"Don't slouch!"
"Why are you slumping?"
"Get your feet off the furniture!"
"Keep your shoulders back!"
"Why are you hunched over that desk?"

Describe the posture you imagine appropriate for a corporate president.

When do you stand erect? When do you slouch? What kinds of nonverbal messages does your posture send to others? What conditions cause you to tense up? What conditions allow you to relax? The way we hold our physical selves when sitting or standing is also a nonverbal broadcast, giving others information that they use to assess our thoughts and feelings.

Although no one bodily position means precisely the same thing to every observer, research has provided us with enough information to reach some general conclusions about how others are likely to interpret our posture. Nancy Henley, in her book *Body Politics*, suggests that "the *bearing* with which one presents oneself proclaims one's position in life." Television and film support this premise by frequently contrasting the upright bearing of a wealthy person with the submissive shuffle of a servant or the slumped demeanor of the "nobody." In line with this, nonverbal theorist Albert Mehrabian has determined that when people are compelled

WEDDED FACES

Holly Hall

As is commonly believed, husbands and wives do grow to look alike, reports psychologist Robert B. Zajonc.

With several of his graduate students, Zajonc collected facial photographs from husbands and wives in 12 Midwestern couples. Half the photos were taken when the couples first married, half about 25 years later. College undergraduates rated youthful and older pairs of these faces for either their resemblance to one another or for the likelihood that the individuals depicted were married.

With younger faces, students did no better than chance would predict at identifying the husbands and wives. However, "after 25 years the two spouses [were] perceived as more similar in appearance . . . and more likely to be married to each other."

Why should married people look more alike with time? Earlier studies suggest that people in close proximity tend to mimic one another's facial expressions, the researchers say. Daily mimicry among spouses, they write, "would leave wrinkles around the mouth and eyes, alter the bearing of the head, and the overall expression. Eventually [it] would produce . . . changes that make spouses appear more similar than they originally were."

Not only do emotions influence our facial expressions, but in a controversial theory Zajonc has proposed that facial expressions also help produce emotions. Tensing or relaxing facial muscles, he says, can alter the flow of blood to the brain, in turn regulating the release of various neurochemicals that may influence our moods. In this way, mimicked facial expressions may aid spouses in empathizing with one another, since such imitation could lead to shared emotions.

If empathy is gained from facial mimicry, couples who have grown more alike in appearance should have better marriages. In fact the researchers found that the greater the resemblance between spouses, the greater their happiness with their marriage.

The researchers believe that their results may also explain similarities in appearance between other family members. As with married partners, sons and daughters also share a close environment and are vulnerable to the effects of mimicry. Resemblance among family members "may be more than a matter of common genes," the researchers say.

Robert B. Zajonc, Ph.D., is at the University of Michigan, Ann Arbor. The research appeared in *Motivation and Emotion* (Vol. 11, No. 4).

Psychology Today, December 1987, p. 10.

to assume inferior roles, they reflect this move by lowering their heads. In contrast, when assuming superior roles, people often raise their heads.

Recall an instance when posture affected your perception of someone else.

Each of us has certain expectations regarding what postures we expect others to display. For instance, a high-ranking military officer would probably adopt an extremely straight and somewhat "official" posture. Henley suggests that "standing tall" in and of itself helps a person achieve dominance. Dame Judith Anderson achieved fame by performing the roles of various dominant women from Shakespeare and Greek tragedies on the stage. Although she was slight in stature, her posture and bearing were such that she seemed to fill the stage.

As a communicator you will want to develop a posture appropriate to and supportive of your goals and aspirations. Whereas stooped shoulders can indicate that you are heavily burdened or submissive, raised shoulders suggest that you are under a great deal of stress. To Americans, square shoulders usually suggest strength. Our emotions or moods and physical bearing are closely related. This relationship is expressed through the verbal idioms that have developed through the years. It is said that we "shoulder a burden," have "no backbone," keep our "chin up," or "shrug it off." The way we carry ourselves can affect the way we feel and the way others perceive us just as much as the way we feel can affect the way we carry ourselves.

The last aspect of posture we will consider is the way we lean, or orient ourselves, when we communicate. If you were speaking to someone and she suddenly turned or leaned away from you, would you consider it a positive sign? Probably not. We usually associate liking and other positive attitudes with leaning forward, not withdrawing. The next time an interesting bit of gossip is discussed in the cafeteria, notice how most, if not all, the listeners lean *forward* to ensure that they do not miss one detail of the story. When communicating with others, a slight forward tilt of your upper body may indicate that you are interested in what your cocommunicator has to say. Mehrabian found in his studies that we lean either left or right when communicating with a person of lower status than ourselves. This right or left leaning is a part of our more relaxed demeanor.[6]

Remember, body posture talks. The messages sent by the way you carry yourself vary and reflect whether you are feeling content and confident, angry and belligerent, or worried and discouraged. Your posture helps signal whether you are ready to approach and meet the world or whether you wish to avoid and withdraw from it. Equally important, how you hold yourself also helps define the way you feel about others with whom you are communicating.

Gestures.   The movements of our arms, legs, hands, and feet constitute another important way in which we broadcast nonverbal, interpersonal data. For instance, the way you position your arms transmits information

Posture Poses

For this exercise members of the class should divide into groups of three. Each of you will assume in turn that you are a photographer and that the other two group members are your models. You will pose your models to demonstrate a variety of relationships. The models' arms will remain at their sides, but you may position them to sit or stand, slump or straighten, to lean forward, backward, or to either side. Position your models to show one of these relationships:

> Servant and employer
> Waiter and customer
> Two people with romantic involvement
> Two boxers before a fight
> Boss and secretary
> Teacher and student who is failing
> Your choice

After each "photographer" sets up the models, the remaining class members should attempt to guess which relationship is being displayed. Discuss the cues you used to portray your choices.

Try on various postures and see what you feel like in each one. To what degree did each posture affect your emotional state?

about your attitudes. Cross your arms in front of you. Do you feel closed off from the world? Stand up and put your hands on your hips. How does this stance make you feel? (You may remind yourself of the old army sergeant stereotype.) Next, clasp your arms behind your back in a self-assured manner. Then hold your arms stiffly at your sides, as in a nervous-speaker or wooden-soldier pose. Finally, dangle your arms at your sides in a relaxed fashion. Become aware of the habitual arm positions you use. What message does each of these various positions communicate?

Our legs also help express information about us to others. Try standing as a model would stand. Next, sit down and put your feet up on a desk or table. Then stand with your feet wide apart. Does this last stance make you feel more powerful? Why? Return to a more comfortable position. Shift your weight forward toward the front of your feet. Then rock back so the weight is on your heels. Watch someone else do this. Does the forward position communicate more energy and enthusiasm? The distribution of your body weight and the placement of your legs and feet can broadcast stability, femininity, masculinity, anger, happiness, and any number of other qualities. Choose the stance that most accurately reflects your goals for an encounter.

It can be said that gestures are the motions of your limbs or body that you use to express or accentuate your moods and ideas. Let us now turn to two other means of delivering nonverbal cues—your physique and your dress style.

Physique and Dress Style

People can generally be divided into one of three body types: endomorphic (heavy), mesomorphic (muscular), and ectomorphic (thin). For some time researchers have tried to establish a relationship between body type and personality. According to psychologists J. B. Cortex and F. M. Gotti,[7] for example, endomorphs, mesomorphs, and ectomorphs tend to be perceived as having the following attributes:

ENDOMORPHIC	MESOMORPHIC	ECTOMORPHIC
dependent	dominant	detached
calm	cheerful	tense
relaxed	confident	anxious
complacent	energetic	reticent
sluggish	impetuous	self-conscious
placid	enthusiastic	meticulous
leisurely	competitive	reflective
cooperative	determined	precise
affable	outgoing	thoughtful
tolerant	argumentative	considerate
affected	talkative	shy
warm	active	awkward
forgiving	domineering	cool
sympathetic	courageous	suspicious
soft-hearted	enterprising	introspective
generous	adventurous	serious
affectionate	reckless	cautious
kind	assertive	tactful
sociable	optimistic	sensitive
soft-tempered	hot-tempered	withdrawn

The same dress is indecent ten years before its time, daring one year before its time, chic, being defined as contemporary seductiveness, in its time, dowdy three years after its time, hideous twenty years after its time, amusing thirty years after its time, romantic 100 years after its time and beautiful 150 years after its time.

James Laver

To what extent do you believe your personality and body type are reflective of these descriptions? To what extent do you believe your physique influences the way you are treated by others or the traits others expect you to exhibit? Although the personality traits in the test are not always associated with the body type under which they appear, the accepted physique-temperament stereotype may have much to do with how you are being treated by others or with the traits others expect you to exhibit.

Since we adorn our bodies with clothes, let us consider this nonverbal cue next. "I can't decide what to wear!" "What should I wear?" "What are you wearing?" Clothing decisions face us every day. Some people choose their clothes very carefully, whereas others just seem to "throw on" whatever is at hand.[8] Some of us enjoy shopping for clothes, whereas others have to be dragged to clothing stores. Even careful attention to dress, however, does not guarantee that we make appropriate choices. Have you ever arrived at a function only to find yourself severely overdressed or underdressed? How did you feel? Were you able to put on or take off some part of your outfit to fit in with the prevalent dress style?

The manner in which we dress ourselves is extremely important in creating a first impression. What first impressions do people receive from your clothes? What impression would you like to create? It should be apparent that your dress and your choice of image should change as your role changes. Auto mechanics must create the impression that they can repair your car, and corporate presidents must give the impression that they can lead the company through an uncertain future. As the caretakers of our health, doctors must inspire confidence. In other words, like it or not, the role we play to some extent dictates the "uniform" we wear. Some organizations, such as fast-food outlets and the military, require their employees to wear specific articles of clothing. Most company-employed individuals are given some latitude in their choice of dress, although the uniform concept, or dress code, is adhered to, to a certain extent. John T. Molloy, the author of *Dress for Success* and *The Woman's Dress for Success*

"Sweetie, will you help me with my tie?"

Drawing by Koren; © 1979 The New Yorker Magazine, Inc.

Something Different

Tomorrow, wear something different to class. Your change in dress style should be very noticeable to others. For instance, if you feel that you are usually sloppily dressed, appear as meticulously neat in attire as possible.

How did people respond to you? What types of questions were you asked? Were people surprised? Compare reactions with others in your class.

Book, gathered his research from numerous studies in which people offered their first impressions of the attire of others. Molloy has identified the kinds of clothing he claims should be worn by people who wish to become managers or executives. For men, he suggests dark blue pinstripe suits to add a feeling of authority. Dark gray is also accepted as executive attire. Molloy has also created a "uniform" for women in business. The basic outfit is summed up in this statement, which many of his female seminar attendees adopted: "I pledge to wear a highly tailored, dark colored, traditionally designed, skirted suit whenever possible to the office." What is your reaction to such dress codes? Would this kind of attire be appropriate for you in your present position? In the future? Use the exercise in the Skill Builder to test how the clothes you wear affect others.

Unquestionably, what you wear causes people to relate to you in particular ways. As a case in point, your authors knew one instructor who wore a black suit and tie to class the first day of each semester just to see how his students would react. His class always believed he was on his way to a funeral. No one spoke a word to him either before or after class. Clothes send forth potent and forceful messages to others. They are one of the important nonverbal stimuli that influence the interpersonal responses to and from others.

Voice

In many ways, you either "play" your voice or are a "victim" of your voice. Researcher Albert Mehrabian estimates that 38 percent of the meaning of a message delivered during face-to-face conversation is transmitted by your voice or vocal cues. Frequently, *how* something is said *is* what is said. How effective are you at playing a voice?

The vocal cues that accompany spoken language are termed *paralanguage*. Among the ingredients of paralanguage are pitch, rate, volume, hesitations, and pauses. Wise communicators realize that the spoken word is never neutral, and they have learned how to use the basic elements of paralanguage to transfer both the emotional and intellectual meanings of their messages. In other words, adept communicators know how to use vocal nuances to help their listeners appreciate and understand the content and "mood tones" of their conversations. They have made their voices adaptable. Let us examine these paralinguistic ingredients more closely.

Pitch is the highness or lowness of the voice on a musical scale. We tend to identify higher pitches with female voices and lower pitches with male voices. We also learn vocal stereotypes. We associate low-pitched voices with strength, sexiness, and maturity and high-pitched voices with helplessness, tenseness, and nervousness. Although we all have what is termed a "habitual pitch," we have also learned to vary our pitch to reflect our mood and generate listener interest. Some individuals, however, overuse one tone to the exclusion of all others. These people have monotonous voices that are characterized by too little variety in pitch. Other individuals speak toward the upper end of their pitch scale, producing very fragile, unsupported tones. One way to discover a pitch that is not overly high is simply to yawn. Try it now. Permit yourself to experience a good stretch; extend your arms to shoulder level and let out a nice vocalized yawn. Do it again. Now count to 10 out loud. To what extent does the pitch of your voice appear to have changed? Is it more resonant? It should be. If you indulge yourself and yawn once or twice before stressful meetings or occasions, you will be able to pitch your voice at a more pleasing level.

Volume is a second paralinguistic factor that affects perceived meaning. Some people cannot seem to muster enough energy to be heard by others. Others blast their voices through encounters. Have you ever sat in a restaurant and heard more of the conversation at a table several feet away than you could hear at your own table? Volume frequently reflects emotional intensity. Loud persons are often perceived as aggressive or overbearing. Soft-spoken individuals are often perceived as timid or polite.

Volume must be varied if it is to be effective. Knowing how to use volume to control meaning is a useful skill. Try your hand at it by participating in this exercise (adapted from Ken Cooper, *Nonverbal Communication for Business Success*): Read the following sentence to yourself: How many animals of *each species* did Moses take aboard the *ark*? (Why is this a riddle? Moses, of course, never had an ark. Noah was the ark builder.) Now tell a friend or acquaintance that you have a riddle. Read the sentence aloud, being careful to increase your volume for each of the italicized words. Keep a tally of the number of people who answer "Two." Try the question again, this time increasing your volume only on the name *Moses*. How did your vocal change affect the reactions of the listeners?

Remember, it is important that the volume you use in communication enhance rather than distort the meaning of your messages. By varying your volume and emphasizing certain words, you can vary and control the meaning attributed to your statements.

The *rate*, or speed, at which we speak is also important. Do you, for example, expect high-pressure salespeople to talk rapidly or slowly? Most often, they speak very quickly. Similarly, "pitch" men and women who are charged with selling all types of gadgets in department stores or on television also speak at a quick clip to retain audience interest and involvement. In contrast, more stately or formal occasions require that communicators use slower speaking rates punctuated by planned pauses. (Politicians at rallies typically litter their speeches with pauses that function almost as applause signs.) Researcher Goldman-Eisler has concluded that two-thirds of spoken language comes to us in chunks of fewer than six words.[9] Therefore, knowing *when* to pause is an essential skill for the effective communicator. Such pauses serve to slow the rate of speech and give both sender and receiver a chance to gather their thoughts. Unfortunately, many people intuitively feel that all pauses must be filled. The question then becomes: How do you fill the pauses? Frequently we fill them with meaningless sounds or phrases, such as "Er—Huh—Uh—" or "You know? You know?" "Right! Right!" or "Okay! Okay!" Such fillers, called *nonfluencies*, disrupt the natural flow of speech. Since pauses are a natural part of communication, we should stop trying to eliminate them. Give the pause a chance to *function*.

How adept are you at employing the paralinguistic factors we have discussed? Try the Skill Builder "Alphabet Recital." This exercise, a variation of a study conducted by researchers Joel Davitz and Lois Davitz, should prove that you do not always need to see people to tell whether they are happy, sad, angry, fearful, or proud.[10] Many of us can judge someone's emotional state by voice alone. Of course, some of us encode emotional messages with our voices better than others, and some of us can decode these messages better than others. Accuracy in sending and judging the nature of emotional messages appears to be related to an individual's sensitivity and familiarity with the vocal characteristics of emotional expression.

How do the voices of 4-year-olds and teen-agers differ? The voices of college-age males and male retirees? Are there differences between the vocal characteristics of, say, a corporation executive and a construction worker?

Besides communicating emotional content, the voice has also been found to be a communicator of personal characteristics. Listening to a person's voice can sometimes help you identify that person's individual characteristics. For instance, when we answer the telephone we are frequently able to determine the speaker's sex, age, and vocation and the region of the country he or she comes from even though we have never met the person. We also tend to associate particular voice types with particular body or personality types. For example, what type of appearance would you attribute to a person who possessed a breathy, high-pitched voice? How do you think a person who had a throaty, raspy voice would look? The chart on page 124 summarizes stereotypes related to vocal cues. As a communicator you should be aware that your vocal quality suggests certain things about you. Whether receivers are interested in identifying your age, occupation, or status, they are likely to make assumptions based

Alphabet Recital

Select a partner. Each of you will choose one of the following emotions for further work. Do not let your partner know which emotion you have chosen. In addition, your partner's eyes should be closed.

happiness	love
sadness	nervousness
anger	pride
jealousy	satisfaction
fear	sympathy

Your task is to communicate the selected emotion to your partner by reciting letters of the alphabet from A to G. As you recite the letters, attempt to make your voice reflect the selected emotion. Your partner's goal is to identify the emotion by listening only to the paralinguistic cues you are sending.

To what extent did the various paralinguistic factors you used (volume, pitch, pause, and rate) help your partner guess the emotion? If your partner was unable to determine the emotion you were sending, what could you have done to make the message clearer?

on what your voice says to them. Although the picture or stereotype they form may be far from accurate, your voice can still influence their assessment of you as an individual and thus affect the way they interact with you.

Space and Distance

How much space on our planet Earth do you call your own? How much space do you carry around with you? Are there times when people encroach on your space? In his book *The Hidden Dimension*, Edward Hall uses the term *proxemics* to mean human "use of space." Thus *proxemics* refers to the space that exists between us as we talk and relate to each other as well as the way we organize the space around us in our homes, offices, and communities. Hall identified four different distances that we keep between us and other people, depending on the type of encounter and the nature of the relationship:

Intimate distance: 0 to 18 inches
Personal distance: 18 inches to 4 feet
Social distance: 4 to 12 feet
Public distance: 12 feet to limit of sight

Can you tell how interested people are in you by where they stand in relation to you? Explain. Think of an instance when you unconsciously expressed your interest in someone else by where you stood in relation to that person.

VOCAL CUES AND PERSONALITY STEREOTYPES

Vocal Cues	Speakers	Stereotypes
Breathiness	Males	Young; artistic
	Females	Feminine; pretty; effervescent; high-strung; shallow
Thinness	Males	Did not alter listener's image of the speaker
	Females	Social, physical, emotional, and mental immaturity; sense of humor and sensitivity
Flatness	Males	Masculine; sluggish; cold; withdrawn
	Females	Masculine; sluggish; cold; withdrawn
Nasality	Males	A wide array of socially undesirable characteristics
	Females	A wide array of socially undesirable characteristics
Tenseness	Males	Old; unyielding; cantankerous
	Females	Young; emotional; feminine; high-strung; less intelligent
Throatiness	Males	Old; realistic; mature; sophisticated; well adjusted
	Females	Less intelligent; masculine; lazy; boorish; unemotional; ugly; sickly; careless; inartistic; humble; uninteresting; neurotic; apathetic
Orotundity (fullness/ richness)	Males	Energetic; healthy; artistic; sophisticated; proud; interesting; enthusiastic
	Females	Lively; gregarious; aesthetically sensitive; proud
Increased rate	Males	Animated and extroverted
	Females	Animated and extroverted
Increased pitch variety	Males	Dynamic; feminine; aesthetic
	Females	Dynamic and extroverted

Adapted from P. Heinberg, *Voice Training for Speaking and Reading Aloud,* 1964.

Intimate distance ranges from the point of touch to 18 inches from the other person. Physical contact is natural at this distance. We can wrestle, and we can make love. At this distance our senses are in full operation. They are easily stimulated but also easily offended if we find ourselves in an uncomfortable situation. Have you ever had someone come too close to you and wanted that person to "back off"? Did you back away? Sometimes we are forced to endure intimate distance between ourselves and strangers in crowded buses, trains, and elevators. How do you feel and respond during such occasions?

The space between people affects how they communicate. This doctor has created a supportive, informal setting that clearly puts the patient at ease.
(J. Berndt/Stock Boston)

Hall considers *personal distance* to range from 18 inches to 4 feet. When communicating at this distance, you can still hold hands or shake hands with another person. This is the most common distance between people talking informally in class, at work, or at parties, and we are apt to conduct most of our conversations within this range. If you reduce personal distance to intimate distance, you are likely to make the other person feel uncomfortable. If you increase it, the other person is likely to begin to feel rejected.

Hall's *social distance* ranges from 4 feet to 12 feet. In contrast to personal distance, at this distance we are not likely to share personal concerns. By using social distance, we can keep people at more than an arm's length. Thus, this is a "safer" distance, one at which we would communicate information and feelings that are neither particularly private nor revealing. Many of our conversations during dinner or at business conferences or meetings occur within this space. In business, the key protector of one's social space is the desk. Of course, the greater the distance between persons, the more formal their encounters. (At a social gathering, you can normally tell how well people know one another by examining how closely they stand to each other.)

Public distance (12 feet and further) is commonly reserved for strangers with whom we do not wish to have an interaction. Distances at the farther end of the range are well beyond the personal involvement limit and make interpersonal communication very unlikely. People waiting in an uncrowded lobby for an elevator frequently use public distance. It can be assumed that if a person opts for public distance when he or she could have chosen otherwise, that person does not care to converse.

The concept to remember regarding intimate, personal, social, and public distances is that "space speaks." Becoming aware of how people use space and of how you can use it can improve your communication effectiveness. Of course the nature of our environment affects the amount of distance we are able to maintain between ourselves and others. Researchers in nonverbal communication divide environmental spaces into the following classifications: informal, semifixed feature, and fixed feature. These categories are based on the perceived permanence of any particular physical space. Thus, *informal space* is seen as a highly mobile, quickly changing space that ranges from intimate to public (from no space between us and others to 25 or more feet). In many ways informal space functions much like a personal "bubble" that we can enlarge to keep people at some distance or decrease to permit them to get closer to us.

In contrast to informal space, *semifixed-feature space* employs objects to create distance. Semifixed features include chairs, benches, sofas, plants, and other movable items. (Today some office walls and partitions can be classified as semifixed features, since they are designed to be relocated as space needs change.) Researchers have found that barriers such as desks can reduce interaction. In a study of doctor-patient relationships, it was determined that patients were more at ease speaking with a physician seated in a chair across from them than they were when the physician was sitting behind a desk.[11] Why do you think this was so? To what extent do you feel the same way about your instructor? Why do you think police interrogators are sometimes advised to eliminate barriers between themselves and the person they are questioning? In many public places, if interaction among persons is desired, the space will usually contain chairs facing each other. Such arrangements are found in bars, restaurants, and lounges. In contrast, the chairs in airport or bus terminal waiting rooms are often bolted together in long parallel rows. In fact, one manufacturer designed a chair to create an uncomfortable pressure on the spine after the sitter has spent a few moments in it. The chair is used in spaces where it is deemed desirable for people not to spend time interacting. How do semifixed features function in homes? Have you ever been in a living room that was created to be "looked at but not lived in"? (Your authors know of one sofa that deteriorated from age rather than from wear because it had been declared "off limits" to an entire household for years!)

Unlike the spatial types we have examined thus far, *fixed-feature space* contains relatively permanent objects that define the environment around us. Included in this category are immovable walls, doors, trees, sidewalks, roads, and highways. Fixed features help guide and control our actions. For example, most classrooms are rectangular with windows along

Mentally redesign your classroom to promote interaction. Next, redesign it to inhibit interaction. Then consider how you could design an office to promote—or inhibit—interaction.

How are the chairs in your classroom arranged? Are they laid out in neat aisles? Is your instructor partially hidden by a desk or lectern? Does she or he speak from a raised area or platform?

one side, usually to the students' left. The window location also determines the front of the room. In like fashion, apartment entrances that open onto a common rotunda increase the chances for tenant communication, as do swimming pools and parks. Fences, however, can serve to inhibit communication. Shopping malls and department stores rely on fixed features to help route pedestrian traffic in certain directions that will increase sales. The next time you shop in a carefully designed environment, examine the location of the store's fixed features. Can you walk unencumbered to a desired department, or are you carefully "directed" through the perfumes, lingerie, and knickknacks? Why?

Territoriality and Personal Space

Also related to proxemics is our need for a defined territory. Animals mark their territory by urinating around its perimeter, and they will protect their area against invaders. We also lay out or stake our space, or territory, and territoriality is an important variable in interpersonal communication. What examples of territoriality can you remember encountering? Are you familiar with "Dad's chair"? "Mom's bureau"? How do you feel when someone invades your room—"your territory"? Is it comfortable to look into your rearview mirror and find you are being tailgated by a tractor-trailer? By a Honda? What happens when someone stands too close to you? How are you treated when you enter another's territory? For example, did your sister ever "throw you out" of her room? Did she ever ask you to keep your hands off the stereo? Has a friend ever thrown you out of his seat?

To establish territory we employ markers. At the library, for instance, you may spread your things out, over, and across the table so that others will not find it easy to enter your territory. In large corporations a person's status is often reflected by the size of his or her space. Thus, the president may be accorded a large top-floor territory, while a clerk is given a desk in a second-floor room amid a number of other desks and copy machines. Regardless of its size, however, we identify with our location and frequently act as if we owned it.

Color

Colors seem to have more than a passing effect on us. Max Luscher, in his book *The Luscher Color Test*, claims that when people look at pure red for long periods, their blood pressure, respiration, and heartbeat all speed up. This is because red tends to excite the nervous system. In contrast, when researchers examined the impact of dark blue, the reverse proved true: Blood pressure, respiration, and heartbeat receded, and people tended to become calmer. Keeping your own reactions in mind, examine the color schemes used in several public areas, including fast-food chains, stores, and

How do various colors make you feel? If you were selected as a color consultant, what colors would you choose for a fast-food operation? An airline? Your classroom? Why?

terminals. What colors are chosen? Do they make you want to move quickly? Do the colors excite you, or are they designed to help you relax?

It has been determined that color affects us emotionally as well as physiologically. One study, conducted by the Color Research Institute, is described by author Vance Packard. The institute was seeking to determine how the color of a package affected consumer buying patterns. Women were given three differently colored boxes of detergent—a yellow box, a blue box, and a blue box with yellow specks. After using the products for three weeks, the women were asked which box of detergent they judged to be most effective for washing delicate clothing. (Although the women thought the boxes contained different detergents, all contained the same product.) The results of the study were revealing. The women reported that the detergent in the yellow box was too strong and that the one in the blue box was too weak. However, the detergent in the blue box with splashes of yellow was felt to be just right. How do the colors on product packages affect you?

Your color *preferences* may even reflect the nature of your personality. In *Color in Your World* Faber Birren suggests that if you like red, you have a tendency to be outwardly directed, active, impatient, and optimistic. If you dislike red, he says that you would probably dislike the qualities exhibited by persons who like red. Do you agree?

Use of Time

Do you have enough time for most of your life's activities? Are you usually prepared for exams or assignments? Do you arrive for appointments on time, early, or late? Edward Hall says that "time talks." What does your use or misuse of time say about you? To what extent do others communicate with you by their use of time? Would you feel insulted if you were asked out for a date at the last minute by someone you did not know very well? (In the United States, at least, some would assume a last-minute invitation to mean that another date fell through or that the inviter is asking only as a last resort.) Some students have a habit of being consistently 15 minutes late to class—even when their previous class was just down the hall! What cues does such habitual lateness transmit to an instructor? Should the instructor conclude that the person is not interested in the class? Does not like the instructor? Is unable to organize activities in such a way as to accomplish even the simplest routine task?

Punctuality is one important form of time communication. There are many jobs that demand that a person be on time. Would you wait 30 minutes for a bank teller to arrive? To a military officer, the concept of being on time really means to arrive 15 minutes early. Thus, the military has created the "hurry up and wait" syndrome familiar to every basic trainee. (Everyone rushes to arrive, but once on site everyone stands around for a while with nothing to do.)

Another important factor in interaction with others is the allocation of certain activities to *appropriate times*. It is acceptable to call a friend for a chat at 3 P.M. However, we know of an attorney who goes to work at 5:30 A.M. and by 6:30 A.M. has already made phone calls to a number of people. (How would you react if you were called by a lawyer at 5:30 in the morning!) He does this, he reports, because he gets effective results because people's "defenses are down" at 5:30 A.M.; consequently they often reveal things they would be prepared to cover up by 9 or 10 o'clock.

We are expected to *structure time* in certain ways to ensure that our activities and our tasks are accomplished efficiently. Americans in business seek to get the greatest return on their "time investment." In other countries, however, time is treated differently in varying degrees. In some cultures, people are accustomed to waiting several hours for a meeting to begin. In others, the meeting begins whenever the second party arrives. Even in the United States we function at different time levels. The authors come from two different areas of the country, and it has taken years of married life to adjust to one another's "internal clocks." One of us can start and nearly complete a task before the other manages to be seated. The term "a long time" can mean one thing to one individual and something completely different to another.

How well do you use your time? In his book *The Time Trap*, Alex MacKenzie lists several barriers to effective time usage:

Attempting too much (taking on too many projects at once)
Unrealistic time estimates (not realizing how long a project will take)
Procrastination (putting it off, and off, and off . . .)
Interruptions (letting yourself be distracted by telephone calls, friends, the media)

Do any of these apply to you? How might you go about improving your use of time?

Touch

The final nonverbal category of communication is touch. We have already mentioned touch in relation to space and distance. As already noted, Edward Hall suggests that intimate space begins at the *point of touch* and moves to 18 inches. How important is touch in your own communication encounters? As children we are admonished not to touch ourselves or things around us: "Don't pick your nose!" and "Don't play with yourself!" are frequent childhood reprimands. Yet all humans need to touch and be touched.[12]

POWER WAITING

E. B. White

> Time is the ultimate symbol of domination. Those who control others' time have power, and those who have power control others' time.
>
> Robert Levine, "Waiting Is a Power Game," Psychology Today, April 1987

While waiting in the antechamber of a business firm, where we had gone to seek our fortune, we overheard through a thin partition a brigadier general of industry trying to establish telephone communication with another brigadier general, and they reached, these two men, what seemed to us a most healthy impasse. The phone rang in Mr. Auchincloss's office, and we heard Mr. Auchincloss's secretary take the call. It was Mr. Birstein's secretary, saying that Mr. Birstein would like to speak to Mr. Auchincloss. "All right, put him on," said Mr. Auchincloss's well-drilled secretary, "and I'll give him Mr. Auchincloss." "No," the other girl apparently replied, "you put Mr. Auchincloss on, and I'll give him Mr. Birstein." "Not at all," countered the girl behind the partition. "I wouldn't dream of keeping Mr. Auchincloss waiting."

This battle of the Titans, conducted by their leftenants to determine which Titan's time was the more valuable, raged for five or ten minutes, during which interval the Titans themselves were presumably just sitting around picking their teeth. Finally one of the girls gave in, or was overpowered, but it might easily have ended in a draw. As we sat there ripening in the antechamber, this momentary paralysis of industry seemed rich in promise of a better day to come—a day when true equality enters the business life, and nobody can speak to anybody because all are equally busy.

The Second Tree from the Corner, Harper & Row. Originally published in *The New Yorker.*

Watch a nursery school teacher as he or she reads a story to 3-year-olds. The children surround the adult, sitting as close to the teacher and to one another as possible. In the nineteenth century, some orphaned young children died in hospitals not because they were ill, but because they were seldom or never touched. In hospitals today, children are picked up and held constantly.

How accessible are you to touch? Psychologist Sidney Jourard counted the frequency of contact between couples in cases in various cities.[13] He reports the following number of contacts per hour:

San Juan, Puerto Rico	180
Paris, France	110
Gainesville, Florida	2
London, England	0

HUGWORK

Russell Baker

Up till now Americans have never been a people to hug each other indiscriminately, but if a California outfit called the Hug Club has its way that will soon change.

The club of course has something to sell—"Hug Club Membership Paks" at $3 per pak—and its sales pitch is based on the same argument that's making millions for the diet and jogging industries; to wit, hugging will make you healthier. Club literature says "medical and lay experts" have found that hugging "helped remove depression," "relieved tension and stress," "created a stronger will to live" and "tuned up the body's support systems." In short, hugging is just as healthful as jogging and dieting, and a lot easier.

Club members are supposed to do "hugwork," which consists of "hugging yourself, hugging a pet, hugging a friend and, most difficult, hugging someone you think you don't like."

I've always been cautious about what and whom I hug, so my first instinct was to throw this mailing in the trash. Still—. Well, it couldn't hurt to try. I closed the door so nobody could see me and hugged myself.

While embracing the back of my left shoulder with my right hand, I detected something new. The shoulder seam of my jacket had split. A new jacket too. It was infuriating. The shoddiness of American tailoring, the swindles perpetrated by haberdashers! Was the whole country going down the drain?

So much for hugging's power to help remove depression. Perhaps hugging a pet could have relieved the tension and stress caused by hugging myself, but I don't have a pet. I once kept a tank in which assorted tropical fish died with sad regularity, but even when not on their last fins they were eminently unhuggable.

Hugging somebody else's pet dog was out of the question. Dogs like to bite me for some reason. Maybe it tunes up their bodies' support systems.

I wonder if the Hug Club has thought this thing through. "Hugging someone you think you don't like," for example—that sounds like a great idea. A lot of movies used to reach happy endings by that device. (Movies don't seem to have endings anymore; like modern skyscrapers, they just seem to stop when the workmen get bored with the job.)

In real life, though, hugging someone you think you don't like can produce terrible trauma. One of my most enduring memories of President Nixon is of the night during the Republican Convention of 1972 when Sammy Davis Jr. hugged him on national television. Nixon's broad smile stayed rigidly in place— he was on national television, after all—but his entire body curled in on itself with an instinctive tremor the way a man's body will when it senses that the end is near.

My analysis of that hug is this: Davis thought he didn't like Nixon but, hoping to create a stronger will to live, decided to hug him for therapeutic purposes. Nixon, suspecting that Sammy Davis Jr. didn't like him, thought the life was about to be squeezed out of him when he felt Davis's embrace.

The terrible thing for Nixon was that, being on television, he couldn't scream for help but had to keep smiling. I've always given him high marks in self-control for his refusal to yield to pure terror in that instant.

Most people you think you don't like are fully aware of how you feel about them and likely to panic if you reach for them with both arms. I suppose a hugger with a lot of personality could carry it off without being painfully kicked and pummeled, but I don't advise it for the average person seeking relief from tension and stress.

Hugging friends, of course, is another matter, but even here it is a trickier business than the Hug Club thinks. Hugging is a lot like waltzing. Somebody has to take the lead. In my limited hugging experience, I've always been uncomfortable in any hug that I didn't initiate. A lot of other people really want to be hugged but absolutely cannot get the thing started. They will stand around frustratedly unhugged all their lives rather than step right up and initiate the hugging.

So we are dealing with two distinct classes: huggers and huggees. The trouble arises when two huggers meet. I have a friend who, like me, is a hugger. Our greetings are like the opening steps of a wrestling match. I know he is going to try to hug me, thus reducing me to the status of huggee, which I hate.

If there is any hugging to be done, I want to start it, so I am ready for him when he comes in the door, and for a few seconds we stalk each other as cunningly as two scorpions with a disagreement.

Occasionally I win and humiliate him by reducing him to a huggee. Being a man of great physical strength, he retaliates by clamping me in a bear hug that shuts down the blood flow between my collarbone and hipbone. I prefer hugging female friends, but rarely do it. Very few of those who are huggers by nature have the muscularity to turn you numb when they're reduced to huggees. On the other hand, whether huggers or huggees, female friends tend to be suspicious when subjected to a robust hugging, which complicates friendship.

Babies are the best of all hugging materials. They smell good, can't squeeze the life out of you, never suspect you of lechery and can't do anything but howl if they resent being treated like huggees.

The evidence seems to indicate that "to touch or not to touch" is partially a cultural question. Where do you touch your father? Your mother? Your brother? Your sister? A friend of the same sex? A friend of the opposite sex? Men seem to touch their fathers' hands—they shake hands—

Embraces communicate joy and enthusiasm. In our culture, the sports field is one of the few public places where men can feel free to embrace one another. (Alan Carey/The Image Works)

and women touch their fathers' arms and faces. In general, women seem more accessible to touch. Both men and women will often kiss women in greeting; men who meet usually shake hands. Physical contact between males is often limited to "contact sports," such as football and soccer.

Touch can also be used to reflect status. The person who initiates touch is usually the one with the higher status. Nancy Henley points out that we are unlikely to go up to our boss and pat her or him on the shoulder. Would you, for example, put your arm around your college or university president? Why? Would your behavior change if you met the president at a party? Probably not. That person, however, might well put an arm around you or another student. The person who initiates the touching usually also controls the interaction.

Touch, of course, functions importantly in sexual communication. If people hold hands, we assume they have a romantic interest in one another. Are we right? The shaving-cream companies have made certain that American males shave every day in order to avoid any embarrassing stubble that would not be touchable. Most American women shave their legs and

How do you feel when shaking hands with a friend? A stranger? An employer? Why? What does a pat on the back communicate to you?

underarms and use a variety of lotions to keep their hands soft to the touch. When you were growing up, did your parents touch in your presence? Many adults avoid any contact in front of their children. It is somewhat paradoxical that we spend a great deal of money on creams, blades, and other products designed to make us "touchable" and then avoid being touched!

Who have you "touched" today? Who has "touched" you?

Of course, how we use touch sends many messages about us. It reveals our status perceptions, our attitudes, and even our needs. For example, in his book *The Broken Heart*, psychologist James L. Lynch establishes a correlation between many diseases, particularly heart disease, and loneliness. Lynch tells the story of one gentleman hooked up to heart-monitoring devices who was in a coma and near death. When a nurse would walk into his room and hold his hand for a few moments, his heartbeat would change from fast and erratic to slow and smooth. Touch communicates. It can make a difference.

HOW TO ASSESS YOUR COMMUNICATION EFFECTIVENESS, NONVERBALLY SPEAKING

As we have seen, nonverbal communication consists of the use of body language, physique and dress style, voice, spaces and distances, colors, times, and touches that can either support or contradict the meaning of the words we speak. Use your knowledge of each of these variables to help you react to the interactions you observe or appropriate pictures in this text. For each, answer the following and identify which cues influenced your response:

1. Who is more trustworthy?
2. Who is more dynamic?
3. Who is more credible?
4. Who has more status?
5. Who is older?
6. Who is more intelligent?
7. Who is more powerful?
8. Who is more friendly?
9. What is their relationship to each other?
10. What predictions can you make regarding the course their relationship will take?

Compare and contrast your responses with those of others in your class. The discussion of your observations will be quite valuable, since many of our important judgments and decisions are based on nonverbal cues. The following guidelines should prove helpful as you continue developing your ability to make valid judgments and decisions based on nonverbal communication.

Examine the Environment

For any particular nonverbal interaction, ask yourself if any environmental stimuli are apt to affect the interaction. Determine if other people present could influence the two communicators. Attempt to assess whether colors and decor will have an impact on the nature and tone of the communication. Analyze the amount of space available to the individuals involved. Evaluate whether architectural factors might alter the outcome. Where are chairs, tables, passageways, and desks situated? Why have the interactors situated themselves as they did? What type of behavior would we expect to see exhibited in this environment?

Watch the Communicators

Ask yourself if the sex, age, or status of the communicators will exert an influence on their relationship. Assess to what extent, if any, attractiveness, clothing style, or physical appearance should affect the interaction. Determine if, in your own mind, the communicators' dress is appropriate to the environment in which they find themselves. Decide if the communicators appear to like each other. Decide if you think they share similar goals.

Watch Facial Expressions, Gestures, Posture, and Eye Behavior

What does each communicator's facial expression reveal? Are the facial expressions of each relatively consistent or fleeting? Do they tend to fluctuate drastically? Assess the extent to which you believe the facial expressions are genuine.

Analyze significant bodily cues. Attempt to decide if hand or foot movements suggest honesty or deception. Decide if either party moves too much or too little. Ask yourself if both individuals are equally involved in the exchange. Is one more eager to continue the communication than the other? Would one prefer to terminate the communication? How do you know?

Assess the extent to which participants in the interaction mirror each other's posture. Ask yourself how posture supports or contradicts the status relationship that exists. Do the interactants appear to be relaxed or tense? Why? Determine if the individuals have used their bodies to include or exclude others from their conversation. Analyze when and why the communicators alter their postures.

Watch the eye behavior of the participants. Determine if one looks away more than the other. Determine if one stares at the other. To what extent, if any, does excessive blinking occur? When is eye contact most pronounced? How does the eye contact of one individual appear to affect the other?

Listen for Vocal Cues

Assess whether the communicators are using appropriate volumes and rates, given their particular situation. Determine if and how the way something that is said supports or contradicts what is being said. Analyze how and when silence is used. Be responsive to signals of nervousness and changes in pitch.

"Target In" on Touch

Watch to see if the participants touch each other at all. Determine, if you can, *why* they touched. How did touching or being touched affect the interactants? Was the contact appropriate or inappropriate to the situation? Why?

SUMMARY

Nonverbal communication consists of all the kinds of human responses not expressed in words. Over 65 percent of the social meaning of the messages we send to others is communicated nonverbally. Perceiving and analyzing nonverbal cues can help us understand what is really happening during a conversation.

Nonverbal messages fall into seven main categories: (1) body language (kinesics), including cues from gestures, body movements, facial expressions, eyes, behavior, and posture, (2) physique and dress style, (3) voice (paralanguage), including pitch, rate, volume, hesitations or nonfluencies, and pauses, (4) space and distance (proxemic factors), including both the space that exists between us when we talk to each other and the way we organize space in our homes, offices, and communities, (5) color, (6) the use of time, and (7) touch.

You can improve your effectiveness as a nonverbal communicator by observing and analyzing both the physical environment of the interaction and the body language, appearance, vocal cues, and touching behavior of the participants.

SUGGESTIONS FOR FURTHER READING

Bandler, Richard, and John Grinder. *Frogs into Princes: Neuro Linguistic Programming.* Moab, Utah: Real People Press, 1979. A readable and practical work about neurolinguistic programming.

Birdwhistell, Ray. *Kinesics and Context.* Philadelphia: University of Pennsylvania Press, 1970. An extensive, scholarly treatment of kinesics and the building blocks of body language.

Birren, Faber. *Color in Your World.* New York: Collier Books, 1962.

Cooper, Ken. *Nonverbal Communication for Business Success.* New York: AMACOM, 1979. An easy-to-read discussion of how the results of research in nonverbal communication can be directly applied to the world of business.

Cortes, J. B., and F. M. Gatti. "Physique and Self-Description of Temperament," *Journal of Consulting Psychology*, Vol. 29 (1965), pp. 408–414. Discusses the classic study.

Eisenberg, Abne M., and Ralph R. Smith. *Nonverbal Communication.* New York: Bobbs-Merrill, 1971. A readable overview of the nonverbal communication area.

Ekman, Paul, and Wallace Friesen. *Unmasking the Face.* Englewood Cliffs, N.J.: Prentice-Hall, 1975. An immensely understandable work about faces and feelings.

Fast, Julius. *Body Language.* New York: M. Evans and Company, 1970. The work that popularized the field of nonverbal communication. Fun to read and full of examples.

Knapp, Mark L. *Nonverbal Communication in Human Interaction.* New York: Holt, Rinehart and Winston, 1972. One of the most thorough surveys of the field of nonverbal communication. Contains a wealth of documented information.

Mehrabian, Albert. *Silent Messages.* Belmont, Calif.: Wadsworth, 1971. An overview of how we communicate liking, power, and inconsistency with nonverbal cues.

Molloy, John T. *Dress for Success.* New York: Warner Books, 1977. A reference work for men in business. Discusses what to wear and why to wear it.

Molloy, John T. *The Woman's Dress for Success Book.* New York: Warner Books, 1977. In this volume Molloy advises women on what to wear to succeed in the business world.

Montagu, Ashley. *Touching: The Human Significance of the Skin.* New York: Harper & Row, 1971. A readable discussion of the value of body touching.

Packard, Vance. *The Hidden Persuaders.* New York: Pocket Books, 1957.

Sommer, R. *Personal Space.* Englewood Cliffs, N.J.: Prentice-Hall, 1969. A description of how we use space to express our feelings and relationships. An analysis of how space controls communication.

Winston, Stephanie. *Getting Organized.* New York: Warner, 1980.

NOTES

1. Ray Birdwhistell, *Kinesics and Context* (Philadelphia: University of Pennsylvania Press, 1970), and Albert Mehrabian, *Silent Messages* (Belmont, Calif.: Wadsworth, 1971).

2. For some practical advice see Rowland Cuthill, "How to Read the Other Guy's Silent Signals," *Quest* (May 1977), pp. 46–51.

3. Paul Ekman and Wallace Friesen, "The Repertoire of Nonverbal Behavior: Categories, Origins, Usage and Coding," *Semiotica*, Vol. 1 (1969), pp. 49–98.

4. E. A. Haggard and K. S. Isaacs, "Micromomentary Facial Expressions as Indicators of Ego Mechanisms in Psychotherapy," in *Methods of Research in Psychotherapy*, edited by L. A. Gottschalk and A. H.

Auerback (New York: Appleton-Century-Crofts, 1966).

5. M. Argyle and J. Dean, "Eye Contact, Distance, and Affiliation," *Sociometry*, Vol. 28 (1965), pp. 289–304.

6. For a summary of Mehrabian's work in this area, see his article "Significance of Posture and Position in the Communication of Attitude and Status Relationship," *Psychological Bulletin*, Vol. 71 (1969), pp. 359–372.

7. J. B. Cortes and F. M. Gotti, "Physique and Self-Description of Temperament," *Journal of Consulting Psychology*, Vol. 29 (1965), pp. 408–414.

8. For a readable survey of nonverbal communicative aspects of clothing, see Leonard Bickman, "Social Roles and Uniforms: Clothes Make the Person," *Psychology Today* (April 1974), pp. 49–51. For a study of the relationship between dress and personality for both men and women, see Lawrence B. Rosenfeld and Timothy G. Plax, "Clothing as Communication," *Journal of Communication*, Vol. 27 (1977), pp. 24–31.

9. F. Goldman-Eisler, "Continuity of Speech Utterance, Its Determinance and Its Significance," *Language and Speech*, Vol. 4 (1961), pp. 220–231.

10. J. R. Davitz and L. Davitz, "The Communication of Feelings by Content-Free Speech," *Journal of Communication*, Vol. 9 (1959), pp. 6–13.

11. See, for example, A. G. White, "The Patient Sits Down: A Clinical Note," *Psychosomatic Medicine*, Vol. 15 (1953), pp. 256–257.

12. An especially persuasive argument is made by Ashley Montagu in *Touching: The Human Significance of the Skin* (New York: Harper & Row, 1971).

13. S. M. Jourard, "An Exploratory Study of Body Accessibility," *British Journal of Social and Clinical Psychology*, Vol. 5 (1966), pp. 221–231.

6

Listening:
A Deliberate
Process

Knowing how to listen takes more than two good ears.

Sperry Corporation

"Are you telling me something?"
"Are you listening?"
"Of course not."

Edward Albee, Lolita

CHAPTER PREVIEW

After finishing this chapter, you should be able to:

Define *listening*
Explain the nature of serial communication
Identify the amount of time you spend listening
Compare and contrast helpful and harmful listening habits
Distinguish between the hearing and listening processes
Explain the Listening-Level Energy-Involvement Scale
Define feedback
Describe the ways in which feedback affects communication
Demonstrate an ability to see different types of evaluative and non-

evaluative feedback
Focus your attention while listening
Set appropriate listening goals
Listen to understand ideas
Listen to retain information
Listen to evaluate and analyze content
Listen empathically

A number of prominent American corporations have run advertising campaigns designed to promote an awareness of the importance of listening. Running through the companies' advertisements are slogans such as:

> "Did you hear that?"
> "Listening is more than just good philosophy. It's vital to our future."
> "How can we expect them to learn when we haven't taught them how to listen?"

Do you believe you listen well? Far too frequently listening is something we take for granted. However, listening is a difficult, intricate skill, and like other skills, it requires training and practice.

WHY LISTEN?

From the time the alarm clock rings until the late news winds up with the weather, we are inundated with things to listen to. As we proceed through our day, as we move from person to person, from class to lunch, from formal discussions to casual conversations, we are constantly called upon to listen. All of us engage in the following activities: We interact face to face with friends and acquaintances, we use the telephone, we attend meetings, we participate in interviews, we take part in arguments, we give or receive instructions, we make decisions based on information received orally, and we both generate and receive feedback. Yet we do all this without paying much attention to the role listening plays in each of our experiences. Consequently, listening problems abound.

A recent poll indicated that half the teenagers in the United States believe that communication between them and their parents is poor and further that one of the prime causes of this gap is deficient listening behavior. As a case in point, one parent was convinced that her daughter had a severe hearing problem. She was so convinced that she took her to an audiologist to have her hearing tested. The audiologist carefully tested both ears and reported back to the distraught parent: "There's nothing wrong with her hearing. She's just tuning you out."

A leading cause of the rising divorce rate (more than half of all marriages end in divorce) is the failure of husbands and wives to interact effectively. They don't listen to each other. Neither person responds to the actual message sent by the other.

In like fashion, political scientists report that a growing number of people believe that their elected and appointed officials are out of touch with the constituents they are supposedly representing. Why? Because they don't believe that they listen to them. In fact, it seems that sometimes our politicians don't even listen to themselves. The following is a true story: At a national legislative conference held in Albuquerque some years ago, then Senator Joseph Montoya was handed a copy of a press release by a press aide shortly before he got up before the podium to deliver a speech. When he rose to speak, to the horror of his press aide and the amusement of his audience, Montoya began reading the press release, not his speech. He began, "For immediate release. Senator Joseph M. Montoya, Democrat of New Mexico, last night told the National Legislative Conference at Albuquerque. . . ." Montoya read the entire six-page release, concluding with the statement that he "was repeatedly interrupted by applause."

Presidents of major companies have likewise identified listening as one of their major communication problems. One executive asked his secretary for 40 Xeroxes and sat there with his mouth open a couple of days later when 40 Xerox copiers were wheeled into the office.

Think back over the years you have spent as a student. Did you receive training in writing? Reading? Speaking? The answer to each of these questions is probably yes. In fact, many children now learn to read and write before they start school; even more important, reading and writing skills are taught and emphasized throughout our educational careers. In addition, courses in writing and speed-reading have recently become popular—if expensive—offerings in adult-oriented programs. We often take public-speaking courses as a part of our educational sequences, and oral presentations are required in many of our classes. But what about *listening*? How much training have you actually received in listening? Even though an International Listening Association now exists, and even though listening is now taught in some schools and colleges, of the four communication skills—reading, writing, speaking, and listening—listening has received the least attention from educators. Yet listening is the fundamental process through which we initiate and maintain our relationships. And it is the primary process through which we take in information. Treat listening as if your very existence depended on it—in many ways it does.

Attaching a dollar value to the price of poor listening is almost impossible, but, for example, with more than 100 million workers in the United States, just one $10 mistake by each of them in a single year would cost a billion dollars.

Studies show that on the average we spend between 42 and 53 percent of our communicative time listening, 16 to 32 percent speaking, 15 to 17 percent reading, and only 9 to 14 percent writing.[1] Listening training is not neglected because we are innately good listeners, nor are we born knowing how to listen. How efficient are your personal listening skills? Estimate what percentage of listened-to information you retain. This figure represents how good a listener you *think* you are, but how good a listener are you really? Let's find out.

Take a moment to review your personal listening situation. Think of interactions you have had that were complicated because you or someone else failed to listen effectively. For example, when was the last time you jumped to a wrong conclusion? Missed an important word? Failed to realize you were not being understood? Reacted emotionally or let yourself become distracted? Far too often, instead of listening we daydream our way through our daily contacts—we take side trips or otherwise tune out what is said to us. In other words, we adopt destructive "unlistening" behaviors. Yet, we are unaware that this is what we are doing. In fact, experience has shown that most people estimate they listen with 70 to 80 percent accuracy. This means that a majority believe they can interact with others and accurately retain 70 to 80 percent of what is said. In contrast, Ralph Nichols, a noted listening researcher, tells us that most of the individuals he has studied actually listen at only 25 percent efficiency—that is, instead of *retaining* 75 percent of what they hear, they *lose* 75 percent![2] How effective do you think your writing would be if 75 percent of your work contained writing errors? What grade would you receive if you misspelled 75 percent of the words you used in an essay or incorrectly punctuated 75 percent of your paper? And yet many of us seem unknowingly to listen at 25 percent efficiency.

> List five problems that could result (or have resulted) from unlistening—that is, from deficient listening skills. List five benefits that could result from improving your listening skills.

PERMUTATION PERSONIFIED

Despite telemetering advances, improvements in mechanical transmission of data and collating total knowledge, there are occasional breakdowns in communication. We're indebted to a traveler recently returned from Miami for this example.

Operation: Halley's Comet.

COLONEL TO EXECUTIVE OFFICER: Tomorrow evening at approximately 2000 hours Halley's Comet will be visible in this area, an event which occurs only once every 75 years. Have the men fall out in the battalion area in fatigues, and I will explain this rare phenomenon to them. In case of rain, we will not be able to see anything, so assemble the men in the theatre and I will show them films of it.

EXECUTIVE OFFICER TO COMPANY COMMANDER: By order of the colonel, tomorrow at 2000 hours, Halley's Comet will appear above the battalion area. If it rains, fall the men out in fatigues. Then march to the theatre, where the rare phenome-non will take place, something which occurs only once every 75 years.

COMPANY COMMANDER TO LIEU-TENANT: By order of the colonel in fatigues at 2000 hours tomorrow evening, the phenomenal Halley's Comet will appear in the theatre. In case of rain in the battalion area, the colonel will give another order, something which occurs once every 75 years.

LIEUTENANT TO SERGEANT: To-morrow at 2000 hours, the colonel will appear in the theatre with Halley's Comet, something which happens every 75 years. If it rains, the colonel will order the comet into the battalion area.

SERGEANT TO SQUAD: When it rains tomorrow at 2000 hours, the phenomenal 75-year-old General Halley, accompanied by the Colonel, will drive his Comet through the battalion area theatre in fatigues.

Reprinted from "Permutation Personified," in *Boles Letter*. Copyright 1962 by Edmond D. Boles and Associates.

Can you cite a similar experience that has actually occurred in your social, school, or job life?

Unfortunately, despite years of supposed listening practice, errors in listening are extremely common. According to communication theorist William Haney, we frequently run into problems when we use serial communication, or chain-of-command transmissions, to relay messages. What happens in *serial communication* is that person 1 sends a message to person 2; person 2 then communicates his or her perception of person 1's message (not person 1's message) to person 3, who continues the process. The example printed below, from an article by communication writer Edmond D. Boles, further clarifies the serial communication concept. Although this example is of course fictional, let's use it to examine what can happen and why. As John R. Freund and Arnold Nelson have noted,

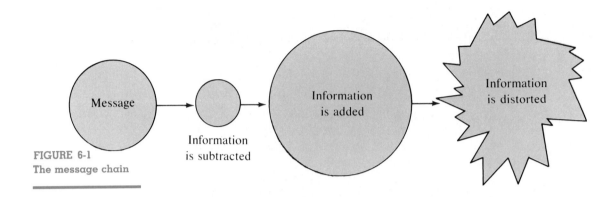

FIGURE 6-1
The message chain

whenever one individual speaks or delivers a message to a second individual, the message occurs in at least four different forms.[3]

1. The message as it exists in the mind of the speaker (his or her thoughts)
2. The message as it is spoken (actually encoded by the speaker)
3. The message as it is interpreted (decoded by the listener)
4. The message as it is ultimately remembered by the listener (affected by the listener's personal selectivities and rejection preferences)

In traveling down this unwieldy "chain of command" from person to person, ideas can get distorted by as much as 80 percent. A number of factors cause this. First, because passing along complex, confusing information poses many problems, we generally like to simplify messages. As a result we unconsciously (and consciously) delete information from the messages we receive before transmitting the information to others. Second, we like to think the messages we pass along to others make sense. (We feel foolish if we convey a message we do not seem to understand or deliver a message that appears to be illogical.) Thus, we try to "*make* sense out of" the message before communicating it to someone else. We do this by adding to, subtracting from, or otherwise altering what we have heard. Unfortunately, once we "make sense out of" the message, it may no longer correspond to the message originally sent to us (see Figure 6-1.) Such errors occur even though we have had years of practice in listening. Communicologist Gerald Goldhaber estimates that a 20-year-old person has practiced listening for at least 10,000 hours, a 30-year-old at least 15,000 hours, and a typical 40-year-old 20,000 or more hours. These figures are mind-boggling, but have we in reality been practicing listening or "unlistening"? Research says the latter.

Listening takes up a very important and very significant portion of your waking day, and since effective listening serves so many purposes, you need to listen as if your life depended on it. People who listen effectively demonstrate a sense of caring and concern for those with whom they interact. In contrast, people who do not listen effectively tend to drive people away. Thus, by listening accurately, you help avoid communication difficulties and breakdowns. Who has the primary responsibility for clear and effective communication—the speaker or the listener? An old proverb says, "Nature gave us two ears and one mouth so we can listen twice as much as we speak." The effective communicator is not afraid to be two parts listener and one part speaker. Actually since we all function as both senders and receivers, we believe that each must assume "51 percent" of the communication responsibility. This practice might not be mathematically sound, but it would certainly increase the effectiveness of our interpersonal, small-group, and public communication.

HEARING VERSUS LISTENING

Hearing and *listening* are not one and the same thing. Most people are born with the ability to hear. Thus *hearing* occurs automatically and requires no conscious effort on your part. If the physiological elements within your ears are functioning properly, your brain will process the electrochemical impulses received, and you will hear. However, what you do with the impulses after receiving them belongs to the realm of listening.

Comedian George Burns once said: "I can't help hearing, but I don't always listen." Provide an example where this statement applied to your own behavior. Describe the outcome.

But what is *listening?* As we will see, it is a deliberate process through which we seek to understand and retain aural (heard) stimuli. Unlike hearing, listening depends on a complex set of skills that we have to acquire. Thus, although hearing simply happens to us and cannot be manipulated, listening requires us to make an active, conscious effort to comprehend and remember what we hear. Furthermore, who we are affects the things we listen to. In your environment, from minute to minute, far too many sounds bombard you for you to be able to pay attention to each one. Thus in listening you *process* the external sounds of your environment to select those which are relevant to you, your activities, and your interests. This is not to say, however, that listening is just an external process. It is also an internal process. We listen to the sounds we hear, and we listen to what others say, but we also listen to what we say aloud and what we say to ourselves in response. (Do you ever talk to yourself? Are you your own best listener? Most of us are!)

We have seen that hearing is a natural and passive process. When we hear, we employ little if any conscious effort. Listening, on the other hand, is a deliberate process. How deliberate is it? How much effort must we expend in order to listen effectively? For example, do you work harder in listening to a professor's lecture on important material or in listening to a

LISTENING LEVEL ENERGY INVOLVEMENT SCALE

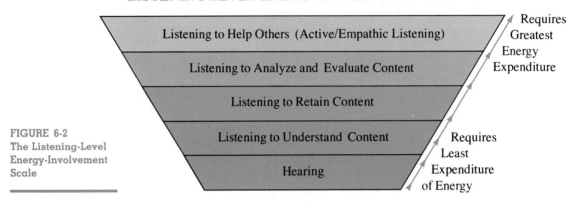

FIGURE 6-2
The Listening-Level
Energy-Involvement
Scale

disc jockey announcing your favorite recording on the radio? In many ways listening is similar to reading. Some material we read very carefully and closely, while other material we scan quickly to abstract only relevant facts. For still other material we need only check the title and author to know we do not care to read it. We approach the information that we receive aurally in much the same way: Some information we pass over lightly, and other information we attend to with more care. If the information is important to us, we work harder to retain it.

To help you begin to develop more effective listening skills, we have identified four levels of receiving. An understanding of these levels should help you assess your own listening effectiveness. Let's begin by examining the *Listening-Level Energy-Involvement Scale* (Figure 6-2).

As the scale indicates, hearing requires little if any energy expenditure or involvement on your part. In contrast, listening to understand requires a greater expenditure of energy. In listening you need to ensure that you comprehend what is being said. Remembering or retaining a message requires even more effort on your part, and working to analyze and evaluate what is said is still more difficult and thus consumes more energy. When we listen to help others (*empathic listening*), we are required to exhibit an even greater degree of involvement and—as we will see—consequently expend even more energy.

A problem shared by many poor listeners is the inability to determine the listening or involvement level appropriate to a given situation. For example, in a course with large lecture sections it is not uncommon to find some students "tuning out"—simply hearing when they should be listening to understand, retain, analyze, and evaluate content so as to improve their performance on examinations. All too frequently the same individuals are later quite adamant in asserting that certain points were "never covered" in class ("I was sitting right there, and I never heard you say that!"). The following is an example of what can happen when people fail to listen effectively at the appropriate level:

> Kevin Daly, founder of Communispond, a company that helps train executives to communicate their ideas more effectively, reports that the president of a steel company in Pittsburgh had aides prepare a news release for him to read at a press conference. The release, as written by his speech writers, was eleven pages. The president did not have time to review the manuscript before arriving at the conference and taking his place at the podium. Nonetheless, he began to read the announcement confidently. As he continued reading the lengthy statement, he realized that page eight had been printed twice. Indeed, he was now reading page eight aloud for the second time. Somewhat flustered, he gazed out at the audience, only to observe that there was "no quiver of recognition" among his listeners. He finished reading the release certain that no one had picked up his error. He was right. The mistake was never reported.

Why didn't the audience—educated individuals, all of them—listen more critically to what they were being told? How could they fail to perceive so blatant an error? How could they effectively evaluate what was being said to them if they were obviously unaware of the content? Are you a more effective listener than the persons referred to in the story? (Are you sure?)

UNLISTENERS: HOW THEY DO IT

While we do not listen at full capacity all the time, we should be aware of the "unlistening" behaviors we adopt that prevent us from understanding what could be important to us or to someone else.

The Ear Nodder.   Ear nodders pretend they are listening. They look at the speaker, nod their heads appropriately in agreement or disagreement, and utter remarks such as "mm" or "uh huh" that imply they are paying attention while in actuality the words are falling on "deaf ears." The ear nodders' façade mirrors the outward appearance of a listener, but they are listening counterfeiters—listening pretenders who let no meaning through. Perhaps they unlisten because they are thinking their own private thoughts, bored with the conversation, or otherwise occupied. Whatever their motivation, the outcome is similar—no listening has occurred.

The Ear Hogger.   Ear hoggers want you to listen to them while they have neither the time nor the desire to listen to you. Intrigued with their own thoughts and ideas, these ear monopolizers deny the validity of your right to be listened to while defending their right to express themselves no matter what the cost.

The Ear Filler.   Ear fillers never quite get the whole story when they listen. To make up for what they've missed or misinterpreted, they manufacture information to fill in the gaps. While the impression is that "they got it all," nothing could be further from the truth.

The Ear Bee.   Ear bees zero in on only those select portions of a speaker's remarks which interest them or have particular importance to them. Everything else the speaker says is rejected, deemed irrelevant, or judged to be inconsequential. Ear bees, in their search for just the honey, often miss the flower.

The Ear Muff.   Ear muffs close their ears to information they would rather not deal with. Sometimes they pretend not to understand what you tell them, act as if they did not hear you, or in short order forget what you told them.

The Ear Dart.   Ear darts wait for you to make a mistake or slip up so they can attack what you have to say.

To be sure, there are a number of other kinds of deficient listeners. But whatever the individual listening malady, the results are less than desirable. Someone spoke, and someone else failed to listen effectively.

FEEDBACK: A PREREQUISITE FOR EFFECTIVE LISTENING

The feedback process is intimately connected with the listening process. Developing an understanding and appreciation of the way feedback works is essential to improving your listening skills.

What Is Feedback?

The expression *feedback* implies that we are feeding someone by giving something back to the person. Simply put, *feedback* consists of all the verbal and nonverbal messages that a person consciously or unconsciously sends out in response to another person's communication. As students, you continually provide your instructors with feedback. Many of you, however, are probably not completely honest when you send feedback. At times when you are confused or bored, you may nevertheless put on an "I'm interested" face and nod smilingly, indicating that you understand and agree with everything your professor has said. Unfortunately, such behavior tends to encourage the sending of unclear messages, whereas if class members admitted confusion, the instructor might be more likely to find alternative ways to present the concepts and formulate new, more interesting examples.

Feedback is part of listening; it supplies the give-and-take necessary for communication. (Lynne Jaeger Weinstein/Woodfin Camp & Associates)

To cite another instance, some individuals will respond more actively and talk at greater length when a listener is smiling at them than they will when the listener appears sad or bored. Whatever the circumstance, we must recognize that the nature of the feedback we give people will affect the communicative interactions we share with them.

Types of Feedback

We constantly provide others with feedback, whether we intend to or not. Everything we do or fail to do in a relationship or interaction with others can be considered feedback. Sometimes we send feedback consciously, intending to evoke a particular response from the person communicating with us. For example, if you laugh or chuckle at a speaker's joke or story, you may be doing so because you want the speaker to feel that you enjoyed the story and hope she or he will tell more jokes. In contrast, some of the feedback we transmit is sent unconsciously and evokes unintentional or unexpected responses. Often, when our words or behaviors prompt another individual to exhibit a reaction that was never intended, we respond with useless phrases such as "That's not what I meant!" or "I didn't mean it that way!" or "What I meant was . . ."

Imagine someone who writes 50 love letters but receives no answer. Did the person receive feedback?

The Expected versus the Unexpected

1. Describe a situation in which a feedback message you sent was interpreted as intended. What effect did your feedback have on the nature of the interaction?
2. Describe a situation when a feedback message you sent was misinterpreted. What effect did your feedback have on the nature of that interaction?

As we can see, what we intend to convey by the feedback we send may not be what others perceive. Sometimes others intentionally choose not to perceive our messages. At other times confusion results because feedback that we mean to be *nonevaluative* in tone is interpreted as being *evaluative*. Distinguishing between these two feedback categories will help us use both types effectively and appropriately.

Evaluative Feedback. When we provide another person with an *evaluative response*, we state our opinion about some matter being discussed. Thus "How did you like my speech?" will almost always evoke a response that will be perceived as evaluative in tone. For example, a slight hesitation before the words "I loved it" might be perceived as connoting a negative response. When we give evaluative feedback we make judgments—either good or bad—based on our own system of values. As we go about the business of daily life, judgments about the relative worth of ideas, the importance of projects, and the classifications of abilities are a necessity.

By its very nature, the effect of evaluative feedback is either positive and rewarding or negative and punishing. *Positive evaluative feedback* tends to keep communication and its resulting behaviors moving in the direction in which they are already heading. If a company places an advertisement and achieves a tremendous growth in sales, the company will tend to place the same or a very similar ad in the same or very similar media in the future. If a person wearing a new hairstyle is complimented, he will tend to keep that hairstyle. If you are speaking to your instructor and she appears receptive to your ideas and suggestions, you will tend to continue offering ideas and suggestions in the future. Thus, positive evaluative feedback serves to make us continue behaving as we are already behaving and enhances or reinforces existing conditions or actions.

Negative evaluative feedback serves a corrective function in that it helps to extinguish undesirable communicator behaviors. When we or others perceive feedback as negative in tone, we tend to change or modify our performance accordingly. For example, if you were to tell a number of off-color stories that your listeners judged to be in bad taste, your listeners might send negative responses to you. They might turn away, attempt to change the subject, or simply maintain a cold, lengthy silence. Each cue would indicate that your message had overstepped the bounds of propriety, and as a result you would probably discontinue your anecdotes.

Whenever you send evaluative feedback messages, whether positive or negative, preface your statements in such a way that your cocommunicator realizes that what you are offering is your opinion only. Such phrases as "It seems to me," "In my opinion," and "I think" are usually helpful, because they allow the target of your remarks to know that you realize that other interpretations and options are available. When possible, avoid using phrases of the "You must" or "That's stupid" type. Such comments almost always elicit a certain amount of defensiveness, whereas couching both positive and negative feedback in less than adamant terms tends to create a more favorable and receptive climate for the relationship.

Formative feedback is a special kind of negative feedback. Don Tosti, an industrial psychologist, utilized timed negative feedback with some interesting results. Tosti discovered that in a learning situation it is best to first provide positive feedback to an individual *immediately after* the individual has displayed a desired behavior. Thus, comments such as "You did a good job" and "Keep up the good work" would be offered immediately following such behavior, because these responses give people a sense of pride and pleasure in themselves and their work. However, Tosti also suggests that a particular negative—or what he calls "formative" feedback—should be given only *just before* the same (or a similar) activity is repeated. In other words, Tosti believes withholding negative feedback until the individual can use it constructively makes the negative, or formative, feedback seem more like coaching than criticism. Comments such as "Okay, team, let's eliminate the errors we made last time" and "When you go out there today, try to . . ." help to alleviate the extent to which negative feedback is perceived as a harmful rather than a helpful force. Thus, saving formative feedback until just before an activity is to be performed again can help eliminate the feelings of rejection that sometimes accompany other negative feedback. In contrast, it should be remembered that the immediate dispensing of positive feedback can do wonders for your cocommunicator's self-image and morale.

The implications of Tosti's findings for communication are many. For example, if you handed in a paper to your instructor, following Tosti's guidelines the instructor would hand you a list containing only positive observations. Not until the instructor made the next assignment would you be offered formative or negative feedback in the form of a list containing errors to avoid. Formative feedback can also be used as a memory refresher or as a motivational tool to improve performance. With formative feedback, it is the timing that counts.

Unlike traditional negative feedback, formative feedback does not tend to discourage an individual from attempting to perform an activity again. Nor does it tend to demoralize the person. Test the theory behind formative feedback by using it in our own communication.

Nonevaluative Feedback. In contrast to evaluative feedback, *noneval- uative* (or *nondirective*) *feedback* makes no overt attempt to direct the actions of a communicator. Thus, we use nonevaluative feedback when we want to learn more about a person's feelings or when we want to aid another person in formulating thoughts about a particular subject. When we offer nonevaluative feedback we make no reference to our personal opinions or judgments. Instead, we simply describe, question, or indicate an interest in what the other person is communicating to us.

Despite its nonjudgmental nature, nonevaluative feedback is often construed as being positive in tone. That is, our cocommunicators' behaviors may be reinforced as we probe, interpret their messages, and offer support as they attempt to work through a problem. Nonevaluative feedback actually reaches beyond the realm of positive feedback, however, by providing others with an opportunity to examine their own problems and arrive at their own solutions. For this reason, carefully phrased nonevaluative feedback can be enormously helpful and sustaining to people as they go through difficult periods.

We will consider four kinds of nonevaluative feedback. Three were identified by David Johnson—probing, understanding, and supporting—and the fourth—"I" messages—was identified by Thomas Gordon.[4]

Probing is a nonevaluative technique in which we ask individuals for additional information to draw them out and to demonstrate our willingness to listen to their problems. For example, suppose a student is concerned with her grades in a particular course and says to you, "I'm really upset. All of my friends are doing better in geology than I am." If you choose to utilize the nonevaluative technique of probing, you might ask, "Why does this situation bother you?" or "What is there about not getting good grades that concerns you?" or "What do you suppose caused this to happen?" Responding in this way gives the other person the chance to think through the overall nature of her problem while providing her with needed oppor- tunities for emotional release. In contrast, comments like "So what. Who cares about that dumb class?" or "Grades don't matter. What are you worrying about?" or "You really were dumb when you stopped studying" would tend to stop the student from thinking through and discussing her problem and instead would probably cause her to experience feelings of defensiveness.

A second kind of nonevaluative response is what Johnson terms *understanding*. When we offer *understanding* we seek to comprehend what the other person is saying to us, and we check ourselves by *paraphrasing* (restating) what we believe we have heard. Paraphrasing shows that we care about other people and the problems they face. Examine the following paraphrases to develop a feel for the nature of the understanding response:

PERSON 1: I don't think I have the skill to be picked for the team.
PERSON 2: You believe you're not good enough to make the team this year?
PERSON 1: I envy those guys so much.
PERSON 2: You mean you're jealous of the people in that group?

If we use understanding responses early in a relationship, in effect we communicate to our partners that we care enough about the interaction to want to be certain we comprehend what they are saying to us. Such responses encourage the relationship because they encourage the other person in describing and detailing personal feelings. By delivering understanding responses both verbally and nonverbally, we also support individuals by showing that we are sensitive to their feelings and are really willing to listen.

A third kind of nonevaluative feedback is referred to by Johnson as *supportive*. *Supportive feedback* indicates that a problem an individual deems important and significant is viewed by the listener also as important and significant. For example, suppose a friend comes to you with a problem that he feels is extremely serious. Perhaps he has worked himself into a state of extreme agitation and implies that you cannot possibly understand his situation. In offering supportive feedback you would attempt to calm your friend down by assuring him that the world has not ended and that you do understand his problem. Offering others supportive feedback is difficult. We have to be able to reduce their intensity of feeling while letting them know that we believe their problems are real and serious. Such comments as "It's stupid to worry about that" or "Is that all that's worrying you?" are certainly not supportive. A better approach might be to say, "I can see you are upset. Let's talk about it. I'm sure you can find a way to solve the problem." A friend who is upset because she just failed an exam needs supportive feedback: "I can see you are worried. I don't blame you for being upset." This is certainly not the time to suggest that she has no valid reason for being upset or that her feelings are inappropriate. It would be foolish to say, "Next time you'll know better. I told you not studying wouldn't get you anywhere." When we use supportive feedback, we judge the problems to be important, but we do not attempt to solve them ourselves; instead, we encourage people to discover their own solutions.

Finally, certain nonevaluative feedback messages are called " 'I' messages," a term coined by Thomas Gordon. When we deliver "*I*" *messages* to others, we do not pass judgment on their actions but instead convey our feelings about the nature of the situation at hand. According to Gordon, when people interact with us, they are often unaware of how their actions affect us. We have an option to provide these persons with either evaluative or nonevaluative feedback. Neither type is inherently good or bad. However, far too often the way we formulate our evaluative feedback adversely affects the nature of our interactions and the growth of our relationships. For example, do any of these statements sound familiar? "You made me angry!" "You're no good!" "You're in my way!" "You're a slob!" What do each of these statements have in common? As you have probably noticed, each one contains the word *you*. Each also places the blame for something on another person. As relationships experience difficulties, the involved parties tend to resort more and more to name-calling and blaming others. Such feedback messages serve to create schisms between people that are difficult and sometimes even impossible to bridge. To avoid this, Gordon suggests that we replace "you" messages with "I" messages. If, for example, a parent tells a child, "You're pestering me," the child's interpretation will probably be, "I am bad," thereby precipitating a certain amount of defensiveness or hostility toward the parent ("I am *not* bad!"). But if the parent tells the child, "I'm really very tired and I don't feel like playing right now," the child's reaction is more likely to be, "Mom is tired." Such an approach is more apt to elicit the type of behavior the parent desires than the name-calling and blaming that "You are a pest" would evoke. Keeping this in mind, which of the following messages do you believe would be more likely to elicit a favorable response?

> SUPERVISOR TO WORKERS: You lazy bums! We'll never meet the deadline if you don't work faster!
>
> SUPERVISOR TO WORKERS: I'm afraid that if we don't work faster, we'll miss the deadline, and the company will lose a lot of money.

Right! The second statement would not produce the feelings of defensiveness that would be engendered by the first.

There is one other quality you should realize about "I" messages and their use. It is quite common for any of us to say "I am angry" to another person. Anger, however, is a secondary emotion. We are angry *because of*, or *due to*, some stimulus or stimuli. In actuality, we *develop* anger. For example, should your child or a child you are watching run into the street, your first response would probably be fear. Only after the child was safe would you develop anger, and then you would probably share your anger with the child. When formulating angry "I" messages during your communicative encounters, be certain to look beyond or below your anger and ask yourself why you are angry. Attempt to determine the forces that precipitate your anger—these are feelings that should be expressed. Thus, if someone says something that hurts you, try to find ways to express the *hurt* rather than simply venting the resulting *anger*. Using "I" messages as feedback will not always evoke the behavior you want from the other party, but it will help to prevent the defensive, self-serving behaviors that "you" messages frequently elicit.

At this point ask yourself which of the types of feedback you have just learned about are best. Which do you feel are most important? As you probably realize, the categories and types of feedback we have discussed are neither good nor bad. Each can be put to good use. Thus, whether you choose to offer evaluative or nonevaluative responses depends on the individual with whom you are interacting and on the nature of the situation in which you find yourself.

Effects of Feedback

How do you think feedback affects interpersonal communication? Suppose, for example, someone is telling you a funny story. What would happen if you should consciously decide to treat this person politely but also to neither smile nor laugh at the story? Such polite but somber reactions can cause the best of storytellers to stop communicating. Sometimes in the middle of a story, the teller will notice that the listener is not amused. At this point, in an attempt to determine if the receiver heard what was said, the sender will repeat or rephrase key phrases of the story: "Don't you understand? What happened was . . ." or "You see, what this means is . . ." The feedback given by the respondent in any encounter strongly influences the direction and outcome of that interaction.[5] You might want to try the "no laugh" procedure the next time someone begins to relate a humorous incident or tale to you. If you do, be sure to note how your not laughing affected the sender's abilities to formulate a message.

The Skill Builder on page 156, adapted from an experiment designed by Harold Leavitt and Ronald Mueller, demonstrates how feedback affects the development of our relationships.[6] Feedback usually increases the accuracy with which information is passed from person to person. However, it also increases the amount of time required to transmit information. Under zero-feedback conditions (phase 1 of the exercise), the speaker requires less time to transmit the information to the receiver than he or she would under either the limited feedback (phase 2) or the free feedback condition (phase 3). Still, most communicators feel that the added time is more than compensated for by the increased accuracy of the replications. In other words, under free feedback conditions, time is not wasted.

HOW TO INCREASE YOUR "EAR POWER": A LISTENING IMPROVEMENT PROGRAM

The first step in developing effective listening habits is to develop an awareness of the importance and effects of listening. The second step is to develop an awareness of the importance and effects of feedback. By now we should have accomplished these objectives. The next step is to develop

Now You Have It, Now You Don't

1. Select a partner.
2. Each of you draw three designs composed of a random series of straight, interconnecting lines on a card or slip of paper.

Do not show the diagrams to each other. The purpose of the exercise is for you to give verbal instructions that will enable your partner to reproduce your diagrams. Deliver your instructions under the following three conditions:

   a. When you explain your first design, you must turn your back to your partner and neither watch nor comment on his or her efforts. Also, your partner is not allowed to speak or look at you during this phase of the experience. This approximates a zero-feedback (no feedback) condition.

   b. When you describe the second design, you may turn and watch your partner work. You may comment on what she or he is drawing, but your partner may not speak to or look at you. This approximates a limited feedback condition.

   c. Finally, when you communicate a description of your third design to your partner, you may interact openly with each other. You may observe and comment on your partner's efforts, and your partner may interact with you by facing you and asking you questions to check on the accuracy of her or his drawing. This approximates a free feedback condition.

   If time permits, partners should reverse roles and repeat the above three steps.

3. Which condition produced the quickest replication? Why? Which condition produced the most accurate replication? Why? During which phase of the experience were you most confident? Least confident? Why? How did functioning as sender or receiver alter your feelings during each phase of the experience?

your listening skills by participating in a series of exercises and experiences. If you really want to improve your listening, these exercises should not merely be done once and put aside. Your listening skills will improve only if you return to try these and similar experiences repeatedly.

Focus Your Attention

Let's begin our listening improvement program by first considering our need to be able to focus our attention. It is apparent that if we are to listen effectively we must be able to pay attention to what is being communicated. However, numerous internal and external stimuli bombard us and compete for our attention.

    The difficulties we experience when attempting to focus attention are confirmed by the number of times, in various situations, we are admonished to "Pay attention!" When was the last time someone uttered something like "He told us that in class. Weren't you paying attention?" All too frequently the response is, "Well, I thought I was." We will explore several ways you can work to improve your ability to consciously attend to information. And before beginning we should emphasize that developing this ability will be a lifelong project.

    If you are to learn to focus your attention and improve your listening skills, one of your main needs is to handle your emotions. Feelings of hate, anger, happiness, and sadness can cause us to decrease our listening efficiency. As we become emotionally involved in a conversation, we simply are less able or less willing to focus our attention accurately. Ralph Nichols in the book *Are You Listening?* notes that single words often cause us to react emotionally and thus reduce the extent to which we are able to pay attention. He terms these "red-flag words." According to Nichols, the latter trigger an emotional deafness that sends our listening efficiency down to zero. Among the words known to function as red flags for certain listeners are *communist*, *punk*, *mother-in-law*, *spastic*, and *income tax*. When particular individuals hear these words, they abandon efforts to understand

Compile a list of words and phrases that tend to distract your attention. Note the reasons for your choices.

and perceive. Instead, they take "side trips," dwelling on endemic feelings and connections. The result is that in effect the emotional eruption they experience causes a listening disruption. It should be noted that, like words, phrases and topics can also make us react emotionally and lessen our ability to concentrate. For these reasons it is important to identify the words, phrases, or topics that tend to distract you emotionally. Your "distraction words" are personal and unique to you and therefore change as you change. An issue that precipitated emotional deafness for you in the past may not distract you even momentarily in the future. For this reason, it is a good practice for you to keep a record of all your attention distractors. If possible, list them on cards, and reexamine them every 3 or 4 months. By constantly updating your red-flag list, you will be better able to recognize and handle distractions during interpersonal encounters.

Physical factors can also act as attention distractors. For example, the room you are in can be too hot or cold for your comfort, the space may be too small or too large, or the seating arrangement can be inadequate. (Have you ever tried to listen politely and efficiently to someone as the springs in your chair were about to poke through the upholstery and pierce you?) In addition to environmental factors, other people can also be a distraction. Individuals you are relating to may speak too loudly or too softly. They may have an accent that you find difficult to comprehend or an appearance that interests or even alarms you. (Have you ever been engaged in conversation with someone wearing such an unusual outfit that you found it difficult to focus your attention on what that person was saying?)

One additional attention determinant should be noted. Simply, we can think faster than we can speak. When communicating we usually speak at a rate of 125 to 150 words a minute. Researchers have found, however, that we can comprehend much higher rates of speech—perhaps even 500 words a minute. What does this mean for you, the listener? It means that when someone speaks at a normal rate you have free time left over and may therefore tend to take mental excursions and daydream. When you return your attention to the speaker, however, you may find that he or she is far ahead of you. Thus we must make conscious efforts to use the speech-thought differential effectively. We can do this by internally summarizing and paraphrasing what is being said *as we listen* and by asking ourselves questions that help focus our attention instead of distracting it from the subject at hand. (Several speech-compression devices on the market use up our excess thinking time by speeding up the rate of ordinary speech without producing distortions in the speaker's voice quality.)

Maintaining or focusing your attention is an act you must constantly perform. Smart communicators periodically check their attention to see if it has wandered. Make the attention check an integral part of your listening improvement regimen. Although the check itself can become an attention

Under what conditions do you "lose consciousness"?

"I'm sorry, dear, I must have lost consciousness.
What were you saying?"

Drawing by Chon Day; © 1982 The New Yorker Magazine, Inc.

distractor, its benefit outweighs the potential deficit. Only after becoming aware that you are not listening can you begin to make the necessary corrections.[7]

Finally, attentive listeners adopt nonverbal behaviors that support the listening effort. Ineffective listeners employ traditionally *passive* listening poses—they do not face the person they are interacting with; they adopt a defensive, tense posture; they lean away from the other person; they avoid eye contact. Attentive listeners exhibit *active* listening behav-

---

SKILL BUILDER

Checking Out, Checking In

1. Begin a conversation with another person. At irregular intervals you and your partner should stop talking and consider where each of you is placing his or her attention. Has it wandered at all? When? To what? Repeat this exercise a number of times.

2. Try a similar attention check when watching the evening news on television or while listening to a long speech broadcast over radio. Keep a tally each time your attention wanders.

iors—they face the other person directly, adopt an open posture, lean slightly toward the other person, and maintain comfortable eye contact.

Set Appropriate Listening Goals

Far too often we find ourselves listening to something without adequately understanding what we are listening for, and as a result we become bored and irritated. One way to combat the "listening blahs" is to set specific listening goals. Research indicates that listening effectiveness increases after goals are identified. How can you make this evidence work for you?

Before beginning an interaction, establish in your own mind the listening goal(s) you would like to achieve. Then analyze the extent to which you were able to attain your goal(s).

Listening goals identify what you personally would like to gain during and after attending to a particular message. When you establish goals, you answer the question, Why am I listening to this? Listening goals are closely related to the levels of listening discussed earlier in this chapter. In general, we listen to understand, to retain, to analyze and evaluate content, and to develop empathic relationships with others. Thus, one way to set your listening goals is to identify which level of listening is most appropriate to a particular situation. For example, if you were an employee who was expected to internalize a series of directions for handling highly explosive materials, you would listen to understand and retain instructions. If you were listening to a series of lectures on types of computer operations and your objective was to select a computer for your company, you would listen to understand and retain but also to analyze and evaluate. In contrast, suppose your friend has lost a parent. In this situation your goal would not be to retain or evaluate information but rather to listen in an empathic manner.

Just as trains frequently switch tracks, so you should be able to switch listening goals. The goals you set are not meant to imprison you; rather, you need to be flexible, able to adapt to the demands of each situation or experience.

Listening to Understand Ideas

After listening to information from another person, have you ever made a statement like "I'm sure I understand the main point" or "The central idea is crystal clear"? When we listen to understand, we listen for the main ideas or central concepts. Let's examine how this works.

Listening to understand may be compared to a simple tooth extraction. When we visit the dentist to have a tooth pulled, we assume the dentist will not simply reach into our mouth and begin pulling our teeth at random. Instead, we operate under the belief that the dentist will locate the tooth that needs to be extracted, take hold of only that tooth, and remove it. When we listen to understand—a process that underlies all higher levels of listening—we, like the dentist, must locate the central concepts contained in the speaker's message and remove them (in this case for further examination). Since it is almost impossible for us to remember every word said to us, we should work to recall only those concepts which are most important—in other words, those ideas which constitute the main points of the person's message. Thus, when you listen to understand, you seek to identify key words and phrases that will help you accurately summarize the concepts being discussed. But remember that unless the ideas you extract from the messages you receive are accurate representations of what was said, you are only hearing, not listening.

Listening to Retain Information

Robert Montgomery, a training expert who has developed a wealth of material on memory for the American Management Associations, says, "The art of retention is the art of attention." If you are to retain what you hear, you must learn first how to focus your attention and second how to make certain that you understand what you have heard. Once you are able to focus your attention on what another person is saying and you are able to understand what the person has said, you are ready to move your listening selector up to the next level—listening to retain.

After receiving travel directions, did you ever find yourself saying to yourself, "Do I turn right or left here? What was I told?" After having a discussion with a friend and assuming that you understood the friend's point of view, did you ever find yourself wondering what that point of view was? Even worse, after being introduced to someone, do you ever find yourself asking, "What was that person's name?" We will now explore several techniques that you can use to help you retain what you hear. Such aids are commonly referred to as *mnemonic devices*. Use the ones that work best for you.

Repeat and Paraphrase. Your basic tool to help retain the information you hear is *repetition*. The more you repeat a concept or idea, the more likely you are to be able to recall it later. Repetition has two faces: We use repetition when we repeat a statement verbatim (exactly reproduce what was said) and when we paraphrase (restate what was said using other words).

One effective way to remember what others say is to reproduce their words in writing. The more proficient you are at note taking, the more information you are likely to be able to retain. Of course, in interpersonal situations, it is neither advisable nor practical to take notes. However, it is a good idea to keep a few index cards or a small notepad handy to record important names, numbers, appointments, and information.

The paraphrase can also be used to improve your personal retentiveness level. By restating what a person has said to you in your own words you

Listening is the first step in retaining information. Taking notes helps you reinforce your learning skills. (Frank Siteman/The Picture Cube)

not only check on your own understanding but also help yourself recall what the other person has said. We will consider the art of paraphrasing in more detail when we consider empathic listening. For now it will suffice if you realize that paraphrasing can help alleviate some of the problems created by the speech-thought time lapse we spoke of earlier. If you use some of your extra thinking time to replicate for yourself what has just been said, you give your mind fewer opportunities to wander.

Visualization. Frequently, we are better able to recall information if we picture something about it. For example, many people are able to associate names, places, and numbers with particular visual images. Often, the more outrageous or creative the picture, the better the image will help them recall a name. For instance, you might picture an individual with the name of John Sanderson as standing atop a large sand pile or sand dune, or a woman named Susan Grant might be pictured as standing inside Grant's tomb.

Listening to Analyze and Evaluate Content

Being able to analyze and evaluate what you listen to calls for even greater skill than retention does. When you learn to analyze and evaluate content effectively, you become adept at spotting fallacies in the arguments and statements you encounter during interpersonal discourse.

Often, we let our prior convictions prevent us from processing and fairly evaluating what we hear. For instance, consider the following conversation:

ALICE: Did you hear? Sandy was arrested by the police for selling drugs.
JIM: Sandy? I don't believe it. The police made a mistake. She isn't that type.

In this interchange Jim is jumping to a conclusion. Instead of analyzing the information he was given, he has reacted on the basis of his prior knowledge. How should Jim have reacted? Should he have agreed that the police were right to arrest Sandy? We don't think so. We think Jim should have asked what evidence the police had to support their claim and what evidence Sandy offered in her own defense. Effective listeners do not let their convictions run away with them but reserve judgment until the facts are in. In other words, they withhold evaluation until their comprehension of the situation is complete.

Attempts at persuasion often find one individual trying to make another believe something because "everyone else believes it." If we accept such drivel, we may find ourselves swept away on the bandwagon. We may end up supporting a candidate simply because we imagine everyone else does. Or we might join a pyramid scheme because we are convinced everyone involved will become rich. Effective listeners, however, realize that they have a choice. They may join the bandwagon, or they may let it pass them by. Effective listeners do not feel compelled to follow the crowd.

If you become proficient at evaluating and analyzing the information you listen to, you will discover that people frequently argue or talk in circles. For example:

ELLEN: Divorce is wrong.
JOSÉ: Why?
ELLEN: Because my minister told me it is wrong.
JOSÉ: Why did he tell you that?
ELLEN: Because it is wrong!

For the next week, keep a record of all circular conversations you hear. Point out the fallacy contained in each example.

We have a tendency to talk circularly when we argue without evidence, particularly if we feel an emotional tie to the topic under discussion or if we believe our stance is closely connected to our value system. When this occurs, we simply insist we are right: "That's all there is to it." We tell ourselves that we do not need reasons. Effective listeners perceive the fallacy inherent in such behavior and weigh the speaker's evidence by mentally questioning it. Effective listeners "listen between the lines."

Listening Empathically, Listening Actively

When questioning witnesses, attorneys listen for contradictions or irrelevancies in testimony: They listen to analyze. In contrast, social workers usually listen to help people work through a personal problem. This, too, is an important level of listening. It is referred to as *empathic,* or *active,* listening and is the last type of listening we will consider in our listening improvement program.

The term *empathic listening* was popularized by the psychotherapist Carl Rogers, who believed that listening could be used to help individuals understand their own situations and problems. When you listen actively, or empathically, you do more than passively absorb the words that are spoken to you. Active listeners also try to internalize the other person's feelings and see life through his or her eyes. The following poem by David Ignatow depicts the nonempathic listener in operation. Are you at all like this person?

TWO FRIENDS

I have something to tell you.
I'm listening.
I'm dying.
I'm sorry to hear.
I'm getting old.
It's terrible.
It is, I thought, you should know.
Of course, and I'm sorry. Keep in touch.
I will. And you too.
And let me know what's new.
Certainly, though it can't be much.
And stay well.
And you too.
And go slow.
And you too.

How often do you put on your "I am listening" mask, nod agreement, and utter the appropriate "Ohs" and "I sees," when in reality you are miles away and self-concerned? We need to be willing to acknowledge the seriousness of other people's problems. We need to take the time required to draw them out so that they can discuss a problem and come to terms with it. We need to show the other person that we understand the problem. We can do this by paraphrasing the person's statements and by reinforcing those statements with genuine nonverbal cues—eye contact, physical contact (touching), and facial expressions.

Active, empathic listeners put themselves in the speaker's place in an effort to understand the speaker's feelings. Active, empathic listeners clearly appreciate both the meaning and the feeling behind what another

---

LISTEN HERE: POSSIBLE MOTTO FOR A MAN WHO IS ALL EARS

Mr. Kirk Martin listens, in person and by appointment only. "I will talk, if a person asks me to, or if he looks like he wants me to," Mr. Martin explains. "I can talk eyeball to eyeball to anyone who comes through my front door." Mr. Martin, 48, a professional truck and taxicab driver who sells one-family homes and farms on the side, began his listening enterprise with a news-paper ad: "I will listen to you talk 30 minutes without comment for $5," the ad said. "I get about 10–20 calls a day now, but only a few of those make appointments." He says his clients are from all walks of life. "Many of them are troubled people who need someone to hear them out, just once."

© The Associated Press.

---

person is saying. Thus, in effect, active, empathic listeners *convey* to the speaker that they are seeing things from the speaker's point of view.

Active, empathic listeners rely heavily on the paraphrase:

PERSON 1: I am so mad at my mother.
PERSON 2: If I'm not mistaken, your mother is giving you trouble. Is that right?
PERSON 1: My boss is really trying to fire me.
PERSON 2: If I understand you, you believe your boss is out to replace you. Do I have it straight?

To paraphrase effectively, follow this three-step process:

1. Make a statement of tentativeness that invites correction; e.g., "If I'm not mistaken. . . ."
2. Repeat the basic idea(s) in your own words.
3. Check it out with the other person; e.g., "Is that correct?"

By paraphrasing the sender's thoughts, listeners accomplish at least two purposes: First, they let the other person know that they care enough to listen; second, if the speaker's message has not been accurately received, they offer the other person the opportunity to adjust, change, or modify the message so that they can understand it as intended:

PERSON 1: I'm quitting my job soon.
PERSON 2: You're leaving your job tomorrow?
PERSON 1: Well, not that soon! But within a few weeks.

In summary, when you listen actively, or empathically, you listen for total meaning, and you listen in order to respond to feelings. When you listen empathically, the following statements will *not* appear in your conversation:

"You must do . . ."
"You should do . . ."
"You're wrong!"
"Let me tell you what to do."
"You sure have a funny way of looking at things."
"You're making a big mistake."
"The best answer is . . ."
"Don't worry about it."
"You think you've got problems! Ha!"
"That reminds me of the time I . . ."

Active, empathic listeners do not judge; they reflect, consider, and often restate in their own words their impressions of the sender's expression. Active listeners also check to determine if their impressions are acceptable to the sender. What kind of a checker are you?

At this point, you should realize why it takes "more than two good ears" to listen.

SKILL BUILDER

What's That You Said?

Choose a partner and select one of the following topics to discuss:

Abortion	Premarital sex
Capital punishment	Socialized medicine
An embarrassing situation	Lying

One person begins the discussion. Before adding ideas, the second person must paraphrase the first speaker's statement. If the paraphrase is accurate, the second person may continue by offering his or her own thought. However, if the paraphrase is inaccurate, the individual must correct any misperceptions. Only when the first speaker agrees that the paraphrase is accurate may the individual continue.

SUMMARY

Listening is a deliberate process through which we seek to understand and retain aural (heard) stimuli. Unlike hearing, which occurs automatically, listening depends on a complex set of acquired skills. The average person listens at only a 25 percent efficiency, losing 75 percent of what is heard. A graphic illustration of the results of inefficient listening is the way a message is distorted in serial communication (when a message is passed from one person to another in a series). A principal reason for poor listening is the failure to determine the listening or involvement level appropriate to a particular situation. Various behaviors we adopt cause us to *unlisten*—that is, they impede true understanding.

A prerequisite for effective listening is effective feedback. Feedback consists of all the verbal and nonverbal messages that a person consciously or unconsciously sends out in response to another person's communication. Through feedback we either confirm or correct the impressions others have of us and our attitudes. There are two main types of feedback: (1) Evaluative feedback gives an opinion, positive or negative, and attempts to influence the behavior of others. (2) Nonevaluative feedback gives emotional support. Probing, understanding or paraphrasing, supportive feedback, and "I" messages are all forms of nonevaluative feedback that help sustain interpersonal relationships.

You can improve your listening skills by learning to focus your attention while listening and by setting appropriate listening goals. Listening to understand ideas, to retain information, to analyze and evaluate, and to empathize each requires progressively more effort and attention.

SUGGESTIONS FOR FURTHER READING

Baker, Larry L. *Listening Behavior.* Englewood Cliffs, N.J.: Prentice-Hall, 1971. This book offers a comprehensive, well-documented analysis of listening and feedback.

Duker, Sam, ed. *Listening: Readings.* New York: Scarecrow Press, 1966. Contains a series of articles relating to listening theory and practice.

Floyd, James J. *Listening: A Practical Approach.* Glenview, Ill.: Scott, Foresman and Company, 1985. An easy to read, experientially based work.

Gordon, Thomas. *Leader Effectiveness Training.* New York: Wyden Books, 1977. A popular book that contains material relevant to the study of listening.

Johnson, David W. *Reaching Out: Interpersonal Effectiveness and Self-Actualization.* Englewood Cliffs, N.J.: Prentice-Hall, 1972. Especially helpful for individuals interested in empathic listening.

Kelly, Charles M. "Empathic Listening." In *Small Group Communication: A Reader.* Boston: William C. Brown, 1974. Discusses what listening is and is not. Presents suggestions for improving listening abilities.

Leavitt, H., and R. Mueller. "Some Effects of Feedback on Communication," *Human Relations,* Vol. 4 (1951), pp. 401–410. One of the classic feedback studies.

Nichols, Ralph G. "Do We Know How to Listen?" *The Speech Teacher,* Vol. 10 (1961), pp. 118–124. Provides a useful overview of the listening process.

Nichols, Ralph G., and Leonard A. Stevens. *Are*

You Listening? New York: McGraw-Hill, 1957. A classic book about listening that helped popularize interest in the field.

Rogers, Carl R. *On Becoming a Person.* Boston: Houghton Mifflin, 1961, Rogers builds his theory of helping others on sound listening skills.

Steil, Lyman K., Larry L. Barker, and Kittie W. Watson. *Effective Listening: Key to Your Success.* Reading, Mass.: Addison-Wesley, 1983. Presents an effective how-to approach to improving listening skills.

Weaver, Carl H. *Human Listening: Processes and Behavior.* Indianapolis, Ind.: Bobbs-Merrill, 1972. Contains useful exercises for improving listening abilities.

Wolf, Florence I., Nadine C. Marsnik, William S. Tacey, and Ralph G. Nichols. *Perceptive Listening.* New York: Holt, Rinehart and Winston, 1983. A comprehensive textbook on listening for both college students and adults.

NOTES

1. Paul Tory Rankin, "The Measurement of the Ability to Understand Spoken Language" (Ph.D. diss., University of Michigan, 1926), p. 43, and Larry Barker, R. Edwards, C. Gaines, K. Gladney, and F. Hally, "An Investigation of Proportional Time Spent in Various Communication Activities by College Students," *Journal of Applied Communication Research*, Vol. 8 (1980), pp. 101–109.

2. For a detailed discussion see Ralph G. Nichols and Leonard A. Stevens, *Are You Listening?* (New York: McGraw-Hill, 1957).

3. John R. Freund and Arnold Nelson, "Distortion in Communication," in *Communication Probes*, edited by B. Peterson, G. Goldhaber, and R. Pace (Chicago: Science Research Associates, 1974), pp. 122–124.

4. See David W. Johnson, *Reaching Out: Interpersonal Effectiveness and Self-Actualization* (Englewood Cliffs, N.J.: Prentice-Hall, 1972), and Thomas Gordon, *Leader Effectiveness Training* (New York: Wyden Books, 1977).

5. For a discussion of the kinds of information conveyed by verbal and nonverbal feedback see Dale G. Leathers, "The Informational Potential of the Nonverbal and Verbal Components of Feedback Responses," *Southern Speech Communication Journal*, Vol. 44 (1979), pp. 331–354.

6. H. Leavitt and R. Mueller, "Some Effects of Feedback on Communication," *Human Relations*, Vol. 4 (1951), pp. 401–410.

7. Ralph G. Nichols, "Listening Is a Ten-Part Skill," *Nation's Business*, Vol. 45 (1957), p. 4.

Communicating
Interpersonally

Understanding Relationships

People meet and separate. But funny things happen in between.

Mark L. Knapp

CHAPTER PREVIEW

After finishing this chapter, you should be able to:

Explain the reasons behind our need for person-to-person contacts

Define *inclusion, control,* and *affection*

Discuss what can happen when our needs for inclusion, control, and affection are not met

Describe relationships according to *breadth* and *depth* characteristics

Explain the theory of *social penetration*

Discuss and distinguish between 10 relationship stages

Explain *cost-benefit* theory

Identify ways to enhance your relationship satisfaction quotient

---

In *Peoplemaking,* Virginia Satir notes: "Once a human being has arrived on this earth, communication is the largest single factor determining what kinds of relationships he makes with others and what happens to him in the world about him. How he manages his survival, how he develops intimacy, how productive he is, how he makes sense . . . are largely dependent on his communication skills."[1] This chapter explores the nature of the relationships we share with others, our satisfaction or lack of satisfaction with them, and how we can enhance them. The one thing all our relationships have in common is communication. Through communication we not only establish and maintain but also withdraw from and end relationships. Through communication we define what we think of ourselves in relationship to others. Through communication we express ourselves and our needs to others. Some relationships we share with others are rich and intense; some are superficial and almost meaningless. In like fashion, so is the communication that characterizes these relationships. Whatever the nature of the experience, what causes us to come together in a relationship is communication, and what happens to the relationship over time is also a result of communication. Communication can function as either the lifeblood or the death knell of a relationship. Let us examine how and why.

THE ROLE OF RELATIONSHIPS

As society becomes increasingly technological, we cannot help but feel that the environment in which we live is becoming less personal. Thus it is only natural that we are impelled to seek warm, personal relationships to compensate; consequently, a major theme of our times has become our desire for closer, more personal ties. As John Naisbitt writes in *Megatrends*, the future may be high-tech, but it must also become "high-touch" if we are to live comfortably in it.[2] We shall now explore why we need such person-to-person contacts. A vast body of research consistently attests that we attempt to meet our needs for inclusion, control, and affection through our relationships.[3]

Our need for *inclusion* involves the varying degrees to which we all need to establish and maintain a feeling of mutual interest with other people—that we can take an interest in others and that others can take an interest in us. We want others to pay attention to us, to take the time to understand us. Wanting to be included is normal. We all remember how it feels to be left out—to be the last person asked to join a team, to not be invited to an important party, or to be ignored during a luncheon conversation. When our need for inclusion is met, we tend to feel worthwhile and fulfilled. If it goes unmet, we tend to feel lonely, and our health may even suffer.

To be sure, loneliness is an all too common affliction of our age. But what exactly is it? A consensus has emerged that loneliness begins with a recognition that the interpersonal relationships we are having are not the kinds we would like to have.[4] When our person-to-person contacts are deficient, we feel alone, and we seek all kinds of substitutes for these contacts, sometimes opting for the company of professional contact persons such as physicians or even radio talk show hosts to fill our person-to-person needs. So interconnected is inclusion with our well-being that in the early 1980s the California State Department of Mental Health spent in excess of $1 million on an advertising campaign designed to convince people that the development of social relationships could enhance their physical and mental health and increase their life spans.

Our need for *control* involves the ability to establish and maintain satisfactory levels of control and power in our relationships with people. To varying degrees, we need to feel that we can take charge of a situation, whereas at other times we need to feel comfortable assuming a more submissive role. When our control need goes unmet, we may conclude that others do not respect or value our abilities and that we are viewed as incapable of making a sound decision or of directing others' or our own future.

Finally, our need for *affection* involves both giving and receiving love and/or experiencing an emotionally close relationship. If the need for affection goes unfulfilled, we are apt to conclude that we are unlovable and that therefore people remain emotionally detached from us (that is, they try to avoid establishing close ties with us). In contrast, if our experiences with affection have been more pleasant, we probably are comfortable handling both close and distant relationships, and most likely we recognize that everyone we come into contact with will not necessarily care for us in the same way.

These three basic needs differ from each other in another significant way: Inclusion comes first; that is, it is our need for inclusion that impels us to establish a relationship in the first place. By comparison, our needs for control and affection are met via our already established relationships. Thus, as psychologist William Schutz notes, "Generally speaking, inclusion is concerned with the problem of *in* or *out*, control is concerned with *top* or *bottom*, and affection with *close* or *far*."[5]

The extent to which the preceding needs are felt and/or met differs from person to person. However, we can categorize people according to need levels. For example, if people do not attempt to satisfy a need, we say that their need level is deficient. In contrast, if people constantly try to satisfy a need, we say that their need level is excessive. Consequently, a person who has a deficient need for inclusion, control, or affection might be described as, respectively, "undersocial," "an abdicrat," or "underpersonal," and a person whose needs were excessive in these areas could be

Do you think males and females differ in their needs for inclusion, control, and affection? Do they differ in the way they express their needs? Why or why not?

The need for warm, personal relationships begins early in life. Such relationships add to both physical and mental well-being. (Erika Stone/Photo Researchers)

labeled as, respectively, "oversocial," "an autocrat," or "overpersonal." Whereas undersocial people tend to avoid interacting with others, insisting instead that they value privacy, oversocial individuals seek to be with people constantly. The fears experienced by each type are similar, however: Both fear being ignored and/or being left out, but the overt behaviors they display to compensate for their fears are different. Similarly, the so-called abdicrat regularly assumes a submissive or subordinate role, whereas autocrats feel that they must dominate at all times. Again, however, both types fear being viewed as incapable or irresponsible; they just compensate in different ways. In like fashion, the underpersonal individual attempts to keep all relationships superficial, but the overpersonal individual always tries to become extremely close to others. Again, both are motivated by the same strong need for affection, and both fear rejection; they just express their needs via opposite behavior. We are not suggesting that people who are satisfied with their relationships are an anomaly; a large number of us have what we might consider to be ideal relationships that satisfy our needs. We are "social" (comfortable with people or alone),

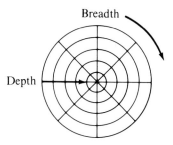

FIGURE 7-1
Breadth and Depth in
Relationships

"democratic" (content to give or take orders depending on the situation),
and "personal" (able to share close or distant relationships). As we try to
understand our own interpersonal needs, as we try to make sense out of
our relationships, we should remember these need classifications and how
we express them through our behavior.

RELATIONSHIP DIMENSIONS

Every relationship we share, whether it involves a friend, a family member,
or a business associate, can be described in terms of two concepts: *breadth*
(how many topics you discuss with the other) and *depth* (how central the
topics you discuss are to your self-concept and how much you reveal about
topics). According to social psychologists Irwin Altman and Dalmas Taylor,
Figure 7-1 shows the two dimensions that characterize our relationships.[6]
Central to their theory of "social penetration" is the idea that relationships
begin with relatively narrow breadth (few topics are spoken about) and
shallow depth (the inner circles are not penetrated) and progress over time
in intensity and intimacy as both breadth and depth increase. Thus our
relationships may develop incrementally as we move from discussing few
to many topics, from superficial discussions (the periphery of the circle) to
intensely personal ones (the center of the circle). Figure 7-2 is an exercise
using these concepts.

The breadth of topics we discuss may be high for casual as well as for
intimate relationships, but the depth of penetration usually increases as
the relationship becomes more intimate. Consequently, a highly intimate

FIGURE 7-2
Use arrows with the
segmented concentric
circles to illustrate
how a casual
relationship you
share with someone
contrasts with one of
your more intimate
relationships.

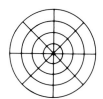

relationship between two people will probably have both high breadth and high depth as they extend the range of topics they discuss and reveal more about how they feel about these topics to each other.

The social penetration model is useful for a number of reasons. First, it can help us visualize the nature of the relationships we share by revealing the range of topics we communicate about and the extent to which we reveal ourselves through our discussions. Second, the model can help explain why certain relationships may seem stronger than others. For example, is there one person to whom you reveal more to than anyone else about a particular topic? Is there someone with whom you would not even consider discussing a particular topic? Do you reveal more of yourself to some people at work than to others? Is the same true for members of your family? What about your friends? Although we may behave in ways that limit some people's access to certain portions of our relationship circle, others may have access to its entire scope; although we may keep some from straying too far from our circle's periphery, we may let others venture close to its core. When your communication with another lacks breadth and/or depth, it should not surprise you that you feel little if any bond to each other; to enhance the strength of your relationship, you would have to alter the nature and extent of your interactions.

How do you feel when someone reveals more to you than you are ready for? Have you ever made anyone feel uncomfortable by revealing too much too quickly? What prompted you to do it? How did that person react?

Sometimes, in an effort to get to know another person quickly, we may discuss topics at a depth that would normally be reserved for those with whom we are more intimate. When such disclosures occur too rapidly or prematurely in a relationship's development, they may create a feeling that "something is wrong" with the disclosing party, signaling that the other party was not ready for the relationship to progress that quickly or to be that intense. For example, employees in one company complained when a supervisor discussed personal aspects of his relationship with his wife with them during the business day. Noting that hearing intimate disclosures made them feel uncomfortable, they requested that he limit the depth and scope of his communications with them.

When interactants are ready to deepen a relationship, they see breadth and depth increases as natural and comfortable developments.

RELATIONSHIP STAGES: FROM BEGINNING TO ENDING TO BEGINNING . . .

All relationships we share are complex (each of us is a unique bundle of experiences, thoughts, fears, and needs) and ever-changing (as we change, our relationships change—they grow stronger or weaker over time). They pass through a number of stages as they strengthen or dissolve.[7]

Stage 1—Initiating. This stage involves the things that happen when we first make contact with each other. At this time, we look for signals that either impel us to initiate a conversation or tell us that we have nothing to gain by interacting. If we decide to make contact, we search for an appropriate conversation opener, for example, "Nice to meet you" or "What's happening?"

What happens when we can't find an appropriate opener? The following passage from *Conversationally Speaking* by Alan Garner describes one such possibility:

> I decided to marry her. Courtship would be a mere formality. But what to say to begin the courtship? "Would you like some of my gum?" sounded too low-class. "Hello," was too trite a greeting for my future bride. "I love you! I am hot with passion!" was too forward. "I want to make you the mother of my children," seemed a bit premature.
>
> Nothing. That's right, I said nothing. And after a while, the bus reached her stop, she got off, and I never saw her again.
>
> End of story.

Stage 2—Experimenting. Once we have initiated contact, we try to find out more about the other person; we begin to probe the unknown. Often we exchange small talk—for example, we tell the other where we're from and who we know in an effort to get acquainted. Although many of us may hate small talk or "cocktail party chatter," according to Mark Knapp it serves several useful functions.

1. It provides a process for uncovering integrating topics and openings for more penetrating conversations.
2. It can serve as an audition for a future friendship or a way to increase the scope of a current friendship.
3. It provides a safe procedure for indicating who we are and how another can come to know us better (reduction of uncertainty).
4. It allows us to maintain a sense of community with our fellow human beings.

In an article on small talk, Michael Korda notes, "The aim of small talk is to make people comfortable—to put them at their ease—not to teach, preach, or impress. It's a game, like tennis, in which the object is to keep the ball in the air for as long as possible."[8]

At this stage our relationships lack the depth we spoke of earlier; they are quite casual and superficial. The vast majority of them never progress beyond this point.

Stage 3—Intensifying. When a relationship does progress beyond experimenting, it enters the intensifying stage. During this stage people become "good friends"—they begin to share things in common, disclose more, become better at predicting the other's behavior, and may even develop

Have you shared some relationships that failed to pass beyond the experimentation phase and that you now wish had done so? What kept them from intensifying?

nicknames for each other or display similar postural and/or clothing cues. In a sense, they are beginning to be transformed from an "I" and an "I" into a "we."

Stage 4—Integrating. The fusion of "I" and "I" really appears to coalesce in stage 4. The two individuals are identified as a pair, a couple, or "a package." Interpersonal synchrony is heightened; those involved may dress, act, and speak more alike or share a song ("our song"), a bankbook, or a project.

Stage 5—Bonding. In this stage interactants announce that their commitment to each other has been formally contracted. Their relationship is now institutionalized, formally recognized. This recognition can be a wedding license or a business contract, for example. The relationship takes on a new character: It is no longer informal. It is now guided by specified rules and regulations. Sometimes this alteration causes initial discomfort or rebellion as the parties attempt to adjust to the change.

Stage 6—Differentiating. Instead of continuing to emphasize "we," in this stage the parties to the relationship attempt to reestablish an "I" orientation in an effort to regain a unique identity. They ask, "How are we different?" "How can I distinguish me from you?" During this phase previously designated joint possessions take on a more individualized character; "our friends" become "my friends," "our bedroom" becomes "my bedroom," "our child" becomes "your son" (expecially when he misbehaves). Although an urge to differentiate the self from the other is not uncommon (we need to be individuals as well as members of a relationship), if it persists it can signal that the relationship is in for trouble or that the process of uncoupling has begun.

Stage 7—Circumscribing. In this stage, both the quality and the quantity of communication between the parties to the relationship decrease. Sometimes an effort is made to carefully limit areas open for discussion to those considered "safe." Other times there is no actual decrease in topic breadth, but subjects are no longer discussed with any real depth. In other words, fewer and less intimate disclosures are made, signaling that withdrawal (mental and/or physical) from the relationship is desired.[9] Dynamic communication between the parties has all but ceased; the relationship is characterized by a lack of energy, a shrinking of interest, and a general feeling of exhaustion.

Stage 8—Stagnating. When circumscribing continues, the relationship stagnates. In stage 8, participants feel that they no longer need to relate to each other because they know how the interaction will proceed; thus,

Relationships go through many stages. As a relationship becomes more personal, more intimate, people share more, disclose more about themselves, and even develop similar patterns of dress, posture, and speech. (Rae Russel)

they conclude that "it is better to say nothing." Communication is at a standstill. Only the shadow of a relationship remains as the participants mark time by going through the motions while feeling nothing. In reality, they are like strangers inhabiting the hollow shell of what once was a thriving relationship. While they still live in the same environment, they share little else.

Stage 9—Avoiding. During this phase, participants actually go out of their way to be apart; they avoid contact with each other. Relating face to face or voice to voice has simply become too unpleasant for one or both to continue "the act." Although sometimes communicated more directly "than others" (sometimes the "symptom" is used as a form of communication; other times an effort is made to disconfirm the other person), the dominant message is "I don't want to see you anymore; I don't wish to continue this relationship." At this point, the end of the relationship is in sight.

Stage 10—Termination. At this point, the bonds that used to hold the relationship together are severed; the relationship ends. Depending on how the parties feel (whether they agree on termination), this stage can be short or drawn out over time, can end cordially (in person, over the telephone, via a letter or legal document) or bitterly. All relationships eventually terminate (the death of a partner is inevitable), but that doesn't mean that "saying good-bye" is easy or pleasant.

What is noteworthy about these stages is that relationships may stabilize at any one of them. For example, as we noted, many relationships never proceed beyond the experimenting stage; others, however, stabilize at the intensifying stage, the bonding stage, etc. When participants disagree about the point of stabilization, additional difficulties can arise. We should also recognize that movement through the preceding 10 stages may be forward or backward. For instance, we may advance and then retreat, deciding that a more superficial relationship is what we really desire. Additionally, we proceed through the stages of a relationship at our own pace. Some relationships, especially those in which time is perceived to be limited, develop more quickly than others; the rate at which the parties to a relationship grow together or apart, however, usually depends on their individual needs.

Although the stages described above may serve as a guide, relationships are not always predictable. No relationship we share is foreordained in heaven or hell for success or failure. Rather, our relationships develop as a consequence of the energy we are willing to commit to them and as a result of what we are willing to do with and for one another.

Unless the individuals who share a relationship are able to continue to grow together and adapt to their continually changing environment, the relationship may begin to deteriorate at any point. For example, according to *cost-benefit theory*, we will work to maintain a relationship only as long as the benefits we perceive for ourselves outweigh the costs.[10] Some of these benefits include a better feeling about the self, personal growth, a greater sense of security, additional resources to accomplish tasks, and an increased ability to cope with problems. In comparison, relationship costs include the time spent trying to make the relationship work, psychological and/or physical stress, and a damaged self-image.

Based on your experiences, identify relationships that have stabilized at one or more of Knapp's "coming together" stages: initiating, experimenting, intensifying, integrating, bonding.

SKILL BUILDER

Relationship Costs and Benefits

Conduct a cost-benefit analysis of a relationship you are now experiencing by identifying both the benefits you receive and the costs you expend as a result of the relationship. Based on your analysis, what is your prognosis for the relationship's future?

The greater our rewards and the lower our costs, the more satisfying the relationship. When costs begin to outweigh benefits, we are more and more likely to decide to terminate the relationship. In contrast, when benefits outweigh costs, relationship development probably will continue.

DECEPTION AND RELATIONSHIP DEVELOPMENT

How do you define the word *lie*? To whom would you lie? What kinds of situations call for a lie? How many times in the past month have you lied to someone with whom you share a relationship? How many times were you caught? What happened as a result?

Why are you lying to me who are my friend?

Moroccan proverb

When we lie to someone, we do not merely deliver wrong information to that person; rather, we intentionally seek to deceive him or her. As described by Sissela Bok, author of *Lying*, when we lie, it is both our hope and our expectation that we will succeed in having the target of our efforts believe something that we do not believe.

It is rare to tell someone only one lie. To sustain our original lie, we usually need to tell more lies. As Bok writes, "The liar always has more mending to do." And the liar has to expend a great deal of energy remembering who he or she told what and why.

Why do people lie? Of course, the reasons are as numerous as the situations that precipitate the felt need to lie in the first place. However, two main reasons appear to dominate: Most people lie to gain a reward or to avoid punishment. What kinds of rewards are we after in our relationships, and what kinds of punishments are we avoiding?

According to researchers Carl Camden, Michael Motley, and Ann Wilson, we lie to continue to satisfy the basic needs fulfilled by our relationships, to increase or decrease desired and undesired affiliations, to protect our self-esteem, and to achieve personal satisfaction.[11] Most often when we lie we benefit ourselves, though a percentage of our lies are designed to protect the person(s) we are lying to and an even smaller percentage benefit a third party (see Table 7-1).

"I don't tell the truth. I tell what ought to be truth."

Blanche DuBois in Tennessee Williams's Streetcar Named Desire

Does this practice help or hinder relationship development? Why?

Why is lying a tactic we use? We may use lying as a tool because lies help us manage what we perceive to be difficult situations, situations that make us more vulnerable than we would like to be.

How do lies affect our relationships once a lie is uncovered? Imagine sharing a relationship, no matter how ideal in other aspects, in which you could never rely on the words or gestures of the other person. Information exchanged in that relationship would be virtually worthless, and the feelings expressed would be practically meaningless. No one likes to be duped. No one likes to appear gullible. No one likes to play the fool. When someone does deceive us, we become suspicious and resentful of that person; we are

TABLE 7-1 TYPES OF WHITE LIES AND THEIR FREQUENCY

	Benefit Self	Benefit Other	Benefit Third Party
Basic Needs	68	1	1
A. Acquire resources	29	0	0
B. Protect resources	39	1	1
Affiliation	128	1	6
A. Positive	65	0	0
1. Initiate interaction	8	0	0
2. Continue interaction	6	0	0
3. Avoid conflict	48	0	0
4. Obligatory acceptance	3	0	0
B. Negative	43	1	3
1. Avoid interaction	34	1	3
2. Leave-taking	9	0	0
C. Conversational control	20	0	3
1. Redirect conversation	3	0	0
2. Avoid self-disclosure	17	0	3
Self-Esteem	35	63	1
A. Competence	8	26	0
B. Taste	0	18	1
C. Social desirability	27	19	0
Other	13	5	0
A. Dissonance reduction	3	5	0
B. Practical joke	2	0	0
C. Exaggeration	8	0	0

From C. Camden, M. T. Motley, and A. Wilson, "White Lies in Interpersonal Communication: A Taxonomy and Preliminary Investigation of Social Motivations," *Western Journal of Speech Communication*, Vol. 48 (1984), p. 315.

disappointed both in the other individual and in ourselves. While molding the truth to sustain relationships may be a common practice, unless trust and truthfulness are present, it is only a matter of time before the relationship dies. Few factors have greater influence on a relationship than does trust.

PERCEPTION OF VULNERABILITY AND RELATIONSHIP DEVELOPMENT

Of course, there is a potential for trouble in any relationship. While one cause of relationship difficulty is lying, another equally important cause is

Lies, Lies, Lies

Report on an experience of being lied to. Indicate who lied to you, the nature of the lie, and your reactions when you found out you had been lied to. How did the lie affect your relationship with the liar?

Report on an experience when you lied to someone else. Indicate who you lied to, the nature of the lie, your reason for lying, and the other person's reaction when she or he found out about being lied to by you. How did your lie affect the relationship you shared?

How is a liar like a counterfeiter?

misreading how deep the other person wants the relationship to go—that is, how much he or she trusts you at a particular point in time. The amount of trust you place in another person to accept information you disclose to him or her without hurting you or the relationship is your "tolerance of vulnerability." Your tolerance of vulnerability varies from person to person, topic to topic, and situation to situation. Researcher William Rawlins designed a matrix we can use to help us analyze the amount of trust we place in different people at different times in a relationship's development.[12]

	High Need To Be Open	Low Need To Be Open
High Amount of Trust in Other's Discretion	I Very Tolerant of Vulnerability (reveal)	III Judgment Required
Low Amount of Trust in Other's Discretion	II Judgment Required	IV Intolerant of Vulnerability (conceal)

We can use this matrix to determine which of our relationships have more stability or staying power than others. A relationship in which partners have difficulty trusting one another is a relationship in trouble.

BUILDING A TRUSTING RELATIONSHIP

Trust gives us the ability to rise above our doubts.

John K. Rempel, John G. Holmes

Some of us are more trusting than others, primarily because of the way we have been treated. British psychologist John Bowlby, for instance, suggests that adult concerns about trust may be related to unresponsive parenting in infancy. Erik Erikson contends that attitudes toward trust continue to develop during early explorations of intimacy. And throughout our adult lives, important relationships can either reinforce our confidence or consolidate our fears about the risks of emotional commitment. But even if our past relationships have sown the seeds of doubt, it may be possible to find ways of building trust.

Clearly, based on past behavior, some people merit our trust and others do not. But the behavior on which we base our judgments cannot always be described in black and white. We have to interpret what the behavior means to us and our relationship. We may not be able to bring about an immediate change in a partner's behavior, but we can change how we interpret his or her actions and begin to build trust.

One thing to guard against is overinterpreting negative behavior, which is most likely to happen when we are reminded of sensitive issues from the past. In a recent study we asked couples to think about times in their relationship when they felt disappointed by their partner. This simple intrusion of negative thoughts had a profound effect on the way they interpreted a subsequent situation. In short, they saw what they expected to see. They became insensitive to their partner's present actions and relied on the past to judge the interaction.

Because our past relationships can so powerfully color our perceptions of the present, we should be especially vigilant for issues that trigger our emotional insecurities. To combat this we can focus on concrete behavior rather than jumping to harsh conclusions about our partner's motives and character. We can also become more sensitive to and appreciative of positive behavior. In essence, we allow ourselves to trust by giving our partner some credit and providing him or her with the necessary room to make mistakes.

These are risky suggestions, and they may not be appropriate for everyone. To believe in someone, especially when there is good reason for uncertainty, means leaving yourself open to hurt and disappointment. Yet the paradox remains: To be able to trust, you must be willing to take the risk of trusting. Indeed, if we try to see new evidence of caring in a partner we risk being wrong, but if we do not try we can never be right.

From "How Do I Trust Thee?" John K. Rempel and John G. Holmes, *Psychology Today*, February 1984, p. 34.

HOW TO IMPROVE YOUR RELATIONSHIP SATISFACTION QUOTIENT

Our relationships can contribute to feelings of happiness or unhappiness, elation or depression. They can enrich us and stimulate us or they can limit us and harm us. To enhance your ability to develop relationships that satisfy, follow these guidelines:

Actively Seek Information from Others and Reinforce Others for Attempting to Seek Information from You. Individuals who fail to initiate contacts and/or fail to reinforce the conversational attempts of others are less likely to build stable foundations for effective relationships. Passive, restrained communicators are simply more apt to remain chronically lonely. Although we will experience short-term loneliness from time to time, sustained chronic loneliness and social apathy feed on each other.

Know the Signs of Friendship. People who share effective friendships report that the following qualities are present: enjoyment (they enjoy each other's company most of the time), acceptance (they accept each other as they are), trust (both assume that one will act in the other's best interest), respect (they each assume the other evidences good judgment in making life choices), mutual assistance (they are willing to assist and support each other), confiding (they share experiences and feelings with each other), understanding (they have a feel for what the other thinks is important and why the other behaves as he or she does), and spontaneity (they each feel free to be themselves).[13]

Recognize That Relationships Evolve. Ours is a mobile society where each change we experience has the potential to bring us different relationships. Be prepared for relationship changes; recognize that in our lives we are apt to experience a certain amount of relationship turnover and change. As we grow and develop, so will our relationships.

Know When to Sever a Relationship. Not all relationships or connections are meant to continue. When a relationship is draining our energies and our confidence, we need to extricate ourselves from the relationship before it destroys us.

Recognize That Communication Is the Lifeblood of a Relationship. Without communication, relationships shrivel and die. Any relationship worth your time and energy depends on effective communication to sustain and nourish it. Your desire and motivation to communicate are key ingredients in relationship establishment and growth.

SUMMARY

Communication is the one variable common to all relationships. As a result of communication, we establish and nurture or withdraw from and end our relationships.

Relationships play many roles in our lives. They fulfill our needs for inclusion, control, and affection. We each need to feel that others take an interest in us, that they view us as capable of exerting control over our lives, and that we are lovable.

Every relationship we share is unique and varies in breadth (how many topics we discuss with the other) and depth (how much we are willing to reveal to the other about our feelings on a topic). Most relationships develop according to a social penetration model, beginning with narrow breadth and shallow depth; over time, some relationships increase in breadth and depth, becoming more intense and/or intimate.

Researchers have identified a number of stages our relationships may pass through: initiating, experimenting, intensifying, integrating, bonding, differentiating, circumscribing, stagnating, avoiding, and terminating. Note that a relationship may stabilize at any stage. When participants disagree about the point of stabilization, relationship problems are apt to arise.

It is important that we recognize that how we communicate plays a key part in determining whether our relationships are as effective and rewarding for us as they could be. Relationships also vary according to the amount of lying or deceiving occurring, and our feelings of vulnerability.

SUGGESTIONS FOR FURTHER READING

Altman, Irwin, and D. Taylor. *Social Penetration: The Development of Interpersonal Relationships*. New York: Holt, Rinehart and Winston, 1973. An in-depth analysis of this frequently referred to theory.

Borisoff, Deborah, and Lisa Merrill. *The Power to Communicate*. Prospect Heights, Ill.: Waveland Press, 1985. Explores the impact of stereotyped gender differences on male and female development, communication, and professional contexts.

Gamble, Teri, and Michael Gamble. *Contacts: Communicating Interpersonally*. New York: Random House, 1982. An introduction to the nature of interpersonal communication and an exploration of the roles we play in developing effective relationships.

Knapp, Mark L. *Interpersonal Communication and Human Relationships*. Boston: Allyn and Bacon, 1984. An examination of how people communicate in developing and deteriorating relationships.

Laing, R. D. *Knots*. New York: Random House, 1970. Each chapter, composed of dialogue scenarios or poems, describes a different kind of relationship. A highly thought-provoking work.

Pearson, Judy Cornelia. *Gender and Communication*. Dubuque, Iowa: William C. Brown, 1985. Synthesizes available research on this topic into a single, manageable, and highly readable source.

Satir, Virginia. *Peoplemaking*. Palo Alto, Calif.: Science and Behavior Books, 1972. A clear and inclusive treatment of family communication and person-to-person interaction.

NOTES

1. Virginia Satir, *Peoplemaking* (Palo Alto, Calif.: Science and Behavior Books, 1972), p. 30.
2. John Naisbitt, *Megatrends* (New York: Warner Books, 1984), pp. 35–52.
3. William C. Schutz, *The Interpersonal Underworld* (Palo Alto, Calif.: Science and Behavior Books, 1966), pp. 18–20.
4. See Robert A. Bell, "Conversational Involvement and Loneliness," *Communication Monographs*, Vol. 52 (September 1985), pp. 218–235.
5. Schutz, p. 24.
6. I. Altman and D. A. Taylor, *Social Penetration: The Development of Interpersonal Relationships* (New York: Holt, Rinehart and Winston, 1973).
7. Mark L. Knapp, *Interpersonal Communication and Human Relationships* (Boston: Allyn and Bacon, 1984), pp. 35–44.
8. Michael Korda, "Small Talk," *Signature*, 1986, p. 78.
9. See Lawrence B. Rosenfield and Daniella Bordaray-Sciolino, "Self Disclosure as a Communication Strategy during Relationship Termination," presented at the national meeting of the Speech Communication Association, Denver, Colorado, November 1985.
10. J. W. Thibaut and H. H. Kelly, *The Social Psychology of Groups* (New York: Wiley, 1959).
11. C. Camden, M. T. Motley, and A. Wilson, "White Lies in Interpersonal Communication: A Taxonomy and Preliminary Investigation of Social Motivations," *Western Journal of Speech Communication* Vol. 48 (1984), pp. 309–325.
12. W. K. Rawlins, "Openness as Problematic in Ongoing Friendships: Two Conversational Dilemmas," *Communication Monograms*, Vol. 50 (March 1983), p. 11.
13. Keith E. Davis, "Near and Dear: Friendship and Love Compared," *Psychology Today*, February 1985, pp. 22–30.

8

Person to Person: Handling Emotions and Expressing Feelings in Relationships

There are no empty people, only people who have deadened their
feelings and feel empty.

Theodore Isaac Rubin

CHAPTER PREVIEW

After finishing this chapter, you should be able to:

Determine how well you "read" and express feelings

Define the terms *emotion state* and *emotion trait*

Identify the physical sensations and facial expressions that
accompany particular emotions

Explain how attraction, proximity, reinforcement, similarity, and
complementarity function as relationship determiners

Explain how the suppression and/or disclosure of feelings can affect the development of a relationship

Compare and contrast emotional display rules pertaining to men and women

Explain how feelings can be handled effectively during conflicts

Explain how assertiveness, nonassertiveness, and aggressiveness differ

Identify behaviors that foster and impede the development of a relationship based on assertiveness

Draw and explain a Relationship Window

Create and explain a DESC script

Explain how you can protect your emotional rights in the relationships you share

---

This chapter is about feelings—your feelings and the feelings of people with whom you share relationships. Although everyone knows feelings exist and although everyone uses terms to identify and label feelings—"anger," "sadness," "fear," or "happiness," for example—few of us really understand how we and others experience these emotions, and even fewer of us realize how these emotions affect our *intrapersonal* and *interpersonal* lives.

Let us begin to examine the communication of emotion. By exploring what feelings "feel" like, "look" like, and "sound" like and by attempting to analyze how people handle their feelings, we will increase our ability to establish and sustain meaningful relationships with others. Since feelings can either enhance or disrupt our interpersonal lives, only when we are able to respond appropriately to our own feelings and to those of others will we be able to communicate effectively.

YOU AND YOUR EMOTIONS

What is it really like to be angry? What does your body feel like when you get angry? What happens to your face? Can you identify the types of situations that make you angry? Can you recall ever enjoying being angry? Can you tell when a friend, family member, or co-worker becomes angry? How well do you read or express feelings? Consider these emotions:

Anger
Happiness
Surprise
Fear
Sadness

For each emotion, answer the following questions:

1. Identify a time when you felt this emotion.
2. On a scale from 1 (mild) to 5 (intense), indicate the feeling's relative strength.
3. Describe what you felt like and what you imagine you looked like when you experienced the feeling.
4. Describe how you attempted to handle the emotion.
5. Describe how others around you reacted to you.
6. Identify a time when you perceived someone you were with to feel this emotion.
7. Describe your perceptions of how the person felt and looked.
8. Describe how he or she attempted to handle the emotion.
9. Describe your reactions to her or his behavior.

Which of the preceding feelings do you experience most frequently? Least frequently? Which of these feelings do you least enjoy expressing? Which do you least enjoy observing in others?

You can use the information you have just gathered in at least three ways: (1) to help you clarify how you feel about emotions, (2) to help you understand other people's emotions, and (3) to help other people understand your emotions.

Whether you realize it or not, you are experiencing some emotion to some degree at all times. In any particular context with any particular people, you almost certainly will have certain thoughts or attitudes about the situation. These thoughts or attitudes will give rise to a particular emotion state. According to theorist Carroll E. Izard, an *emotion state* refers to a particular emotion process of limited duration, lasting from seconds to hours and varying from mild to intense. However, Izard also notes that "chronically intense emotions, or frequent episodes of intense emotion may indicate psychopathology."[1] Thus it is the unusual person who *always* feels an emotion intensely—who is always in an extreme state of joy, depression, or anger. In addition to emotion states (for example, the sadness state) individuals may also exhibit *emotion traits*. For instance, if you were described as exhibiting a sadness trait, this would indicate that you had a tendency to experience this particular emotion frequently in your daily interactions.[2] What emotion traits have you experienced or observed in others in the past 24 hours? Does any particular emotion trait punctuate either your interpersonal behavior or the behavior of those with whom you habitually relate? Every emotion you experience is accompanied by physiological changes in your body and physical changes in your appearance. Are you "fine-tuned" to the physiological and visual signals the body and face send as a person experiences an emotion?

What Do Feelings Feel Like?

Feelings can be accompanied by a wide range of physical sensations and changes. Sometimes, as with anger, blood rushes to your face and your face reddens, your heartbeat and pulse quicken, and you may experience a desire to wave your arms and legs, raise your voice, and use strong words to express to others what you are feeling. Likewise, when you are exposed to a threat or become anxious or frightened, your body will respond by releasing certain hormones into your bloodstream. According to Dr. David Viscott, in times of stress the blood supply to muscles is increased while the supply to the abdomen and skin is decreased.[3] Thus, cold feet and skin pallor are two physical symptoms of the feeling of anxiety. In these and similar ways, your feelings let you know how people, ideas, and the environment affect you. In other words, they reveal to you what is important to you.

Becoming aware of our feelings can help us understand our reactions to ourselves and to those with whom we interact. Understanding bodily reactions to emotion can help us understand how we try to cope with emotion. Not everyone experiences feelings in the same way. Your ability to accept the reactions of other people indicates that you realize that they can experience unique physical sensations—responses quite separate and distinct from your own. Emotions affect us in many different ways. As we have seen, they may cause changes to occur in the circulatory or respiratory system. Increases or decreases in blood pressure and breathing rate can in turn affect the perceptions, outlook, and actions of the person experiencing the feeling. As Carroll E. Izard observes, "The joyful person is more apt to see the world through 'rose colored glasses,' the distressed or sad individual is more apt to construe the remarks of others as critical, and the fearful person is inclined only to see the frightening object (tunnel vision)."[4] Feelings are our reaction to what we perceive; they function to define and color our image of the world.

What Do Feelings Look Like?

Your face is the prime revealer of your emotions. In fact, although the rules for displaying emotions vary from culture to culture, the facial

All these faces vividly express the emotions of loss and sadness. Emotion is often revealed in facial expression—our faces are usually accurate reflections of our inner state at any given moment. (Topham/The Image Works)

expressions of certain emotions (specifically fear, happiness, surprise, anger, and sadness) appear to be universal to at least some degree. As early as 1872 Charles Darwin, in *The Expression of the Emotions in Man and Animals*, observed that people the world over express basic feelings in similar ways. Thus, without understanding a person's language, you can frequently determine whether he or she is angry, frightened, or amused. It appears that certain basic facial expressions are innate. Paul Ekman, a prominent researcher in the area of nonverbal emotion, has gone so far as to assert that the face will eventually become the most important source of information on human emotion. Ekman states: "[The face is] the one social fact that accurately reflects our subjective experience. It's the only reflection of man's inner emotional life that is visible to the world."

Both Ekman and Izard have identified the facial patterns (facial muscle changes) that are specific to basic emotions. According to these researchers, *surprise* is a transient state and the briefest of all emotions, moving on and off the face quickly. Surprise is typically expressed by lifted eyebrows that create horizontal wrinkles across the forehead, slightly raised upper eyelids, and usually an open, oval-shaped mouth. Surprise can turn to happiness if the sudden or unexpected event that precipitated it promises something favorable, but it can turn to fear or anger if the event poses a threat or foretells aggression.

Describe some of the ways in which face reading might affect work atmosphere and worker productivity.

In contrast to surprise, *anger* results most typically from interference with the pursuit of our goals. Being either physically or psychologically restrained from doing what you would like to do can produce anger. So can being personally insulted or rejected. Thus an action that shows someone's disregard for our feelings and needs may anger us. When angry, a person's eyebrows are usually lowered and drawn together, creating a frown. The eye appears to stare at the object of anger, and the lips are tightly compressed or are drawn back in a squarish shape, revealing clenched teeth. Often the face reddens, and veins on the neck and head become more clearly visible.

The appearance of *happiness* differs from the two preceding emotions in a number of ways. It is the easiest emotion for observers to recognize when expressed on the face. Happiness is the feeling that pulls the lips back and curves them gently upward. The raised cheek and lip corners create wrinkles, or dimples, that run down from the nose outward beyond the lips and from the eyes outward around the cheeks. *Sadness*, the opposite of happiness, often brings about a loss of facial muscle tone. Typically, the inner corners of the eyebrows are arched upward and may be drawn together. The lower eyelid may appear to be raised, the corners of the mouth are drawn down, and the lips may begin to tremble.

The last emotion whose appearance we will consider here is *fear*. During fear the eyebrows appear to be slightly raised and drawn together. The eyes are opened more widely than usual, and the lower eyelid is tensed. The lips may be stretched tightly back, and wrinkles appear in the center of, rather than across, the entire forehead.

Think of an instance when you read and responded to the feelings of another. Think of an instance when you failed to do so. How was the relationship you shared affected?

When these feelings reveal themselves on your face, do other people observe, listen to, and react to them? When they reveal themselves on the faces of persons with whom you interact, do you observe, listen, and react to them? We cannot communicate effectively if we fail to respond to the feelings of others or if others fail to respond to our feelings. This is why it is important to be highly attuned to facial expressions. We cannot afford to let emotions pass by unattended or unnoticed.

RELATIONSHIP DETERMINERS

It is our feelings that make us human. It is our feelings that color our relationships, adding warmth, vitality, and spirit to them. It is feelings that cause us to be moved or to move. In fact, feelings are at the heart of each of our established interpersonal relationships. In order to create liking, build trust, engage in self-disclosure, resolve conflicts, and influence others, it is necessary to communicate feelings. The first step in the study of how feelings affect our relationships is to recognize what causes us to seek out the company of some people and not others.

Attraction

What is *interpersonal attraction*? Why are we attracted to one person and not another? Why do we develop a positive attitude toward one individual and a negative attitude toward another?

A number of researchers have identified the major variables that influence how attracted people feel toward one another. Attractiveness, proximity, similarity, reinforcement, and complementarity are consistently named as attraction determiners.[5] In fact, the first kind of information we process when we interact with someone is that person's *outward attractiveness.* For the most part, we tend to like physically attractive people more than physically unattractive ones, and we tend to like people who exhibit pleasant personalities more than those who exhibit unpleasant personalities. Of course, judgments of what is physically attractive and what constitutes a pleasant personality are subjective. However, whatever we perceive as pleasing functions as an important element in creating and sustaining interpersonal attraction.

A second factor influencing attraction is *proximity.* If we were to survey the people with whom we enjoy interacting, we would find that for the most part they are people with whom we work or who live close to us. Apparently the physical nearness of persons affects the amount of attraction we feel for them. Living physically close to or working near another person gives us ample opportunity to interact, talk, or share in similar activities and thus form attachments. For these reasons, research tells us that the closer two individuals of the opposite sex are situated geographically, the more likely it is that they will be attracted to each other and marry. In all fairness, however, we should examine the opposite side of the proximity coin. According to Ellen Berscheid and Elaine Walster, authors of *Interpersonal Attraction*, the closer people are located, the more likely it is that they can also come to dislike each other. Berscheid and Walster note, "While propinquity may be a necessary condition for attraction, it probably is also a necessary condition for hatred." What do you think?

Reinforcement is the third factor that finds its way into practically all

MISS PEACH by Mell Lazarus. Courtesy of Mell Lazarus and Field Newspaper Syndicate.

Explore the relationship you have shared with a person who was critical of you, one who praised you, one who cooperated with you, and one who competed with you. Which relationship caused the most problems? Which was the most satisfying? The most productive?

theories of interpersonal attraction. Simply put, the reinforcement principle tells us that we will feel positive about those individuals who reward us or are associated with our experiences of reward, whereas we will feel animosity or dislike for those individuals who punish us or are associated with our experiences of punishment. Thus, for the most part, we like people who praise us more than people who criticize us, we like people who like us more than those who dislike us, and we like people who cooperate with us more than those who oppose us or compete with us. Of course, reinforcement can backfire if reinforcers become overzealous in their praise of us and fawn over us too much, thereby causing us to question their sincerity and motivation. As the social psychologist Eliot Aronson affirms, "We like people whose behavior provides us with a maximum reward at minimum cost."[6]

Similarity also affects our attachments to others. We are attracted to persons whose attitudes and interests are similar to our own and who like and dislike the things we like and dislike. Thus, we usually like people who agree with us more than we do those who disagree with us, especially when we are discussing issues we perceive to be salient or significant. In effect, similarity helps provide us with social validation by giving us the evidence we need to evaluate the "correctness" of our opinions or beliefs. We also expect people who hold attitudes similar to our own to like us more than people who hold attitudes that are dissimilar to ours. Perhaps if we believed that everyone we met could not help but like us, we would more readily associate with unfamiliar persons who held attitudes different from our own. By seeking the company of "similars," we play it safe.

Not all the evidence suggests that we seek to relate only to "carbon copies" of ourselves, however. In fact, *complementarity*, the last factor influencing interpersonal attraction, suggests just the opposite. Instead of being attracted to people who are similar to us, we frequently find ourselves attracted to people who are dissimilar in several ways. Both the psychologist Theodore Reik and the sociologist Robert Winch note that persons often tend to fall in love with people who possess characteristics that they admire but do not themselves possess. Thus, a dominant woman might seek the company of a submissive man, and a socially awkward female might seek the companionship of a socially poised male.

The Role of Feelings in Relationships

In *Interpersonal Attraction* Berscheid and Walster noted that in our lifetime we will come into contact with only a few of the billions of people who inhabit the earth. Our relationships with most of the persons we contact will be transitory and will not amount to much. At times, however, and for one reason or another, we find that our interchanges continue, and then it becomes quite important to be able to determine what the person with

Likes and Dislikes

1. Identify five people to whom you are very attracted. How might each of the preceding factors help to explain the attraction?
2. Identify five people to whom you are not attracted. Again, using the factors provided, attempt to explain why you do not find each person attractive.

whom we are communicating is feeling. At that point, it is just as necessary for us to understand the world of the other person as it is for us to understand ourselves. We need to realize that other people are as easily able to experience happiness, sadness, anger, fear, or surprise as we are, and indeed, the feelings we express toward another are apt to be reciprocated by that individual.

Feelings by themselves are inherently neither good nor bad. Feelings do not disrupt relationships, "build walls," or add problems to your life. Rather, it is what you think and how you act *when experiencing a particular feeling* that can affect a relationship for better or worse. For example, emotions such as anger or fear are not necessarily harmful. As Izard notes, "Anger is sometimes positively correlated with survival, and more often with the defense and maintenance of personal integrity and the correction of social injustice." Fear, likewise, may also be associated with survival and at times even serves to help us regulate destructive aggressive urges. Thus, it is not the emotion itself that is an issue but how you deal with the emotion and the effect that it has on you and on those who are important to you.

According to John Powell, author of *Why Am I Afraid to Tell You Who I Am?* our feelings tell us about our needs and the state of our relationships.[7] Individuals who share healthy relationships are able to pay direct attention to the emotional reactions that occur during their interactions with others. They take time to become aware of these emotions by periodically asking, "What am I feeling?" Once the feeling has been identified, the next step is to estimate its strength: "How strong is this feeling?" Next, the following queries are investigated: "How did I get to feel this way?" "Where did the feeling come from?" "How did I contribute?" In healthy relationships, the emotion would be reported as experienced; for instance, "I'm getting angry, and I'm beginning to say things I really don't mean."

Everything that we have just said notwithstanding, it must be understood that healthy relationships are not composed totally of positive feelings. Other feelings are important to relationships, too. Unfortunately, however, too many of us lack the commitment, courage, and skill needed to express our feelings to others and to have others express theirs to us. People are reluctant to work feelings through, choosing to ignore or deny them until they become unmanageable. Thus, we often keep our feelings in check too much, or when we do express them, we express them ineptly and incompletely. Did you realize that the majority of people fired from jobs are asked to leave not because of incompetence but because of "personality conflicts"? It may well be that many of the problems we have with friends, parents, or employers are due to a mutual inability to express or accept feeling-related messages. Efforts to sacrifice or disregard feelings inevitably lead to relationship problems or failures. In the next section, we will examine how this happens.

THE SUPPRESSION AND DISCLOSURE OF FEELINGS

Sometimes the way we handle feelings impedes the improvement of relationships with others instead of helping those relationships. For example, we may bury our real feelings, hesitate to express them, or unleash them uncontrollably.

Censoring Your Feelings

Feelings are not the enemies of healthy human relationships. However, for some reason we are taught to act as if this were so, and as a result many of us grow up afraid of feelings.

Have the important people in your life ever expressed sentiments similar to the following to you?

"You shouldn't feel depressed about what happened."
"Don't ever let me hear you say you hate your boss."
"If you can't tell me you're pleased with the way it looks, then don't say anything."
"Don't you scream at me! You have no right to get angry with me!"
"If you were strong, you would turn the other cheek and smile."
"There's nothing to be afraid of! Why are you such a baby?"

Compile a list of feelings you try, or have tried, to avoid exhibiting. Explain why you feel it necessary to conceal them.

As these examples clearly imply, feelings and emotions are frequently perceived as dangerous, harmful, and something to be ashamed of. When this is the case, we in effect censor our feelings and become overly hesitant to express our feelings to others or to have others express theirs to us. We allow ourselves to exhibit only socially approved feelings for fear of being judged to be irrational or emotionally volatile. This leads to communications with others that are shallow, contrived, and frequently inappropriate. Often, in a desire not to "make waves," both males and females act the part of "nice guy" to avoid alienating others. At times people desperately want others to like them and so are willing to go along with pretending to feel, or pretending not to feel, a particular emotion. At other times, people may become what Theodore Isaac Rubin calls "emotional isolationists." That is, they may try to protect themselves from the exchange of feelings by minding their own business and thereby avoiding relationship entanglements or involvements. Or they may overintellectualize every experience in an attempt to render their emotions impotent. Each of these techniques is counterproductive and can ultimately cause relationship problems.

Display Rules

Various types of unwritten laws guide us in deciding when or when not to show emotions. For instance, when we were younger we may have been told not to cry at school, not to yell in front of strangers, or not to kiss in public. Today we may be advised not to flirt at office parties, not to display anger when disciplined, or not to be too outspoken during a meeting. Although feelings do not discriminate between the sexes, and although members of both sexes obviously are equally capable of emotions of all kinds, our society for some reason deems it appropriate for men and women to behave differently from one another emotionally. For example, among the confused ideas Theodore Isaac Rubin, author of *The Angry Book*, has heard expressed with regard to the feeling of anger are the following:

Big anger displays are not feminine.

Big anger displays are only feminine and are not masculine.

Gentlemen simply don't show anger.

Ladies must not get angry at gentlemen.

Gentlemen must not get angry at ladies.

Very loud anger displays are evidence of homosexuality.

Despite the fact that, as Rubin observes, "members of both sexes get equally angry" and "are equally expressive," different rules and taboos regarding the expression of anger and other emotions have been internalized by males and females. According to Sidney Jourard, males in our society are compelled to play a dangerous role—they are taught not to disclose. Because of this, Jourard believes, their tension accumulates and they die an early death. Marc Feigen-Fasteau, author of *The Male Machine*, echoes this. He puts it this way with regard to the emotional restraints placed on males: "If others know how you really feel, you can be hurt, and that in itself is incompatible with manhood." Do you agree with this statement? Why?

"Do you know how masculine it is to risk crying?"

Drawing by Koren; © 1981 The New Yorker Magazine, Inc.

In our society, men are generally viewed as more rational, objective, and independent than women. Women, in contrast, are perceived to be more dependent, subjective, and emotional than men. Women are also supposed to do more disclosing than men. When asked, people indicate that the traits the male exhibits are more desirable than those of the female. Kay Deaux notes in *The Behavior of Women and Men* that this is not to suggest that the supposedly female characteristics are seen as all bad:

> There is a cluster of positively valued traits that people see as more typical of women than men; these traits generally reflect warmth and expressiveness. Women are described as tactful, gentle, aware of the feelings of others, and able to express tender feelings easily. Men in contrast are viewed as blunt, rough, unaware of the feelings of others, and unable to express their own feelings.

Thus for the most part women are perceived as warm, while men are perceived as competent. Which do you feel is the more desirable trait?

Another important determinant of display rules for emotions is national culture. For example, in some African societies, people assume you are friendly until you prove to them you are not. When they smile, it means they like you; if they don't smile, it means they distrust or even hate you. We know that the Japanese often employ laughing and smiling to mask anger, sorrow, or disgust. And people from Mediterranean countries often intensify felt emotions such as grief, sadness, and happiness, whereas the British deintensify, or understate, these emotions.

In addition to display rules prescribed by a culture, males and females alike tend to formulate *personal* display rules. In effect, we decide for ourselves under what conditions and with whom we will freely share or inhibit our emotional expressions. You might, for instance, feel it inappropriate to show anger before a parent, but you might readily reveal it to a boyfriend, girlfriend, or spouse. You might be hesitant to express your innermost fears to a professor or employer, but you might readily disclose them to a close friend.

> To whom do you feel free to say, "I'm scared about that," or, "What you just did disappointed me," or, "I really care about you"?

Our personal display philosophy might also cause us to use a certain characteristic style of emotional expression. We might become "withholders" and try never to show how we feel, or we might become "revealers" and try to always let others know how we feel. We could, however, also become what researchers Paul Ekman and Wallace V. Friesen term an "unwitting expressor," a "blanked expressor," or a "substitute expressor." In the first case, we reveal our feelings without being aware that we have done so. (We then wonder how someone could read our emotions.) In the second case, we are certain we are communicating our feelings to others when we are not. (We are then confused or upset when people fail to "pick up on" the cues we imagine we are sending.) In the third case, we substitute the appearance of one emotion for another emotion without realizing that we have done so. (We then can't understand why people react in ways we had not expected.) Thus, personal display rules sometimes work to impede the establishment of effective interpersonal relationships.

Effects of Suppressed Feelings on Relationships

As Jerry Gillies, author of *Friendship*, writes, "You are not making contact if you are not putting out what you really are." The late interpersonal communication theorist Sydney Jourard noted that dissembling, concealing, and displaying a hesitancy to reveal feelings are "lethal" habits for males. Jourard believed that men, because they are not as apt to express their feelings as women are, encounter stresses that actually cause them to have a shorter life span than women. Now that women are assuming what were formerly traditionally male roles, will they too feel more compelled to keep their feelings to themselves? Whatever the answer, it is acknowledged that *all* individuals are likely to experience intrapersonal and interpersonal difficulties when they try to repress or disguise feelings.

According to communicologist David Johnson, many people mistakenly assume that all that is needed to ensure the development of effective interpersonal relationships is to be rational, logical, and objective. "To the contrary," writes Johnson, "a person's interpersonal effectiveness increases as all the relevant information (including feelings) becomes conscious, discussable, and controllable." Thus Johnson affirms that the suppression of feelings results in ineffective interpersonal behavior. This position is supported further by the psychologist Thomas Gordon, who notes that besides reducing your interpersonal effectiveness, continually "bottling up" your feelings can cause you to develop ulcers, headaches, heartburn, high blood pressure, a spastic colon, and various psychosomatic problems. Medical doctor David Viscott adds to this belief by stating, "When we lose touch with our feelings, we lose touch with our most human qualities. To paraphrase Descartes, 'I feel, therefore, I am.'"

How might suppressing your feelings affect your ability to perform effectively in school? On the job?

If either party in a relationship attempts to suppress his or her feelings, one or more of the following consequences may result. First, it may become increasingly difficult to solve interpersonal problems. Research reveals that in a relationship the quality of problem solving improves when individuals feel free to express both positive and negative feelings. When either of the persons is inhibited, the quality of the communication between them is diminished. Second, unresolved feelings foster a climate in which misinterpretation, distortion, and nonobjective judgments and actions can thrive. Unresolved feelings create or increase blind spots in our interpretation of people and events. Third, the repression of emotions can lead to serious relationship conflicts and blowups. Intense feelings that are not dealt with fester beneath the surface until they erupt as a result of mounting internal (self) and external (other) pressures. (Holding in such feelings can make it impossible for you to think clearly.) Fourth, maintaining an effective relationship means that the parties to it are honest with each other. To penalize or reject a person for expressing emotions honestly is to tell that person you refuse her or him the right to reveal an authentic self. You also deny yourself the ability to know the person. Finally, the continued repression of feelings can in time cause you to obliterate your capacity to feel anything.

Effects of Disclosed Feelings on Relationships

Certainly there are people to whom you may not choose to reveal your feelings, and most assuredly there are also situations in which you decide that the disclosure of your feelings would be inappropriate. However, consider this. When you do take the risk of revealing your feelings to others, your relationship stands to reap certain definite benefits.

By honestly revealing feelings, first you reduce the threat of making a similar revelation for the other person. You demonstrate that you care enough about that person to share your feelings with him or her, and thus risk taking becomes a reciprocal process. Second, you acknowledge that

SEX ROLES REIGN POWERFUL AS EVER IN THE EMOTIONS

Daniel Goleman

Despite two decades of assaults on sexual stereotypes, new research shows that when it comes to emotional life, men and women seem as bound as ever by traditional sex roles.

The differences are starkest in the suppression of feeling. Psychologists are finding that men generally are still more reticent when it comes to emotions like sympathy, sadness and distress, while women are more inhibited when it comes to anger and sexuality.

Yet studies are finding that men and women differ little, if at all, in the actual physiology of these feelings; the differences appear only when it comes to their expression.

Beyond the expression of feeling, men and women also differ in how they explain an emotional outburst—especially intense feelings like anger and sadness—and what the appropriate response might be.

And these differences seem destined to last. Recent studies show that parents still treat boys and girls differently in regard to their emotional life.

"The stereotypes of emotionality for men and women are as strong as ever, in spite of two decades of efforts to break them down," said Dr. Virginia O'Leary, a psychologist at Radcliffe College. Dr. O'Leary was one of several psychologists presenting findings on sex differences in emotions at a meeting of the American Psychological Association last week.

Some of the most compelling laboratory research shows, for instance, that when provoked, men and women had equivalent reactions in terms of heart rate and other physiological responses. But when questioned, the men usually said they were angry while the women usually said they were hurt or sad.

In a study, men and women viewed scenes of accidents and their victims. The men's faces showed no expression, while the women expressed sympathy. Physiological measures, meanwhile, showed that both men and women were equally affected by the scenes.

"Although women don't admit to feeling angry as much as do men, they may feel just as angry inside," said Leslie Brody, a psychologist at Boston University. "It's their early training that tells women not to be as open about their anger. And the same is true for men with emotions like sympathy."

Dr. Brody has reviewed much of the research on sex differences in emotion in "Gender and Personality," published by Duke University Press. In Dr. Brody's own research, men and women are presented with situations intended to elicit various emotions. In those that elicit anger—for instance, descriptions of betrayal or criticism—men simply react with anger. Women, on the other hand, were as likely to say that they would be sad, hurt or disappointed.

"Men are about four times more likely to commit acts of violence than are women, while women are about twice as likely to become depressed as men," Dr. Brody said. "When men are in conflict, they turn their anger against the other person, while women tend to turn it against themselves by taking the blame."

The inhibitions in expressing emotion seem strongest in social situations, and weakest in situations where a person is most at ease. For instance, in a study where people were asked to reveal an emotionally upsetting secret, men did so as readily as women when they could tell the secret by talking into a tape recorder or by writing in a private journal.

But in face-to-face situations, differences emerge between men and women, said James Pennebaker, a psychologist at Southern Methodist University, who did the research on confessions. "It's more threatening for men to express emotion that shows they are troubled," he said.

In the emotional politics of life, the relative ease with which men express their anger may lead to unsuspected difficulties. In a survey of women who work as secretaries, the single most disliked characteristic of male bosses was anger, Dr. O'Leary said.

Sexuality is another arena where there is a marked difference between the sexes in inhibition. One study found that as many as 42 percent of women said they were not sexually aroused, even as readings of vaginal temperature showed that they were responding physiologically. The women in the study were listening to a tape of an erotic story while the measurements were made. In the same study, not a

single man was unaware of his sexual arousal.

More recent studies have had similar findings, said Dr. Patricia Morokoff of the University of Rhode Island. Dr. Morokoff has found that, particularly among women with less sexual experience, there tended to be a disparity between physiological arousal and the arousal they reported, measured during both erotic films and sex fantasies.

"Girls are taught to restrict knowledge of their genitals and genital responses," while boys are freer to explore their genitals, Dr. Morokoff said.

"Society presents an ambivalent message to women about sex: It is desirable to be sexually responsive with one's partner, but it is not desirable to be interested in sex for gratification of one's own sexual needs," she added. "One way out of this double-bind is physiological response without awareness of arousal."

For men, the greatest suppression is for a range of emotions that, in terms of gender stereotypes, are seen as "unmanly," said Dr. O'Leary of Radcliffe.

In research with Devorah Smith, a psychologist at Boston University, Dr. O'Leary found that men and women differ in the causes they attribute for emotions like anger, fear or sadness in themselves or others.

"Men are more likely to explain a strong emotion in terms of some impersonal event, something that happened in the situation, while women are more likely to see the cause as something in a personal relationship or the person's mood," Dr. O'Leary said.

This difference between men

and women has greatest implications for arguments between the sexes, she said.

"If a couple fight, the man is likely to make an instrumental response—to look for something in the situation to change and make things better," Dr. O'Leary said. "But the woman is likely to read the argument as an index of trouble in the relationship itself, and become critical of their relationship."

The difference between the sexes in the causes they use to explain life's difficulties may be one reason women tend to be more susceptible to depression than men, said Ellen McGrath, a psychologist in New York City who addressed the psychology meeting on women and depression.

"If men fail at something, they tend to attribute it to some external cause, like the challenge being impossible, or not enough support from their boss," Dr. McGrath said. "For women, though, the tendency is to see a failure as due to something about themselves, as the result of some personal inadequacy."

The influence of sex roles on depression was reported in another study at the psychology meeting by Rosalind Cartwright, a psychologist at Rush-Presbyterian-St. Luke's Medical Center in Chicago. The research, which is continuing, involves 157 men and women who are going through separation or divorce. So far, half of the men and women in the study have become severely depressed.

While the usual sex ratio for those being treated for depression shows a rate of twice as many women as men, the Chicago study found that the rates were identical for men and women.

But when the volunteers were asked questions to assess how they conform to the traditional sex roles, the 2-to-1 ratio emerged. Among the most traditional men and women, there were twice as many depressed women as men. Among the least traditional, the ratio was reversed.

The emotional differences seem destined to remain, researchers say, since the ways parents treat boys and girls appear to be as distinctive as ever. Studies at Pennsylvania State University have shown that parents ask their 18-month-old girls how they are feeling more often than they ask boys of the same age. Mothers were also found to talk to their 2-year-old daughters about feelings more than they do to their 2-year-old sons.

The patterns of emotional inhibition among adult men and women seem in large part attributable to how parents treat their children. Parents insist more that boys control their emotions, for instance, but with girls emphasize emotional closeness, studies have found. And research shows, too, that when parents tell stories to children, they tend to use more emotional words with girls, with one exception: they refer more to anger in stories they tell to boys.

emotions are okay. You do not censor the feelings the other person experiences, nor do you select which feelings she or he may feel and which she or he may not. You express an interest in the whole person, and instead of using emotions as weapons, you evidence a willingness to use them as tools. Third, by describing feelings and by sharing "feeling reports" and perceptions with others, you become more aware of what it is *you* are actually feeling. Fourth, you give yourself the opportunity to resolve relationship difficulties or conflicts in a productive way. Finally, by revealing your feelings you can help educate others about how you wish to be treated. In contrast, by keeping quiet—by saying nothing—you encourage others to continue exhibiting behavior of which you may disapprove. Feelings, when respected, are friendly, not dangerous.

HANDLING FEELINGS DURING CONFLICTS

One of our objectives in this chapter is to investigate conflict to discern how we can learn to handle it effectively. This makes sense when you consider that you have been, and will be, faced with conflicts all your life. Consequently, observing your own conflicts and giving more thought to them can be a positive experience.

Conflict develops for a multitude of reasons and takes a variety of forms. It can arise from individuals' different needs, attitudes, or beliefs. We can say that conflict tests each relationship we share with another individual and in so doing helps measure each relationship's health or effectiveness. Handled well, conflict can help each party develop a clearer picture of the other as well as strengthen and cement a relationship. If handled poorly, conflict can create schisms, inflict psychological scars, inflame hostilities, and cause lasting resentments. Thus, conflicts have the ability to produce both highly constructive and highly destructive relational consequences.

We need to realize that every relationship worth maintaining, every relationship worth working at, is certain to experience moments of conflict. As David Johnson notes, "A conflict-free relationship is a sign that you really have no relationship at all, not that you have a good relationship."[8] Thus, to say there should be no conflict is akin to saying we should have no relationships. If a relationship is healthy, conflicts will occur regularly. If a relationship is healthy, conflicts will also be handled effectively. In the June 1976 issue of *Redbook* magazine it was noted that how people express themselves in conflict situations is frequently more important than what they disagree about. *Redbook* asked female readers how they were most likely to behave when displeased with their husbands and how their husbands were most likely to behave when displeased with them. Readers were

What conflicts have you been involved in recently—in class, at work, or at home? Why did you define the situation as a conflict?

LIFE BOAT STATION

*"Since there are no women or children on board, Mr.
Aaron here has suggested that we go in alphabetical order."*

queried as to whether they were most apt to "say nothing, brood about it, hint they were unhappy, express their feelings, or start an argument." They were also questioned regarding the ways they handled themselves when they did argue with their spouses. For instance, were they most likely to "leave the room, sulk, sit in silence, swear, shout, hit out, cry or break things"? Survey results indicated that the most happily married wives were those who responded that both they and their husbands were able to reveal when they were displeased with each other, discuss it, and try to resolve the problem in a calm and rational manner. They also noted that they rarely if ever felt compelled to resort to active aggressive fighting (swearing, shouting, hitting out, crying, or breaking things) or to passive aggressive fighting (leaving the room, sulking, or keeping silent). Thus it appears that avoiding conflicts, trying to settle them prematurely, or prohibiting the discussion of differences can lead to serious relationship problems.

At this point, reexamine your personal conflict inventory to determine your style of managing conflict. Do you or people you know use any of the ineffective or "pseudo" methods of dealing with conflicts just mentioned? Do you feel a need to deny that a conflict exists, withdraw, surrender,

The Conflict Inferno

1. Pretend you and the other members of your class are a group of people trapped by fire on the top floor of a skyscraper. An explosion could occur at any time. Only the narrowest of stairways remains to lead the group to freedom. You decide to form a line, single file, in an effort to reach the ground level. Of course, those nearest the front of the line will have the greatest chance of survival. Your task is to determine the order in which individuals will exit the burning building. You must give reasons why the person you are portraying should head the line.

2. How successful were you in handling the conflicts that arose? What communication strategies did you use? What effects did they have?

placate, or distract by introducing irrelevancies? Do you intellectualize, blame, find fault, or force another to accept your ideas by physically or emotionally overpowering that person? Why? What elements of your relationship elicit these kinds of responses instead of a rational discussion of the pros and cons of the issues in dispute?

Of the strategies available, only discussion, or "leveling," can break impasses and solve difficulties. Thus, the fate of any conflict is related to the communication strategies employed. Conflict of necessity forces individuals to select from available response patterns in order to forge an effective network of communication. An individual can choose either disruptive or constructive responses. Try using constructive strategies as you participate in the Skill Builder above.

We see that in any situation problems can develop if we fail to deal with conflict appropriately. We can see equally that there are certain definite benefits to be derived from handling conflict effectively. Alan Filley, in the book *Interpersonal Conflict Resolution*, identifies four major values arising from conflict. First, many conflict situations can function to eliminate the probability of more serious disharmony in the future. Second, conflict can increase our innovativeness by helping us acquire new ways of looking at things, new ways of thinking, and new behaviors. Third, conflict can develop our sense of cohesiveness and togetherness by increasing our closeness and trust. Fourth, it can provide us with an invaluable opportunity to measure the strength or viability of our relationships.[9] Conflict, after all, is a natural result of diversity.

My idea of an agreeable person is a person who agrees with me.

Benjamin Disraeli

Can you think of situations in your own life that illustrate the four functions of conflict discussed here?

HOW CONFLICT ARISES: THE TUG-OF-WAR

We have examined what conflict is and how we feel about it. Now let us explore how and why it arises. We can begin by saying that conflict is apt to occur wherever human differences meet. As we have seen, conflict is the clash of opposing beliefs, opinions, values, needs, assumptions, and goals. It can result from honest differences, from misunderstandings, from anger, or from expecting either too much or too little from people and/or situations. Conflicts can be handled rationally or irrationally. Also, conflict does not always require two or more to argue; we can sometimes be in conflict with ourselves. This occurs when we find ourselves having to choose between two or more mutually exclusive options—two cars, two classes, two potential spouses, two activities. The internal struggle we experience while deciding is *intrapersonal conflict*. In contrast, *interpersonal conflict* occurs when the same type of opposition process occurs between two or more individuals. Such encounters can be prompted by differences in perceptions and interests; by a scarcity of resources such as money, time, or position; or by rivalries in which we find ourselves competing with someone else. Those involved in either an intrapersonal or an interpersonal conflict usually feel "pulled" in different directions at the same time.

SKILL BUILDER

"Tied in Knots"

This exercise was suggested by an experience included in *Peoplemaking* by Virginia Satir.

1. Think of an idea, belief, value, need, or goal that has involved you in a conflict situation.
2. Identify the aspects of yourself or the other individual(s) involved in the conflict situation. Briefly summarize each position.
3. Select class members to play the part(s) of those you perceived yourself to be in conflict with.
4. Cut heavy twine or rope into 10-foot lengths, one for each player. Also cut a number of 3-foot lengths to tie around each individual's waist, including your own. Next, tie your 10-foot "lead" rope to the rope around your waist. Then, hand your rope to the person(s) with whom you perceive yourself to be in conflict, who will also hand his or her rope to you.
5. While tied to each other, begin to talk about the issue that is the cause of conflict.

Consider the Skill Builder on page 209. How did the experience feel? Of course, when engaged in conflict you do not have real ropes tugging at you, but we are certain you sometimes feel as if you did. When you are able to handle the conflict, the ropes do not get in the way. At other times, however, the conflict escalates out of your control. Before you know it, you are "tied up in knots" and unable to extricate yourself. In any case, the exercise probably demonstrated that those who see themselves in conflict with each other are interdependent and have the power to reward or punish one another. Thus whenever two or more people get together, conflicts serious enough to damage their relationship may develop.

We can categorize conflict in different ways. First, we can identify the type of *goal* or *objective* about which a conflict revolves. Goals or objectives can be nonshareable (for example, two teams cannot win the same basketball game) or they can be shareable (your team wins some games and the other team wins some). Or they can be fully claimed and possessed by each party to the conflict. You can each win everything—members of the rival Teamsters and Independent Truckers Unions both get a raise.

Second, conflicts can be categorized according to their *level of intensity*. In low-intensity conflicts, the interactants do not want to destroy each other; they devise an acceptable procedure to help control their communications and permit them to discover a solution that is beneficial to each. In medium-intensity conflicts each party feels committed to win, and winning is seen as sufficient. No one feels that the opposition must be destroyed. In high-intensity conflicts, however, one party intends to destroy or seriously hurt the other. It is in these conflicts that winning is only part of the game; to mean anything, victory must be total.

A conflict can also be classified as a *pseudoconflict*, a *content conflict*, a *value conflict*, or an *ego conflict*. Although not really a conflict, a *pseudoconflict* gives the appearance of a conflict. It occurs when a person mistakenly believes that two or more goals cannot be simultaneously achieved. Pseudoconflicts frequently revolve around false either-or judgments ("Either I win or you win") or simple misunderstandings (failing to realize that you really agree with the other person). A pseudoconflict is resolved when the parties realize that no conflict actually exists.

A *content conflict* occurs when individuals disagree over the accuracy of a fact, the implications of a fact, a definition, or the solution to a problem. If the opponents realize that facts can be verified, inferences tested, definitions checked, and solutions evaluated against criteria, they can be shown that a content conflict can be settled rationally.

In contrast to a pseudoconflict and a content conflict, a *value conflict* arises when people hold different views on some issue of a particular nature. As an example, take the welfare system in this country. A person who values individual independence and self-assertiveness will have very differ-

Describe and give examples (real or hypothetical) of low-, medium-, and high-intensity conflicts. At which "temperature" do you prefer to keep your conflict thermometer? Why?

ent opinions about public welfare than will one who believes we are ultimately responsible for the well-being of others. The realistic outcome of such an encounter would be that the parties to the conflict would disagree without becoming disagreeable—that is, they would discuss the issue and learn something from one another, even though they might continue to disagree. In effect, they would agree that it is acceptable to disagree.

In contrast to pseudoconflicts, content conflicts, and value conflicts, ego conflicts have the greatest potential to destroy a group. An *ego conflict* occurs whenever the opposing parties believe that "winning" or "losing" is a reflection of their own self-worth, prestige, or competence. When this happens, the issue itself is no longer important because each person perceives himself or herself to be on the line. This in turn makes it almost impossible to deal with the situation rationally.

At this point you should understand that conflict can develop for a number of different reasons. We are aware of the types of disagreements and the types of problems that can arise during intrapersonal and interpersonal encounters. What we need to realize is that particular conflict-generating behaviors affect each of us differently. We can see this in the following excerpt from Neil Simon's play *The Odd Couple*.

THE ODD COUPLE

Neil Simon

(FELIX comes out of the kitchen carrying a tray with steaming dish of spaghetti. As he crosses behind OSCAR to the table, he smells it "deliciously" and passes it close to OSCAR to make sure OSCAR smells the fantastic dish he's missing. As FELIX sits and begins to eat, OSCAR takes can of aerosol spray from the bar, and circling the table sprays all about FELIX, puts can down next to him and goes back to his newspaper.)

FELIX. (Pushing spaghetti away.) All right, how much longer is this gonna go on?

OSCAR. (Reading his paper.) Are you talking to me?

FELIX. That's right, I'm talking to you.

OSCAR. What do you want to know?

FELIX. I want to know if you're going to spend the rest of your life not talking to me. Because if you are, I'm going to buy a radio. (No reply.) Well? (No reply.) I see. You're not going to talk to me. (No reply.) All right. Two can play at this game. (Pause) If you're not going to talk to me, I'm not going to talk to you. (No reply.) I can act childish too, you know. (No reply.) I can go on without talking just as long as you can.

OSCAR. Then why the hell don't you shut up?

FELIX. Are you talking to me?

OSCAR. You had your chance to talk last night. I begged you to come upstairs with me. From now on I never want to hear a word from

What types of problems would Felix and Oscar experience if they worked together in the same office?

that shampooed head as long as you live. That's a warning, Felix.

FELIX. *(Stares at him.)* I stand warned. . . . Over and out!

OSCAR. *(Gets up taking key out of his pocket and slams it on the table.)* There's a key to the back door. If you stick to the hallway and your room, you won't get hurt. *(Sits back down on couch.)*

FELIX. I don't think I gather the entire meaning of that remark.

OSCAR. Then I'll explain it to you. Stay out of my way.

FELIX. *(Picks up key and moves to couch.)* I think you're serious. I think you're really serious. . . . Are you serious?

OSCAR. This is my apartment. Everything in my apartment is mine. The only thing here that's yours is you. Just stay in your room and speak softly.

FELIX. Yeah, you're serious. . . . Well, let me remind you that I pay half the rent and I'll go into any room I want. *(He gets up angrily and starts towards hallway.)*

OSCAR. Where are you going?

FELIX. I'm going to walk around your bedroom.

OSCAR. *(Slams down newspaper.)* You stay out of there.

FELIX. *(Steaming.)* Don't tell me where to go. I pay a hundred and twenty dollars a month.

OSCAR. That was off-season. Starting tomorrow the rates are twelve dollars a day.

FELIX. All right. *(He takes some bills out of his pocket and slams them down on table.)* There you are. I'm paid up for today. Now I'm going to walk in your bedroom. *(He starts to storm off.)*

OSCAR. Stay out of there! Stay out of my room! *(He chases after him. FELIX dodges around the table as OSCAR blocks the hallway.)*

FELIX. *(Backing away, keeping table between them.)* Watch yourself! Just watch yourself, Oscar!

OSCAR. *(With a pointing finger.)* I'm warning you. You want to live here, I don't want to see you, I don't want to hear you and I don't want to smell your cooking. Now get this spaghetti off my poker table.

FELIX. Ha! Haha!

OSCAR. What the hell's so funny?

FELIX. It's not spaghetti. It's linguini! *(OSCAR picks up the plate of linguini, crosses to the doorway, and hurls it into the kitchen.)*

OSCAR. Now it's garbage! *(Paces around the couch.)*

FELIX. *(Looks at OSCAR unbelievingly.)* What an insane thing to do. You are crazy! . . . I'm a neurotic nut but *you are crazy!*

OSCAR. *I'm* crazy, heh? That's really funny coming from a fruitcake like you.

FELIX. *(Goes to kitchen door and looks in at the mess. Turns back to OSCAR.)* I'm not cleaning that up.

OSCAR. Is that a promise?

FELIX. Did you hear what I said? I'm not cleaning it up. It's your mess. *(Looking into kitchen again.)* Look at it. Hanging all over the walls.

OSCAR. *(Crosses up on landing and looks at kitchen door.)* I like it. *(Closes door and paces right.)*

FELIX. *(Fumes.)* You'd just let it lie there, wouldn't you? Until it turns hard and brown and . . . yich. . . . It's disgusting. . . . I'm cleaning it up. *(He goes into the kitchen. OSCAR chases after him. There is the sound of a struggle and falling pots.)*

OSCAR. *(Off.)* Leave it alone! . . . You touch one strand of that lin-

> guini—and I'm gonna punch you right in your sinuses.
> FELIX. *(Dashes out of kitchen with* OSCAR *in pursuit. Stops and tries to calm* OSCAR *down.)* Oscar. . . . I'd like you to take a couple of phenobarbital.
>
> OSCAR. *(Points.)* Go to your room! . . . Did you hear what I said? Go to your room!

Felix and Oscar function almost as a prototype of roommate relationships. Through them, the human contrasts that precipitate conflict are exposed. Are you a Felix or an Oscar? Both? Neither?

Some of us perceive ourselves to be involved in a conflict if we are deprived of a need, whereas others do not. Some of us perceive ourselves to be involved in a conflict if someone impinges on our territory or disagrees with us about the way we define a particular role; others do not. Take some time to discover your own personal sources of conflict. Making such observations will help you understand the types of issues that draw you into harmony with yourself and others. It will also let you see how you tend to respond when faced with a conflict situation. We will now examine constructive and destructive ways of handling conflict in greater detail.

YOUR RELATIONSHIPS AND CONFLICT RESOLUTION: A LOOK AT EXPRESSION STYLES

As we have seen, your emotions and how you handle them can help "make or break" the relationships you enter into. In other words, you can make your feelings work for or against you. There are three possible ways of handling the emotionally charged or conflict-producing situations of your life: nonassertively, aggressively, and assertively. Let's examine the characteristics of each approach.

The Nonassertive Style

Have there been moments in your life when you believed you had to suppress your feelings to avoid rejection or conflict or when you felt unable to state your feelings clearly? Are you ever afraid to let others know how you feel? If you have ever felt hesitant to express your feelings to others, intimidated by another person, or reluctant to speak up when you believed you were being treated unfairly, then you know what it is to be *nonassertive*. When you behave nonassertively, you force yourself to keep your real feelings inside. Frequently, you function like a weather vane or "change colors like a chameleon" in order to fit the particular situation in which you find yourself. In other words, you become an echo of the feelings around you. Unfortunately, nonassertive individuals rarely take the steps needed to improve a relationship that is causing problems, and as a result they frequently end up with something they really don't want. With so much at stake, why do people refrain from asserting themselves?

Experience shows that we hesitate to assert ourselves in our relationships for a number of different reasons. Sometimes inertia or laziness intervenes, and the easiest response to adopt is simply no response at all. (After all, assertion can be hard work.) At other times apathy and a lack of interest are the factors that lead us to exhibit nonassertive responses; we simply do not care enough to become actively involved. Frequently, interpersonal fears can produce nonassertiveness. In particular, we may fear the rejection we believe might result from active self-assertion. (We become convinced that speaking up may make someone angry.) Or we may feel we are not sufficiently equipped with the interpersonal skills needed for assertiveness.

Another important cause of nonassertiveness is shyness. Each of us experiences feelings of personal inadequacy from time to time. We may feel exploited, or perhaps we feel stifled or imposed upon. These feelings manifest themselves in a variety of ways—as depression, as weakness, as loneliness—but most of all, according to psychologist Philip G. Zimbardo, as shyness. A survey reported in the May 1975 issue of the magazine *Psychology Today* disclosed that more than 80 percent of the U.S. high school and college students interviewed revealed that they had been disturbingly shy for a great portion of their lives. What effect does this have? Zimbardo sums it up in his work *Shyness*, where he states: "The shy person shrinks from self-assertion."

According to Zimbardo and Shirley L. Radl, coauthors of *The Shyness Workbook*, few shy people judge their shyness to be a positive trait, but view it as evidence that something is wrong with them. Actually, note Zimbardo and Radl, "shyness is not a permanent trait but rather is a response to other people evoked by certain situations. The unpleasant feelings of shyness come from having low self-esteem and worrying about what other people will think of you."

According to Lynn Z. Bloom, Karen Coburn, and Joan Pearlman, authors of *The New Assertive Woman*, in our society shyness or nonassertive behavior is often perceived to be an asset for women but a liability for men. To what extent do your experiences support this? Do you think women gain more from being nonassertive than men lose? Why?

There are many degrees of shyness. For example, shyness can affect you as mild bashfulness, or it can cause you to increase the distance you like to keep between yourself and others, as we see in the article by Jack Horn.

Identify reasons why you might be hesitant to protect your rights—that is, why you would be reluctant to assert yourself. Under which circumstances would such nonassertiveness occur?

Which situations and people in your life make you feel shy? What are the consequences of your shyness?

MEASURING SHYNESS—THE 12-INCH DIFFERENCE

Jack C. Horn

Shyness can be measured in inches as well as blushes. Or so psychologists Bernardo Carducci and Arthur Webber concluded when they had 73 California college students (42 men and 31 women) approach other people in a recent experiment.

Carducci and Webber employed a standard psychological method of measuring the distance people like to keep between themselves and others. As each volunteer entered the room where the experiment took place, he or she was met by an experimenter and asked to stand on a certain spot while the experimenter moved 18 feet away. The student was then asked either to walk toward the other person until the student reached a point that felt comfortable, or to stand still while the experimenter approached, saying "Stop" when the experimenter reached a comfortable distance.

After the experimenter measured this distance, the process was reversed—students who had walked, stood still, and those who had stood still, walked—and the preferred distance was measured again. Students then filled out the Stanford Survey on Shyness, a measure developed by psychologist Philip Zimbardo. . . . Based on the shyness scores, Carducci and Webber split the students into very-shy and less-shy groups, and compared the interpersonal distances chosen by each.

They found that when the experimenter was doing the walking, shy people did not say "Stop" at a farther distance than less shy people did, apparently because they were just too shy to say it when they wanted to. But when Carducci and Webber averaged the two distances to get a single measure for each student, they found that shyer people preferred a distance 8 inches farther apart, on the average, than did the less shy—33.4 inches rather than 25. The difference grew to a foot (36.3 inches rather than 24.4) when the shy student and the experimenter were of opposite sexes.

Unfortunately, shyness can ultimately make you fear entering into any social relationships at all, just as it can inhibit you from acknowledging or expressing your emotions.

Let us next examine the polar opposite of the shy, nonassertive individual—the aggressor.

The Aggressive Style

Describe an interpersonal situation in which someone took advantage of you and you permitted it. What do you believe motivated the person to act in this fashion? What motivated you to respond as you did? Describe a situation in which you took advantage of someone else. Why do you believe the person allowed the victimization?

Unlike nonassertive people, who often permit others to victimize them and are reluctant to express feelings, aggressive people insist on standing up for their own rights while ignoring and violating the rights of others. Thus, whereas aggressive individuals manage to have more of their needs met than do nonassertive individuals, they generally accomplish this at someone else's expense. The aggressor always aims to dominate and "win" in a relationship; breaking even is not enough. The message of the aggressive person is selfish: "This is the way I feel. You're dumb for feeling differently. This is what I want. What you want doesn't count and is of no consequence to me." In contrast to the nonassertive person, who ventures forth in communication hesitantly, the aggressive person begins by attacking, thereby precipitating conflict. It is therefore not surprising that conversations with aggressive persons often escalate out of control because the target of the aggressor frequently feels a need to retaliate. In such situations no one really wins, and the end result is a relationship stalemate.

People feel a need to act aggressively for a number of different reasons. According to assertiveness counselors Arthur J. Lange and Patricia Jakubowski, we display a tendency to lash out when we feel ourselves becoming vulnerable to another; we simply attempt to protect ourselves from the perceived threat of powerlessness. Second, often unresolved, emotionally volatile experiences may cause us to overreact when faced with a relationship difficulty.

Third, we may firmly believe the only way for us to get our ideas and feelings across to the other person is through aggression. For some reason, we may think people will neither listen to nor react to what we say if we take a merely mild-mannered approach. Fourth, we simply may never have learned how to channel or handle our aggressive impulses. (In other words, we may not have mastered a number of necessary interpersonal skills.) Finally, our aggression may be related to a pattern of repeated nonassertion in the past; thus the hurt, disappointment, bewilderment, and sense of personal violation that accompany previously *nonassertive* responses may have mounted to a boiling point. No longer able to keep these feelings inside, we abruptly vent them as aggressiveness. Needless to say, damaged or destroyed relationships are a frequent result of aggression.

As we have seen, neither the nonassertive nor the aggressive person has many meaningful relationships. For this reason we must find the middle ground or "golden mean" between the extremes of nonassertion and aggression.

The Assertive Style

Whereas the intent of nonassertive behavior is to avoid conflict of any kind and the intent of aggressive behavior is to dominate, the intent of assertive behavior is to communicate honestly, clearly, and directly and to support your beliefs and ideas without either harming others or being harmed yourself. If we can assume that both nonassertion and aggression are due at least partly to learning inappropriate ways of reacting in interpersonal encounters, we should be able to improve our interpersonal relationships if we work to develop appropriate ways of behaving. Understanding the meaning of assertiveness will help us accomplish this.

When you assert yourself, you protect yourself from being victimized; you meet more of your interpersonal needs, make more decisions about your own life, think and say what you believe, and establish closer interpersonal relationships without infringing on the rights of others. To be assertive is to recognize that all individuals have the same fundamental rights and that neither titles nor roles alter this fact. We all have a right to influence the way others behave toward us; we all have a right to protect ourselves from mistreatment. Furthermore, we all have the right to accomplish these objectives without guilt.

Assertive individuals have learned how to stop themselves from sending nonassertive messages or aggressive messages when such behavior would be inappropriate. Thus assertive people announce what they think and feel without apologizing but equally without dominating. This involves learning to say "No," "Yes," "I like," and "I think." In this way neither one's own self nor that of the other person is demeaned; both are respected.

The focus of assertiveness is *negotiation*. Assertive persons try to balance social power in order to equalize the nature of the relationships they share. Whereas aggressive individuals often hurt others and nonassertive people often hurt themselves, assertive people protect themselves as well as those with whom they interact. This means attending to feelings and using specific verbal and nonverbal skills to help solve interpersonal problems.

Remember, to be assertive does not mean you must be insensitive or selfish, nor does it mean you must be stubborn or pushy. It does mean that you are willing to defend your rights and communicate your needs, and it does mean that you are willing to attempt to find mutually satisfactory solutions to interpersonal problems or conflicts that arise. It is time now to decide whether you would like to redefine some of the ways in which you relate to others. It is time now to determine whether you would like to shake off any inappropriate and unproductive ways of behaving in favor of assertiveness.

The Impact of Assertion Encounters

In this section we will examine some of the difficulties you may face as you attempt to promote more successful and open communication with others. Sherwin B. Cotler and Julio J. Guerra point out that most assertion

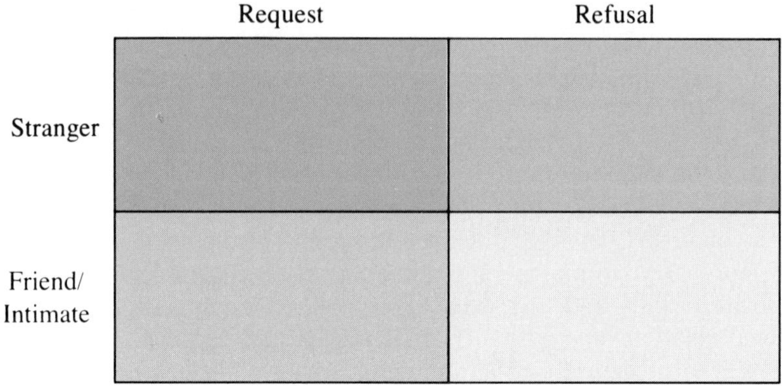

Request   Refusal

Stranger

FIGURE 8-1   Friend/
The Relationship   Intimate
Window

situations fall into at least one of the following four categories: an interaction with a stranger where you are requesting something, an interaction with a friend or intimate where you are requesting something, an interaction with a stranger where you are refusing something, an interaction with a friend or intimate where you are refusing something.[10] These situations may be represented in a Relationship Window (see Figure 8-1).

Most persons experience the majority of their assertion difficulties in one or more of the quadrants shown in the figure. For example, some people may find it easy to refuse a stranger's request but difficult to deny that of a friend. For others, refusing close friends or strangers alike may pose few problems; instead, these individuals may experience great anxiety when making requests of others. Where do you experience the most difficulty?

It is important for you to realize that at one time or another we all have some difficulty in at least one of the relationship quadrants. Now that you have identified your problem areas, however, you can begin to examine your behavior more closely. You can begin to assess when you feel a need to fight, when you feel a need to flee, and when you feel you must assert yourself. Fighting or fleeing makes sense for animals and is therefore characteristic of their behavior, but these alternatives do not necessarily make sense for human beings in dealing with one another. Yet you and I do flee from each other, and we do fight with each other. Sometimes we display these behaviors because we want to, sometimes because we feel we must, and other times because we don't know what else to do or may think we are not equipped with the social skills to do anything else. What we can do, however, is use our problem-solving ability to develop assertive means of handling these interpersonal difficulties. We can learn to be *socially adept*.

In order for any interpersonal relationship to grow, both individuals need to demonstrate at least a minimal level of assertiveness in their

The Relationship Thermometer

Whereas the emotional response index of nonassertive persons is usually too low or "below normal" (they do not permit themselves to react) and the emotional response index of the aggressive person is usually too high or "above normal" (they overreact), the emotional response index of the assertive person is "normal." Examine your own relationship "temperature" by trying to send the following messages using each style of behavior discussed.

1. You would like a stranger seated near you to stop smoking.
   a. Nonassertive
   b. Aggressive
   c. Assertive
2. You do not wish to drive a friend to the airport.
   a. Nonassertive
   b. Aggressive
   c. Assertive
3. You do not want to move your seat on an airplane so that two friends whom you do not know can sit together.
   a. Nonassertive
   b. Aggressive
   c. Assertive
4. You would like a friend to help you plan a club function.
   a. Nonassertive
   b. Aggressive
   c. Assertive

At which "temperature setting" did you find it easiest to operate? Why? Which type of style was hardest for you to formulate? Why?

communication with each other. The important thing is to try to let your actions be dictated by the circumstances and the people. There is no one right way for you to act in every interpersonal encounter, and the choice of how you act should be your own. We can all increase our feelings of self-worth by learning to be more assertive.

HOW TO EXPRESS FEELINGS EFFECTIVELY IN RELATIONSHIPS

As we have seen, many of us have trouble expressing our feelings. Either we behave nonassertively and keep our emotions too much in check, or we behave aggressively and become excessively demanding or belligerent. The net result is that our emotions impede the development of healthy relationships, fostering instead the development of unhealthy ones.

It is sad that we are rarely if ever taught how to reveal our emotions in ways that will help our relationships. The key to being able to use our feelings to promote effective relationships is to learn to express them effectively. The following guidelines should help you communicate feelings in positive ways and thereby enrich the quality of your interpersonal encounters and relationships.

Work On Feelings You Have Difficulty Expressing or Handling

By now you should have a pretty good idea of what feelings you have trouble expressing or responding to. Now concentrate on expressing or responding to these feelings when they arise. A first step is to let others know what feelings cause problems for you.

Stand Up for Your Emotional Rights

When we sacrifice our rights, we teach others to take advantage of us. When we demand rights that are not ours, we take advantage of others. Not revealing your feelings and thoughts to others can be just as damaging as disregarding the feelings and thoughts of others. Here is what we conceive to be Every Person's Bill of Rights:

1. The right to be treated with respect
2. The right to make your own choices or decisions
3. The right to make mistakes and/or change your mind
4. The right to have needs and have these needs considered to be as important as the needs of others
5. The right to express your feelings and opinions
6. The right to judge your own behavior
7. The right to set your own priorities
8. The right to say no without feeling guilty
9. The right not to make choices for others
10. The right not to assert yourself

These rights provide the structure upon which you can build effective relationships. Internalizing them will enable you to learn new habits and formulate new expectations. Accepting your personal rights and the personal rights of others is an important first step.

Check Your Perceptions

So far we've spoken about your feelings, but what about the other person's? Sometimes our interpretations of another's feelings are determined by our own. Checking your perception requires that you *express* your assessment of the other's feelings in a tentative fashion. You want to communicate to other people that you would like to understand their feelings and that you would like to refrain from acting on the basis of false assumptions that you might later regret. Sample perception checks might include the following:

"Were you surprised at what Jim said to you?"
"Am I right you feel angry that no one paid attention to your ideas?"
"I get the feeling what I said annoyed you. Am I right?"
"I'm not certain if your behavior means that you're confused or embarrassed."

Display a Respect for Feelings

Refrain from attempting to persuade yourself or other people to deny honest feelings. Statements like "Don't feel that way," "Calm down," and "Don't cry over spilt milk" communicate that you believe the other person has no right to feel that way. (As we have seen, you should avoid advising yourself or others to repress or ignore feelings.) Feelings are potentially constructive and should not be treated as destructive forces.

Handle Feelings Assertively

In their book *Asserting Your Self*, Sharon Bower and Gordon Bower present a technique you can use to help you handle interpersonal dilemmas effectively. This approach utilizes what is called a "DESC script" (*DESC* stands for *D*escribe, *E*xpress, *S*pecify, *C*onsequences). A script contains characters (you and the person with whom you are relating), a plot (a happening that has left you dissatisfied), a setting (the time and place the interaction occurred), and a message (the words and nonverbal cues of the actors). You begin the script by describing, as specifically and objectively as possible, the behavior of another that troubles you and makes you feel inadequate. By describing the bothersome occurrence you give yourself a chance to examine the situation and define your personal needs and goals. Once you have identified what there is about the other person's behavior you find undesirable, you are in a better position to handle it. However, use simple, concrete, specific, and unbiased terms to describe the other's actions. For example, instead of saying, "You're always overcharging me, you dirty cheat!" try, "You told me the repairs would cost $50, and now you're charging me $110." Instead of saying, "You're ignoring me, you don't care about me," substitute, "You never look at me when we speak." Instead of guessing at motives and saying, "You resent me and want Lisa," use, "The last two times we've gone out to eat with Jack and Lisa you've criticized me in front of them."

Write a direct description of a particular behavior that bothers you. Identify also the characters, the plot, and the setting. Now add a few sentences to describe how you feel and think about the behavior. To do this, get in touch with your emotions and use personal statements. Using personal statements makes it clear you are referring to what *you* are feeling and what *you* are thinking. The cue to a personal statement is a pronoun such as *I*, *me*, or *my*; for example, "I feel," "I believe," "My feelings," "It appears to me. " Thus, when hurt by the behavior of an unthinking friend, you might say, "I feel humiliated and demeaned when you make fun of me." Realize there are a number of ways in which feelings can be described. You can name a feeling: "I feel disappointed. I feel angry." You can use comparisons: "I feel like mashed potatoes without salt" or "I feel like a rose whose petals have been ripped off one by one." Or you can indicate the type of action your feelings are prompting you to exhibit: "I feel like leaving the room" or "I feel like putting cotton in my ears." By disclosing such feelings tactfully, you can make your position known without alienating the other person.

Once you have described the bothersome behavior and expressed your feelings or thoughts about it, your next step is to write down your request for a different specific behavior. This means that you *specify* the behavior you would like substituted. In effect, you are asking the other person to stop doing one thing and start doing something else. As before, make your request concrete and particular. It would be more effective to say, "Please stop playing the drums after 11 P.M." than to yell, "Stop being so damn noisy!" Review your script and rehearse it until you feel that your verbal and nonverbal cues support your goal.

Practice These Basic Assertive Behaviors

Practice the following assertive behaviors:

1. Stop automatically asking permission to speak, think, or behave. Instead of saying, "Do you mind if I ask to have this point clarified?" say, "I'd like to know if . . ." In other words, substitute *declarative statements* for permission requests.

2. Establish eye contact with individuals with whom you interact. Instead of looking down or to the side (cues that imply uncertainty or insecurity), look into the eyes of the person you are speaking to. This lets people know you have the confidence to relate to them honestly and directly.

3. Eliminate hesitations and fillers (the "uhs," "you knows," and "hmms") from your speech. It's better to talk more slowly and deliberately than to broadcast lack of preparedness or lack of self-assurance.

4. Say no calmly, firmly, and quietly; say yes sincerely and honestly; and say "I want" without fear or guilt.

SUMMARY

Our emotions have an impact on our intrapersonal and interpersonal lives. They can enhance our relationships or disrupt them. They can help increase our understanding of other people or they can prevent us from relating to them effectively. We are experiencing some emotion to some degree at all times. A temporary emotional reaction to a situation is an emotion state; a tendency to experience one particular emotion repeatedly is an emotion trait.

Feelings can be accompanied by a wide range of physical sensations. A number of basic feelings (including surprise, anger, happiness, sadness, and fear) are also reflected by characteristic facial expressions that are similar around the world. We can improve our communication abilities by learning to read the facial expressions of others to discover their feelings and by letting our expressions convey our emotions to them.

Feelings are at the heart of all our important interpersonal relationships. Among the factors that can cause us to establish relationships with some people but not others are attractiveness, proximity, reinforcement, similarity, and complementarity. How we deal with our emotions often influences the course of our relationships. When we censor or fail to disclose our feelings, we are apt to engage in interactions that are shallow or contrived rather than fulfilling and real. Sometimes we are simply obeying unwritten display rules—usually sexually or culturally based—when we decide which feelings we will reveal or conceal. Not expressing our feelings honestly to others can lead to misunderstandings and even breakdowns in our relationships.

There are three ways of expressing feelings in emotionally charged or conflict-producing interpersonal situations: nonassertively, aggressively, and assertively. Only the assertive style enables us to express our beliefs and ideas without harming others or being victimized ourselves. We can use the Relationship Window to identify the kinds of interactions in which we find it most difficult to be assertive. We can then analyze and learn to handle a typical situation by using a DESC script.

SUGGESTIONS FOR FURTHER READING

Aronson, Eliot. *The Social Animal*. San Francisco: Freeman, 1980. Contains an excellent chapter on attraction; explores why people like each other.

Bach, George R., and Ronald M. Deutsch. *Stop! You're Driving Me Crazy*. New York: Putnam, 1979. This readable work explains how to recognize the "crazy-making" behavior of those closest to you as well as how to put an end to it.

Berscheid, Ellen, and Elaine Hatfield Walster. *Interpersonal Attraction*, 2d ed. Reading, Mass.: Addison-Wesley, 1978. A scholarly examination of theories of interpersonal attraction.

Bloom, Lynn Z., Karen Coburn, and Joan Pearlman. *The New Assertive Woman.* New York: Dell, 1975. A highly readable and in-depth description of assertion.

Bower, Sharon Anthony, and Gordon H. Bower. *Asserting Yourself.* Reading, Mass.: Addison-Wesley, 1976. An easy-to-follow assertiveness training program; explains DESC scripts.

Deaux, Kay. *The Behavior of Women and Men.* Belmont, Calif.: Brooks/Cole, 1976. Brings together a considerable amount of information about the behavioral styles of women and men. Among the topics explored are emotional stereotypes, aggression, and attraction.

Dyer, Wayne. *Pulling Your Own Strings.* New York: Avon, 1978. A best-seller; identifies effective ways of dealing with people. Dyer offers strategies for eliminating self-defeating behaviors.

Egan, Gerard. *You and Me: The Skills of Communicating and Relating to Others.* Monterey, Calif.: Brooks/Cole, 1977. Contains a readable chapter on expressing feelings and emotions. Good exercises are suggested.

Gaylin, Willard. *Feelings.* New York: Ballantine Books, 1979. Establishes the thesis that feelings are not barriers to a happy life but an integral part of it.

Gillies, Jerry. *Friends: The Power and Potential of the Company You Keep.* New York: Coward McCann, 1976. This book explores what friends mean to you and what roles they play in your life.

Goleman, Daniel. "The 7000 Faces of Dr. Ekman," *Psychology Today*, February 1981, pp. 42–49. Updates the work of this important nonverbal researcher into nonverbal expression.

Izard, Carroll E. *Human Emotions.* New York: Plenum Press, 1977. A scholarly, thoughtful look at human emotions and their management.

Johnson, David W. *Reaching Out.* Englewood Cliffs, N.J.: Prentice-Hall, 1972. Discusses the verbal and nonverbal expression of feelings clearly and understandably.

Lange, Arthur J., and Patricia Jakubowski. *Responsible Assertive Behavior.* Champaign, Ill.: Research Press, 1976. A guide for trainers. Contains useful, structured exercises.

Powell, John. *Why Am I Afraid to Tell You Who I Am?* Niles, Ill.: Argus Communications, 1969. Contains a composite of suggestions for dealing with our emotions.

Rubin, Theodore Isaac. *The Angry Book.* New York: Macmillan, 1969. Describes how to use anger to build a stronger and happier personality. Discusses the problems that can result from unreleased anger.

Viscott, David. *The Language of Feelings.* New York: Pocket Books, 1976. An in-depth examination of the feelings that guide our lives.

Zimbardo, Philip G. *Shyness.* New York: Jove Books, 1977. A highly readable work. Discusses what we can do about the "social disease" that is reaching epidemic proportions.

Zimbardo, Philip G., and Shirley L. Radl. *The Shyness Workbook.* New York: A&W Visual Library, 1979. Contains worksheets for analyzing the role shyness plays in your life.

NOTES

1. Carroll E. Izard, *Human Emotions* (New York: Plenum Press, 1977), p. 5.
2. Ibid.
3. David Viscott, *The Language of Feelings* (New York: Pocket Books, 1976), p. 54.
4. Izard, p. 10.
5. See, for example, Ellen Berscheid and Elaine Hatfield Walster, *Interpersonal Attraction*, 2d ed. (Reading, Mass.: Addison-Wesley, 1978).
6. Eliot Aronson, *The Social Animal*, 3d ed. (San Francisco: Freeman, 1980), p. 239.
7. John Powell, *Why Am I Afraid to Tell You Who I*

Am? (Niles, Ill.: Argus Communications, 1969).

8. David W. Johnson, *Reaching Out: Interpersonal Effectiveness and Self Actualization* (Englewood Cliffs, N.J.: Prentice-Hall, 1972), p. 203.

9. Alan C. Filley, *Interpersonal Conflict Resolution* (Glenview, Ill.: Scott, Foresman, 1975).

10. Sherwin B. Cotler and Julio J. Guerra, *Assertive Training* (Champaign, Ill: Research Press, 1976), pp. 15–22.

9

Interviewing: From Both Sides of the Desk

Dear . . . ,
We enjoyed having you visit us here (last week) (last month)
(recently). Everyone who talked with you was most impressed, and I
personally feel that you are one of the most promising young (men)
(women) I've seen in a long time.
We all wish we could make you an offer at this time. However . . .

From a corporation's form letter

CHAPTER PREVIEW

After finishing this chapter, you should be able to:

Define *interview*

Explain how an interview differs from a casual conversation

Identify the types of information both parties to an interview share
with each other

Explain the fears interviewer and interviewee may bring to the
interview situation

Determine your own level of "interviewphobia"

Describe the key stages of an interview

Explain the role played by questions during an interview

Demonstrate an ability to formulate closed, open, primary, and secondary questions

Compare and contrast the roles and responsibilities of interviewer and interviewee

Demonstrate the ability to create a favorable impression while functioning as an interviewer or interviewee

Determine how to enhance your *interview quotient*

A t various points during the course of our lives we will be expected to take part in interviews by assuming the role of interviewer or interviewee. The interview incorporates many of the communication characteristics and principles we have discussed. Self-concept, perception, listening and feedback, nonverbal communication, language and meaning, and assertiveness all play a part in determining the effectiveness of communication in the interview setting.

The time you spend interviewing or being interviewed can be critical. It can determine whether you give or get a loan, sell or purchase a product, hire the right person, get the job you want, or keep the job you have. By exploring the interview process you can prepare yourself to participate in any interview—from either side of the desk.

THE INTERVIEW: BEYOND CONVERSATION

Just like other forms of communication, interviews usually involve face-to-face interaction. However, unlike ordinary person-to-person communication, in an interview at least one of the participants has a purpose for the conversation that goes beyond informally interacting with or talking to somebody for simple enjoyment. The conversation that occurs during an interview is planned and is designed to achieve specific objectives. In fact, you could say that the interview is the most common type of purposeful, planned, decision-making, person-to-person communication (although sometimes three or more persons are involved). Thus, in the interview, interaction is structured, questions are asked and answered, and behavior is interchanged in an effort to explore predetermined subject matter and realize a definite goal.

The description just provided is in keeping with the frequently referred to definition by Goyer, Redding, and Richey, authors of *Interviewing Principles and Techniques: A Project Text*. They state that an interview is "a form of oral communication involving two parties, at least one of whom has a preconceived and serious purpose and both of whom speak and listen from time to time."[1] No matter how an interview is defined, its participants are involved in a process of contact and information exchange; they meet to both give and receive information in order to make educated decisions. Ideally, there should also be a participation *balance* in the interview: Both interviewer and interviewee should give themselves the opportunity to learn from the data given and received during the interchange.

Interviews serve a variety of purposes. People engage in interviews to gather information (the information-gathering interview), participate in an evaluation (the appraisal interview), change someone's attitudes or behavior (the persuasive interview), determine why someone is leaving a position (the exit interview), provide guidance (the counseling interview), and gain employment or select the right person for a job (the hiring/ selection interview). The participants in each of these interview types have different goals. Let us compare and contrast them.

The Information-Gathering Interview.   In the information-gathering interview, the interviewer's goal is to collect information, opinions, or data about a specific topic or person. It is the interviewer's job to ask the interviewee questions designed to add to the interviewer's knowledge, questions that reveal the interviewee's views, understandings, insights, and/or predictions, for example. Interviews conducted with expert sources to complete an assignment and interviews conducted for popular magazines or television shows illustrate this interview type. Whether the interviewer is Barbara Walters, Mike Wallace, or you, the aim is to gather specific information from someone who has knowledge that you do not yet have.

The Appraisal Interview.   During an appraisal interview, the interviewee's performance is assessed by an interviewer, usually a superior from management. The goal is to evaluate what the interviewee is doing well and what she or he could do better. Through this means, expectations and behaviors are better matched. Interviewees gain perspective on how others view their work, and they also reveal how they see themselves performing.

The Persuasive Interview.   The goal of the interviewer during a persuasive interview is to change the interviewee's attitudes or behavior. As the interview progresses, it is hoped that the interviewee will come to a desired conclusion or reveal a desired response. Salespersons traditionally conduct such interviews with customers in an effort to close a sale.

The Exit Interview.   Frequently, an exit interview is conducted when an employee leaves an organization; it is an effort to determine why the match between employer and employee did not work or why the employee made

What types of information have you shared during interviews? What information have you received from the other party to the interview? How do you think the information exchanged affected the decision-making process?

a decision to leave voluntarily. The information obtained during the interview can be used to refine the hiring process, to help prevent other employees from leaving, or merely to increase the pleasantness of the departure experience for employer and employee.

The Counseling Interview. The counseling interview traditionally is conducted by someone trained in psychology and is designed to provide guidance and support for the person being interviewed. Interviewees are helped to solve problems facing them, work more productively, interact with others more effectively, improve their relationships with friends or family members, or simply cope more successfully with daily life.

The Hiring Interview

The hiring interview is among the best known and most widely experienced types of interview and probably is the next major interview you will face. For that reason we will focus on it. It is as a result of this type of interview that we find ourselves accepted or rejected for work by an individual employer, a business, or a corporate organization. The employment interview offers the unique opportunity for the potential employer and employee to share meaningful information that will permit each to determine whether the mutual association will be a beneficial and productive one. In a sense, the employment interview gives both parties a chance to test each other by asking and answering relevant questions. The better prepared you are for the employment interview, the better your chances of performing effectively and realizing your job objectives. Remember, an interview is certainly not "just talk."[2]

There is only one person who can tell you whether any candidate is right for the job: the candidate him- or herself.

Kevin J. Murphy, Effective Listening: Your Key to Career Success

Preparation: Reducing "Interviewphobia"

How do you feel about interviewing someone? About being interviewed?

1. Listed below are some of the fears commonly expressed by new interviewers. Read them and identify the number beneath each statement that most accurately reflects your own level of apprehension, where 0 represents "completely unconcerned"; 1, "very casual concern"; 2, "mild concern"; 3, "more apprehensive than not"; 4, "very frightened"; and 5, "a nervous wreck."

   a. I won't be able to think of good questions to ask.

       0   1   2   3   4   5

   b. I will appear to be very nervous.

       0   1   2   3   4   5

   c. I will give the interviewee too little or too much information.

       0   1   2   3   4   5

d. I will not be judged to be a credible source.

                                  0   1   2   3   4   5

e. I will be asked questions about the company I can't answer.

                                    0   1   2   3   4   5

f. I will be a poor judge of character.

                                    0   1   2   3   4   5

g. I will not have good rapport with the interviewee.

                                    0   1   2   3   4   5

h. I will not appear organized.

                                    0   1   2   3   4   5

i. I will be ineffective at probing for more information.

                                    0   1   2   3   4   5

j. I will not hire the right person for the job.

                                    0   1   2   3   4   5

Total your selected numbers to arrive at your interviewerphobia score.

2. Listed below are some of the fears frequently expressed by inexperienced interviewees. Read them and identify the number that most accurately reflects your own level of interviewee apprehension (see item 1 for the level of emotion expressed by each number).

a. I will be asked questions I am unable to answer.

                                  0   1   2   3   4   5

b. I will not dress right for the interview.

                                  0   1   2   3   4   5

c. I will appear to be very nervous.

                                  0   1   2   3   4   5

d. I will not appear to be competent.

                                  0   1   2   3   4   5

e. The interviewer will cross-examine me.

                                  0   1   2   3   4   5

f. I will be caught in a lie.

                                  0   1   2   3   4   5

g. I will talk too much or too little.

                                  0   1   2   3   4   5

h. I will not have good rapport with the interviewer.

                                  0   1   2   3   4   5

i. I will undersell or oversell myself.

                                  0   1   2   3   4   5

j. I won't be hired.

                                  0   1   2   3   4   5

Total your selected numbers to arrive at your intervieweephobia score.

3.   Your scores give an indication of how frightened you are of assuming the role of interviewer or interviewee. If you accumulated 45 to 50 points, you are "a nervous wreck"; 35 to 44 points, you are too frightened; 20 to 34 points, you are somewhat apprehensive; 11 to 20 points, you are too casual; and 0 to 10 points, you just don't care at all.

Contrary to what you might assume, not being concerned at all about participating in an interview is just as much of a problem as being a nervous wreck, and being casual about the experience can do as much damage as being very frightened. An effective interviewer or interviewee should be apprehensive *to a degree*. If you're not concerned about what will happen during the interview, then you won't care about making a good impression and as a result will not perform as effectively as you could. Both the interviewer and the interviewee must plan and prepare to participate in an interview. Only in this way will important questions and answers be shared and interviewphobia eliminated. Let's begin by familiarizing ourselves with a number of interview variables.

Interview Stages

For the next few days, keep track of the verbal and non-verbal messages people use when they say hello or good-bye. Which beginnings and endings were particularly communicative? Which were ineffective? Which false starts or endings did you observe? How could they have been avoided?

Most effective interviews have a discernible structure. Simply, they have a beginning, a middle, and an end. The *beginning*, or *opening*, is that segment of the process that provides an orientation to what is to come. The *middle*, or *body*, is the largest segment and the one during which both parties really get down to business. The interview's *end*, or *close*, is the segment during which the parties prepare to take leave of one another.

Just as the right kind of hello at the start of a conversation can help create a feeling of friendliness between interactors, so the opening of the interview should be used to help establish rapport between interviewer and interviewee.[3] The primary purpose of this phase is to make it possible for both to participate freely and honestly by creating an atmosphere of trust and goodwill and by explaining the purpose and scope of the meeting. Conversational icebreakers and orientation statements perform key interview-opening functions. Typical icebreakers include comments about the weather, here-and-now surroundings, and current events or a compliment. The idea is to use small talk to help make the interview a human rather than a mechanical encounter. Typical orientation remarks include identification of the interview's purpose, a preview of the topics to be discussed, and statements that motivate the respondent and act as a conduit or transition into the body of the interview.

In the body of the interview, the interactors really get down to business. Here the interviewer and interviewee might discuss work experiences, including those things the applicant does best, his or her weaknesses, major accomplishments, difficult problems tackled in the past, and career goals. Educational background and activities or interests are relevant areas to probe during this phase of the interview. Breadth of knowledge and time-management abilities are also common areas of concern.

During the close of the interview, the main points covered are reviewed and summarized. Since an interview that ends well can enhance any future meetings the interactors may have, care must be taken to make the leave-taking comfortable.[4] Expressing appreciation for the time and effort given is important; neither interviewee nor interviewer should be made to feel discarded. In other words, the door should be left open for future contacts.

Questions: The "Heartbeat" of the Interview

How many times a day are you asked questions? How many times a day do you ask questions? Questions are obviously a natural part of our daily discourse. Let's see why.

Questions asked in the course of typical interpersonal encounters during a typical day perform a number of functions. They help us find out needed information, satisfy our curiosity, demonstrate our interest, and test the knowledge of the individual questioned; at the same time they permit those questioned to reveal themselves to us. For these reasons,

> The only way to get the accurate answers is to ask the right questions.
>
> *Kevin J. Murphy,* Effective Listening: Your Key to Career Success

SKILL BUILDER

Question Track

In the next 24 hours, keep a record of five questions you ask others and five questions others ask you. For each question you ask, list the following:

1. The question
2. The person asked
3. The purpose of the question
4. The information revealed

For each question another person asks you, list the following:

1. The question
2. The person asking
3. The perceived reason
4. What I revealed

questions are the primary medium for data collection in an interview. Not only do questions set the tone for the interview, they also determine whether the interview will yield valuable information or prove to be practically worthless. As James M. Lahiff, author of *Interviewing for Results*, notes, "The correlation between appropriate questions and a successful interview cannot be overemphasized."

The effective interviewer, like the effective newswriter, can benefit from this famous Rudyard Kipling verse:

> I keep six honest serving-men
> (They taught me all I know).
> Their names are what and why and when
> And how and where and who.

The interrogatives *what*, *where*, *when*, *who*, *how*, and *why* are used throughout the interview because they help to lay a foundation of knowledge on which to base decisions or conclusions.

During the course of an interview, closed, open, primary, and secondary questions may all be used, and in any combination.[5] *Closed questions* are highly structured and can be answered with a simple yes or no or a few brief words. The following are examples of closed questions:

> "How old are you?"
> "Where do you live?"
> "What schools did you attend?"
> "Did you graduate in the top quarter of your class?"
> "Would you work for the salary offered?"
> "What starting salary do you expect?"

In contrast to closed questions, *open questions* are broader in nature and are less restricting or structured; hence, they offer the respondent

Closed

Open

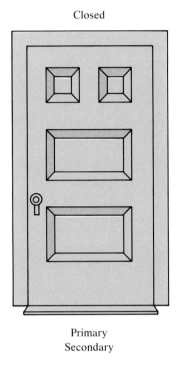
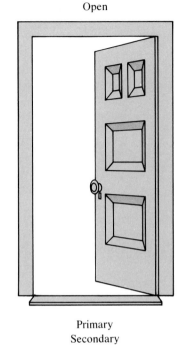

Primary
Secondary

Primary
Secondary

FIGURE 9-1
Interview questions

more freedom in the choice and scope of an answer. The following are examples:

"Tell me about yourself."

"What are your feelings about our industry?"

"How do you judge success?"

"Why did you choose to interview for this particular job?"

"What are your career goals?"

Open questions give individuals a chance to express their feelings, attitudes, and values. Furthermore, they let individuals know the interviewer is interested in understanding their perspective.

Open and closed questions may be either primary or secondary (see Figure 9-1). *Primary questions* are used to introduce topics or to begin exploring a new area. "What is your favorite hobby?" and "Tell me about your last job" are examples of primary questions; the first is closed, and the second is open. A smart interviewer will prepare a list of primary questions before coming to the interview, and smart interviewees will anticipate the primary questions they may be asked.

The Follow-Up

What secondary questions would you use to follow up this series of interviewer-interviewee exchanges?

1. INTERVIEWER: How do you feel about a job that requires 50 percent travel?
   INTERVIEWEE: That depends.
   INTERVIEWER:

2. INTERVIEWER: Why are you leaving your present position?
   INTERVIEWEE: It's time for a change.
   INTERVIEWER:

3. INTERVIEWER: What kind of job are you seeking?
   INTERVIEWEE: An interesting one.
   INTERVIEWER:

4. INTERVIEWER: What are your attitudes toward overtime?
   INTERVIEWEE: A lot of employees object to overtime.
   INTERVIEWER:

5. INTERVIEWER: What do you expect to be earning in 5 years?
   INTERVIEWEE: A decent wage.
   INTERVIEWER:

Secondary questions are used to follow up primary questions and are sometimes referred to as *probing questions*. They ask that the respondent explain the ideas and feelings behind answers, and they are frequently used when the answers to primary questions are vague or incomplete. The following are examples:

"Go on, what do you mean?"
"Would you explain that further?"
"Could you give me an example?"
"What did you have in mind when you said that?"

"Uh huh" and "Hmmm" are typical secondary-question comments. Charles J. Stewart and William B. Cash, Jr., note in their book *Interviewing: Principles and Practices* that the effective use of secondary questions distinguishes skilled from unskilled interviewers.

To be an effective follow-up questioner requires that you be an effective listener. You must be sensitive to and on the lookout for the feelings and attitudes of the interviewee in addition to the facts and opinions stated. You will need to develop techniques that will permit you to see the world through the other person's eyes. Of course, it goes without saying that the interviewee must also be an effective listener. At this point, let's examine more closely the roles and responsibilities of each party to the interview.

Roles and Responsibilities

Both interviewer and interviewee come to the interview with certain goals in mind. Interviewers usually have a threefold objective. They hope to (1) gather information that will enable them to judge accurately the interviewees' future performance, (2) persuade applicants that the business or organization is a good one to work for, and (3) ascertain whether the applicants and the people with whom they will work will be compatible. Interviewers also work to keep their own jobs. Remember, a company invests both time and money in the hiring and training of a new employee. If the employee doesn't work out, the investment is sacrificed and some of the blame obviously falls on the original interviewer.

To fulfill their objectives, interviewers need to master the art of structuring a successful interview, use effective questioning techniques, and approach each interview situation with flexibility and sensitivity. Good interviewers work hard during an interview. They wear three "hats": information seeker, information giver, and decision maker (see Figure 9-2). They recognize good answers, are aware of word choices, and pick up on silences and hesitations. They are active, not passive, participants.

Interviewees also bear a great responsibility in the interview. They too need to speak and listen and provide and collect information to decide whether to accept the job. To accomplish these goals, interviewees need to research the company to which they are applying and try to anticipate the questions they will be asked. They also need to plan to ask questions themselves. It's unfortunate and unproductive when only the interviewer gains information from the interview experience. The interviewee can often learn much about work conditions and the prospects for job advancement by asking questions and probing for answers. To the extent that interviewees have a right to share the control of the interview, they can affect its direction and content. Like interviewers, interviewees need to be good listeners, adaptable and sensitive to the image they project.

Effective interviewees work hard at self-assessment. In effect, they take stock of themselves in order to determine who they are, what their career needs and goals are, and how they can best sell themselves to the company of their choice. As a prospective interviewee, you will find it useful to prepare by thinking about and answering the following questions:

1. For what types of positions has my training prepared me?
2. What has been my most rewarding experience?

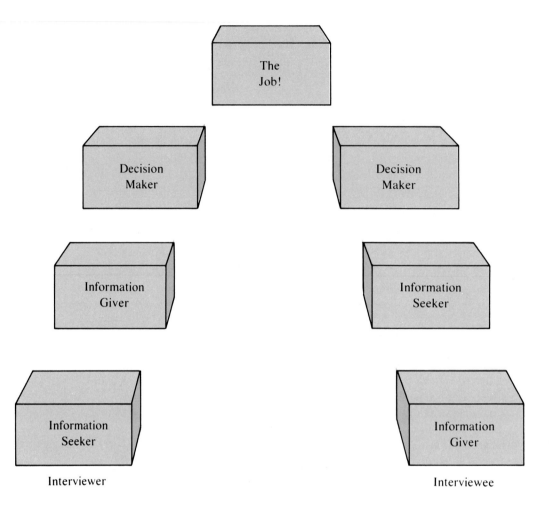

Interviewer   Interviewee

FIGURE 9-2
Interview
responsibilities

3. What type of job do I want?
4. Would I be happier working more alone than with others?
5. What qualifications do I have that make me feel I would be successful in the job of my choice?
6. What type(s) of people do I want to work for?
7. What type(s) of people do I not want to work for?
8. How do I feel about receiving criticism?
9. What salary will enable me to meet my financial needs?
10. What salary will enable me to live comfortably?
11. What will interviewers want to know about me, my interests, my background, and my experiences?

In addition to conducting a self-survey, the interviewee needs to work to withstand the pressure of the interview situation. Are you prepared to maintain your composure while being stared at, interrupted, spoken to abruptly, or asked difficult questions? How do you think you would react? The following questions are interviewer favorites. How would you answer them?

1. Tell me about yourself.
2. What do you think you're worth?
3. If we hired you, what about this organization would concern you most?
4. What attributes do you think an effective manager should possess?
5. What are your short-term goals? How are they different from your long-term goals?
6. How has your background prepared you for this position?
7. What are your major strengths and weaknesses?
8. How would a former employer or instructor describe you, if asked?
9. What do you consider to be your greatest accomplishment?
10. How long do you plan to remain with us should you get this job?
11. What would you like to know about us?

Practice in answering questions like these—under both favorable and unfavorable conditions—is essential.[6] It is important that you know what you want to say during the interview and that you use the questions you are asked as a springboard for saying it. Along the way, you can flatter the interviewer by offering comments like "That's a really good question" or "I think you've touched on something really important."

It should be realized that the interviewer can use the interviewee's résumé to ascertain factual information about the applicant, educational background and previous positions held, for example. However, gathering enough information to make a decision about the personal qualities of the applicant is more difficult. Following is a list of personal qualifications and the questions that interviewers typically use to determine if the individual possesses the skill or trait they are looking for.

What other qualities do you believe interviewers look for in interviewees? If you were the interviewer, what questions would you ask to determine if a person possessed those qualities?

QUALITY: Career management skill
QUESTION: What specific things have you deliberately done to bring yourself to where you are today?
QUALITY: Management skill
QUESTION: Give me some examples of things you do and do not like to delegate.

QUALITY: Sense of responsibility

QUESTION: What steps do you take to see that things do not fall through the cracks when you are supervising a project?

QUALITY: Skill in working with people

QUESTION: If we assembled a group of people you have worked with in one room and asked them to describe what it was like to work with you, what would they be apt to reply? What would your greatest supporter say? What would your severest critic say?

To be effective, an interview requires that both parties work hard. Realize that questioner and respondent constantly exchange information. When either the interviewer or the interviewee speaks, the other is still sending forth nonverbal information through posture, facial expression, head nodding, and so on. Because you stop talking during an interview does not mean you stop communicating. Know what you're trying to accomplish with your verbal and nonverbal messages.

FOCUS ON IMPRESSION MANAGEMENT

The word *interview* is derived from the French word *entrevoir*, meaning "to see one another" or "to meet." What happens when an interviewer and an interviewee meet for the first time? What variables influence the impressions the interviewer forms of the interviewee? We know, for example, that most interviewers make their decisions about the job applicant during the course of the actual interview; in fact, although most decide in the last quarter of the interview whether to invite the applicant back, a bias for or against the candidate is established earlier in the interview, often during the first 4 minutes.

In *Your Attitude Is Showing*, Elwood N. Chapman notes:

> First impressions are important because they have a lasting quality. People you meet for the first time appear to have little radar sets tuned into your attitude. If your attitude is positive, they receive a friendly, warm signal, and they are attracted to you; if your attitude is negative, they receive an unfriendly signal, and they try to avoid you.

Studies reported in the *Job-Seeking Skills Reference Manual* support this observation. Recent studies have revealed that if an employer formed a negative impression of an interviewee during the first five minutes of an interview, 90 percent of the time that person did not get the job. In contrast, if the employer's first impression was positive, 75 percent of the time the interviewee was hired. What happens is that once interviewers form an initial impression, they selectively pick up on whichever information supports the initial impression. In effect, interviewers set up self-fulfilling prophecies and then act to ensure that they come true.

According to researcher Lois Einhorn, the amount of available interview time consumed also sends an important message. Interviewees who failed to get hired participated in shorter interviews than did successful applicants. The successful interviewees also spoke a greater percentage of the time than did their unsuccessful counterparts. In fact, the successful applicants spoke for some 55 percent of the total interview time available to them while the unsuccessful interviewees accounted for only 37 percent of the words spoken during their interviews. Seeming to control the interview also leaves an impression. Successful applicants initiated 56 percent of the comments made during their interviews, while unsuccessful applicants were viewed as followers and initiated only 37 percent of the comments made. Consequently, it is important for an interviewee to send messages that announce that he or she is an active, not a passive, respondent.

The Interviewee

It is important that you realize that as a job applicant you will have to work to manage the initial impression you give others. You will be evaluated on how you come across during the interaction and on how you present yourself. What you say and how you say it are your basic resources—the key tools you have to work with. In effect, you are your own marketing manager; therefore, it's up to you to sell yourself to the interviewer. How you communicate your assets, your values, your attitudes, and your overall

---

SKILL BUILDER

My Marketing Profile

1. Identify the assets and talents you would bring to the position of your choice. In other words, attempt to enumerate the qualities and skills that would make you a good investment for an employer.

2. Identify your shortcomings and developmental needs. Enumerate the qualities and skills you wish to develop further and plan how you would do this.

3. Identify those personality strengths you will attempt to communicate during an interview.

4. Identify the communication skills you will use.

5. Now, using the above information, compose a "Position Wanted" advertisement for yourself.

WHY DIDN'T I GET THE JOB?

What are the reasons why you as an applicant sometimes receive only a thundering silence from prospective employers after your interview has been completed? A placement director at Northwestern University recently made an interesting survey of 405 well-known firms to find these reasons.

1. Poor personality and manner: lack of poise; poor presentation of self; lack of self-confidence; timid; hesitant approach; arrogance, conceit.
2. Lack of goals and ambitions, does not show interest, uncertain, and indecisive about the job in question.
3. Lack of enthusiasm and interest, no evidence of initiative.
4. Poor personal appearance and careless dress.
5. Unrealistic salary demands, more interest in salary than opportunity, unrealistic about promotion to top jobs.
6. Poor scholastic record without reasonable explanation for low grades.
7. Inability to express yourself well, poor speech habits.
8. Lack of maturity, no leadership potential.
9. Lack of preparation for the interview—failure to get information about the company and therefore unable to ask intelligent questions.
10. Lack of interest in the company and the type of job they have to offer.
11. Lack of extracurricular activities without good reason.
12. Attitude of "What can you do for me," etc.
13. Objection to travel; unwilling to relocate to branch offices or plants.
14. Immediate or prolonged military obligation.
15. No vacation jobs or other work experience; did not help finance own education.

Reprinted by permission of Bruce K. Bennett, T/M Associates, Orange, California.

---

credibility will affect whether you are hired. Your resources and your ability to share what you are come with you to every interview.

Of necessity, interviewers need to find out a great deal about you in a short period of time. They want to evaluate your communication strengths, general personality, social effectiveness, and character. The interviewer also wants to determine what your needs and wants are—including your career goals, educational interests, and developmental aspirations. Interviewers will want to assess your appearance, your ability to use body language effectively, and your ability to maintain control during the interview.

To a large extent, the interviewer's assessment of you will determine whether you get the job.

At least in part, interviewers will judge you on the basis of the nonverbal cues you send. Interviewers consistently give higher general ratings to applicants who rank high at nonverbal expression than to those who rank low. The high-ranking nonverbal presentation consists of (1) maintaining comfortable eye contact with the interviewer rather than looking away, (2) varying the pitch and volume of your voice rather than speaking in a monotone, a whisper, or a shout, (3) eliminating hesitations rather than uttering numerous "Uhs" and "Ums," (4) leaning forward from the trunk rather than slumping in your seat, and (5) communicating a high energy level supported by smiles, hand gestures, and appropriate body movements. In like fashion, the absence of tightly held hands, a twitching foot or finger, and various other signs of physical tension all help to influence the interviewer positively.

Obviously, appropriate dress is also important to the impression you make during the interview. Consultant John Molloy reports that when interviewing for a job it is advisable to dress as if you were a candidate for a position one or two steps higher than the one for which you are interviewing.[7] He notes that a man is safe if he wears a dark-color suit (navy blue, dark gray, blue, or gray pinstripe); a white, blue, or pale yellow shirt; and a conservative, nondescript tie. Molloy finds that gray suits worn with pale blue shirts and dark blue suits worn with pale yellow shirts help increase likability. He also comments that a solid gray or a conservative

What type of dress would you deem to be inappropriate for a job interview? What type of outfit would you wear to a job interview?

STUDY SHOWS NEATNESS PAYS OFF IN JOB HUNT

Neat, well-dressed college graduates have a better chance to land a job than those who appear in jeans or refuse to wear a bra, according to a Stanford University study.

The wearing of jeans, shorts, sandals, or dispensing with bras creates an impression ranging from "mildly" to "strongly negative," the survey shows.

Applicants who use jargon, have dirty fingernails or fiddle with objects on the desk also earned negative ratings, according to the study by two Stanford students who received doctoral degrees in educational counseling and guidance.

The researchers, Jane Anton and Michael Russell, questioned more than 100 recruiting officers from 17 different industry groups, ranging from accounting and aerospace to government and utilities.

They found that a male creates a mildly positive impression if he wears a sport coat, shirt, tie and slacks. But he creates a stronger impression if he wears a suit.

And the shorter, more neatly trimmed the hair and beard on males, the better the impression on recruiters.

© 1975 United Press International

blue or gray pinstripe suit, preferably a three-piece one, is the most powerful and authoritative suit and should therefore be saved for the crucial interview with the most important person you will see. In like fashion, Molloy believes every woman applying for a professional job should wear a dark-colored, skirted suit and a white or blue blouse; she should avoid wearing tight-fitting clothing or pants. And for both sexes, as the accompanying article shows, neatness counts.

Since every aspect of your nonverbal communication clearly affects the interviewer's judgment of you, you need to work to send out appropriate nonverbal signals. If you consciously or unconsciously send out signals that indicate you're bored, disinterested, or apathetic, you put the interview process in jeopardy. For example, TV interviewer *par excellence* Barbara Walters reported the following incident in her book *How to Talk with Practically Anybody about Practically Anything.*

> Some years ago I interviewed Warren Beatty on "Today." It was before his Bonnie and Clyde fame, and he was fast achieving a reputation among interviewers for being sullen and difficult. However, he was on our program to promote a picture he was currently starring in, and I figured how bad could it be? I smiled warmly and chatted animatedly and asked Mr. Beatty every provocative question I could think of. He answered me monosyllabically with an expression of extreme boredom bordering on distaste. Finally, I resorted to the hackneyed but spoilproof, "Tell me, Mr. Beatty, what is your new picture about." Well, he slumped in his seat and scratched his chest and rubbed his scalp and yawned and finally after an endless pause he said, "Now that's really a very difficult question."
>
> I'd had it. Right on the air, in front of ten million, I am certain, very sympathetic viewers, I said, "Mr. Beatty, you are the most impossible interview I have ever had. Let's forget the whole thing and I'll do a commercial."

Although the preceding example was not a *job* interview, the message is clear. If you do not appear to be a cooperative and willing party to the interview, interviewers will feel that you are wasting their time and effort. Even the most qualified candidate can ruin an interview (and thus forfeit a job opportunity) by communicating a negative rather than a positive image to the interviewer.

You can help cement a positive image by sending a brief thank-you note to the person or persons who interviewed you. Richard Bolles, author of *What Color Is Your Parachute?* writes: "This is one of the most essential steps in the whole job-seeking process—and the one most overlooked by job-seekers." In fact, one of the authors actually was told that a person who interviewed her for a teaching position recommended her for the job because she was the only interviewee to send him a thank-you note after the interview.

Success in a job interview depends on both your verbal skills and on the nonverbal cues and messages you send. (Van Bucher/Photo Researchers)

The Interviewer

It should be remembered that in any interview the interviewer who judges is also judged by the interviewee. To the extent that this judgment is favorable, the interviewer can elicit the interviewee's fullest cooperation in accomplishing the aims and objectives of the interview. The interviewer's ability to set the tone by reducing the initial anxiety of the interviewee is extremely important in influencing the interviewee's initial impression. During the main body of the interview, the interviewer must work to (1) maintain control of the interchange, (2) deliver content so that it is clearly understood, (3) listen for content as well as feelings, (4) build trust, and (5) distinguish relevant from irrelevant information. Finally, at the interview's conclusion, it is up to the interviewer to explain to the applicant the next course of action to be taken and to terminate the encounter smoothly and graciously.

Like interviewees, interviewers must be adept at using nonverbal cues. They must know when to pause and when to speak. For example, 3- to 6-second silences initiated by interviewers have been found effective in getting interviewees to provide more in-depth information. Thus, the interviewer can easily influence the amount of time an applicant spends answering a question. Another means of increasing the length of applicant responses is for the interviewer to murmur "Mm-hmm" while nodding affirmatively. In fact, the answers to questions posed by interviewers who say "Mm-hmm" have been found to be up to two times as long as the replies given to interviewers who offer no "Mm-hmms." Whenever interviewees perceive the interviewer's vocal communication and ability to listen to be of high quality, they tend to enjoy the interview more and rate the interviewer favorably.

As we can see, the interview, like any other interpersonal relationship, requires the cooperation, skill, and commitment of both parties in order to be effective.

HOW TO IMPROVE YOUR INTERVIEW QUOTIENT

Both the interviewee and the interviewer can benefit by following these guidelines:

1. Be prepared. Understand the purpose of the interview, plan or anticipate the questions you will ask and be asked, understand your goals, and be able to communicate them clearly.
2. Practice sending and receiving messages. By its very nature the interview demands that each party to it be adept at sending and receiving verbal and nonverbal messages. Not only must both interactants clearly encode their messages, each must be skilled at reading the reactions and checking on the perceptions of the receiver.
3. Demonstrate effective listening skills. Problems occur in interviews when either the interviewer or the interviewee fails to listen closely to what the other is saying. As is noted in John Brady's *The Craft of Interviewing*, if participants listen carefully and are not thinking merely about what they plan to say next, the interview has a better chance of being productive.
4. Have conviction. Ask and answer questions and express your opinions with enthusiasm. If you aren't excited by your ideas, skills, and abilities, why should anyone else be?
5. Be flexible. Don't overprepare or memorize statements. Think things through thoroughly, but be prepared for questions or answers you didn't anticipate. Be able to adjust to the other person's style and pace.
6. Look. Pay attention to the nonverbal signals sent to you and by you. Be sure they convey positive, not negative, messages. Give the other person your total attention.
7. Consider. Both interviewer and interviewee need to consider the ramifications of a job offer. A typical 40-hour-a-week job done for approximately 50 weeks a year adds up to 6,000 hours in only 3 years. Be sure your choice is one you and the organization can both live with.

8. Chart your progress. Finally, each time you participate in an interview, fill out a copy of the following interview evaluation graph by circling the number that most closely describes your response.

   a. How prepared were you for the interview?

   Not at all prepared   1   2   3   4   5   Fully prepared

   b. What kind of climate did you help create?

   Hostile climate   1   2   3   4   5   Friendly climate

   c. Were the questions you posed clear?

   Not clear   1   2   3   4   5   Clear

   d. Were the responses you offered complete?

   Incomplete   1   2   3   4   5   Complete

   e. How carefully did you listen to the other person?

   Not at all   1   2   3   4   5   Very carefully

   f. How carefully did you pay attention to nonverbal clues?

   Not at all   1   2   3   4   5   Very carefully

   g. To what extent were you distracted by external stimuli?

   Very much   1   2   3   4   5   Not at all

   h. How self-confident were you during the interview?

   Not at all   1   2   3   4   5   Very

   i. How flexible were you during the interview?

   Not flexible   1   2   3   4   5   Very flexible

   j. How would you like to change or improve your behavior for your next interview?

SUMMARY

During the course of our lives we will each take part in a number of different types of interviews as either interviewee or interviewer. The interview is the most common type of purposeful, planned, decision-making, person-to-person communication.

Effective interviews are well-structured interactions. They have a beginning, which provides an orientation to what is to come; a middle, when the parties get down to business; and an end, when the main points are reviewed and the parties take leave of one another.

Questions are the heartbeat of the interview and the primary medium for data collection. Four basic types of questions are asked in an interview: closed, open, primary, and secondary. Closed questions are highly structured and can be answered with a yes, a no, or a few words; open questions are broader and offer the interviewee more freedom in the choice of a response. Primary questions introduce topics or begin exploring a new area; secondary questions (probing questions) follow up primary questions by asking for further information.

Good interviewers and interviewees work hard during an interview, functioning simultaneously as information seekers, information givers, and decision makers. To be a successful interviewee also requires preparation. Honest self-assessment, practice in answering typical interview questions, and mastery of the techniques of impression management are of prime importance.

SUGGESTIONS FOR FURTHER READING

Benjamin, Alfred. *The Helping Interview*. Boston: Houghton Mifflin, 1981. Explores the central issues of the helping interview. Useful for both the lay reader and the specialist.

Bolles, Richard Nelson. *What Color Is Your Parachute?* Berkeley, Calif.: Ten Speed Press, 1978. An interesting, involving manual for job hunters and career changers.

Brady, John. *The Craft of Interviewing*. New York: Vintage Books, 1977. A helpful guide; covers all aspects of the interview process. Especially strong on the art of questioning.

Chapman, Elwood N. *From Campus to Career Success*. Chicago: Science Research Associates, 1978. An easy-to-read career-planning manual.

Donaho, Melvin W., and John L. Meyer. *How to Get the Job You Want*. Englewood Cliffs, N.J.: Prentice-Hall, 1976. The authors offer readable, practical, results-oriented tips on the job-getting process.

Meltzer, Ken. *Creative Interviewing*. Englewood Cliffs, N.J.: Prentice-Hall, 1977. A resource that reveals how to be a successful interviewer. Explains how to pose questions and gather essential data.

Robertson, Jason. *How to Win in an Interview*. Englewood Cliffs, N.J.: Prentice-Hall, 1978. Explains how to make who you are and what you know work for you.

Stewart, Charles J., and William B. Cash, Jr. *Interviewing: Principles and Practices*. 3d ed. Dubuque, Iowa: William C. Brown, 1982. A thorough examination of the interviewing principles applicable to all interview settings. Easily translatable into practice.

Walters, Barbara. *How to Talk with Practically Anybody about Practically Anything*. New York: Doubleday, 1970. A description of this famous interviewer's personal rules for successful conversation.

NOTES

1. Robert S. Goyer, W. Charles Redding, and John T. Rickey, *Interviewing Principles and Techniques: A Project Text* (Dubuque, Iowa: William C. Brown, 1968), p. 6.

2. For example, Lois J. Einhorn reports in "An Inner View of the Job Interview: An Investigation of Successful Communicative Behavior," *Communication Education*, Vol. 30 (1981), pp. 217–228, that successful candidates were able to identify with employers, support arguments, organize thoughts, clarify ideas, and speak fluently.

3. Leonard Zunin and Natalie Zunin, *Contact: The First*

Four Minutes (Los Angeles: Nash Publishing, 1972), pp. 8–12.

4. See Mark L. Knapp, Roderick P. Hart, Gustav W. Friedrich, and Gary M. Shulman, "The Rhetoric of Goodbye: Verbal and Nonverbal Correlates of Human Leave-Taking," *Speech Monographs*, Vol. 40 (1973), pp. 182–198.

5. Charles J. Stewart and William B. Cash, Jr., *Interviewing: Principles and Practices*, 3d ed. (Dubuque, Iowa: William C. Brown, 1982), pp. 75–85.

6. For a study confirming that employers use a candidate's speech characteristics to judge competence and likability, see Robert Hopper, "Language Attitudes in the Employment Interview," *Speech Monographs*, Vol. 44 (1974), pp. 346–351.

7. See John T. Molloy, *Dress for Success* (New York: Warner, 1977), and John T. Molloy, *The Woman's Dress for Success Book* (New York: Warner, 1977).

Communicating in the Small Group

10

The Role of the Group in Problem Solving

Talented administrators know that they do not know all there is to know.

Anonymous

After finishing this chapter, you should be able to:

Define a *group*

Explain the role groups play in your life

Identify those occasions when it is more appropriate to have a group rather than an individual attempt to solve a problem

Enumerate the potential advantages and disadvantages of group problem solving

Provide examples of how *climate* affects the operations of a group

Compare and contrast a variety of decision-making methods

Demonstrate an ability to use the decision-making grid

Demonstrate an ability to apply the reflective-thinking framework to increase your problem-solving effectiveness

Describe and use the technique of *brainstorming*

I f you think about it, you probably spend a great deal of time interacting in groups. A large part of your socialization, or adapting to society, occurred in your family group. Much of your leisure time is spent in the company of groups of friends. When you attend a religious service you become part of a group. As a class member you belong to a group. Even at work you are probably expected to function as part of a team of some sort. Thus, from your earliest days to the present, and from today on, you have had and will continue to have a variety of group memberships. The simple fact is that there are more groups than people in the United States. Most of us belong to a number of different groups. For example, are you a member of two groups? Ten groups? Twenty groups? Take a moment to assess the nature of your group memberships.

Compile a list of the groups to which you belong, the groups to which you aspire to belong, and the groups to which you would refuse to belong; give your reasons for accepting, seeking, or refusing membership.

As you probably realize, groups are everywhere. Some groups you belong to for fun, some for profit. Some you join to attain prestige, others because you have to. Some help you fulfill personal or professional objectives, and others feed your moral and ethical needs and give you a sense of well-being. Groups help you define who you are. The groups to which you belong or aspire to belong tell you about your likes, preferences, and goals. The groups you shy away from or refuse to join tell you about your dislikes, fears, and values. The simple fact is that groups exert a great impact on your daily life, and you need to belong to a number of them to survive in today's world.

Some of your most important communication time will take place in one group or another. For example, it is estimated that over 11 million meetings are held each day and that at least 40 percent of your work life will be spent attending such group meetings and conferences. A recent survey showed that the typical executive spends about 700 hours per year interacting in groups. That means that two out of every five days on the job could be spent communicating in a group. Thus, whereas knowing how to relate to others in a group setting is vital if you are to attain personal success, it is critical if you are to attain professional success.[1] For this reason, although we realize that social or friendship groups are important, in this and coming chapters we will focus on the work-related problem-solving or task group. By the time you conclude your study of small-group communication, you will have internalized the information you need to understand the forces that shape and modify group behavior. We hope you also will have gained the skills you need to improve the quality of task-group interaction. And of course the knowledge and abilities you gain will be transferable to other areas of your life. Let's continue by inquiring into the nature of small-group communication. Why do we need to use small groups to begin with?

WHY INTERACT WITH OTHERS TO SOLVE PROBLEMS?

We form small groups to share information that will permit us to solve common problems and make particular decisions in order to achieve certain identified common goals. But why use small groups of people instead of a single individual?[2]

The Group versus the Individual

The purpose of this exercise is to explore the differences between individual and group decisions.

1. First complete the following tasks working alone; then complete each one as a member of a problem-solving group.

2. At the end of the exercise answer these probes: How did the group's responses differ from your own? Which were you more satisfied with? Why?

TASK 1: THE STATES
Your task is to geographically arrange the following 20 states from the easternmost (number 1) to the westernmost (number 20). Disregard north and south as factors. (Do not use maps.)

Alabama	Maine	Oklahoma
Arkansas	Minnesota	Utah
Colorado	Mississippi	Washington
Delaware	New Jersey	Wisconsin
Georgia	New Mexico	Wyoming
Idaho	New York	
Illinois	North Dakota	
	Ohio	

TASK 2: THE FOUNDATION
You are empowered to grant an award of $1 million to one and only one of the following persons. The money may not be divided among the candidates, nor may it be personally kept by the grantee. The following profiles are the only information you have about the candidates. Rank order your choices for the award from 1 (most deserving) to 10 (least deserving).

Angela is a 52-year-old nun who teaches in a depressed area. She says she will use the money to clothe, feed, house, and educate the poor.

Jamie is a 7-year-old boy who has been suffering from bone cancer for 4 years. Jamie will die unless new and expensive lifesaving procedures are used. In addition, Jamie's family would like to use the money to provide Jamie with some of the joys of childhood he has missed—including a trip to Disneyland. They say they will donate the remaining money to the Cancer Research Fund.

John is the 45-year-old director of the School for Human Resources, an organization that educates muscle-diseased youths. He needs the money to improve the school's facilities, increase its educational offerings, and hire a full-time psychologist for the students.

Jim is a 60-year-old union president and founder of the Needy Children's Scholarship Fund. He says he would use the money to send disadvantaged minority youths to college.

Simone is a 40-year-old prosperous real estate developer. She says she will use the money to become a partner in real estate deals that will return 10 times the initial investment in 5 years. With part of the profit she expects to build a modern housing project for the elderly.

Alex is a 37-year-old paraplegic who received his injuries during the Vietnam war. Although his handicap qualifies him for disability benefits, Alex refuses to accept them. Alex would use the money to help other disabled veterans lead a more normal life.

Mickey is an orphaned college student majoring in physics. He supports himself and his two younger sisters by taking odd jobs. Mickey hopes to become a nuclear physicist. He would use the money to take care of his family and pay for his education.

Amy is 24 years old and a promising medical student. When she was 2 days old she was adopted by the Nelsons. Although she loves her family, Amy would like to find and meet her natural parents. She needs the money to fund her search and help with her medical school expenses.

Lynn is a 20-year-old struggling artist who refuses to use her family's money to further her career. She says she would use the award to lease or build space and purchase the materials that would enable her and a group of other aspiring artists to have the security they need to develop and show their work.

Karen is a 6-month-old mildly retarded child whose parents were killed in an automobile accident. She has been adopted by her aunt and uncle. The money would be placed in a trust and awarded to her when she reaches her twenty-first birthday.

Advantages of the Small Group

In many ways, using a group to solve a complex problem is more logical than relying on one individual working alone. Group problem solving offers a number of important advantages. First, it permits a variety of people

WHY TEAMWORK?

Advantages	Disadvantages
Facilitates pooling of resources	Encourages laziness
Increases motivation	Conflicting personal and group goals
Makes error identification easier	Domination by a few
Decisions are better received	Stubbornness leads to deadlock
Provides rewards of working with others	Riskier decisions are made
	Takes longer to reach decision

with different amounts of information and points of view to have input into the problem-solving, decision-making process, thus facilitating the pooling of resources. The broader the array of knowledge on any one particular problem, the more likely an effective solution. Second, group participation apparently increases individual motivation. Group effort often leads to greater commitment to finding a solution and then to a greater commitment to the solution itself once it has been arrived at. Third, group functioning makes it easier to identify other people's mistakes and filter out errors before they can become costly or damaging. Groups are frequently better equipped than a single person to foresee difficulties, detect weaknesses, visualize consequences, and explore possibilities. As a result they tend to produce superior decisions and solutions. Fourth, the decisions or solutions of a group tend to be better received by others than are those of an individual. As the old adage says, "There is strength in numbers." The person to whom a group solution is reported tends to respect the fact that a number of people working together came to one conclusion. Fifth, group effort is generally more pleasant and fulfilling than working alone. The group provides companionship, a chance for the affirmation of ideas and feelings, and an opportunity for self-confirmation. It is rewarding to know that others respect us enough to listen and react to what we have to say. It is even more rewarding to have our thoughts and concerns accepted by others.

> You know . . . everybody is ignorant, only of different subjects.
> *Will Rogers*

Disadvantages of the Small Group

This is not to suggest that using a group does not carry with it certain potential drawbacks. The following disadvantages of group problem solving have been identified. First, when working with a number of other people, it sometimes becomes very tempting to "lay back" and let someone else perform your duties and responsibilities. Thus, the lazy group member maintains a low profile and simply coasts along on the efforts of others. Second, personal goals sometimes conflict with group goals. As a result, people may seek to use the group to fulfill particular self-oriented objectives despite the fact they might interfere with or sabotage the realization of group objectives. Third, the decision-making, problem-solving process may be dominated by only a few forceful, persistent members who do not take the time to ensure that all members have a chance to speak and be heard. Actual or perceived status plays a part here as well. Group members may be hesitant to criticize the comments of high-status individuals, and low-status individuals may be reluctant to participate at all. Consequently, position and power can affect whether ideas are offered, listened to, or incorporated into group decisions. Fourth, certain individuals who are set upon having their ideas and only their ideas accepted may be unwilling to compromise. When this happens, the group decision-making "machinery" breaks down, and frequently no solution is agreed upon. In other words, the group becomes deadlocked. Fifth, the decisions reached and the actions taken after a group discussion are often riskier than the decisions individuals would have made and the actions they would have taken prior to discussion. This phenomenon has been termed "the risky shift." Sixth, it often takes longer to reach a group solution than to formulate an individual one. In business and industry, since time is frequently equated with money, the group turns out to be a costly tool.

When to Use a Group to Solve a Problem

As a new employee, what problems might you experience when interacting with others in a problem-solving group?

In view of the foregoing pros and cons, we may now ask: When does it make sense to use a group? At what point do the advantages outweigh the possible disadvantages? Experience has demonstrated that a group rather than an individual should be used to solve a problem if the answers to most of the following questions are yes instead of no.

1. Is the problem complex rather than simple?
2. Does the problem have many parts or facets?
3. Would any one person be unlikely to possess all the information needed to solve the problem?
4. Would it be advisable to divide up the problem-solving responsibilities?
5. Are many potential solutions desired rather than a single potential solution?
6. Would the examination of diverse attitudes be helpful?
7. Are the group members more likely to engage in tasklike than nontasklike behavior?

In these complex times, it often makes sense for individuals of varied expertise to join together and pool their knowledge and insight to help solve the problems confronting them. Note that we said "pool their *knowledge* and *insight*." Group effort is futile if the members are able to pool only ignorance and obstinacy. As we shall see, the kind of interaction that yields an array of relevant data is an essential ingredient in successful group work. The more information gathering and sharing the members can do, the more likely they are to rid themselves of bias, and in turn the more objective their work becomes.

Thus far we have established when and why it makes sense to use a group. It is time now to attempt to answer the following two questions: What exactly is a group? How can you tell when you are part of a group?

GROUP CHARACTERISTICS
AND COMPONENTS

Is explaining what the word *group* means easy? Try your hand at it now. Generate five different responses for each of the following sentence starters:

1. A *group* is . . . .
2. A *group* is not . . . .

Defining a group is tricky business.[3] First, a *group* is a collection of people. It is not just a random assemblage of independent individuals, however, but is composed of individuals who interact verbally and nonverbally, occupy certain roles with respect to one another, and cooperate to accomplish a definite goal. The members of a group recognize the other individuals who are part of the activity, have certain kinds of attitudes toward these people, and obtain some degree of satisfaction from belonging to or participating in the group. The interactants within the group acknowledge the dos and don'ts of group life, the norms that specify and regulate the behavior expected of members. Furthermore, communication within a group involves more than the casual banter that occurs between strangers at bus stops or in department stores.

Just because a number of people are present in a particular space at the same time does not mean a group exists. Thus, under ordinary conditions, the passengers in a train or elevator are not a group. (However, should the train or elevator break down or experience difficulty, they might become a group in order to meet the demands of the new situation.) Rather, the members of a group consistently influence and are influenced by each other; that is, interaction in the form of mutual influence occurs. The individual members of the group affect the character of the group and are also affected by it. Researchers have found that for most tasks, groups of five to seven people work best. This size enables members to communicate directly with each other as they work toward accomplishing a common task or goal, such as problem solving, information exchange, or the development of improved interpersonal relationships.

Every group establishes its own goals, its own structure and communication patterns, its own norms, and its own "climate." Every participant in the group usually has a stake in the outcome, will develop relationships with the other members of the group, and will assume roles that relate to group tasks and/or interpersonal relationships that either foster or impede group effectiveness. Thus the interaction styles of members will have an impact on the kind of atmosphere or climate that develops in the group. Conversely, the climate will affect what members say to each other as well as the way they say it. For example, have you ever belonged to a group that had "too hot" a climate—one in which members were intolerant of each other and tempers flared? Have you ever belonged to a group that had "too cold" a climate—one in which members were aloof, sarcastic, unconcerned about hurting one another's feelings, or too self-centered to notice that the needs of others were not being adequately met?

If the predominant group climate is cold, closed, mistrustful, or uncooperative, individual members will frequently react in ways that sustain the feeling. In contrast, if the predominant group climate is warm, open, trusting, and cooperative, members will usually react in ways that reinforce those characteristics. In the book *Communication within the Organization*, Charles Redding has suggested that an effective climate consists of the following ingredients: (1) supportiveness, (2) participative decision making, (3) trust among group members, (4) openness and candor, and (5) high performance goals.[4] The healthier the group climate, the more cohesive the group.

Select two groups you belonged (or belong) to that are representative of what you believe to be an effective climate and an ineffective climate. For each group, identify the types of behavior exhibited by members. How did each climate affect your own participation in the group? How did each climate affect your relationship with other group members?

Many decisions that affect your life are made in group meetings. Some aspect of this man's health or life style may be the topic of this discussion between patient and doctors, and the result of the discussion could be a decision that will affect his daily life. (J. Berndt/Stock Boston)

Group climate also affects group norms, the explicit and implicit rules that members internalize concerning their behavior. In some groups we would exhibit certain behaviors that we would not dare exhibit in others. For example, in which groups that you belong to would you feel free to ask a question that might be considered "dumb," interrupt someone who is talking, express disagreement with another member, openly express support for an unpopular position, point out that someone isn't making sense, offer a comment unrelated to the topic, or simply not attend a meeting? In some groups interaction is formal and stuffy; in others it is informal and relaxed. Groups invariably create standards that they expect members to live up to. In this way a group is able to foster a certain degree of uniformity. In coming chapters we'll take a closer look at the communication patterns, roles, leadership behaviors, and problems that develop in groups. For now, let us recognize that certain attributes can help implement the group process whereas others work against it. Organizational communication theorist Douglas McGregor summarizes the characteristics of an effective and well-functioning group:

1. The atmosphere tends to be informal, comfortable, relaxed.
2. There is a lot of discussion in which virtually everyone participates, but it remains pertinent to the task of the group.
3. The task or objective of the group is well understood and accepted by the members. There will have been free discussion of the objective at some point until it was formulated in such a way that the members of the group could commit themselves to it.
4. The members listen to each other. Every idea is given a hearing. People do not appear to be afraid of being foolish by putting forth a creative thought even if it seems fairly extreme.
5. There is disagreement. Disagreements are not suppressed or overridden by premature action. The reasons are carefully examined, and the group seeks to resolve them rather than to dominate the dissenter.
6. Most decisions are reached by a kind of consensus in which it is clear that everyone is in general agreement and willing to go along. Formal voting is at a minimum; the group does not accept a simple majority as a proper basis for action.
7. Criticism is frequent, frank, and relatively comfortable. There is little evidence of personal attack, either openly or in a hidden fashion.
8. People are free in expressing their feelings as well as their ideas both on the problem and on the group's operation.
9. When action is taken, clear assignments are made and accepted.
10. The chairman of the group does not dominate it, nor on the

contrary does the group defer unduly to him. In fact, the leadership shifts from time to time, depending upon the circumstances. There is little evidence of a struggle for power as the group operates. The issue is not who controls but how to get the job done.

11. The group is self-conscious of its own operation.[5]

As we mentioned earlier, every group has a goal—a reason for existing. We turn next to examining how groups reach these goals.

DECISION MAKING: REACHING GOALS

In our society critical decisions are usually relegated to a group; depending on the group, a wide variety of decision-making strategies or approaches may be used. Let us investigate the diverse methods members can adopt to arrive at a decision as well as the advantages and disadvantages of each approach. Start by considering these questions. How do the groups to which you belong make decisions? Do different groups use different strategies? Why? Does the method any one group employs change from time to time? Why? Are you happy with each group's decision-making approach?

Methods of Decision Making

As we mentioned, there are a number of different methods that groups use in making decisions. Before we examine them, use the following list to decide which decision-making strategy or strategies a group you belong to would employ most often if you had your way. Do this by ranking the possibilities from 1 (most favorable) to 8 (least favorable).

Ask an expert on the topic to make the decision.

Flip a coin.

Let the majority rule.

Let the group leader make the decision.

Stall until a decision no longer needs to be made.

Let the minority rule, because that's sometimes fair.

Determine the "average" position, since this will be least offensive to anyone.

Reach a decision by consensus, that is, be certain all have had input into the discussion, understood the decision, can rephrase it, and will publicly support it.

After considering these alternatives, examine the implications of your responses.

As the preceding list reveals, among the methods employed by groups to make decisions are (1) decision by an expert, (2) decision by chance, (3) decision by the majority, (4) decision by the leader, (5) total deferral of decision, (6) decision by the minority, (7) decision by averaging individual decisions, and (8) decision by consensus. Each method has certain advantages and is more appropriate and workable under certain conditions than others. An effective group bases its decision-making strategy on a number of variables, including (1) the nature of the problem, (2) the time available to the group to solve the problem, and (3) the kind of climate in which the group enjoys operating. Try the exercise in the Skill Builder "Lost on the Moon" to see how effective each strategy is for your group.

Experience has shown that the decision-making methods of groups vary considerably in their effectiveness. *Majority vote* is the method used most frequently. Most elections are decided in this way, many laws are passed using this approach, and a large number of decisions are made on the basis of the vote of 51 percent of a group's members. Lest we overlook the importance of the *minority*, however, we should note that it too can carry weight. Think of how often committees subdivide responsibilities with the result that subgroups actually end up making the key recommendations and thus the key decisions. Another popular decision-making strategy is *averaging*. Under the rule of averaging, the most popular decision becomes the group's decision. (In the case of "Lost on the Moon," p. 264, the average response of each group could have been obtained by summing all member answers and then dividing by the number of members in the group.) Letting the *expert* member decide what the group should do is also used at times. In this case the group simply defers its decision-making power to its most knowledgeable member. In many other groups the *leader* retains all the decision-making power. Sometimes this is done after consultation with group members, at other times prior to consultation.

Although each method just mentioned has been used successfully by a variety of groups, the most effective decision-making strategy has been found to be *decision by consensus*. When a group achieves consensus, all members agree what the decision should be. Even more important, all help formulate the decision by voicing their feelings and airing their differences of opinion. Thus all understand the decision and will support it. Research also shows that the greater the *involvement* of members in the decision-making process, the more effective the decision will be. Of course, decisions by the leader, by the expert, or by majority or minority vote all take less time than consensus; however, it should be remembered that after all, it is the group that will usually be responsible for implementing the decision. If members disagree with a decision or do not understand it, they may not work very hard to make it succeed. A leader may make routine decisions

Identify the methods of decision making that are employed most often in your class. At home. At your place of employment. Are you satisfied with them? Why?

or may be called on to make decisions when little time is available for a real discussion of the issues, but under most circumstances, one person cannot be the best resource for all decisions. In addition, a drawback of the decision-by-expert method is that it is sometimes difficult to determine who the expert is. Also, it, like the decision by the leader system, fails to provide for the involvement of other group members. Averaging, on the whole, is superior to both the designated-leader and the expert methods. The average position doesn't dissatisfy anyone too much, but neither does it satisfy anyone too much. Thus, although averaging permits individual errors to cancel themselves out and, at the least, all members to be consulted, commitment to the decision usually is not very great.

Thus, under most circumstances the quality of decision making and the satisfaction of the participants are higher when the consensus approach is used. Why? Because consensus puts the resources of the entire group to effective use, permits the discussion of all issues and alternatives, and ensures the commitment of all members to the decision's implementation. From this we can see that it is not just decision adequacy that is important in group interaction; we must also be concerned with the reactions and feelings of group members.

SKILL BUILDER

How do you influence a group? What behaviors let some people exert more influence than others?

"Lost on the Moon"

You are a member of a space crew originally scheduled to rendezvous with a mother ship on the lighted surface of the Moon. Mechanical difficulties, however, have forced your ship to crash-land at a spot some 200 miles from the rendezvous point. The rough landing has damaged much of the equipment aboard your module. Since survival depends on reaching the mother ship, the most critical items available must be chosen for the 200-mile trip. Below are listed the 15 items left intact after landing. Your task is to rank them in order of their importance to you and your crew in attempting to reach the rendezvous point. Your number 1 choice should be the most important item, your number 2 choice the next most important, and so on, up to number 15, the least important item.

One box of matches
Food concentrate
Nylon rope (50 feet)
Parachute silk
Two .45-caliber pistols
One case of dehydrated milk
Two 100-pound tanks of oxygen
Stellar map of Moon's constellations

Life raft
Magnetic compass
Five gallons of water
Signal flares
First-aid kit with injection needles
Solar-powered FM receiver-transmitter
Portable heating unit

1. Divide your class into groups. For each group, designate one individual as leader and another (the one with the most knowledge on the topic) as expert.

2. Next, working first individually and without discussion, rank the items listed above in terms of their importance in reaching your destination.

3. Make a copy of your individual ranking. (Leaders should write "Leader" on their copies, and the most knowledgeable members should write "Expert" on their copies.) Submit your sheets to your instructor, who will then compute leader, expert, average, majority, and minority scores for the total class.

4. Attempt to reach a group ranking of the items described above by employing the strategy of consensus.

5. At the end of the work period your instructor will provide you with the correct ranking.
   a. Determine the numerical difference between your group's score and the correct answer.
   b. Add all differences together to determine the overall rating of your group. The lower the score, the more accurate the ranking.

6. Compare and contrast the effectiveness of the various decision-making methods.

A problem can develop when you have a group meeting and the boss acts as if he or she is sitting on a "15" when actually it's an "89." What can be done to prevent this from damaging the group's effectiveness?

Remember, at issue is how well the group handles all its resources.

The Decision-Making Grid

How do you behave when engaged in collective problem solving? The next list will provide you with a generalized indication of your own behavior in a problem-solving group. From the following set of possibilities, choose the approach that best characterizes your personal decision-making style. Rank your behavior from 1 (most characteristic) to 5 (least characteristic).

When my group is engaged in the decision-making process, I:

Sit back and let others make the decision for me.
Am concerned that a decision work, not whether others like it.

Am concerned that members are satisfied with the decision, not whether it will work.

Sacrifice my own feelings in order to reach a decision that can be implemented.

Work for everyone to discuss, understand, agree to, and be satisfied with a decision.

The decision-making grid, adapted from the work of Jay Hall, Vincent O'Leary, and Martha Williams, can help you understand your responses (see Figure 10-1). It offers a visual depiction of the relationship between concern that a decision work (concern for decision adequacy) and concern for the commitment of others to the decision (concern for commitment).[6] As we see from the grid ratings, if you characteristically sit back and let others do the decision making, you exemplify a 1/1 decision-making style (i.e., low concern for decision adequacy/low concern for commitment). If you insist that the quality of the decision is more important than the "happiness" of group members, you represent a 9/1 decision-making style. The exact opposite of this type of person is the individual who is more concerned about group support for the decision than about its quality or workability. Such an individual illustrates the 1/9 style. The middle position, the 5/5 decision-making style, is typical of the sacrificer/compromiser, who is willing to give in in order to get the job done. Finally, if you characteristically employ a 9/9 decision-making style, you adhere to the belief that a consensus is possible if all group resources are used, if members feel free to express their opinions and ideas, and if importance is given both to the task itself and to the maintenance (social and emotional, or member-satisfaction) dimension of the decision-making process.

Questions for Decision Making

Three key kinds of questions constitute the content of decision making: questions of fact, questions of value, and questions of policy.

Questions of fact are concerned with the truth or falsity of a statement. Existing information may conflict, and group members are required to ferret out the truth. For example, a group might be asked to determine whether evidence proved beyond a doubt that Bruno Hauptmann kidnapped and murdered Charles Lindbergh's child or whether Sam Shepherd murdered his wife. Questions might be phrased like this: What evidence supports the guilt or innocence of _____? Similarly, a group might wrestle with questions like these: What is the likelihood of a nuclear winter following a nuclear war? What are the effects of depletion of the ozone layer of the atmosphere? As you can see, answering questions like these requires that a group examine and interpret the available data carefully.

In contrast, *questions of value* are not fact-based; rather, they involve

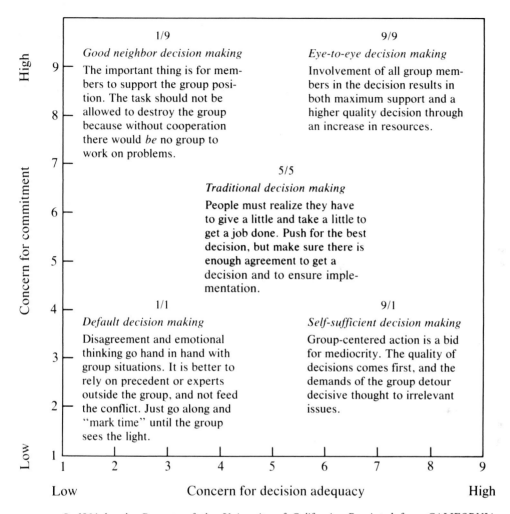

1/9

Good neighbor decision making

The important thing is for members to support the group position. The task should not be allowed to destroy the group because without cooperation there would *be* no group to work on problems.

9/9

Eye-to-eye decision making

Involvement of all group members in the decision results in both maximum support and a higher quality decision through an increase in resources.

5/5

Traditional decision making

People must realize they have to give a little and take a little to get a job done. Push for the best decision, but make sure there is enough agreement to get a decision and to ensure implementation.

1/1

Default decision making

Disagreement and emotional thinking go hand in hand with group situations. It is better to rely on precedent or experts outside the group, and not feed the conflict. Just go along and "mark time" until the group sees the light.

9/1

Self-sufficient decision making

Group-centered action is a bid for mediocrity. The quality of decisions comes first, and the demands of the group detour decisive thought to irrelevant issues.

Concern for commitment (High / Low) — vertical axis 1–9

Concern for decision adequacy (Low / High) — horizontal axis 1–9

© 1964 by the Regents of the University of California. Reprinted from CALIFORNIA MANAGEMENT REVIEW, Vol. VII, No. 2, pp. 45–46 by permission of the Regents.

FIGURE 10-1
The Decision-Making Grid.

the issuance of subjective judgments. Who was the best President to serve in the last 100 years? is a question of value. So are the following: To what degree is a college education valuable to all Americans? What is the desirability of physical fitness programs? To what extent, if any, is the use of laboratory animals for scientific research justified?

On the other hand, *questions of policy* are designed to help us determine what future action(s), if any, should be taken. In fact, the key word in a question of policy is the word *should:* What should colleges do to prevent student suicides? What should the United States do to discourage terrorism? What should federal policy be regarding the sale of semiautomatic military-style weapons to members of the general public?

A Decision-Making Framework

The quality of a group's decision making depends at least partly on the nature of the particular decision-making system that members use to arrive at a decision. There is a generally agreed upon structure containing a number of stages which, if used properly, can help increase the problem-solving effectiveness of most groups. This is called the reflective-thinking framework, and it was first proposed by John Dewey in 1910. It probably still is the sequence most commonly used by problem-solving groups.[7]

The reflective-thinking framework contains six basic components: (1) *What is the problem?* Is it clearly defined? Do we understand the general situation in which it is occurring? Is it stated so as not to arouse defensiveness? Is it phrased so as not to permit simply a yes or no answer? (For example, "What should the college's policy be toward final exams for seniors?" instead of "Should the college stop wasting the time of its seniors and eliminate final exams for them?" or "What should the government's policy be toward gun control?" instead of "What can the government do to put an end to trigger-happy hunters?") (2) *What are the facts of the situation?* What are its causes? What is the problem's history? Why is it important? Whom does it affect, and how? (3) *What criteria must an acceptable solution meet?* By which and/or whose standards must a solution be evaluated? What are the principal requirements of the solution? How important is each criterion? (4) *What are the possible solutions?* How would each remedy the problem? How well does each satisfy the criteria? What are the advantages and/or disadvantages of each? (5) *Which is the best solution?* How would you rank the solutions? Which offers the greatest number of advantages and the smallest number of disadvantages? Would some combination of solutions be beneficial? (6) *How can the solution be implemented?* What steps need to be taken to put the solution into effect?

To make this framework function, it is necessary for every member of the group to cultivate an attitude of suspended judgment. This means the interactants must be open to all available ideas, facts, and opinions. Instead of insisting on the rightness of your own position and closing yourself to new information, you will need to adequately explore all the major variables that contributed to the creation of the problem and investigate all the major issues that may be involved in producing a workable solution. As you make your way through the framework, ask yourself if (1) the resources of all the group members are being well used, (2) the group uses its time to advantage, (3) the group places optimum emphasis on fact-finding and inquiry, (4) members listen to and respect one another's opinions and feelings, (5) pressure to conform is kept to a minimum while an honest search for diverse ideas is made, and (6) a supportive (noncritical), trusting (nonthreatening), cooperative (noncompetitive) atmosphere prevails. Remember, if group members are afraid to speak up, close-minded, reluctant to search for information, or not motivated to solve the problems at hand, they will not perform effectively.

Brainstorming: The Search for Better Ideas

According to a number of researchers, the best way to have a *good* idea is to have *lots* of ideas. Frequently, however, instead of suspending evaluation and permitting ideas to develop freely, problem solvers tend to grasp at the first solution that comes to mind. Recognizing that this practice inhibits the search for new avenues of thought, Alex Osborn devised a technique called *brainstorming*.[8] This method is used primarily to promote a free flow of ideas and can be incorporated into the problem-solving process itself. For instance, although brainstorming is used most frequently when group members are attempting to identify a solution, it can also be used to help identify the factors that caused the problem, the criteria that a solution should meet, and ways to implement the solution.

To ensure that brainstorming sessions are successful, group members need to adhere to certain guidelines:

> I had an immense advantage over many others dealing with the problem inasmuch as I had no fixed ideas derived from long-established practice to control and bias my mind, and did not suffer from the general belief that whatever is, is right.
>
> *Henry Bessemer (discovered a new method of producing steel)*

1. Temporarily suspend evaluation and criticism of ideas. Instead, adopt a "try anything" attitude. This will encourage rather than stifle the flow of ideas.

2. Encourage freewheeling. The wilder the ideas offered, the better. It is easier to tame an idea later than to invent or invigorate one. At this point, the practicality of an idea is not of primary importance.

3. Think of as many ideas as you can. At this stage the quantity, not quality, of ideas is important. The greater the number of ideas, the better the chance of finding a good one. Thus, no self-censorship or group censorship is permitted. All ideas should be expressed.

4. Build on and improve or modify the ideas of others. Work to mix ideas until they form interesting combinations. Remember, brainstorming is a group effort.

5. Record all ideas. This ensures that the group will have available all the ideas that have been generated during the session.

How is brainstorming related to what researcher Rosabeth Moss Kanter calls "kaleidoscope thinking"? According to Kanter:

A kaleidoscope takes a set of fragments and forms them into a pattern. But when the kaleidoscope is twisted or approached from a new angle, the same fragments form a different pattern. Kaleidoscope thinking, then, involves taking existing data and twisting it or looking at it from another angle in order to see and analyze the new patterns that appear.

Brainpower

CASE 1: A STITCH IN TIME . . .

A woman was surprised to discover that her somewhat eccentric uncle had left her over 1 million empty spools of thread in his will. Since she was an enterprising individual, she decided to turn her inheritance into a business. Working with four to six other individuals, your group's task is to use the next few minutes to generate as many uses for empty spools of thread as you can.

CASE 2: WARNING SIGNS

What methods can we employ to warn people who are alive 10,000 years from now that they should stay away from today's nuclear waste-dumping areas? Again, working with your group, your task is to generate as many ways to warn people as you can.

After completing these activities, answer the following probes:

1. How satisfied were you with the group effort? Why?
   a. Case 1:   Satisfied   1   2   3   4   5   Dissatisfied
   b. Case 2:   Satisfied   1   2   3   4   5   Dissatisfied

2. Which brainstorming guidelines were adhered to? How do you know?

3. Which brainstorming guidelines were ignored or not fulfilled? Why?

6. Only after the brainstorming session is finished should group members evaluate the ideas for usefulness and applicability.

Brainstorming is effective because it lessens the inhibitions of members and makes it easier for them to get their ideas heard; promotes a warmer, more playful, enthusiastic, and cooperative atmosphere; and encourages each individual's potential for creativity. But perhaps the most unique benefit of brainstorming is suspended judgment.

Too often, one or two group members stifle the creative thinking effort of a brainstorming group. Despite the lip service they may pay to the importance of suspending judgment, such persons come to the problem-solving experience with an "evaluative set." According to creative-thinking researcher Sidney Parnes, this attitude surfaces in the form of "killer phrases" or groups of words that stop the flow of ideas. This practice strikes at the very heart and nature of the brainstorming process. It replaces the "green light" of brainstorming not merely with the "yellow light" of criticism or thoughtful evaluation but with the "red light" of frozen judgment. We should note that "killer phrases" are often accompanied or replaced by "killer looks"—looks that discourage or inhibit the generating of ideas. (How often do killer phrases or looks intrude upon your group experiences?) By gaining insight into the types and effects of creative-thinking killers, you can increase your ability to analyze your own small-group behavior and change it if you wish.

HOW TO IMPROVE YOUR PROBLEM-SOLVING SKILLS

For a problem-solving group to be effective, certain characteristics need to be present, and concerned individuals must work to realize these qualities when functioning as group members. By developing an awareness of the difference between optimal or ideal problem-solving behaviors and the behaviors with which you and your fellow group members approach problem solving, you can begin to improve your group's method and style of operation. An effective group exhibits these characteristics:

1. Group goals are clearly understood and cooperatively formulated by the members. Goals are not merely imposed. If group members are confused about the nature of the problem, they will not be able to solve it. (As group theorists Bobby R. Patton and Kim Giffin stress, "If we aim at nothing, we are pretty apt to hit it.")

2. All members of the group are encouraged to communicate their ideas and feelings freely. Ideas and feelings are valued; they are neither ignored nor suppressed. Keynote personalized phrases to use are "I think," "I see," and "I feel." These elements reveal a personal point of view and indicate that you recognize that someone else may feel, think, or see differently from the way you do.

3. Group members seek to reach a consensus when the decision is an important one. Input from all members is sought. Each member's involvement is considered critical. Thus, the decision is not left to an "authority" to make on the basis of little or no discussion.

4. Consideration is given to both the task and maintenance dimensions of the problem-solving effort. Both the quality of the decision and the well-being of the group members are considered important.

5. Group members do not set about haphazardly to solve a problem. A problem-solving framework is used, and an outline is followed that aids the group in its search for relevant information.

6. The motivation level is high. Group members are anxious to search for information, speak up, listen to others, and engage in an active and honest search for a "better" solution. They neither jump

impetuously at the first solution that presents itself nor prematurely criticize and evaluate ideas.

7. An effort is made to assess the group's problem-solving style to identify and alleviate factors that impede its effectiveness as well as to identify and foster factors that enhance its effectiveness.

SUMMARY

In communication theory, a *group* is defined as a collection of people who interact verbally and nonverbally, occupy certain roles with respect to one another, and cooperate with each other to accomplish a definite goal. Some of our most important communication experiences occur in small groups. Small groups are used to solve common problems and make decisions by sharing information.

The advantages of using a group of people instead of an individual are that resources can be pooled, individual motivation is increased, errors are more likely to be detected, decisions are more readily accepted by those outside the group, and the group members have an opportunity to enjoy the companionship and rewards of working with others. There are, however, potential disadvantages of group problem solving: It may encourage laziness among particular members, conflict may arise between personal and group goals, the group may be dominated by a few, the stubbornness of one or two members may lead to deadlock, the group may make an excessively risky decision, and the decision itself usually takes longer to reach.

To operate effectively, group members need to be supportive; exercise participative decision making; show trust, openness, and candor; and set high performance goals. The healthier the group climate, the more cohesive the group.

There are a number of different methods groups use to make decisions—decision by an expert, by chance, by majority, by the leader, by the minority, by averaging individual decisions, and by consensus—or the group can defer a decision entirely. Making decisions by consensus is considered the most effective strategy. When a group achieves consensus, all members have helped formulate the decision, all have agreed what the decision should be, and all will support the decision.

The behavior of group members can be plotted and analyzed on the decision-making grid, which provides a visual depiction of the relationship between the concern that a decision will actually work and the concern that the other group members will be committed to the decision. Most groups can improve their problem-solving effectiveness by using the reflective-thinking framework, a systematic six-step approach to decision making. Another technique that is useful in some situations is brainstorming, which encourages each member's potential for creativity.

SUGGESTIONS FOR FURTHER READING

Bormann, Ernest G. *Discussion and Group Methods: Theory and Practice*, 2d ed. New York: Harper & Row, 1975. A thorough examination of small groups.

Jay, Anthony. "How to Run a Meeting," *Harvard Business Review*, Vol. 54 (March–April 1976), pp. 43–57. This interesting article describes the types of things that can go wrong in meetings and how to right them.

Johnson, David W., and Frank P. Johnson. *Joining Together: Group Theory and Group Skills*. Englewood Cliffs, N.J.: Prentice-Hall, 1975. Provides both theory and practice opportunities. Readable examination of the dynamics of small-group communication.

McGregor, Douglas. "The Human Side of Enterprise." In *Human Relations and Organizational Behavior*, edited by K. Davis and W. Scott. New York: McGraw-Hill, 1969. Clearly compares and contrasts "theory X" with "theory Y."

Phillips, Gerald M., Douglas J. Pedersen, and Julia T. Wood. *Group Discussion: A Practical Guide to Participation and Leadership*. Boston: Houghton Mifflin, 1979. A practical resource for problem solvers.

Redding, Charles. *Communication within the Organization*. New York: Industrial Communication Council, 1972. Very readable and comprehensive, but hard to find.

NOTES

1. Vincent DiSalvo, "A Summary of Current Research Identifying Communication Skills in Various Organizational Contexts," *Communication Education*, Vol. 29 (1980), pp. 281–290.

2. For a discussion of the issue of individual versus group decision making see G. Walson and D. W. Johnson, *Social Psychology: Issues and Insights*, 2d ed. (Philadelphia: Lippincott, 1972).

3. There are numerous definitions of the word *group*. For a sampling, see *Small Group Communication: A Reader*, 3d ed., edited by Robert S. Cathcart and Larry A. Samovar (Dubuque, Iowa: William C. Brown, 1979); David W. Johnson and Frank P. Johnson, *Joining Together: Group Theory and Group Skills* (Englewood Cliffs, N.J.: Prentice-Hall, 1975); and Marvin E. Shaw, *Group Dynamics: The Psychology of Small Group Behavior*, 3d ed (New York: McGraw-Hill, 1981).

4. Charles Redding, *Communication within the Organization* (New York: Industrial Communication Council, 1972).

5. Douglas McGregor, *The Human Side of Enterprise* (New York: McGraw-Hill, 1960).

6. J. Hall, V. O'Leary, and M. Williams, "The Decision-Making Grid: A Model of Decision-Making Styles," *California Management Review* (Winter 1964), pp. 45–46.

7. John Dewey, *How We Think* (Boston: Heath, 1910).

8. A. F. Osborne, *Applied Imagination* (New York: Scribner, 1957).

Group Networks, Membership, and Leadership

I will pay more for the ability to deal with people than any other ability under the sun.

John D. Rockefeller

CHAPTER PREVIEW

After finishing this chapter, you should be able to:

Explain how networks affect group interaction

Define *group role*

Compare and contrast task, maintenance, and self-serving roles

Define *leadership*

Distinguish between the following leadership styles: type X, type Y, the autocratic leader, the democratic leader, and the laissez-faire leader

Describe how trait theory, situation theory, and functional theory contribute to our knowledge of leadership

Explain how cooperation and competition manifest themselves in group interactions

Identify behaviors that contribute to the formation of defensive and supportive group climates

Demonstrate your ability to improve communication among the members of a group

I n this chapter we will explore the various dimensions of group membership and the meaning of leadership; we will also elaborate on the characteristics of effective group communication. By gaining insights into the various roles performed by members and leaders, by familiarizing ourselves with the communication styles open to us, and by seeing how role expectations, leadership, and networks (communication patterns) affect group performance, we will be better equipped to analyze our own behavior in problem-solving groups.

NETWORKS: WHO TALKS TO WHOM

Very few ideas and very few projects of any significance are implemented by one person alone.

Rosabeth Moss Kanter

Any group's ability to accomplish its task is related to the interactions of its members. It is all but impossible for a small group to communicate well unless the members are comfortable in speaking with one another, feel free to express their ideas and feelings to each other, and have an opportunity to receive feedback about how they are coming across. If you are able and willing to communicate with most, if not all, the members of your group, you can be said to occupy a *central position* in the group. In contrast, if you relate to only one or at the most a few people in your group, you occupy a *peripheral position*. It is the group's networks that determine the communication paths open to members and the effectiveness of their interactions. Figure 11-1 illustrates representative types of networks.

The first group network studies were conducted by the sociological researchers Bavelas and Leavitt.[1] Bavelas studied four communication patterns: the circle, the line, the star (or wheel), and the Y. For each pattern, he measured the time it took group members to solve a simple problem and the satisfaction of group members with the operation of the group. Bavelas discovered that the Y pattern was the most efficient; that is, it enabled the members to solve the problem presented to them in the shortest time. However, he also discovered that members who belonged to the circle group had the highest morale. In addition, results indicated that persons who occupied central positions in group networks were more satisfied with the group's operation than were members who occupied peripheral positions.

Like Bavelas, Leavitt studied four patterns of communication: the circle, the chain (or line), the Y, and the wheel (or star). In Leavitt's experiments, the members in each of these groups had to discover a common symbol included on cards provided to them. Leavitt's results indicated that

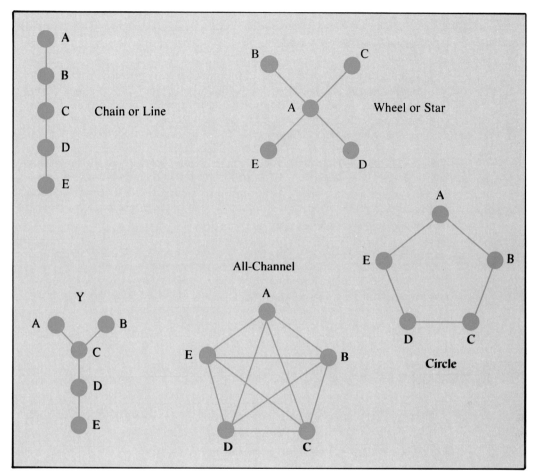

FIGURE 11-1
Communication networks

the network with the greatest degree of shared centrality (the circle) produced the highest morale among group members; members limited to using the network with the lowest degree of shared centrality (the wheel) required the shortest time to come up with an accurate solution. In addition, in most groups the person who occupied the centralmost position was declared to be the leader. Thus, the circle was said to possess shared leadership, whereas other groups had one clearly emergent leader.

   We can see that the particular type of communication network employed by a group determines which communication channels are open

Central or Peripheral?

The purpose of this exercise is to increase your awareness of the effect networks have on the satisfaction level and efficiency of problem-solving groups. Your instructor will divide the class into groups containing from five to six individuals each. Each group will be required to use one of the networks shown in Figure 11-1. You may communicate with only the members to whom you are directly linked. Thus, in the wheel formation, for example, only if you are A can you communicate with all the members of the group; if you are B, C, D, or E, you may communicate with other members through A only. (Note that only in the all-channel network are the lines of communication completely free and open to each member.) Complete the following:

1. Using only written messages sent directly to the person(s) with whom you are permitted to communicate, your task is to reach unanimous agreement on the number of squares contained in the following diagram. Your group will be considered to have completed the task when each person in the group has reported the group's decision to your instructor.

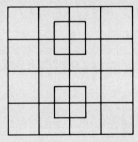

2. Maintaining the same group formations assigned for item 1, rank the following list of a small-group communicator's attributes from 1 (most important) to 10 (least important). Your group will be considered to have completed the task when each person has reported the group's decision to your instructor.

> High self-esteem
> Ability to express oneself fluently
> Ability to get along well with others
> Goal-oriented
> Highly intelligent
> Prolific generator of ideas
> Strong problem-solving ability
> Strong leadership qualities
> Does not automatically agree with superiors
> Self-disciplined

3. When tasks 1 and 2 have been completed, answer these probes:
   a. Network my group used:
   b. Time we required to complete the task:
   c. How did the time your group used compare with the time consumed by other groups?
   d. Rank the extent to which you enjoyed being a member of your group:

      Very much   1   2   3   4   5   Not at all

   e. What was your group's average level of enjoyment score? (To compute this, add the individual scores together and divide by the number of persons in your group.)
   f. How did your group's enjoyment level compare with the enjoyment level of the other groups?
   g. Do you think your group had a leader? If so, who?
   h. To what extent do you think your group's network helped or hindered your own performance? Explain.

or closed and thus helps determine who talks to whom. When people are cut off from relating to each other, individual satisfaction suffers. Thus it makes sense that overall group morale increases when decentralized networks (networks with *shared centrality*) are used. In addition, other studies have shown that although centralized networks (networks high in isolate, or peripheral, members) produce faster solutions to a simple problem, decentralized networks are more efficient if the problem is more complex. (It seems that if a problem is complex and the group network is centralized, the member in the central position begins to suffer from "information overload," thus decreasing efficiency.)

From the studies just described we see that if we can trace the types of communication patterns that groups use when attempting to solve problems, we will more readily understand why some group members feel frustrated while others feel content, why some feel they are able to exert power while others feel powerless, and why some enjoy the group experience while others abhor it. Having an opportunity to interact with others, give and gain information directly from others, and exert some control over the operation of the group is essential if members are to believe they can contribute to the group, are to be satisfied with the group process, and are to be motivated to continue their participation in the group. For a group to be effective, the members need to realize that it is up to them to elicit contributions from one another and to encourage effective communication among all members. Thus, a completely connected pattern of group communication is usually the most desirable.

MEMBER RESPONSIBILITIES: GROUP ROLES

What type of group member do you consider yourself? In order to be an effective member, you need to consider the assets or liabilities you bring with you to the group experience, the roles you perform in your group, and how your behavior either contributes to or detracts from your group's effectiveness.

List three positive and three negative qualities you bring to groups. What could others do to make you a more effective group member? How could they make you an ineffective member?

At this point it will be useful for us to examine a number of different group roles in order to determine how each contributes to or detracts from a group's performance. First, however, let us clarify that a *group role* is a type of behavior, that is, a particular kind of communicative act exhibited by a group member. Naturally, a group will perform more effectively when group members assume positive roles (functions that help accomplish the group's purpose) and avoid negative roles (behaviors that distract or frustrate the group). We may perform a number of different roles in a group, or we may prefer to perform a particular role. We may also perform certain roles in one group and completely different roles in another. For example, sometimes we may contribute in ways that promote the accomplishment of the group task, at other times we may function in ways that help maintain relationships among group members, and at still other times we may de-emphasize group objectives by exhibiting self-serving behaviors and actively seeking to meet only personal needs or goals.

Even though their role-classification model was formulated more than 30 years ago, the system proposed by Kenneth Benne and Paul Sheats is still commonly used today. It describes the functions participants should seek to assume and avoid during the life of a group.[2] Benne and Sheats considered *goal achievement* (completing the task) and *group maintenance* (relationship building) the two basic objectives of any group. They further reasoned that eliminating nonfunctional behaviors is a requirement or condition that must be met if the preceding goals are to be realized. With this premise to guide them, these researchers identified three role dimensions: (1) task-oriented roles, (2) maintenance-oriented roles, and (3) self-serving roles.

Among the task behaviors that group members may perform are the following:

Initiating: The member defines the problem; suggests methods, goals, and procedures; and starts the group moving along new paths or in different directions by offering a plan.

Information Seeking: The member asks for facts and opinions and seeks relevant information about the problem.

Opinion Seeking: The member solicits expressions of feeling and value in order to discover the values underlying the group's effort.

Information Giving: The member provides ideas and suggestions and supplies personal experiences as well as factual data.

Opinion Giving: The member supplies opinions, values, and beliefs and reveals what he or she feels about what is being discussed.

Clarifying: The member elaborates on the ideas of others, supplies paraphrases, offers examples or illustrations, and tries to clear up confusion and enhance clarity.

Coordinating: The member summarizes ideas and tries to constructively draw together various contributions.

Evaluating: The member evaluates the group's decisions or proposed solutions; she or he helps establish standards for judgment.

Consensus Testing: The member checks on the state of group agreement to see if the group is nearing a decision.

Among the maintenance behaviors members may perform are the following:

Encouraging: The member is warm, receptive, and responsive to others and praises others and their ideas.

Gate Keeping: The member attempts to keep the communication channels open; he or she helps reticent members contribute to the group and works to keep the discussion from being dominated by only one or two members.

Harmonizing: The member mediates differences between participants and attempts to reconcile misunderstandings or disagreements; she or he also tries to reduce tension levels in the group by using humor or other relief measures at appropriate junctures.

Compromising: The member is willing to compromise his or her position to maintain group cohesion; she or he is willing to admit error and modify beliefs to achieve group growth.

Standard Setting: The member assesses whether group members are satisfied with the procedures being used and indicates that criteria have been set for evaluating group functioning.

Finally, among the self-serving roles members may perform are the following:

Blocking: The member is disagreeable and digresses in an effort to ensure that nothing is accomplished.

Aggressive: The member criticizes or blames others and works to deflate the egos of other group members in an effort to enhance his or her own status.

Recognition Seeking: The member attempts to become the focus of attention by boasting about her or his own accomplishments rather than dealing with the group task; she or he may speak loudly and exhibit behavior that is unusual.

Withdrawing: The member appears indifferent, daydreams, and/or sulks.

Dominating: The member insists on getting her or his own way, interrupts others, and gives directions in an effort to "run" the group.

Joking: The member appears cynical and/or engages in horseplay or other "out-of-field" behaviors.

Self-Confessing: The member uses other group members as an audience and reveals personal, non-group-oriented "feelings" or "insights."

Help Seeking: The member tries to elicit sympathy or pity from fellow members.

SKILL BUILDER

Role Call

1. Form groups containing from five to seven individuals each. Select two members of each group to serve as group-process observers.

2. While the observers chart the roles members perform during the life of the group, each set of group members is to complete the following tasks:
   a. Use materials like cotton, pipe cleaners, construction paper, tape, glue, scissors, and string to build a container that will support and catch an uncooked egg dropped from a height of five feet without damaging the shell.
   b. Choose a group name and design a group symbol to affix to your egg container.

3. With the aid of your process observers, answer these probes:
   a. How did the group organize for work?
   b. To what extent was participation evenly distributed?
   c. Which task or maintenance functions did various members perform?
   d. Which task or maintenance functions were lacking or not sufficiently present, inhibiting the group's performance?
   e. Which self-serving roles were present? How did they affect the group's operation?
   f. Summarize what the group needs to do to enhance its ability to function in the future.

Which roles in each of the preceding categories do you find yourself performing most frequently? What group conditions or personal needs do you believe help precipitate such behavior on your part?

As we have seen, every group member affects the operation of his or her group; sometimes the members exhibit behaviors that improve task performance, and sometimes they exhibit behaviors that reflect their concern for human needs and feelings. Sometimes they exhibit helpful behaviors, and sometimes they behave in ways that announce their minimum regard for the group experience. Developing an understanding of membership roles and behavior preferences is essential if we are to be able to meaningfully evaluate the effectiveness of the groups to which we belong, as is developing an understanding of group leadership. After all, membership and leadership go hand in hand.

APPROACHES TO LEADERSHIP: THE LEADER IN YOU

What is leadership? Are you a leader? Do you have leadership potential? What qualities does a good leader possess? Are effective leaders born or made?

What Is Leadership?

Leadership is the ability to influence others. Thus, every person who influences others can be said to exert leadership.[3] Leadership can be either a positive or a negative force. When its influence is positive, leadership facilitates group-task accomplishment. If the leadership influence is negative, group-task accomplishment is inhibited. Every group member has leadership potential. Whether this potential is used wisely or abused, used effectively or ineffectively, depends on each individual's skills, personal objectives, and commitment to the group.

Groups, especially problem-solving ones, need effective leadership in order to achieve their goals. Effective leadership can be demonstrated by one or more of the members in the group. We should point out here that there is a difference between being appointed a leader—that is, serving as a designated leader—and exhibiting leadership behaviors. When you function as the designated leader, you have been "dubbed" the group's leader; this means that an outside force has given you the authority to exert your influence within the group. When you simply engage in effective leadership behavior without being appointed or directed to do so, you achieve leadership, that is, automatically perform the roles that help a group attain its task and/or maintenance objectives. Effective leaders perform combinations of the roles we described earlier. They demonstrate *role versatility*.

Explore what leadership means to you by completing these sentences:
A leader is a person who . . .
I like a leader who . . .
I am a leader when . . .
It is essential that a leader . . .
I possess the following leadership skills . . .
I lack the following leadership skills . . .

Such leaders help establish a group climate that encourages and stimulates interaction; they make certain that an agenda is planned for a meeting; they take responsibility for ensuring that group communication proceeds smoothly. When group members get off the track, it is this type of leader who asks relevant questions, offers internal summaries, and keeps the discussion going. This is also the kind of leader who encourages continual group-member evaluation and improvement. But where does leadership ability come from? Why do some people exert more leadership than others? Why are some people more effective leaders than others?

Leadership Styles

The successful organization has one major attribute that sets it apart from unsuccessful organizations: dynamic and effective leadership.

*P. Hersey and
K. Blanchard*

The assumptions we make about how people work together will influence the type of leadership style we adopt. Here are eight assumptions that a leader might make about how and why people work. Choose the four you are most comfortable with.

1. The average group member will avoid working if she or he can.
2. The average group member views work as a natural activity.
3. The typical group member must be forced to work and must be closely supervised.
4. The typical group member is self-directed when it comes to meeting performance standards and realizing group objectives.
5. A group member should be threatened with punishment to get him or her to put forth an adequate effort.
6. A group member's commitment to objectives is not related to punishment but to rewards.
7. The average individual prefers to avoid responsibility and would rather be led.
8. The average individual not only can learn to accept responsibility but actually seeks responsibility.

If you picked mostly odd-numbered items in the list above, you represent what management theorist Douglas McGregor calls a type X leader. In contrast, if you checked mostly even-numbered items, you possess the perceptions belonging to his type Y leader.[4] The type Y leader is more of a risk taker than is the type X leader. A Y leader is willing to let the members of her or his team grow and develop in order to realize their individual potentials. An X leader, however, does not readily delegate responsibility; unlike the Y leader, he or she is not concerned with the personal sense of achievement that members receive as a result of their experiences. (Are you satisfied with the set of assumptions in which you expressed belief? What consequences could they have?)

In most discussions of leadership styles, three categories in addition to type X and type Y also usually come up: the autocratic leader ("the boss"), the democratic leader ("the participator"), and the laissez-faire leader ("the do-your-own-thing-er").[5] Let's examine each briefly.

Autocratic or *authoritarian leaders* are dominators who view their task as a directive one. In a group with an autocratic leader, it is the leader who determines all policies and gives orders to the other group members. In other words, one boss typically assumes almost all leadership roles; thus in effect this person becomes the singular decision maker. Although such an approach may be effective and efficient during crisis situations, the usual outcome of this behavior is low group satisfaction.

The opposite of the authoritarian leader is the *laissez-faire leader*. This type of leader employs a "leave-them-alone" attitude. In other words, this person diminishes the leadership function to the point where it is almost nonexistent. The result is that group members are free to develop and progress on their own; they are indeed free to "do their own thing." Unfortunately, the members of a laissez-faire group may often be distracted from the task at hand and suffer loss of direction, with the result that the quality of the work they produce suffers.

The middle leadership position—and the one that has proved to be most effective—is *democratic leadership*. In groups with the democratic leadership style, members are directly involved in the problem-solving process; the power to make decisions is neither usurped by "the boss" nor abandoned by the laissez-faire leader. Instead, behavior representing a reasonable compromise between these two extremes is practiced. Whereas these leaders do not dominate the group with one point of view, they do attempt to provide direction to ensure that both task and maintenance leadership functions are met. The group is free to identify its own goals, follow its own procedures, and reach its own conclusions. Most people prefer belonging to democratic groups. Member morale, motivation to work, group-mindedness, and the desire to communicate all increase under the guidance of a democratic leader.

It should be emphasized that although the democratic style of leadership is traditionally preferred, all three leadership styles can be effective under the appropriate conditions. Thus, when an urgent decision is required, the autocratic style may be in the group's best interest. When a minimum of interference is needed for members to work together effectively, the laissez-faire style may be more effective. When commitment to the group decision is of the greatest importance, the democratic style should be practiced.

Divide into groups. Create a problem-solving situation and explain how an authoritarian, a laissez-faire, and a democratic leader might handle it. For example, imagine that a corporation needs to purchase data-processing equipment. What behaviors might each type of leader exhibit when in charge of a group discussion on the topic? In turn, each group will role-play discussion-style examples.

Theories of Leadership

Are some people born to be leaders? Or does every situation "find" its own leader? Or is leadership a matter of abilities and skills that are learned?

Over the years, theorists have given both yes and no answers to each of these questions.

The Trait Theory. The earliest view of leadership was the *trait theory*, which maintained that leaders were people who were born to lead.[6] (Do you know any "born-to-lead" men or women?) Theorists further believed there were special built-in leadership traits that could be identified, and an attempt was made to design a test that would predict whether an individual would become a leader. After many years of research, however, proof of this hypothesis is still lacking. Simply put, personality traits are not surefire leadership predictors. For one thing, no one set of characteristics is common to all leaders, and leaders and followers alike share many of the *same* characteristics. Finally, the particular situation one finds oneself in appears at least in part to determine which individual comes forward to exert leadership. This is not to suggest that trait research did not yield valuable findings. In fact, while the statement "Leaders *must* possess the following personality traits . . ." is not valid, the research that was conducted does enable us to note that certain traits are indeed *more likely* to be found in leaders than in nonleaders.

On a separate paper, use the following scale to measure the extent to which you possess these attributes:

	Low			High	
Dependability	1	2	3	4	5
Cooperativeness	1	2	3	4	5
Desire to win	1	2	3	4	5
Enthusiasm	1	2	3	4	5
Drive	1	2	3	4	5
Persistence	1	2	3	4	5
Responsibility	1	2	3	4	5
Intelligence	1	2	3	4	5
Foresight	1	2	3	4	5
Communication ability	1	2	3	4	5
Popularity	1	2	3	4	5

Calculate your leadership score by adding up the numbers you have chosen. Next, use the scale to rate a person you perceive to possess definite leadership ability. Finally, use the scale to rate a person whom you definitely perceive *not* to be a leader. To what extent did you perceive yourself to possess the preceding traits? The highest possible score is 55. Such a score probably indicates strong leadership potential and means that the individual definitely perceives himself or herself to be a leader or is so perceived by others. How does your total score compare to that of the person you felt was a leader? To that of the nonleader? If desired, you can compute an

Describe a person who you believe was born to be a leader. Note the attributes and qualities that you believe ensured this individual's success and destined her or him to lead.

average score for men and women. Which sex do you think would score higher? Why do you think each set of results turned out as it did?

According to leadership researcher Marvin Shaw, the characteristics identified in the preceding exercise are those which are indicative of leadership potential. In contrast, Shaw notes that a person who does not exhibit these traits is unlikely to be a leader. Of course, just because you have leadership potential doesn't guarantee that you will emerge a leader. This means that although a number of group members may have the qualities of leadership, the final assertion of leadership will depend on more than the possession of merely the potential.

The Situational Theory. The second theory of leadership is the *situational theory*. This theory stresses that whether an individual displays leadership skills and behaviors and exercises leadership roles is dependent on the situation.[7] In other words, the development and emergence of leadership can be affected by such factors as the nature of the problem itself, the social climate, the personalities of the group members, the size of the group, and the time available to accomplish the leadership task. As organizational behavior theorist Keith Davis notes in the book *Human Relations at Work*, "The leader and his group interact not in a vacuum, but at a particular time and within a specific set of circumstances." A leader is not necessarily a person "for all seasons."

The Functional Theory. The third theory of leadership is the *functional theory*. In contrast to the preceding two theories, which emphasize the emergence of one particular individual as the group leader, the functional theory suggests that a number of different group members should be ready

---

SKILL BUILDER

How Are You Situated?

1. What conditions are necessary for you to feel comfortable exerting leadership? Explain.
2. What conditions could inhibit you from making an attempt to become a leader? Explain.
3. Describe an instance when either you or someone you knew tried to lead a group but failed. What factors can you point to as contributing to the failure?
4. Describe an instance when either you or someone you knew emerged as the leader of a group. What factors can you point to as contributing to such leadership development?

to show leadership because various actions are needed if a group is to achieve its goals. Advocates of functional leadership believe that any of the task or maintenance activities identified previously in this chapter can be considered leadership functions. In other words, when you perform any needed task or maintenance function, you are assuming a leadership role. Thus, according to functional theory, leadership changes from person to person and is shared. Of course, sometimes one or two group members perform more leadership functions than do others. Consequently, it is often the case that one member might become the main task leader, whereas another might assume the role of main socioemotional leader. However, the point is that we can enhance our leadership potential by learning to perform needed group functions more effectively.

From the functional viewpoint, then, leadership is not necessarily a birthright; nor is it simply a matter of being in the right situation at a critical juncture. Instead, we are all capable of leadership, and what is required is that we have enough self-assertion and sensitivity to perform the functions that are needed *as* they are needed. In effect, this is asserting that good membership is good leadership. And the converse is also true: Good leadership is good membership.

GROUP INTERACTION AND THE SOCIAL ENVIRONMENT: ARE YOU COOPERATIVE OR COMPETITIVE, DEFENSIVE OR SUPPORTIVE?

A number of other variables affect the quality of group interaction. Chief among these is the fact that the nature of the relationships shared by the members of the group is highly important in determining whether the group will operate effectively. For this reason, the following questions also deserve our attention: To what extent do members of the group cooperate or compete with one another? To what extent do members help to foster a defensive or a supportive environment?

Cooperation or Competition: The Name of the Game

Obviously, the personal goals of each individual have an impact on the operation of the group of which that person is a member. If individual members view their goals as congruent or coinciding, an atmosphere of group cooperation can be fostered. However, if individual members see their goals as mutually contradictory, a competitive atmosphere will be engendered. Too frequently, group members attempt to compete with one another when cooperating with one another would be more beneficial to the group. Psychologists Linden L. Nelson and Spencer Kagen believe that competing when cooperating would make better sense is actually irrational and self-defeating.[8] If a group experience develops into a "dog-eat-dog" phenomenon, all members may go "hungry."

Few variables do more to damage a group's ability to maintain itself in operation and complete a task than competition among members. Yet highly competitive individuals do belong to groups and do in fact affect the group's communication climate and emergent goal structure. The term *goal structure* describes the way members relate to each other. Under a *cooperative goal structure*, in which the members of a group work together to achieve their objectives, the goals of each person are perceived to be compatible or complementary with those of the others. Group members readily pool resources and coordinate their efforts to obtain what they consider mutual aims. In contrast, when a group develops a *competitive goal structure*, members do not share resources, efforts are not coordinated, and, consciously or unconsciously, individuals work to hinder one another's efforts to obtain the goal. According to the psychologist Morton Deutsch, members who have a competitive orientation believe they can achieve their goals only if other members of the group fail to do so.[9]

How do you act in group situations you define as cooperative? In situations you define as competitive? To what extent does the sex of the other person appear to make a difference?

In order for the members of a group to cooperate with each other, certain requirements need to be met. First, group members need to agree that each has an equal right to satisfy needs. Second, conditions must be such that each person in the group is able to get what she or he wants at least some of the time. Third, plays for power that rely on techniques such as threatening, yelling, or demanding are viewed with disdain and are avoided. Finally, members do not attempt to manipulate each other by withholding information or dissembling. Consequently, when you cooperate as a group member, you do not aim to "win" or to "beat" or "outsmart" others. Unlike competition, cooperation does not require that you "gain an edge" over the other members of your group; for this reason, unlike competition, cooperation does not promote defensiveness.

Supportiveness or Defensiveness: "As the Wheel Turns"

For our purposes, *defensive behavior* can be said to occur when a group member perceives or anticipates a threat.

Whenever you feel yourself becoming defensive, you may experience one or more of the following symptoms: a change in voice tone (as you become nervous, your throat and vocal mechanism grow tense and your vocal pitch tends to rise), a tightening of your muscles and a degree of rigidity throughout your body, and a rush of adrenaline accompanied by a desire to fight or an urge to flee. Now let us examine the behaviors that can precipitate such reactions.

In general, we tend to become defensive when we perceive others

On the Defensive

Think of a number of group experiences you have shared with others during which you found yourself becoming defensive. Use this format to help you record your reactions. Under column 1, identify the nature of the group experience. Under column 2, include a detailing of group happenings or group-member actions that you believe led to your feeling threatened, anxious, or frightened. Under column 3, include a description of the feelings you experienced and the behaviors you adopted during the group meeting.

attacking our self-concept. In fact, when we behave defensively, we devote a great amount of our energies to defending the *self*. We become preoccupied with thinking about how the self appears to others, and we become obsessed with discovering ways to make others see us more favorably. Whenever a member of a group becomes overly concerned with self-protection, he or she may compensate either by withdrawing or by attacking the other members. When this happens, the conditions necessary for the maintenance of the group begin to deteriorate. In short, defensive behavior on your part gives rise to "defensive listening" in others. Also working to raise the defense levels of the cocommunicators are the postural, facial, and vocal cues that accompany words. Once the defensiveness of a group member has been aroused, that person no longer feels free to concentrate on the actual meaning of messages you are trying to send. Instead, the defensive recipient feels compelled to distort your messages. Thus as group members become more and more defensive, they experience a corresponding inability to process accurately the emotions, values, and intentions of those with whom they are relating. For this reason the consequences of defensiveness include destroyed or badly damaged person-to-person relationships, continuing intragroup conflicts and increased personal anxiety, and wounded egos and hurt feelings.

Before we can work to eliminate or even minimize the arousal of defensiveness in our group relationships, we must understand the stimuli that can cause us to become defensive in the first place. The sociological researcher Jack R. Gibb identified six such defense-causing behaviors and also isolated six contrasting behaviors that, when exhibited, help to allay or reduce the level of threat experienced.[10] Let us examine these.

Intragroup relationships can run into trouble if a group member makes judgmental or *evaluative statements*. As Gibb notes in an article, "Defensive Communication," "If by expression, manner of speech, tone of voice, or verbal content the sender seems to be evaluating or judging the listener,

The success of group interaction depends in large part on the relationships among its members. Do they cooperate, do they show respect for each other, or do they compete? (Richard Wood/The Picture Cube)

then the receiver goes on guard." Far too often, we are apt to offhandedly label the actions of others "stupid," "ridiculous," "absurd," "wonderful," or "extraordinary" because we simply are predisposed to use judgmental terms. Although some people we communicate with do not mind having their actions praised, the anticipation of judgment can hinder the creation of a positive communication climate. In contrast to evaluative behaviors, *descriptive behaviors* recount particular observable actions of a communicator without labeling those behaviors as good or bad, right or wrong. When you are descriptive, you do not advise receivers to change their behaviors. Instead, you simply report or question what you saw, heard, or felt.

BEHAVIORS CHARACTERISTIC OF DEFENSIVE AND SUPPORTIVE CLIMATES

Defensive Climate	Supportive Climate
1. Evaluation	1. Description
2. Control	2. Problem orientation
3. Strategy	3. Spontaneity
4. Neutrality	4. Empathy
5. Superiority	5. Equality
6. Certainty	6. Provisionalism

Communication that group members see as seeking to *control* them can also arouse defensiveness rather than trust. In other words, if your intent is to control other group members, to get them to do something or change their beliefs, you are apt to evoke resistance. The amount of resistance you meet will depend partly on the openness with which you approach these individuals and on the degree to which your behavior causes them to question or doubt your motives. When we conclude that someone is trying to control us, we also tend to conclude that that person thinks we are ignorant or unable to make our own decisions. A *problem orientation*, however, promotes just the opposite type of response from a receiver. When senders communicate that they have not already formulated solutions and will not attempt to force their opinions on us, we feel free to cooperate in solving the problems at hand.

Our level of defensiveness will also be increased if we feel another group member is using a *strategy* or is trying to "put something over on us." No one likes to be "conned," and no one likes to be the victim of a hidden plan. We are suspicious of strategies that are concealed or tricky. We do not appreciate others making decisions for us and then attempting to persuade us that we made the decisions ourselves. Thus when we perceive ourselves being manipulated, of necessity we become defensive and self-protective. In contrast, *spontaneous* behavior that is honest and free of deception reduces defensiveness. Under such conditions the receiver does not feel a need to question the motivations of the source, and trust is engendered.

Another behavior that can function to increase defensiveness in group members is *neutrality*. For the most part we need to feel that others empathize with us, that we are seen as worthwhile, valued, and well liked. We need to feel that others care about us and will take the time to establish a meaningful relationship with us. If, instead of communicating empathy, warmth, and concern, a fellow group member communicates neutrality or indifference, we may well interpret this as being worse than rejection. We feel that such an individual is not interested in us, and we may even conclude that the individual perceives us as a "nonperson."

The fifth pair of behaviors related to the development of defensiveness or trust in intragroup relationships is *superiority* and *equality*. Our defensiveness will be aroused if another group member communicates feelings of superiority about social position, power, wealth, intellectual endowment, appearance, or other characteristics. When we receive such a message, we tend to react by attempting to compete with the sender, by feeling frustrated or jealous, or by disregarding or forgetting the sender's message altogether. On the other hand, a sender who communicates equality can decrease defensive behavior in us. We perceive such an individual as willing to develop a shared, problem-solving relationship with us, as willing to trust us, and as concluding that any differences that exist between us are unimportant.

The last two behaviors identified by Gibb are *certainty* and *provision-alism*. The expression of absolute certainty or dogmatism on the part of a group member will probably succeed in making us defensive. We are simply suspicious of those who believe they have all the answers, view themselves as our guides rather than as our fellow travelers, and reject all information that we attempt to offer. In contrast, an attitude of provisionalism or open-mindedness encourages the development of trust. Instead of attempting to win arguments, to be right, and to defend their ideas to the bitter end, individuals who communicate a spirit of provisionalism are perceived as flexible and open rather than rigid and closed.

Gibb described the behaviors associated with a defensive or supportive climate, and Linda Heun and Richard Heun, in *Developing Skills for Human Interaction*, and Anita Taylor, in *Communicating*, identified the nonverbal cues that usually accompany such behaviors. The chart on page 294 is adapted from their work.

Take some time to examine the ways in which you feel you elicit defensiveness or support in the groups to which you belong.

HOW TO IMPROVE COMMUNICATION AMONG GROUP MEMBERS

Here are a number of things you can do to help ensure that the members of your group communicate and function effectively:

1. *Encourage an open, supportive environment.* Group members must feel free to contribute ideas and feelings. They must also believe that their ideas and feelings will be listened to. Unless members feel free to exchange information and feelings, it is unlikely they will achieve their objectives. It is only through the transmission and accurate reception of task- and maintenance-related content that groups progress toward goal realization. Thus, experienced group members realize how essential it is to elicit contributions from all members and to encourage communication among all members.

2. *Establish a cooperative "climate."* As we have seen, a competitive goal structure can impede effective group interaction. Instead of dealing honestly with each other, as is the practice in a cooperative group, members sometimes begin to dissemble and deliberately mislead each other. In order to guard against this and foster a cooperative orientation, members need to work to demonstrate mutual trust and respect. Thus, participative planning is essential. The key is coordination, not manipulation.

NONVERBAL CUES CONTRIBUTING TO THE DEVELOPMENT
OF A SUPPORTIVE OR DEFENSIVE CLIMATE

Defensive Behavior	Supportive Behavior
1. *Evaluation* Maintaining extended eye contact Pointing at the other person Placing hands on hips Shaking your head Shaking your index finger	1. *Description* Maintaining comfortable eye contact Leaning forward
2. *Control* Sitting in the focal position Placing hands on hips Shaking your head Maintaining extended eye contact Invading the personal space of the other person	2. *Problem Orientation* Maintaining comfortable personal distance Crossing your legs in the direction of the other person Leaning forward Maintaining comfortable eye contact
3. *Strategy* Maintaining extended eye contact Shaking your head Using forced gestures	3. *Spontaneity* Maintaining comfortable eye contact Crossing your legs in the direc- tion of the other person Using animated natural gestures Leaning forward
4. *Neutrality* Crossing your legs away from the other person Using a monotone voice Staring elsewhere Leaning back Maintaining a large body dis- tance (4½–5 feet)	4. *Empathy* Maintaining a close personal dis- tance (20–36 inches) Maintaining comfortable eye contact Crossing your legs in the direc- tion of the other person Nodding your head Leaning toward the other person
5. *Superiority* Maintaining extended eye contact Placing hands on hips Situating oneself at a higher elevation Invading the other person's personal space	5. *Equality* Maintaining comfortable eye contact Leaning forward Situating oneself at the same elevation Maintaining a comfortable personal distance
6. *Certainty* Maintaining extended eye contact Crossing your arms Placing hands on hips Using a dogmatic tone of voice	6. *Provisionalism* Maintaining comfortable eye contact Nodding your head Tilting your head to one side

3. *Be ready to perform needed leadership and membership roles.* Members can help the group accomplish its tasks if they contribute to rather than detract from effective group functioning. To the extent that (1) task roles are "present and accounted for," (2) maintenance roles are effectively carried out, and (3) negative, individual, or self-centered roles are deemphasized, member satisfaction with the group experience will increase and the group will prosper.

4. *Encourage continual improvement.* Since there is no such thing as being *too effective* at communicating with others in a group setting, we should continually make every effort to improve our communication ability. Become a group communication-process observer. Pay careful attention to how your behavior affects others and how theirs affects you. Only in this way can you develop the insights needed to facilitate more effective group interaction.

SUMMARY

A group's ability to complete its task depends on the way its members interact with each other. The five most common kinds of communication networks in groups are the chain (or line), star (or wheel), circle, Y, and all-channel networks. The all-channel network is usually the most effective and satisfying, since each group member communicates directly with all the others and no one occupies a peripheral position.

Every group member performs a specific group role. We contribute to the group's objective when we play a task-oriented role (behaving in a way that promotes the accomplishment of the group task) or a maintenance-oriented role (helping to maintain the relationships among group members). However, we can undercut the group's effectiveness by playing a self-serving role—seeking to satisfy only our own needs or goals.

In order to achieve their objectives, groups need effective leadership. Leadership is simply the ability to influence others, and there are many different leadership styles. For example, the autocratic leader dominates and directs all the other members of the group, but the laissez-faire leader lets them "do their own thing." Preferable in most situations is the democratic leader, who encourages all the members to be involved constructively in decision making and problem solving. There are three principal explanations of how people become leaders. The trait theory asserts that some men and women are simply born to lead; the situational theory maintains that the situation itself—the nature of the problem and the characteristics of the group—determines who assumes the leadership role; the functional theory argues that a number of group members can and should share the various leadership functions that have to be performed if the group is to achieve its goals.

In addition to effective leadership, a group needs cooperation among its members and a supportive group climate to be able to work toward achieving its objectives.

SUGGESTIONS FOR FURTHER READING

Appelbaum, Ronald L., Edward M. Bodaken, Kenneth K. Sereno, and Karl W. E. Anatol. *The Process of Group Communication*. Chicago: Science Research Associates, 1979. Successfully integrates theory and application.

Bavelas, A. "Communication Patterns in Task-Oriented Groups," *Journal of the Acoustical Society of America*, Vol. 22 (1950), pp. 725–730. Describes early network studies.

Benne, Kenneth, and Paul Sheats. "Functional Roles of Group Members," *Journal of Social Issues*, Vol. 4 (1948), pp. 41–49. Classic explanation of role functions.

Fiedler, Fred. *A Theory of Leadership Effectiveness*. New York: McGraw-Hill, 1967. Gives the reader a chance to understand this psychologist's situational theory of leadership.

Gibb, Jack R. "Defensive Communication," *Journal of Communication*, Vol. 2 (1961), pp. 141–148. This article identifies behaviors that help elicit defensive or supportive reactions from others.

Heun, Linda R., and Richard E. Heun. *Developing Skills for Human Interaction*, 2d ed. Columbus, Ohio: Merrill, 1978. Offers a clear discussion of the nonverbal cues that contribute to the establishment of a defensive or supportive climate.

Leavitt, H. J. "Some Effects of Certain Communication Patterns on Group Performance," *Journal of Abnormal Social Psychology*, Vol. 46 (1951), pp. 38–50. Provides clear examples of how networks affect interaction.

Nelson, Linden L., and Spencer Kagen. "Competition: The Star-Spangled Scramble," *Psychology Today*, September 1972, pp. 53–56, 90–91. A readable study of how culture influences the development of the competitive spirit.

Patton, Bobby R., and Kim Giffin. *Decision-Making Group Interaction*, 2d ed. New York: Harper & Row, 1978. Offers a comprehensive overview of relevant research and theory.

Shaw, Marvin E. *Group Dynamics: The Psychology of Small Group Behavior*, 3d ed. New York: McGraw-Hill, 1981. A valuable resource for those interested in a comprehensive guide to small-group research.

Taylor, Anita, Teresa Rosengrant, Arthur Meyer, and Thomas B. Samples. *Communicating*. Englewood Cliffs, N.J.: Prentice-Hall, 1977. Like Heun and Heun, provides a clear description of the nonverbal cues that characterize supportive and defensive interactions.

NOTES

1. See A. Bavelas, "Communication Patterns in Task-Oriented Groups," *Journal of the Acoustical Society of America*, Vol. 22 (1950), pp. 725–730, and H. J. Leavitt, "Some Effects of Certain Communication Patterns on Group Performance," *Journal of Abnormal Social Psychology*, Vol. 46 (1951), pp. 38–50.

2. Kenneth Benne and Paul Sheats, "Functional Roles of Group Members," *Journal of Social Issues*, Vol. 4 (1948), pp. 41–49.

3. For a summary and critique of 114 studies on small groups, focusing on leadership, discussion, and pedagogy, see John F. Cragan and David W. Wright, "Small Group Communication Research of the 1970's: A Synthesis and Critique," *Central States Speech Journal*, Vol. 31 (1980), pp. 197–213.

4. Douglas McGregor, *The Human Side of Enterprise* (New York: McGraw-Hill, 1960).

5. For a classic study on leadership style, see K. Lewin, R. Lippit, and R. K. White, "Patterns of Aggressive Behavior in Experimentally Created Social Climates," *Journal of Social Psychology*, Vol. 10 (1939), pp. 271–299.

6. For an early study on the trait theory, see Frederick Thrasher, *The Gang: A Study of 1313 Gangs in Chicago* (Chicago: University of Chicago Press, 1927).

7. See Fred Fiedler, *A Theory of Leadership Effectiveness* (New York: McGraw-Hill, 1967).

8. Linden L. Nelson and Spencer Kagen, "Competition: The Star-Spangled Scramble," *Psychology Today*, September 1972, pp. 53–56, 90–91.

9. Morton Deutsch, "A Theory of Cooperation and Competition," *Human Relations*, Vol. 2 (1949), pp. 129–152.

10. Jack R. Gibb, "Defensive Communication," *Journal of Communication*, Vol. 2 (1961), pp. 141–148.

12

Handling Group Conflict: How to Disagree without Becoming Disagreeable

Man is the only animal that can remain on friendly terms with the victims he intends to eat until he eats them.

Samuel Butler

You can't eat your friends and have them too.

Budd Schulberg

CHAPTER PREVIEW

After finishing this chapter, you should be able to:

Define *conflict*

Explain how you feel when involved in a group conflict

Define *groupthink* **and explain its consequences**

Identify the benefits that can be derived from effective handling of group conflict

Provide examples of what can happen if group conflicts are
handled poorly

Distinguish between healthy and unhealthy conflict-management
styles or strategies

Demonstrate an ability to use constructive strategies to
resolve conflicts

Discuss how conflicts can be categorized

Explain the difference between a competitive and a cooperative conflict orientation

Identify behaviors that can be used to help resolve conflicts
effectively

Conflict is an inevitable part of the life of any group, and sooner or later it touches all group members. A conflict can be started by anyone and can occur at any point in a group's existence. Forces within us that oppose each other can build conflicts, or we can find ourselves experiencing tension as external forces build and create conflicts. Thus, a conflict can originate within a single group member or between two or more group members.

A group experiences *conflict* whenever a member's thoughts or acts limit, prevent, or interfere with the thoughts or acts of that member or another. If you think about your recent group experiences, you will probably discover that you have been involved in conflict situations. Some involved only you; some involved you and another. Some were probably mild and subtle; others were intense and hostile. In any case, all were probably interesting.

Our goal in this chapter is to explore what conflict is, how it arises, how it affects us as group members, and how we can handle it productively. In doing so, we will develop skills to help us deal more effectively with group problem-solving and decision-making experiences.

HOW DO YOU VIEW CONFLICT?
"GROUPTHINK" VERSUS "FREETHINK"

The word *conflict* means different things to different people. What does conflict mean to you? Use a separate sheet to take the following test.

1. State your personal definition and indicate how you feel when involved in a conflict situation.

2. Next, use the following scale to measure the extent to which you judge conflict in a small group to be a positive or a negative force:

Good	1	2	3	4	5	Bad
Rewarding	1	2	3	4	5	Threatening
Normal	1	2	3	4	5	Abnormal
Constructive	1	2	3	4	5	Destructive
Necessary	1	2	3	4	5	Unnecessary
Challenging	1	2	3	4	5	Overwhelming
Desirable	1	2	3	4	5	Undesirable
Inevitable	1	2	3	4	5	Avoidable
Healthy	1	2	3	4	5	Unhealthy
Clean	1	2	3	4	5	Dirty

   a. Add your circled numbers together. If you scored between:
      10–14 You believe conflict is definitely a positive experience.
      15–20 You believe that conflict can be helpful.
      21–30 You do not like to think about conflict; you have very ambivalent feelings.
      31–40 You believe conflict is something to try to avoid.
      41–50 You believe conflict is definitely a negative experience.
   b. Determine the average male and female scores in the class. How do they compare? If they are different, what do you believe caused the difference? How does your score compare with the average score for your sex?
   c. Compute the average score for your class. Where do you stand as a group? How does your score compare with the class average?

3. Finally, complete these sentence starters:
   a. The time I felt worst about dealing with conflict in a group was when . . .
   b. The time I felt best about dealing with conflict in a group was when . . .
   c. I think the most important outcome of group conflict is . . .
   d. When I am in conflict with a group member I really care about, I . . .
   e. When I am in conflict with a group member I am not close to, I . . .
   f. When a group member attempts to avoid entering into a conflict with me, I . . .
   g. My greatest difficulty in handling group conflict is . . .
   h. My greatest strength in handling group conflict is . . .

FEIFFER

How would being given the silent treatment affect your ability to function on the job?

The dictionary defines *conflict* as "disagreement . . . war, battle, and collision. . . ." These definitions suggest that conflict is a negative force that of necessity leads to undesirable consequences. To what extent does your conflict appraisal score support this premise? To what extent do you believe that conflict is undesirable and should be avoided at all times and at all costs? Do you feel conflict is taboo? Why? Unfortunately, many of us have been led to believe that conflict is "evil," one of the prime causes of divorce, disorder, or violence, and that to disagree, argue, or fight with another person will either dissolve whatever relationship exists or prevent one from forming. Somehow many individuals grow up thinking that nice people do not fight, do not make waves. They believe that if they do not smile and act cheerful, people will not like them and they will not be accepted or valued as a group member.

What is *groupthink*? How does it come about? According to Irving Janis, author of *Victims of Groupthink*, this form of behavior occurs when groups let the desire for consensus override careful analysis and reasoned decision making.[1] In effect, then, groupthink is an extreme form of conflict avoidance. While cohesiveness is normally a desirable group characteristic, when carried to an extreme it can actually become dysfunctional or destructive. Are you a groupthinker? To find out, answer yes or no to each of the following questions and then explain your responses.

Research the space shuttle disaster that occurred on January 28, 1986. To what extent, if at all, do you believe that groupthink contributed to the problem?

1. Have you ever felt so secure about a group decision that you ignored all warning signs that the decision was wrong? Why?
2. Have you ever been party to creating a rationalization to justify a group decision? Why?

3. Have you ever defended a group decision by pointing to your group's inherent sense of morality?

4. Have you ever participated in feeding a "we-versus-they" feeling— that is, in depicting those opposed to you in simplistic, stereotyped ways?

5. Have you ever censored your own comments because you feared destroying the sense of unanimity in your group?

6. Have you ever applied direct pressure to dissenting members in an effort to get them to agree with the will of the group?

7. Have you ever served as a "mind guard"—that is, have you ever attempted to preserve your group's cohesiveness by preventing disturbing outside ideas or opinions from becoming known to other group members?

8. Have you ever assumed that the silence of other group members implied agreement?

Each time you answered yes to one of these questions, you contributed to the illusion of group unanimity. In effect, you let the tendency to agree interfere with your ability to think critically. By so doing, you acted like a groupthinker. We contend that groupthink impedes effective group functioning; we believe that when every group member tries to think alike, no one thinks very much. In our opinion, conflict is neither a positive nor a negative phenomenon. For this reason, we will not show you how to avoid it. We do believe, however, that how you view conflict and how you handle it in any group to which you belong will determine the nature of the group's experience and your satisfaction with it. Conflict can be productive if you meet its challenge, but it can be counterproductive if you deal with it

In a group situation, conflict is inevitable. But whether the results are harmful or constructive depends entirely on how the conflict is handled. (Michael Hayman/Photo Researchers)

improperly. In other words, whether a group conflict is helpful or harmful, destructive or facilitative, depends on how constructively you cope with it.

COMBATING THE WIN-LOSE SYNDROME: COOPERATIVE VERSUS COMPETITIVE CONFLICT

A lion used to prowl about a field in which four oxen used to dwell. Many a time he tried to attack them; but, whenever he came near, they turned their tails to one another, so that whichever way he approached them he was met by the horns of one of them. At last, however, they fell a-quarreling among themselves, and each went off to the pasture alone in a separate corner of the field. Then the lion attacked them one-by-one and soon made an end to all four.

What useful applications does this story from *Aesop's Fables* have for our study of conflict? Let's find out by trying the Skill Builder "Brown Paper." What happened in the exercise you just enacted? The "goal" was probably ripped to shreds. Like the oxen, instead of cooperating, you all pulled in separate directions. Unlike the oxen, however, you can learn to handle your conflicts constructively and can learn to disagree without becoming disagreeable. To do this you need to cast conflict in a mutual, noncompetitive frame. Unfortunately, sometimes this is more easily said than done. In many conflict situations we are too quick to view our own position as "correct" or "true" while condemning and misperceiving the other person's position.

SKILL BUILDER

Brown Paper

1. Divide into groups of three to five individuals.
2. A 3- by 5-foot length of brown wrapping paper will be distributed to each group.
3. At a given signal, each individual will take hold of a section of the brown paper.
4. On receiving a second signal, the members of each group will pull the brown paper toward themselves and away from the other members of the group. Each member's personal goal is to get as much brown paper as he or she can.

FROM COMPETING

Harvey L. Ruben

Everybody likes to win.

There is something about coming in first, about achieving a victory over a rival, which seems to fulfill a deep need of the human psyche. Accomplishments of many different kinds give human beings satisfaction, but the ones which are most cherished are often those which are carried through in the face of competitive resistance from others.

The medal we honor most is not the one given for a job well done, but the one given for a job done better than some other job. The immense popularity of competitive sports, the attraction of political contests, and the pervasiveness of social "gamesmanship" . . . all bear witness to the importance of competition as a means of enhancing position, pride, and prestige.

Competition can function in many different ways, at times acting as a kind of social glue, at other times severing the most intimate of bonds. It can be blatant or subtle, aggressive or ingratiating, conscious or unconscious. The ways in which we strive to win are almost as varied as human personalities themselves.

Yet we all do strive to win, in one way or another, and that is of central importance. In almost every culture and at every stage of individual development, people seem to have an urge to achieve victory over others. So omnipresent is this condition that we might be justified in relabeling *homo sapiens;* perhaps *homo contendens* would be a better name for us all.

Besides causing us to be too hasty in defending our own position and condemning someone else's, conflicts can also make us compete when we should cooperate. When a conflict first develops, one of the key variables affecting the outcome is whether the participants' attitudes are *cooperative* or *competitive.* (Will one person achieve victory while the position of others is destroyed? Will they argue to a draw? Or will they share the goal?)

If individuals bring a competitive orientation to the conflict, then each will tend to be ego-involved and will view winning as a test of personal worth and competence. In contrast, if individuals bring a cooperative orientation to the conflict, then each will tend to look for a mutually beneficial way to resolve the disagreement. The exercise on page 304 explores how situations come to be defined as either cooperative or competitive. The "auction" was competitive if at any time you and your group's members bid against one another or raised the bidding level. The situation was

"Gold Rush"

1. Divide the class into groups of six to eight persons. Designate one person as "group auctioneer." This individual is given an unlimited supply of "gold bars" (represented by rectangular pieces of yellow poster board) to "auction off" to group members.

2. The group members sit in a row as the auctioneer puts a gold bar up for sale, and each person offers a bid in turn. Bidding is done in pennies, and each group member has a bank of 100. The gold bar is considered sold when all group members but one have passed on it in turn.

3. Whenever a new gold bar is placed on the auction block, the first chance to bid is passed down the line of group members. Keep a record of how much each member ends up paying for each bar. Members may meet to discuss their strategy after each round of play, that is, after each person has had a turn to bid or pass. At the end of play, those who have purchased the most gold bars are the winners. (Note: A group can contain no winners, one winner, two winners, or any number of winners.)

4. Once 10 complete rounds have been played or 20 minutes has elapsed, the group should discuss what has just occurred. Members should attempt to answer these questions:
    a. Who behaved cooperatively? How do you know?
    b. Who behaved competitively? How do you know?
    c. What factors affected the way your group defined the situation?

cooperative if you and the group's members permitted each bidder to buy an equal number of gold blocks at the minimum price of one penny each.

In general, we can say that individuals come to a conflict situation with one of two orientations or perspectives: competition or cooperation. People who have a competitive set perceive a conflict situation in all-or-nothing terms and believe that to attain victory they must defeat the other parties. A person who has a cooperative set believes that a way to share the rewards of the situation can be discovered.

For a conflict to be defined as *cooperative*, each party to it must demonstrate a willingness to resolve it in a mutually satisfactory way. In other words, each party must avoid behaving in a way that would escalate the conflict. If the parties to a conflict are treated with respect by all the others involved, if they are neither demeaned nor provoked, and if communication is free and open instead of underhanded and closed, the disagreement may be settled amicably.

However, if a conflict is perceived as *competitive*, the "combatants" believe that to attain victory they must defeat the other party. Unfortunately, competing with or defeating another person with whom we are interacting is a characteristic of encounters in our society. The phrases we use reflect this orientation: We speak of "outsmarting" others, of putting people "in their place," of getting ourselves "one up" and someone else "one down."

We can define a conflict as a win-lose situation, or we can define it as a win-win situation. If we interpret it as *win-lose*, we will tend to pursue our own goals, misrepresent our needs, attempt to avoid empathizing with or understanding the feelings of others, and use threats or promises to get others to go along with us. If we define a conflict as *win-win*, we will tend to view it as a mutual problem, try to pursue common goals, honestly reveal our needs to others, work to understand their position and frame of reference, and make every effort to reduce rather than increase defensiveness levels.

To transform a conflict from a competitive situation into a cooperative one, you must use effective communication techniques.[2] One of our goals is to help you discover workable strategies and give you an opportunity to practice them until you can use them for yourself. You should aim to become a conflict processer and develop the ability to view a conflict encounter from the eyes of others.

The role-reversal technique can help parties to a conflict understand each other, find creative ways to integrate their interests and concerns,

Conflict Corner: Can You See It My Way?

Select a current topic of interest that is controversial (for example, abortion, the war on drugs, capital punishment, nuclear energy). You will be assigned to defend or oppose the issue under consideration. Defenders and opposers will have a chance to meet in order to prepare their cases. Each defender (A) will be paired with an opposer (B). Person A will have 5 minutes to present the defense's position of the controversy to person B. Person B then has 5 minutes to present the opposition's perceptions to person A. Players will then switch roles so that B presents A's case and A presents B's case.

1. To what extent did reversing roles permit you to understand and appreciate another point of view?

2. How could utilizing such a procedure help turn an individual with a win-lose orientation into one with a win-win orientation?

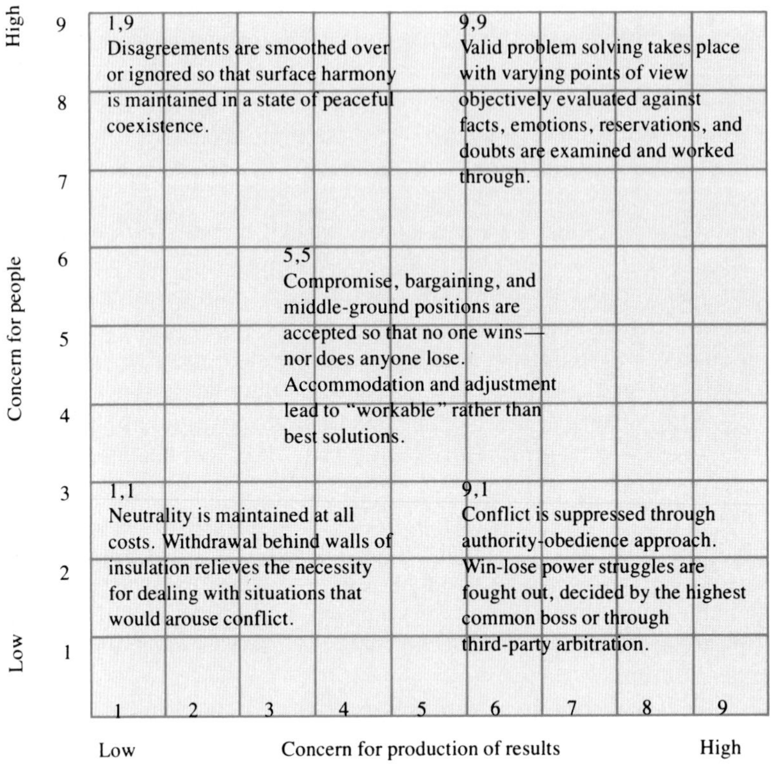
High
Low
Concern for people
9
8
7
6
5
4
3
2
1
1,9
Disagreements are smoothed over or ignored so that surface harmony is maintained in a state of peaceful coexistence.
9,9
Valid problem solving takes place with varying points of view objectively evaluated against facts, emotions, reservations, and doubts are examined and worked through.
5,5
Compromise, bargaining, and middle-ground positions are accepted so that no one wins—nor does anyone lose. Accommodation and adjustment lead to "workable" rather than best solutions.
1,1
Neutrality is maintained at all costs. Withdrawal behind walls of insulation relieves the necessity for dealing with situations that would arouse conflict.
9,1
Conflict is suppressed through authority-obedience approach. Win-lose power struggles are fought out, decided by the highest common boss or through third-party arbitration.
1
2
3
4
5
6
7
8
9
Low
Concern for production of results
High

FIGURE 12-1
Conflict Grid® (Blake and Mouton)
Reproduced by special permission from The Journal of Applied Behavioral Science, *"The Fifth Achievement," by Robert R. Blake and Jane Srygley Mouton, Vol. 6, No. 4, p. 418, copyright 1970,* NTL Institute.

and work toward a common goal. Reversing roles helps you avoid judging others by enabling you to see things from their perspective. Once you can replace a statement like "You're wrong" or "You're stupid" with one like "What you believe is not what I believe," you will be on your way to developing a cooperative orientation.

A number of different paradigms, or models, representing the ways in which we try to resolve conflicts have been proposed. Among these are Blake and Mouton's Conflict Grid[3] (See Figure 12-1). The graph has two scales. The horizontal scale represents the extent to which an individual wishes to realize his or her personal goals. The vertical scale represents the extent to which an individual is concerned for people. The interface between the measures indicates how strongly an individual feels about these concerns, that is, how concern is apportioned.

As we can see, concern for the production of results is scaled from 1 (low) to 9 (high), representing its increasing degree of importance in the mind of the individual; likewise, concern for people is scaled from 1 (low) to 9 (high). Based on this scaling, Blake and Mouton identify five main conflict styles. As you explore the grid, try to identify where your style would fall. If you have a "1, 1" style, your goal is to maintain neutrality at all costs. As a 1, 1 (lose-and-walk-away avoider), you probably view conflict as a useless and punishing experience, one that you would prefer to do without. Thus, rather than tolerate the frustrations that sometimes accompany conflict, you simply physically or mentally remove yourself from the conflict situation.

If you are a 1, 9 (give-in-and-lose accommodator), your behavior demonstrates that you overvalue the maintenance of relationships and undervalue the achievement of your own goals. Your main concern is to ensure that others accept you, like you, and "coexist in peace" with you. You are afraid to make others angry, and you will do anything to avoid being perceived as a troublemaker. Although conflicts may exist in your world, you refuse to deal with them. You feel a need to maintain the appearance of harmony at all costs. This discrepancy leads to the creation of an uneasy, tension-filled state characterized by a great deal of smiling and nervous laughter.

> Why would people who are competitors (9,1s) enjoy being surrounded by "yes people" (1, 9s)? What dangers could such a mix pose?

If you are a 5, 5 (middle-ground compromiser), your guiding principle is compromise. Thus, you work to find a way to permit each party to the conflict to gain something. While compromise is a valid strategy in some cases, it can be a problem if you always try to find only workable solutions because you are afraid the conflict may escalate if you try to find the best solution. Although you adhere to the maxim that "half a loaf is better than none," such an approach, besides leaving participants half-satisfied, can also be said to leave them half-dissatisfied. Thus this is sometimes referred to as the "lose-lose" approach.

If you are a 9, 1 (win-lose-competing forcer), attaining your personal goals is far more important to you than a concern for people. You have an overwhelming need to win and dominate others; you will defend your position and battle with others, whatever the cost or harm to them. In contrast, if you are a 9, 9 (win-win, problem-solving collaborator), you actively seek to satisfy your own goals (result-oriented) as well as those of others (person-oriented). This, of course, is the optimum style to use when seeking to reduce conflict. As a problem solver, you realize that conflicts are normal and can be helpful; you also realize that each party to a conflict holds legitimate opinions that deserve to be aired and considered. You are able to discuss differences without issuing personal insulting statements or making personal attacks. According to Alan Filley, effective conflict resolvers rely to a large extent on problem solving (9, 9) and smoothing (1, 9), whereas ineffective conflict resolvers rely extensively on forcing (9, 1) and withdrawal (1, 1).

> Which conflict-resolving strategies do you use? Why?

If we are to develop and sustain meaningful group relationships, we need to learn to handle conflicts constructively. According to psychologist Morton Deutsch, a conflict has been productive if all the parties to it are satisfied with the outcomes and believe they have gained as a result of the conflict. In other words, no one loses, everyone wins. In contrast, a conflict has had a destructive outcome if all parties to it are dissatisfied with the outcomes and believe they have lost as a result of the conflict. Perhaps one of the most important questions facing each of us today is whether we can turn our conflicts into productive rather than destructive interactions.

When individuals or groups fail to achieve cherished goals, they may feel a need to strike out. Consider this.

DREAM DEFERRED

Langston Hughes

What happens to a dream deferred?
  Does it dry up
  like a raisin in the sun?
  Or fester like a sore—
  And then run?
  Does it stink like rotten meat?
  Or crust and sugar over—
  like a syrupy sweet?

  Maybe it just sags
  like a heavy load.

  Or does it explode?

We will be most likely to succeed in creating constructive rather than destructive interactions if our conflicts are characterized by cooperative problem-solving methods, attempts to reach mutual understanding, accurate and complete communication, and a demonstrated willingness by each party to trust the other. We will be most likely to fail, however, if our conflicts become win-lose encounters characterized by misconceptions and misperceptions; inaccurate, sketchy, and disruptive communication, and a demonstrated hesitancy by each party to trust the other. It is apparent that in a conflict situation the best approach to a constructive resolution is cooperation.

MANAGING CONFLICT SUCCESSFULLY: SKILLS AND STRATEGIES

Conflict can be resolved productively by applying principles of effective communication. When you use effective communication techniques, you reduce the likelihood that your comments will escalate a conflict by eliciting angry, defensive, or belligerent reactions from others. Learning to handle conflict successfully is an attainable goal that can lead to increased self-confidence, improved relationships, and a greater ability to handle stressful situations. All that is required is a commitment to practice and apply the necessary skills. Anyone who is willing can learn creative and effective ways of managing conflict—ways that will increase the likelihood of future harmony and cooperation. Let us examine the behaviors that can turn conflict situations into problem-solving situations. The following suggestions will function as a basic guide to conflict resolution.

Recognize That Conflicts Can Be Settled Rationally

A conflict stands a better chance of being settled rationally if you do not do any of the following:

Pretend it does not exist (act like an ostrich)

Withdraw from discussing it (act like a turtle)

Placate or surrender to the individual(s) with whom you are in conflict (act like a sheep)

Try to create distractions so that the conflict will not be dealt with (act like a cuckoo)

Overintellectualize or rationalize the conflict (act like an owl)

Blame or find fault with the other parties to the conflict (act like a screeching parrot)

Attempt to force all others to accept your way of seeing things (act like a gorilla)

Conflicts can be settled rationally if you act like a capable, competent problem solver and adopt a person-to-person orientation.

Recognizing unproductive behaviors is a first step in learning to handle your conflict situations more effectively. Being willing to express your feelings openly, directly, and constructively without resorting to irrational techniques that destroy mutual trust and respect is a prerequisite to becoming a productive conflict manager. Thus, instead of insulting or attacking others or withdrawing from a conflict, be willing to describe the action, behavior, or situation you find upsetting. Do this without negatively evaluating other people or causing them to become defensive. Focus on *issues*, not *personalities*. Be willing to listen to and react to what the other person is saying.

Define the Conflict

Now that you have recognized that conflict situations can be handled rationally, you are ready to ask: Why are we in conflict? What is the nature of the conflict? Which of us feels more strongly about the issue? What can

To Be Rational or Irrational? "That is the Question"

1. Identify two group-conflict situations that you attempted to settle through nonrational and/or rational means. Use the questions and charts below to help you identify the behaviors you and the other parties to the conflicts employed. For example, did you begin the interaction by acting like a screeching parrot or an overly intellectual owl? Did you switch strategies during the interaction? Why? What was your behavior like at the conclusion of the interaction?

CONFLICT INTERACTION 1

ISSUE:

	My Behavior		My Perception of Other Person's Behavior	
	BEGINNING OF INTERACTION	TERMINATION OF INTERACTION	BEGINNING OF INTERACTION	TERMINATION OF INTERACTION
human				
gorilla				
parrot				
owl				
cuckoo				
sheep				
turtle				
ostrich				

we do about it? Here again, it is crucial to send "I" messages ("I think it is unfair for me to do all the work around here"; "I don't like going to the library for everyone else") and to avoid sending "blame" messages to other people ("You do everything wrong"; "You are a spoiled brat"; "You will make us fail yet"). Be very clear that you would like to join with your fellow group members in discovering a solution that will be acceptable and beneficial for all of you—a solution where none of you will lose and each will win.

Check Your Perceptions

A conflict is a conflict when it is perceived to be one. Conflict-ripe situations, however, frequently give rise to internalized distortions of the behavior, position, or motivations of the other person involved. We prefer to attribute

To Be Rational or Irrational? "That is the Question (Continued)

CONFLICT INTERACTION 1

ISSUE: _____

	My Behavior		My Perception of Other Person's Behavior	
	BEGINNING OF INTERACTION	TERMINATION OF INTERACTION	BEGINNING OF INTERACTION	TERMINATION OF INTERACTION
human				
gorilla				
parrot				
owl				
cuckoo				
sheep				
turtle				
ostrich				

2. If possible, ask the other individuals involved in the conflict to fill out similar charts. Then compare and contrast your perceptions.
3. For each situation, answer the following questions:
   a. Which ineffective behaviors did you find yourself using during the course of the interaction?
   b. What consequences did these behaviors have?
   c. Which factors or occurrences do you believe kept you from functioning in a human-to-human or person-to-person manner?

one set of motivations rather than another to an individual because it meets our own need to see the situation that way. When we do this, we deny the person the legitimacy of any other position. Thus, it is not uncommon for each party in a conflict to believe, mistakenly, that the other is committing underhanded and vicious acts. It is not extraordinary for each party to make certain erroneous assumptions regarding the other's feelings, nor is it unusual for individuals to think they are disagreeing with each other simply because they have been unable to communicate their agreement. For these reasons, it is important that each party take some time to explain his or her assumptions and frame of reference to the others. It is also important that all the parties involved feel that their contributions are listened to and taken seriously.

After each of you has identified how you feel, it is time to determine whether you understand one another. This calls for active empathic listening techniques. Each of you should be able to paraphrase what the other has said in a way the other finds satisfactory. Doing this before you respond to the feelings expressed can help avert conflict escalations. Along with active listening, the role-reversal techniques we spoke of earlier are also effective in helping individuals in conflict understand one another. Like active listening, role reversal permits us to see things as others in the group see them. If we are willing to listen to and experience another person's point of view, that person will be more likely to listen to and experience ours.

Suggest Possible Solutions

The goal during this phase is for you and your fellow group members to put your heads together and come up with a variety of solutions. Most important, neither you nor anyone else in the group should evaluate, condemn, or make fun of any of the solutions suggested. You must suspend judgment and honestly believe that the conflict can potentially be resolved in a variety of ways.

Assess the Alternative Solutions and Pick the Best One

After the possible solutions have all been generated, it is time to see which each person thinks are best. It is legitimate to try to determine which solutions will let one party "win" at the other's expense, which will make all parties "lose," and which will let all parties "win." Your objective is to discover which solutions are totally *unacceptable* to each party and which are *mutually acceptable*. (It is crucially important to be honest during this stage.) Once all the solutions have been assessed, you are in a position to determine if one of the mutually acceptable solutions is clearly superior to all the others—that is, if it has the most advantages and the fewest disadvantages. Also, be sure to explore whether it is the most constructive solution.

Try Out the Solution and Evaluate It

During this stage we see the extent to which the chosen solution is working. We try to ascertain who is doing what, when, where, and under what conditions, and we ask how all this is affecting each person in the group. We want to know if the parties involved were able to carry out the job as planned, whether the adopted solution solved the problem, and whether the outcomes have been mutually rewarding. If not, we know it is time to begin the conflict resolution process again.

Remember, conflict situations can be learning experiences; if handled properly, they can help us discover ways of improving our ability to relate to others. Thus, your goal should not necessarily be to have fewer conflicts but rather to make the conflicts you do have *constructive*. Instead of eliminating conflicts from our group relationships, we simply need to learn how to use them.

SUMMARY

Conflict is an inevitable part of the life of any group. A group experiences conflict whenever a member's thoughts or acts limit, prevent, or interfere with the thoughts or acts of that member or another. However, conflict is not always a negative force. In fact, the absence or avoidance of conflict can result in the problem of groupthink, which occurs when a group allows the desire for consensus to override careful group analysis and reasoned decision making.

Whether a conflict helps or hinders the group's operation depends on how the members react to it. If they resort to strategies such as blaming, withdrawing, intellectualizing, distracting, or forcing, group effectiveness will be impaired. However, if they use a leveling strategy (agreeing to have a calm discussion of the issues), they can break group impasses and solve group difficulties. The various styles of handling conflict can be plotted on Blake and Mouton's Conflict Grid. The most effective style is that of the win-win problem-solver collaborator, who has high concern both for producing results and for the feelings of other people.

A number of communication techniques can help us resolve conflicts. The first step is simply to recognize that conflicts can be settled rationally—by focusing on the issues, not on personalities. Next we should define the conflict and check the accuracy of our perceptions, using "I" messages, empathetic listening, and role-reversal techniques, as appropriate. Then we should suggest and assess a variety of solutions to the conflict, pick the best one that is mutually acceptable, and try it out.

SUGGESTIONS FOR FURTHER READING

Blake, Robert, and Jane Mouton. "The Fifth Achievement," *Journal of Applied Behavioral Science*, Vol. 6 (1970), pp. 413–426. Contains an explanation of the Conflict Grid.

Deutsch, Morton. "Conflicts: Productive and Destructive," *Journal of Social Issues*, Vol. 25 (1969), pp. 7–43. Compares and contrasts constructive and destructive conflicts.

Filley, Allan C. *Interpersonal Conflict Resolution.* Glenview, Ill.: Scott, Foresman, 1975. The author describes how to handle conflict in the organizational setting.

Jandt, Fred E. *Conflict Resolution through Communication.* New York: Harper & Row, 1973. A compilation of 10 articles; theoretical in nature.

Janis, Irving. "Groupthink," *Psychology Today*, Vol. 5 (1971), pp. 43–46, 74–76. A readable and useful overview of this dangerous phenomenon.

Janis, Irving. *Victims of Groupthink: A Psychological Study of Foreign Policy Decisions and Fiascoes*. Boston: Houghton Mifflin, 1972. Offers a more detailed treatment and careful analysis of groupthink.

Johnson, David W. *Reaching Out: Interpersonal Effectiveness and Self-Actualization*. Englewood Cliffs, N.J.: Prentice-Hall, 1972. Demonstrates that conflict is necessary to the development of a healthy relationship.

Ruben, Harvey L. *Competing*. New York: Lippincott & Crowell, 1980. A popular, insightful account of the role competition plays in our lives.

NOTES

1. Irving Janis, *Victims of Groupthink: A Psychological Study of Foreign Policy Decisions and Fiascoes* (Boston: Houghton Mifflin, 1972).

2. For a description of how to promote a win-win approach to conflict, see Deborah Weider-Hatfield, "A Unit in Conflict Management Communication Skills," *Communication Education*, Vol. 30 (1981), pp. 265–273.

3. Robert Blake and Jane Mouton, "The Fifth Achievement," *Journal of Applied Behavioral Science*, Vol. 6 (1970), pp. 413–426.

Communicating
to the Public

13

The Speaker and the Audience

In the United States there are more than twenty thousand different ways of earning a living and effective speech is essential to every one.

Andrew Weaver

CHAPTER PREVIEW

After finishing this chapter, you should be able to:

Identify the characteristics shared by effective public speakers

Enumerate steps to be taken in approaching public speaking systematically

Explain why self-analysis is a prerequisite to effective speechmaking

Conduct a thorough audience analysis

Explain how the attitudes of audience members can affect their reception of a presentation

P ublic speaking. Two seemingly harmless words. Public speaking. The act of preparing, staging, and delivering a speech to an audience. We speak every day. Under ordinary circumstances we rarely give our speaking abilities a second thought—that is, until we're asked to deliver a speech, until we're asked to speak in public. Once we know that this is what we're going to have to do, if we're like most Americans, we fear it more than we fear bee bites, heights, being involved in an accident, or our own demise.[1] When we are told that we will have to speak in public, a whole series of terrifying thoughts and feelings consume us. But just as we can learn to handle ourselves more effectively in our interpersonal relationships and group relation-relationships if we take the time that is needed to analyze and practice successful behaviors, we can do the same with our public-speaking abilities. With practice, we can master the skills and understanding needed to turn us into articulate speakers who are organized, confident, and competent and can communicate ideas in such a way that others cannot help but be interested in them and/or persuaded by them.

Unfortunately, far too few of us ever bother to analyze our public-speaking effectiveness until after we have stepped into the speaker's spotlight; we believe that it is time to correct such errors. With that end in mind, the chapters in Part IV have been designed to help you master the skills and understanding you need to speak like a pro and to feel like a winner after addressing an audience. We believe that harnessing these skills and understanding and putting them to work for you can set you another step above the crowd.

Consider this. Although there are countless ways to earn a living in the United States, your ability to communicate will play the greatest role in determining whether you are as successful in your chosen career as you could be. A typical individual speaks over 34,000 words each day; that adds up to more than 218,000 words per week, or 12 million words per year. A percentage of those words will be delivered via the public-speaking mode. If we do not want to waste our words, have them ignored or misunderstood, we must learn to use the tools that will help people understand us, believe us, and respond to us. We must prepare to meet the speechmaker's challenge.

PREPARING TO MEET THE SPEECHMAKER'S CHALLENGE

People respond to the challenge of becoming public communicators in a variety of ways. Some believe speechmaking is an inborn skill: "I talk a lot, so this public-speaking business poses no difficulty for me." Others view the situation as torture: "I'm scared stiff! This will be traumatic!" Both extremes of attitude can cause problems. Overconfident people run the risk of being less than adequate speakers because they conduct little research and thus are ill prepared. Similarly, the person who is overly anxious or fearful may find it terribly trying and nerve-racking to stand before an audience and deliver a talk. The most effective speaker is the one who displays a healthy respect for the challenges involved in speaking before others and works in a systematic manner to create, prepare, and deliver an admirable presentation.

How can you become an effective speaker? Of course you must work at it. To help you, we will put the entire speechmaking process into a logical format that you can examine and follow in detail. The process we will describe should serve you as a speechmaking "road map"—one you can use to prepare every public presentation you will ever make! Then we will help you learn to control your nervous energy so that you make it work for and not against you as you deliver your speeches. In effect, we can provide you with speechmaking procedures; however, it will be up to you to supply the material and creative energy that will help develop your materials into an effective presentation. Let's begin!

What Do You Expect from a Speaker?

When you listen to a speaker either in person or via media, how do you expect that person to behave? What do you want that person to do for you? We believe it is helpful to view the speech-presentation process from the standpoint of the listeners. After all, without listeners, we would be speaking to ourselves, and that is not what public speaking is all about. Good speakers share a number of behaviors that you may want to keep in mind as you prepare your own presentations.

SKILL BUILDER

From the Listener's Point of View

1. Describe the behaviors exhibited by the most effective speaker you have ever had the good fortune to hear.
2. Contrast that description with a description of the most ineffective speaker you ever had the misfortune to hear.

First, good speakers have insight. They know their strengths and their limitations. They understand and have considered the reservoir of experience upon which they may draw. Second, good speakers know their audiences. They work to understand the nature and concerns of the particular public they have been called upon to address. They are able to tap into the pulse of this public, to stand in the shoes of their audience members, and to view the speaking event or occasion through their eyes so that they are able to share with them something that will be of value to them. Third, good speakers believe that what they are doing is important; they know why they are speaking, and they know what they hope to accomplish by speaking. They are clear as to their purpose and the main ideas they want to communicate. In addition, they are adept at formulating and delivering a message that is organized and supportive of their purpose. Fourth, good speakers always practice. They conduct dry runs of their presentation, each time adapting to potential changes in audience needs. They also prepare well for questions audience members may ask. Fifth, good speakers think of the speaking event as if it were a performance. They know they will need to work hard to keep audience members interested in what they have to say; they understand the essential fickleness of the audience, and so they make it easy and pleasurable for listeners to "stay tuned" to their ideas. Finally, good speakers conduct a critique or postpresentation analysis of their speech. They know that there is much to learn from each experience, much that they may be able to apply the next time they enter the speaker's spotlight.

It is noteworthy that because of the media explosion, our society has grown accustomed to high-quality speech presentations in everyday life. Talk shows, television news programs, and entertainers constantly bring professional speechmaking into our homes. Newscasters, for example, have had years of speech training and practice. Public relations practitioners are often carefully schooled in public speaking to ensure that they know how to communicate an appropriately positive image to an audience. Similarly, many corporate executives employ speech writers and speech coaches to aid them in communicating with diverse audiences. Over 1 million speeches will be given by business people this year alone. All this presents a difficult but not impossible task for the student who is about to step into the public speaker's spotlight. The communication environment you find yourself in is a challenging one. Without doubt, you too will be called upon to add the skills of information sharing and persuasion to your credentials, for only then will you possess the expertise that will allow you to communicate effectively in the multidimensional environment in which you find yourself. From the classroom to the corporation, from the boardroom to the television studio, from the steps of city hall to the podium in your local auditorium, your challenge is to develop the skills and confidence you need to deliver messages important to you and important to the people you represent in a clear and persuasive fashion.

Approaching Public Speaking Systematically

It is important to realize that public speaking is a creative undertaking and not something that just happens when you stand before a group of people. The process actually begins when you first consider addressing a group of people, and it is not finished until you have completed a postpresentation analysis of your work. We believe this creative process can be approached systematically, as shown in the chart "The Systematic Speaking Process." The chart divides speechmaking into four main stages: topic selection, topic development, presentation, and postpresentation analysis.

During the *topic selection stage* your job is to analyze yourself, your audience (in this case, your fellow students), and the nature of the occasion; choose a general subject area; focus in on the subject; and narrow its scope until you hit upon a particular aspect of the topic you can handle in the time allotted. This then becomes your purpose or reason for speaking. During the *development stage* you gather your evidence, organize the evidence according to your purpose, prepare visuals, and rehearse. During the *presentation stage* your main task is to control your anxiety level so that you will be able to deliver your ideas clearly and effectively. During the *postpresentation analysis stage* you determine (with the aid of your instructor or fellow class members or on your own) the strengths and weaknesses of your presentation in order to be better prepared to meet the speechmaker's challenge when another public-speaking occasion arises.

THE SYSTEMATIC SPEAKING PROCESS

Stage	Activity
TOPIC SELECTION	Analyze yourself ▼ Analyze your audience ▼ Consider the occasion ▼ Select your subject area ▼ Narrow your topic ▼
TOPIC DEVELOPMENT	Gather support ▼ Organize materials ▼ Conduct an oral tryout and revise ▼
PRESENTATION	Work to control anxiety ▼ Rehearse the presentation ▼ Deliver the presentation ▼
POSTPRESENTATION ANALYSIS	Conduct a postpresentation analysis

It is important to realize that not every phase of the preparatory sequence consumes the same amount of time; in fact, the preparation time you will need for developing each stage will vary from speech to speech. Sometimes you will need to spend a great deal of time analyzing your audience and identifying the needs of your listeners. At other times you will know your audience members well and will need to expend relatively little time determining whether your speech and its contents are appropriate for them. Sometimes the subject of your talk will be provided for you. At other times, you will be required to come up with your own topic. Sometimes you will be asked to fill a brief time period; other times you will be allotted as much time as you need to share your ideas effectively with others. For example, as a manager you may be required to deliver a detailed report on work that your unit has been doing with the instruction to "take as much time as you require to inform us of your progress." On the other hand, you may find yourself asked to "say just a few words" or to "give a brief progress report." For some speeches you may find you need to spend a great deal of time researching and gathering material, while for others the primary problem will lie not in gathering the materials but in organizing them so the speech flows smoothly and accomplishes its objectives.

In view of the wide variety of circumstances and occasions that require speechmaking, we suggest that you consider each step of the systematic speaking process for every speech that you prepare. Skipping over any phase without at least being certain that you have adequately considered it can lead to embarrassing and discomforting moments for you and your audience. Let's begin now to work our way through the speechmaking process.

TURNING THE SPOTLIGHT ON THE SPEAKER

A thorough self-analysis is a prerequisite to effective speechmaking. Although there is no doubt that at times speaking subjects or topics may be assigned to you, under many circumstances the choice will be left to you, the speaker. Even when the topic is spelled out, it is recommended that you conduct a self-analysis to help you uncover any aspects of the subject that you may find particularly interesting or appealing. Such an analysis could later become the basis for a number of personal stories or anecdotes that can eventually be integrated into your presentation.

There are more topics and subject areas to put into a speech than you could possibly exhaust in a lifetime.[2] Still, the line "But I just don't know what to say" is an all too familiar lament.

A systematic approach to public speaking includes rehearsals of the presentation. The feedback will strengthen the final speech. (McGraw-Hill photo by Elyse Rieder, courtesy of Pace University)

But where was I to start? The world is so vast, I shall start with the country I know best, my own. But my country is so very large. I had better start with my town. But my town, too, is large. I had best start with my street. No: my home. No: my family. Never mind, I shall start with myself.

Elie Wiesel, *Souls on Fire*

We suggest that at the outset of your preparation you take some time for what corporate trainers call a "front-end analysis," or preliminary examination of the possibilities. Begin by reviewing your life from the perspective of potential topics.

1. Divide your life to date into thirds: early, middle, more recent. Compose one sentence to sum up what your life consisted of during each segment. (For example, "I lived in ——— with my two brothers and mother and went to elementary school.")
2. Under each summary statement, identify your main interests and concerns at that particular time in your life.
3. Examine your interest lists. Which interests keep recurring? Which have you left behind? Which have you developed recently?

Now that you have briefly reviewed your life and generated a list of possible interests, you are ready to begin considering this very moment as a potential source of topic ideas.

1. On the left side of a sheet of paper, compile a list of sensory experiences; that is, list everything you are able to see, hear, taste, smell, or touch from your present vantage point.

2. Once you have amassed a list of 10 to 15 items, go back over it and note subject(s) or topic(s) that might be suggested by each observation or experience. Arrange these in a corresponding list on the right side of the paper. For example, if you listed "a passing train" in the left column, you might enter "mass transportation" in the right column. Note: If you are unhappy with the topics you identified, simply move to another location and begin the process again.

A third way to find an idea is to work with the newspaper:

1. Take today's newspaper and, beginning with the front page, read a story and compile a list of speech topics suggested by it.

2. Do not prejudge your ideas. Simply work your way through the paper looking for possibilities.

Your "autobiography," your "right now" observations, and today's news should provide you with an ample number of potential subjects. You may wish to go over the list, ranking these ideas in order of potential interest value (A for the most promising, B for the next, C for less promising, and so on). This approach should be considered tentative, but it will provide you with the raw data you need as you move ahead in the speech-preparation process. Having conducted a search of yourself, it is now time to establish where your audience fits in.

TURNING THE SPOTLIGHT ON THE AUDIENCE

Unfortunately, many speakers fall prey to the pitfall of "speaking to please themselves only," approaching speechmaking with only their interests and their point of view in mind, neglecting the needs and interests of audience members. Because of mistakes like these, speakers often choose to speak on an inappropriate topic, dress improperly, or deliver a presentation that is either too simple or too technical for the audience. We have all heard medical experts discuss diseases with general audiences using such complex language that people were baffled and bored. We have also heard speakers address highly educated groups with such simple language and about such mundane topics that everyone was equally bored and insulted.

If your focus during the initial stages of speech preparation should not be placed solely on yourself, where should it be placed? Be prepared to consider a potential topic from the point of view of your audience. Just as you bring your background and experiences to a presentation, so audience members bring theirs. Thus, it is important for you to consider what your listeners are thinking about, what their needs are, and what their hopes are. You may start with a consideration of where you are, but you must not be so self-centered as to stop there. Successful communicators enlarge the size of the speaker's spotlight so that it lights the members of the audience as well. To pay proper attention to the members of your audience, you must know something about them. For example, how familiar are they with what you are going to talk about? What attitude do they hold toward your topic? What are they anxious about? What would they like to know? What are their expectations? If you don't find out the answers to questions like these, you run the risk of having your words fall on deaf ears. Unfortunately, audience analysis is the most overlooked step in the public-speaking process. Not falling into the "speaking to hear yourself speak" trap is something you will want to take steps to avoid every time you are called to speak before others. In other words, when preparing any speech, you must be audience-centered. Without an audience, you're in trouble. Without an audience, you can of course speak in a room alone—to yourself—

SKILL BUILDER

Brainstorm

You can generate literally hundreds of speech topics by taking simple everyday objects and listing all the topics that come to mind. For example, list topics that come to mind for these objects:

A safety pin
A watch
A diamond
A paper clip

If you are not generating 25 or more topics for each object, you need to allow your mind to wander and flow more freely. You may wish to work with a partner and share lists.

Once your lists are complete, take time to identify the five most interesting topics which might be developed into speeches for your class.

but this will be of little value if your goal is to change the attitudes, values, beliefs, or behavior of others. No one will be enlightened by your ideas, no one will chuckle at your humor, no one will give you a pat on the back for a job well done unless he or she has listened to you. Making a speech without considering the audience would be much like a chef cooking a banquet and then dining alone or an artist storing a painting of great beauty in a garage. Therefore, it is from behind the eyes of your audience that you must also approach your speechmaking task. Let's see how this works.

Beginning Your Audience Analysis: Who Are They?

Although discovering information about the people you will speak to is a simple task, it can also often appear to be a nearly impossible one. After all, how can you know or hope to determine precisely who will attend your presentation? For example, do you expect some interested groups of people to arrive together? Will others whom you do not expect surprise you and show up? Maybe. Despite this seeming unpredictability, it is important to try to make educated guesses about the makeup of your intended audience. What you are doing at this stage of the process is creating a mental picture of the people to whom you are going to speak.[3] Once you have created such an image or "snapshot" for yourself, you will be better able to continue planning your presentation.

Speech . . . preserves contact—it is silence which isolates.

Thomas Mann

Fortunately for most speakers, people seldom "happen" into audience situations. Unless they are in a park or a shopping mall or walking down a street when someone—perhaps a politician—begins to speak out about some issue, people tend to gather to hear speakers for particular reasons. People meet to listen to speakers in a number of different settings, including lecture halls, auditoriums, parties, and houses of worship, as well as in front of radio and television sets. They meet to gain information, to praise or pay homage to others, to evaluate ideas and proposals, to assess attitudes and beliefs, to be entertained, to be spiritually uplifted, and to be comforted in sorrow. Although each of these reasons merits attention, our primary emphasis in this book is on learning to devise speechmaking materials that will appeal to audiences who have gathered to listen to an *informative* or *persuasive address*.

Just as an economist must gather data, synthesize them, and use them to attempt to predict the future reaction of the dollar on the world market, so you must gather, synthesize, and use data to predict the reaction of your audience to your presentation. Unfortunately, we cannot be right 100 percent of the time. As any stockbroker will tell you when you have just lost money on a recommended investment, "No one can foretell the future!" Nonetheless, it would be foolhardy not to at least attempt to make accurate predictions. To stay in business, the stockbroker or economist must make more correct forecasts than incorrect ones. Equally, you must aim to predict audience reactions accurately more times than not. Otherwise, in the future you may find your promotion, your career, or perhaps even your grade on the line.

Information about your audience should come from two key sources: (1) your prior personal experience with the group and (2) original research. Let's consider each of these.

Prior Experience. The best source of information about your audience is your personal experience with the group—either as a speaker or as an audience member. If you have attended several functions or are a member of the class or organization you are expected to address, you have a personal knowledge of the audience members. Thus you will probably be able to formulate reasonably accurate predictions about the appropriateness of your material for that particular group.

Original Research. But what if you have had no prior contact with the group you are to address? If this is the case, you might ask the program planner to provide you with relevant information. For instance, if asked to speak at a professional convention, you would be concerned with information regarding the makeup of the audience. How many will attend the lecture? Will there be students present? Government officials? All these factors must be taken into account when you are preparing and customizing your presentation.

Another way to gather needed information about a group is to obtain copies of public relations material. Recent news releases highlighting the organization may help put you on the same "track" as the members of your audience. Corporate newsletters can also be valuable, as can a trip to the local library for information describing the organization.

Many times original research takes the form of discussions with members of the potential audience. Robert Orben, speech consultant and writer for former President Gerald Ford, tells this story. A presidential address had been planned for delivery at a college campus in Minnesota. The speech writers knew that many of the students there were not supporters of the President. They therefore spent a great deal of time on the telephone with students and school officials in an effort to obtain specific bits of information that could be included in the speech to help create a friendship bond between the President and the student body. Finally, a somewhat disgruntled student provided the writers with the "gem" they felt they needed, and they completed the speech confident that they had done their jobs well. And they had. When President Ford arrived to deliver his address, he began by saying, "Washington may have the new subway, Montreal may have the monorail, but this campus has the Quickie!" Students in the audience went wild with laughter, and thunderous applause filled the hall. Why? It seems that the drinking age in that particular state was 21. However, a neighboring state's drinking age was 18. Thus the 15-mile trip students often took to get to the first bar across the state line was referred to on campus as "the Quickie." In this instance, talking at length to potential members of the audience had provided information that helped establish an atmosphere in which students, although not necessarily in agreement with the speaker, were at least rendered friendly enough to listen to his views.

Zeroing In on Demographics: What Are They Like?

Since the background and composition of your audience are important speech-planning ingredients, every effort must be made to determine audience demographics. Determining *demographics* means you must work to acquire information regarding such factors as age, sex, marital status, religion, cultural background, occupation, economic status, education, and special organizational memberships. Despite the fact that no one audience is significantly uniform in all these categories, you should consider each one during your initial planning sessions.

Age.   Would you give precisely the same presentation to a group of children that you would give to your class? Probably not. How might your presentations differ? Could you deal with the same subject? Would it be developed in the same way? The adult student would bring many more years of experience to your presentation than would the child. Adults may have been through economic hassles and even a war—experiences that a child has probably not yet had to face. Of course, the maturity levels of the adult and younger audiences would also differ. These contrasts may appear obvious, yet age is a factor often overlooked in speech planning. Although you might choose to speak on draft registration or birth control to a college audience, the same material would probably have less intrinsic appeal to a group of senior citizens.

It's also wise to consider how your own age will affect your presentation. How close are you to the mean or average age of your anticipated listeners? If you are about the same age as the potential audience members, your job may be a little easier. If you are much older or much younger than they, you will need to attempt to see your topic through their eyes and adjust it accordingly.

In addition to inducing you to make certain adaptations in the content of your speech, the average age level of audience members might cause you to consider making certain adaptations in your manner of presentation. A study by Donald Kausler and Charles Lair indicated that age can affect information-processing abilities. According to these researchers, younger people can process oral information at a somewhat faster rate than older

Choose a topic of current interest. How would you approach the topic for a presentation to people your age? How would you change your approach to appeal to an older or younger audience?

persons can. Thus audiences of older citizens might prefer that you use a slower, more evenly paced step-by-step delivery than would appeal to younger people.[4]

Sex.   Sex can also influence your audience's reaction to your speech. For example, in the past researchers believed that women could be more easily persuaded than men.[5] Do you think this is a valid statement today? Regardless of your answer, you need to consider sex differences, especially if you speak to an audience composed mainly of one sex. However, be sure to study your potential audience before drawing any conclusions. Although the same topics may appeal to both men and women, biological considerations may affect the ways in which audiences composed predominately of males or females respond. For example, a discussion of rape or abortion may precipitate a stronger emotional reaction from the women in your class, whereas a discussion of vasectomy or animal castration may elicit a stronger response from the men. (Veterinarians in fact report that men, not women, tend to overfeed castrated male dogs in order to overcome the owners' sense of guilt!) Still, the so-called traditional roles of men and women are changing, and old stereotypes once attributed to both groups are beginning to crumble.

Marital Status.   Are most of the members of your audience single? Married? Divorced? Widowed? These factors might also influence their reactions to your presentation. The concerns of one group are not necessarily the concerns of another.

Religion.   If you are speaking to a religious group with whom you have little familiarity, make a point of discussing your topic with some group members in advance. Some groups have formulated very clear guidelines regarding issues such as divorce, birth control, and abortion. It is important for you to understand the audience and its feelings if you are to be able to relate effectively to its members.

Cultural Background.   Use your knowledge of your audience's culture and mind set to create a bond with the members. During the Iranian hostage crises of 1980–1981, for example, one Iranian student at a U.S. university decided to handle the cultural difference problem in a unique and effective manner. From his perspective, his U.S. audience was composed of foreigners who had been provoked to resent his presence. In fact, anti-Iranian graffiti had become a common sight on his campus. Thus he began his speech—called "Stereotypes"—by noting, "I am an Iranian student. I am not holding anyone hostage. I have not demonstrated against the United States. I am simply trying to better myself by receiving a college education just like you are." In this way the speaker established an understanding with his audience. He reached beyond nationality to the human factor—a tactic that helps unite speaker and audience.

Occupational Role. People are interested in issues that relate to their employment and the employment of those important to them. Consequently, if possible, relate your subject to the occupational concerns of your audience. Also, if you are speaking before an audience whose members belong to a particular occupational group, you must attempt to find or create examples and illustrations that reflect the job concerns of that audience.

Education. Although it is important to determine the educational level of potential listeners, you cannot let your findings trap you into making unwarranted assumptions—either positive or negative—regarding the audience's intellectual ability. You will probably find that the higher people's level of education, the more general their knowledge and the more insightful their questions. In addition, the more knowledgeable members of your audience may have specific data to dispute your stand on controversial issues. They may be far more aware of the impact of various political and social programs than, say, a group composed of high school dropouts. The less educated may need to be provided with additional background information that more educated audience members may find trivial.

Whatever the education level of your listeners, here are three precepts to keep in mind:

1. Don't underestimate the intelligence of your listeners; don't speak down to them.
2. Don't overestimate their need for information; don't try to do too much in the time you have available to you.
3. Don't use jargon if there's a chance your listeners are unfamiliar with it; listeners will quickly turn off to what they don't understand.

Additional Factors. You may find that you need to consider several additional variables as you prepare your presentation. Do class members belong to a particular campus organization, for example? Do members of the class involve themselves in any particular types of projects? Do the interests of the group relate in any way to your speech? Do members have any goals, fears, frustrations, loves, or hates that could be tied in? How has their environment influenced their perception of key issues?

If used wisely, your knowledge of audience demographics can help you achieve your speech purpose. It can permit you to draw inferences about the predispositions of audience members and their probable responses to your presentation. Thus, when planning your next class presentation, fill out a chart like this one:

*"I am here tonight, gentlemen, to speak to you not
of guns but of, God help me, butter."*

Drawing by Ziegler © 1981 The New Yorker Magazine, Inc.

Do you think it would
be possible for the
speaker to obtain a
fair hearing from
such an audience?
How?

Average age of audience members:

Sexual makeup:

Marital status:

Religious preferences:

Cultural background:

Education:

Occupation:

Additional relevant factors:

Your topic:

Examples of ways I will use the previous information:

Zeroing In on Attitudes: How to Determine What They Care About

Once you have understood audience demographics, your next step is to try
to predict the attitudes the listeners will have toward you and your
presentation. For example, you should consider whether audience members
are being coerced to attend, whether the audience is homogeneous in nature,
and whether the members favor your stand or are actively opposed to it.[6]

Coercion. People attend or "tune in on" a presentation because they want
to (that is, they do so willingly), because they have to (they are coerced to

It is always easier to address a homogeneous audience; attitudes and views on fundamental issues will be the same. (Ulrike Welsch)

do so), or because they are curious. One person attending a town council meeting might do so because a proposed increase in property taxes is being considered; others may attend a parents' meeting at school out of a sense of duty or because their spouses made them go; still others might attend a lecture on the fur industry out of curiosity about what might be discussed.

Try to rate your class audience on the following scale:

Coerced to attend 1   2   3   4   5 Possess great desire to attend

Since the audience's willingness to attend can affect how your presentation is received, it is important that you make educated guesses regarding its enthusiasm level. (Of course, just because audience members want to attend your talk does not ensure that they will agree with what you have to say.)

Homogeneity.   A second factor worthy of your consideration is the degree of audience *homogeneity*, that is, the extent to which everyone possesses similar values and attitudes. Of course, it is easier to address a homogeneous audience than a heterogeneous one. In addressing heterogeneous groups, appeals need to be more varied to ensure that all segments of the audience spectrum are considered. Use the following scale to measure the extent to which the members of your audience share similar characteristics and values:

Homogeneous 1   2   3   4   5 Heterogeneous

Level of Agreement.   Does your audience agree with your position? Whatever your topic, you must attempt to predict your audience's reaction to the stance you take. For example, they may oppose you, they may support you, or they may be neutral or disinterested. The accuracy of your prediction will to some extent determine the reception your presentation will receive. Use the following scale to help you assess your perception of your audience's present position and its similarity or dissimilarity to your own.

Agree with me 1   2   3   4   5 Disagree with me

Your objective when speaking to an audience that *agrees* with your position is to maintain its support. Your aim when speaking to a *neutral* audience is to gain your listeners' attention and show them how your presentation can be of value to them. When facing an audience that *disagrees* with you, you need to be especially careful and diplomatic in your approach. Remember, your goal is to move audience members closer to the in-agreement-with-you side of the continuum. This task becomes easier if you establish common ground with audience members, that is, if you stress values and interests that you share first. Keep in mind that your goal is to increase the likelihood that a voluntary audience will attend to your message and that a "captive" audience will give you a fair hearing.

Level of Commitment.   Finally, how much does the intended audience care about your topic? Is it very important to them? Do they feel strongly enough to be moved to action? Or are your concerns irrelevant to your listeners? Use the following scale to represent your perception of audience commitment.

Passive 1   2   3   4   5 Active

Together the attitudinal scales you have filled out will indicate how much background and motivational material you need to include in your presentation.

Once you have completed your audience research, you will be in a position to predict that group's reception of any topic you select. Consider the following questions:

1. What do the audience members now know about my topic?
2. To what extent are they interested in my topic?
3. What are their current attitudes toward this topic?

Thus, as you develop your presentation, you must keep in mind audience knowledge of, interest in, and attitude toward the subject matter. These important factors will help you select and shape material specifically for the audience members.

Attitude Check

1. For practice, select from three to five current controversial topics of local concern.
2. Each member of the class should fill out the following scale for each topic:
   a. If you were to attend a speech on this topic, would you:

      Have to be coerced   1 2 3 4 5   Have a great desire
      to attend   to attend

   b. Do you feel your attitudes and values are similar or dissimilar to those of other members of your group?

      Similar (homogeneous)   1 2 3 4 5   Dissimilar (hetero-
                                                geneous)

   c. Are you a supporter or disapprover of the issue?

      Favor   1 2 3 4 5   Disapprove

   d. Are you passively or actively involved in or committed to your stance?

      Passive involvement   1 2 3 4 5   Active involvement

3. Using your knowledge of class members, estimate where on each scale the average response will fall.
4. Compute the scores for each issue and divide by the number of class members participating to determine the actual class average for each issue.
5. How accurate were your predictions? Would you have been off base if you had spoken to the class on one or more of the identified topics? Why? How can the gathered information help you become a more effective speaker?

SUMMARY

Public communication, unlike interpersonal communication, occurs in a somewhat formal setting and requires the communicator to be well prepared. Effective speakers understand the challenges involved in speaking before others and work in a systematic manner to create, prepare, and deliver their presentations.

The public-speaking process begins when you first consider addressing a group of people. The four main stages of speechmaking then follow: topic selection, topic development, the presentation itself, and the postpresentation analysis.

A thorough analysis of yourself and a thorough analysis of your audience are the essential preliminary steps in topic selection. Information about your audience should come from your prior personal experience with the group and/or original research (e.g., news releases or interviews). First, you need to determine audience demographics, including such factors as age, sex, marital status, religion, cultural background, occupation, economic status, education, and special organizational memberships. Then you should try to predict the attitudes the listeners will have toward you and your presentation. It will help you to know whether audience members are being coerced to attend, homogeneous in their attitudes, favorably or unfavorably disposed toward your position, or uninterested in your topic altogether.

SUGGESTIONS FOR FURTHER READING

Eisenberg, Abné, and Teri Kwal Gamble. *Painless Public Speaking*. New York: Macmillan, 1982. A workbook approach; guides the speechmaker easily through the audience-analysis process.

Frank, Milo. *How to Get Your Point across in 30 Seconds or Less*. New York: Pocket Books, 1986. A concise book, directed at business speakers, written by a former media specialist and film producer.

Gibson, James W., and Michael S. Hanna. *Audience Analysis: A Programmed Approach to Receiver Behavior*. Englewood Cliffs, N.J.: Prentice-Hall, 1976. Presents an understandable, easy-to-follow method of audience analysis.

Holtzman, Paul D. *The Psychology of Speakers' Audiences*. Glenview, Ill.: Scott, Foresman, 1970. Provides the speechmaker with a perspective on the speaking situation from the audience's point of view. Stresses that audience analysis is a continuous process.

Tarshis, Barry. *The "Average American" Book*. New York: Atheneum, 1979. Highly readable; contains a wealth of audience-analysis-related information.

Van Ekeren, Glenn. *The Speaker's Source Book*. Englewood Cliffs, N.J.: Prentice-Hall, 1988. A refreshing compilation of stories, anecdotes, and quotations about many topics. They can be adapted to fit many topics.

Wilson, John F., and Carrol C. Arnold. *Public Speaking as a Liberal Art*. Boston: Allyn & Bacon, 1974. Contains valuable information about both the speaker and the audience.

NOTES

1. David Wallechinsky, Irving Wallace, and Amy Wallace, *The Book of Lists* (New York: William Morrow, 1977), p. 469.

2. For an overview of the speech selection process, see Martin P. Andersen, E. Ray Nichols, Jr., and Herbert W. Booth, *The Speaker and His Audience*, 2d ed. (New York: Harper & Row, 1974), chap. 10, "Determining the Subject and Thesis Statement"; and John F. Wilson and Carroll C. Arnold, *Dimensions of Public Communication* (Boston: Allyn & Bacon, 1976), chap. 2, "First Considerations."

3. The following sources expand on our discussion of audience analysis: Douglas Ehninger, Alan H. Monroe, and Bruce E. Gronbeck, *Principles and Types of Speech Communication*, 8th ed. (Glenview, Ill.: Scott, Foresman, 1978); and Steven W. King, *Communication and Social Influence* (Reading, Mass.: Addison-Wesley, 1975).

4. Donald H. Kausler and Charles V. Lair, "Information, Feedback Conditions and Verbal Discrimination Learning in Elderly Subjects," *Psychonomic Science* (1968), pp. 193–194.

5. Thomas M. Scheidel, "Sex and Persuasability," *Speech Monographs*, Vol. 30 (1963), pp. 353–368.

6. See Lawrence R. Wheeless, "The Effects of Attitude Credibility and Homophily on Selective Exposure to Information," *Speech Monographs*, Vol. 41 (1974), pp. 329–338.

14

The Occasion and the Subject

The study of man is the study of talk.

Kenneth Boulding

CHAPTER PREVIEW

After finishing this chapter, you should be able to:

Explain how the nature of the occasion influences the speech event

Demonstrate an ability to narrow your topic appropriately

Demonstrate an ability to evaluate a topic according to its worth, appropriateness, interest potential, and research material availability

Formulate clear and precise purpose statements and audience behavioral objectives

Whenever you give a speech, you should have a clear idea of the nature of the speechmaking occasion and how your topic relates to it. Clearly, both the occasion and your selected subject will affect the way you develop your presentation, stage it, and deliver it.

CONSIDER THE OCCASION: WHERE ARE WE? WHY ARE WE HERE? HOW LONG WILL WE STAY?

If asked to speak before a group—including your own class—your first response might well be, "Why? What's the occasion?" Determining the occasion and your role in it are essential steps in the speech-preparation process. Fortunately much, if not all, the information you need to know about the occasion is relatively easy to obtain. Essentially, only the following need be identified:

DATE AND TIME OF PRESENTATION
LENGTH OF PRESENTATION
NATURE OF THE OCCASION
LOCATION OF PRESENTATION
AUDIENCE SIZE

Date and Time

Date and time are the most obvious and yet two of the most important bits of information you need to acquire. We have seen student speakers and professional speakers alike arrive a day early or a day late, an hour early or an hour late. (Of course, it's far better to be early than to be late!)

One well-known mentalist who was to speak at a New York college arrived late to deliver his presentation only to find a hostile audience—one that had waited nearly an hour for his arrival. Some professional speakers schedule their engagements so close together—handling two or three a day—that they must rudely rush out the door almost before they have completed their talks. To be sure, audiences can react quite angrily to such scheduling procedures.

Time can affect your speaking effectiveness in other ways as well. For example, one student speaker decided to deliver a 10-minute informative speech, "The History of the Corvette." Although it was suggested that he limit his consideration of the topic to two or three major model changes, the student rejected this option and instead attempted to discuss every minute body and grill alteration in the Chevrolet Corvette from 1954 to the present. Despite the fact that the instructor attempted to stop him on numerous occasions, 40 minutes into the speech he was still going strong. At this point the instructor announced a class break, to which the student responded, "That's fine. I'll just continue." And he did—although the majority of his audience had departed.

Sometimes instead of being permitted to talk longer than our time limit, we are not given as much speaking time as we had been led to expect.

For example, luncheon or after-dinner speakers are often told they will have 45 minutes to fill, but after introductions and discussions by preliminary speakers they suddenly are left with 30 minutes or less. In his book *Public Speaking for Private People* Art Linkletter states that he tells officers of groups that he will speak the full allotted time, no more and no less. If he is originally asked to speak for 45 minutes and only 5 minutes remains when he is introduced, he will nevertheless speak for 45 minutes.[1] Most speakers are not in a position to make such a demand. Are you able to plan your presentation to ensure that you run neither over nor under your time limit?

Location and Participants

Reminding yourself of the location of your presentation and of the people directly connected with it is an important preparation aspect. The location may well be mentioned during the speech itself. We recall being present to listen to a speech delivered by a world-famous psychologist whose audience consisted of members of the host college and members of the surrounding community. Early in his speech, the eminent Dr. M——— mumbled what seemed to be the name of another college, but the majority of those in attendance failed to notice. The second time, however, he clearly announced how happy he was to be here at X———, and he again clearly mentioned the wrong college. (Doubly unfortunate was the fact that the latter institution was an archrival of the group being addressed.) Some members of the audience appeared embarrassed for the speaker, and others evidenced hostility. The third time, the psychologist mentioned not only the wrong school but the wrong town as well. There was sufficient commotion in the audience at that point for him to realize his error, and in a moment of embarrassment he turned to the college president to ask where he was!

How can you avoid such problems as a speaker? When we were married, the minister who officiated at our ceremony provided a possible solution. During the wedding rehearsal we noticed that a page in his Bible was marked with a paper clip that held a small slip of paper. After the rehearsal we inquired about the purpose of the slip of paper. The minister showed us that it had our names clearly written on it. He explained that because he was somewhat nervous when conducting a wedding, he frequently tended to forget the names of the bride and groom, even if they (in our case the bride) had belonged to the congregation for years. The slip of paper provided an unobtrusive way of preventing such an error. Taking our cue from this experience, we now each attach a slip of paper to the first page of our notes whenever we address a group. The slip bears the name of the organization, its location, the name of the person introducing us, the names of top-level officers, and other miscellaneous information of an important nature. Thus we have the needed data at our disposal, to be

---

MR. KENNEDY, YOU REMEMBER MRS. . . . UH . . .

For at least one of the participants, a trip down memory lane yesterday proved just a bit too far back.

Barbara B. Kennelly, daughter of the late John M. Bailey, the Democratic leader in Connecticut, is a candidate to fill the unexpired term of a deceased United States Representative, and she invited Senator Edward M. Kennedy, an old family friend, to a campaign rally in Hartford.

Mrs. Kennelly said she remembered vividly how the two had met in 1958, when her father was a valued supporter of John F. Kennedy's Presidential aspirations.

But Senator Kennedy's memory proved not quite so keen as his old friend's.

At one point he called her "Mrs. Connelly."

At another, he referred to her as "this outstanding candidate, Barbara McNelly."

While Irish eyes are smiling or crying over the bloopers, Mrs. Kennelly corrected her old friend each time.

Then Mr. Kennedy referred to her as "Barbara Kanally" and someone in the crowd shouted, "It's Kennelly."

"South Boston," said the Senator, sheepishly referring to his home town to explain the gaffes.

But by the end of his speech endorsing Mrs. Kennelly, Mr. Kennedy had adapted a safe means of referring to the woman he called "my old friend."

"Elect Barbara your Congresswoman," he said.

© 1982 by The New York Times Company. Reprinted by permission.

---

appropriately integrated when needed. In the future you may also wish to adopt this simple procedure in order to avoid unnecessary embarrassment or loss of speaker credibility.

On December 1, 1982, during an official state visit to South America, President Ronald Reagan delivered a few words at the airport: "It was so nice to be here in Bolivia." Unfortunately, he was in Brazil. Realizing his mistake, he noted, "Bolivia is my next stop." Unfortunately, Bolivia wasn't on his itinerary.

Of course, there are other aspects to location besides merely the site and the people located there with you. Also of concern is the nature of the physical space you are to speak in. Whether the space is nicely or shabbily decorated, hot, cold, or comfortable, quiet or noisy also merits your attention. If appropriate, you might even refer to the environment in your talk, as one student speaking on the effects of AIDS (acquired immune deficiency syndrome) did:

Take a look around you. What do you see? Desks, chairs, fluorescent lights, a chalkboard, your friends? Sights you take for granted every day. Eight-year-old Jane Doe doesn't take these sights for granted though. Not any more. Jane has AIDS, and has been barred by a court order from attending a public school. No more will she sit at a desk as you are, glance at the board as you do, share the fun of learning with friends. AIDS is changing her life.

Type of Occasion

Why have you been asked to speak? Although every speechmaking occasion is unique to some extent, you can ask some questions to clarify the situation in your own mind. For example, is it a class function? Right now it probably is, but in the future it could well be a sales meeting, a routine management planning session, a convention, or even a funeral. Determine if your presentation is part of the observance of a special event. For example, is the function in honor of a retirement? A promotion? Some other type of recognition? Who else, if anyone, will be sharing the program with you? Making such determinations can affect the nature of your presentation. An appropriate speech topic for a retirement party may be considered inappropriate for a more formal occasion.

Determining how many people will show up to listen to any particular presentation is difficult. Given the classroom situation, for example, on some days the room may be filled, whereas on other days the speaker may arrive only to find a number of students out sick or off on a special project for another course. The same problem confronts the professional speaker. In our work we always multiply and divide the sponsor's estimate by two. Thus we are prepared to speak to a small group—that is, possibly 20—if 40 were expected, or to a large group—possibly 100—if 50 was the estimate. We also make it a policy to be prepared with large visuals and ample handouts, although we are likewise psychologically ready to decrease the formality of the presentation if only a smaller number of listeners arrive.

If you are speaking in a situation that requires that chairs be set up, we recommend that a small number of chairs be put in place and others stacked nearby. If a small group arrives, it appears the audience was just the size anticipated; if a larger crowd shows up, people come away with the impression that you were prepared for an overflow. Consider the example on page 342 related by Jerry Bruno, "advance man" for the late Robert Kennedy.

Of course, you are not likely to have an "advance" person at your disposal when preparing to deliver your presentation—at least not yet. Thus you must do all the advance thinking for yourself. Make it a habit to complete an analysis of both your audience and the occasion before completing work on any presentation. The predictions you make will serve you well as you continue preparing your speech. Now let's move on to the next phase of a speechmaker's preparation—subject selection.

FROM THE ADVANCE MAN

Jerry Bruno

There's nothing really rewarding about being denounced in front of five thousand people by a congressman. . . . It's just one of those things—or two or five of those things—that I ran into in politics. It just seemed that, working for Robert Kennedy, I happened to run into them all the time. . . .

The particular denunciation was the result of a fight with Congresswoman Edith Green of Oregon. . . . Edith Green is a very tough politician—one of the toughest anywhere—and as a lot of badly scarred people in Washington will tell you, when she wants something, she knows how to fight for it. She's also somebody Robert Kennedy felt a debt to, because of her help to John Kennedy in 1960.

Now my business is crowds: how to get them in, how to get them out, even how to count them. . . . Edith Green had her ideas about what Bob Kennedy should do—namely, speak at this new auditorium in Portland that seated 14,000. Remember the first rule of crowds: 25,000 people in a 50,000-seat stadium is a half-empty turnout. But 4,000 people in a hall that seats 3,000 is an overflow crowd. And it works that way on a crowd. People want the sense of being somewhere special, somewhere a lot of people are trying to get to. It depresses people to see empty seats all around them, makes them feel they've been conned into turning out for an event that wasn't all that special.

In this case I took a look around and realized that you couldn't fill those fourteen thousand seats if Raquel Welch and Paul Newman put on a stag show as a warm-up.

So I called the Washington office.

"Joe," I said to Dolan, "you just can't fill this hall Edith wants us to go to. It'll be just terrible."

"Well," Dolan said, "don't do it."

So I looked around and found a Labor Temple that was perfect. It held maybe four thousand people and I knew we could get an overflow crowd out to that auditorium. It was just right. At least, that's what I thought until I spoke to Edith Green.

"That Temple can't hold the crowd that's going to turn out for Kennedy," she said.

"How many do you think will come out?" I asked.

"Maybe six thousand people," she said.

"Yeah, but that won't even half fill the new hall," I said. "It'll be terrible."

"Why can't we hang a curtain over the empty seats?" she said.

This is a common trick in political advance, and it really works great in places like the old Madison Square Garden where you can barely see the balcony from the floor. The press never notices those things. But when we went out to look at this new hall, it was one of those well-lit modern places, with no posts and no hidden corners. There was just no way to hide eight thousand empty seats, not from newsmen, and God knows not from Robert Kennedy.

The argument showed no signs of settlement, so I settled it myself. I had thousands of flyers printed up announcing that Robert Kennedy and Edith Green would appear at the Labor Temple. Edith Green just about hit the ceiling and threatened to cancel the whole affair.

"I don't think you can do that," I said. "You've got fifty thousand flyers saying you and Kennedy will be there. That could mean a lot of disappointed voters."

So Bob Kennedy came to Portland, and at the Labor Temple they were hanging from the rafters, and I mean literally up there in the rafters. There were two thousand people or so outside, the hall was packed, the press was impressed by the turnout, and it was the kind of evening Kennedy loved. And then Edith Green stood up to introduce Kennedy.

"I want all you people to know," she said, turning in my direction, "that had I had my way, we would all have been comfortable and been able to hear Bob Kennedy. But because of that man there"—and she points to me—"we're in this crowded, sweaty room. And I want you to know, Senator Kennedy, that it was that man who caused this problem."

There I am—my first public recognition in all my years in politics! And there's Bob Kennedy, his head down as though in deep thought, trying to keep from bursting out laughing on the stage. . . .

A STIRRING BREEZE SPARKS FEELINGS, THEN WORDS FOR A PRESIDENT'S VISION

Maureen Dowd

Washington, Jan. 20—Peggy Noonan was sitting on a couch in a West Wing office at the White House two weeks ago, her black fake crocodile notebook in her lap. She was tired and drained. She had just finished working on Ronald Reagan's farewell speech, and now she was beginning to scribble notes for George Bush's Inaugural Address.

With an unorthodox time-sharing scheme, both men had chosen the 38-year-old speech writer to help them express themselves, one with his partisan musings as he left the Oval Office and the other

Peggy Noonan.
(Julie Gottesman/The New York Times)

with his bipartisan dreams as he entered it.

Ms. Noonan began day-dreaming about her privileged perch. "I thought this must be the most special place in history, 40 feet down from the retiring President and 20 feet from the incoming President," she recalled at lunch Thursday. "And here I am, sitting on this couch between this President and that one."

Down the hall in the direction of the Oval Office, there was still-ness that day two weeks ago. Down the other way, toward Mr. Bush's Vice-Presidential office, there was noise and laughter and aides and secretaries and Secret Service agents bustling about.

"It felt like a new breeze," she recalled. "There was a literal movement of air. A new history beginning today."

And so President Bush's in-augural message was born. "A new breeze is blowing, and a nation refreshed by freedom stands ready to push on," he told America today.

Ms. Noonan was one of a handful of people, watching from the reviewing stand as Mr. Bush took the oath of office, who were pivotal in helping the new President win the prize he had sought so long and so hard.

It was an odd pairing in some ways, the passionate and eloquent writer from an Irish working-class family in New Jersey interpreting the proper and less-than-articulate politician from an upper-crust, Anglo-Saxon clan.

But, from "warts and all" and "read my lips" to "a quiet man" and "kinder, gentler," the partnership worked so well that many of the phrases Ms. Noonan coined for Mr. Bush became so famous so fast that they are now clichés.

Ms. Noonan began her career in Newark as a premium adjuster at the Aetna Insurance Company and wrote radio commentaries for Dan Rather at CBS News before moving to the Reagan White House staff.

She provided some of Mr. Reagan's most moving moments, including his speech in Normandy in 1984 to mark the 40th anniversary of the D-Day invasion and his re-marks in 1986 after the explosion of the space shuttle Challenger. So moving were her words that she was dubbed "La Pasionaria" after Dolores Ibarruri, whose fiery speeches in the Spanish Civil War rallied Communists against Franco.

Ms. Noonan had left the White House and was at home nursing her infant, Will, and working on a book about Washington politics and mores when she heard Mr. Bush on the radio campaigning in New Hampshire. He was "recycling" Bob Dole's I-am-one-of-you slogan, she recalled.

She asked her husband, Rich-ard Rahn, and her mother if they could take care of the baby for a week. Then she flew north.

She found Mr. Bush impa-tient. Tapping his fingers on his chest, he told her, "They gotta get to know me out there." She traveled with him and ate with him and watched him with his children and grandchildren. She got a pad and pen and interviewed him like a reporter, asking him how he imag-ined his Presidency and what events had shaped his ideas on social issues.

Accustomed to the response

from the public that President Reagan received, she was struck by the different way people reacted to Mr. Bush. Waitresses kissed him and locals stopped by the table to shake hands and say, "Hang in there, George."

"When you traveled with Reagan, it was like traveling with a God," she said. "People were struck by his radiance and looked at him with slack jaws. With Bush, it was cuter."

Ms. Noonan, who detests "faux Kennedy speeches rendered in gummy hands," dissected Mr. Bush and gave him a simpler, self-deprecating style—not high drama and trumpets, as he said today.

"He doesn't have the rolling roundness of Reagan," Ms. Noonan said. "He's more of a brisk bounder."

Ms. Noonan, who says she always tries "to hit a home run," said she was "the most scared I ever was" as she watched Mr. Bush give his speech at the Republican National Convention. The speech was widely hailed as the best of his career and the one that helped change the tide for his lagging campaign.

"Before he had even finished, a lady in the Delaware delegation held up a placard saying 'Read my lips,' " she recalled, "and I said to myself, 'O.K., we have a hit, ladies and gentlemen.' "

One Bush aide had asked her to take the word "gentle" out of the speech. "Don't you think this will start up the wimp thing again?" he complained. Ms. Noonan explained, with barely restrained anger, that "only a man utterly confident of his own strength can talk like this."

For those who had watched Mr. Bush talk with his own words and then talk with Ms. Noonan's, the effect was eerie. Pre-Noonan, if Mr. Bush wanted to talk about drugs, he would talk about "narced-up terrorist kind of guys," not, as he did today under Ms. Noonan's influence, "deadly scourge."

Pre-Noonan, Mr. Bush could answer only, "Challenges, rewards," when asked why he was in politics. Today he could talk about being the man who could help a country "celebrate the quieter, deeper successes that are made not of gold and silk."

Other Bush aides may refer to his speeches as "rah, rah," but Ms. Noonan, who is returning full time to her book and baby after today, has a more lofty view of a great political speech: "It makes people less lonely. It connects strangers with simple truths."

New York Times, January 21, 1989.

SUBJECT SELECTION: WHAT'S THERE TO SAY?

To continue preparing your speech without having selected a subject suggested by your self-analysis inventory and your audience-occasion analyses would be like trying to buy an airline ticket without knowing your destination. You must carefully examine the list of possible topics you

Topic Evaluation Time

1. Working individually or in groups, develop a list of criteria by which you believe a topic for an in-class speech should be measured.
2. Share your criteria with others. Which criteria seem to be most important in the selection process? Which appear to be least important? Why?
3. Compare the criteria you developed with those we have identified. How are they similar or different?

generated during the self-analysis and audience-analysis phases of your preparation. What you do during such an examination is to evaluate your topic ideas according to a number of specific speechmaking criteria. Included among these criteria are (1) apparent worth, (2) appropriateness, (3) interest, and (4) material availability. When you keep these criteria in mind, selecting a topic to speak on will be easier if only because few of your choices will fulfill each of the criteria equally well in regard to the needs of particular audiences.[2]

Criteria for Topic Selection

Is the Topic Worthwhile?   At this point you need to determine if the topic is important to you and to the people who will listen to you. College and business speakers alike often fall into the trap of choosing topics that are of little value to their intended audiences. One of the authors recalls a time in a military training institute when he heard one colonel tell another colonel, "After 25 years in the military they are wasting my time telling me how to inspect a fork!" To the audience of high-ranking officers, the topic "Fork Inspection Techniques" was clearly viewed as trivial. You may find speech topics chosen by others similarly trivial from your perspective. They may be of such commonplace occurrence—how to set a table, for example—as to not actually merit the time and energy you must expend in listening to them. Although many subjects may be acceptable for interpersonal discourse, they may become inconsequential when presented in a public setting where audience members have gathered for the purpose of attending to a speaker whose avowed purpose is to inform or persuade them. Which topics do you judge to be worth your time? Which, in your opinion, are unworthy of consideration?

What Is It Worth?

1. Working individually or with a group, create a list of 10 topics that you believe are worthy of your time and attention.
2. Next, compile a list of 10 seemingly worthless or trivial topics.
3. Compare your list with those made by others.

Is the Topic Appropriate?   We have already discussed how important it is for you to determine if a topic is appropriate to you and your personal interests. However, two additional facets of this criterion must also be considered: (1) Is the topic appropriate to the audience? (2) Is it appropriate to the occasion? Let's examine each in turn.

By this time you should have developed a profile of your audience. That is, you have either determined precisely or made educated guesses regarding the age, sex, and educational level of the majority of the people who are going to hear your speech. It then becomes imperative for you to ask which of your possible topics is most appropriate for such a mix of people. Sometimes this determination is an easy one to make. For instance, it is not every day that you would give a talk about the evils of television to a group of network representatives. You equally might opt not to speak on the advantages of a women's college to an audience already attending a women's college. Likewise, you might choose not to speak on the subject of baseball trivia to an audience of highly intelligent women. Or would you? Is there a way to make seemingly inappropriate topics appropriate? Every subject area must be approached through the eyes of its intended audience. Just as an automobile is customized for a particular owner, so a subject area must be customized to reflect the needs of a particular group of listeners. Just as the automobile is painted, pinstriped, and upholstered with an owner or type of owner in mind, so you as a speaker must "outfit" your speech topic to appeal to the audience members you hope to reach. This takes work, but it can be done.

The appropriateness of the speech topic to the occasion must also be considered. For example you can probably think of any number of occasions on which a humorous topic would appear ill conceived. Can you think of occasions where a humorous topic would be an asset? Although a highly humorous topic would probably be an inappropriate choice for an event commemorating people who have given their lives for their country, a funny subject would be welcomed at a "roast."

Make a list of 10 subjects you believe would be inappropriate for delivery to your class. Discuss ways each topic might be approached to make it appropriate.

Is the Topic Interesting? Speechmakers often make the mistake of selecting topics they *think* they should speak about rather than topics they *want* to speak about. Student speakers, for instance, will sometimes turn to the latest copy of a newspaper or news magazine and, without further thought, select a story at random. This story then becomes the basis for their speech. We know one student who insisted on talking about labor-management relations. Why? Because he thought it sounded like an important subject. Unfortunately, he had spent little time in the labor force and no time in management. And because he cared to do little if any research, the entire subject remained foreign to him. Not surprisingly, the speech he delivered was dull, "tired," and disjointed. A lazy, unenthusiastic speaker can make almost any topic uninteresting—even a potentially interesting one.

It cannot be overemphasized that for others to believe that what you are speaking about is important, you must first believe that it is important. General Dynamics spokesperson John Silverstein put it this way, "You need to believe in your idea. This is very important. What a listener often gauges is how convinced the speaker is. If he has lived it, breathed it, and is himself really sold on it, it generally is enough to sell the argument.[3] Of course, selecting a topic that is appealing to you is a personal matter and can be relatively simple, but determining what will interest your audience can be somewhat more challenging.

Here you also have an advantage. You know your fellow students, and you should therefore be able to identify topics that will interest them. When addressing less familiar audiences, however, feel free to return to your audience analysis data and make some educated guesses. Determining audience interests is a never-ending challenge—one that some unadventurous speechmakers prefer not to accept. One corporate executive, for example, had delivered a speech that was well received—5 years previously. Unfortunately, he has been delivering essentially the same presentation ever since, although times and needs have changed. Needless to say, his current audiences are not interested in his topic. As times change, the interests of people change, and so should the topics selected by speakers. Thus public communication topics must be updated to match the moods, needs, and concerns of listeners; only then do you help ensure that your topic treats an issue of interest to your audience.

Advertising executives discovered long ago that people are interested primarily in themselves and in how products (or in our case subjects) relate to them. Keep this in mind when considering the interests of your audience members. Ask yourself how your subject relates to them. Ask yourself what they stand to gain from listening to you. Create an "inventory" for each of your possible speech subjects. If you are unable to identify significant ways your audience will benefit from listening to you, there is good reason for you not to speak on that topic.

We like to hear what makes us feel comfortable and self-assured. Yet this is exactly what we have no need of hearing; only those who disturb us can improve us.

Sydney J. Harris

What's In It For Them?

Why might each of the following topics interest the identified audiences?

Topic: "Gun control"
Audience: Senior citizens
Audience: Your class

Topic: "Teenage suicide"
Audience: Members of a parent-teachers association
Audience: Your class

Topic: "The art of Chinese cooking"
Audience: Members of Weightwatchers
Audience: Your class

Is There Sufficient Research Material Available?   Before choosing a topic, you must be certain that material on the subject exists and that you can find it in the library. Many a speaker has fallen into the trap of writing for material that was unavailable in a school or local library only to have the needed subject matter arrive too late or turn out not to be as promising as expected. Such an occurrence causes last-minute panic, and the result is a less than adequately prepared speechmaker and a less than adequate presentation. Avoid this pitfall by giving careful attention to your library during the subject selection phase of your preparation.

Narrowing the Topic

It is essential to consider how much time is available for your speech. We know a military chaplain who more than once demonstrated how adept he was at handling the time constraints placed on him. The chaplain's job was to address groups of recruits during basic training, and on each occasion he was given only 3 minutes to get his message across. One day his objective was to persuade soldiers not to use foul language. (It was his belief that such a practice degraded both the individuals and the military.) Realizing that he could accomplish only so much in the time permitted, he chose to focus on a single word—the particular word that he found most offensive. During his 3-minute talk he suggested that the troops avoid using that one particular term. By doing this the chaplain demonstrated that he understood how important it is to narrow a topic to manageable proportions and, incidentally, succeeded in realizing his objective. (After his speech the abused word was heard much less frequently around the base.)

Careful library research helps you get enough material to present an organized, well-focused speech. (Michael Kagan/Monkmeyer)

Far too many speakers attempt to give audiences "the world" in 5 minutes. (Even Mel Brooks, in his satiric film *History of the World*, limited himself to *Part One*.) It is essential to narrow your topic to fit the constraints imposed by your particular speaking situation. Don't try to take on too much. Five minutes is not sufficient to discuss the history of Russia, the Industrial Revolution, or even pedigreed dogs. Let us share with you a strategy you can use to avoid "biting off more than you can chew"—or talk about.

Select a topic and place it at the top of a "ladder":

Then subdivide the topic into constituent parts; that is, break it down into smaller and smaller units. The smallest unit should appear on the lowest step of the ladder. This process is like whittling or carving a stick of wood.

Selection Manageability Scale

Respond to each of the following queries about your subject by awarding yourself a score from 1 to 10, where 1 represents poor and 10 represents excellent. The highest score possible is 100.

1. Is your subject worthwhile?
   From your perspective? _____
   From your audience's perspective? _____
2. Is your subject appropriate?
   From your perspective? _____
   From your audience's perspective? _____
3. Is your subject interesting?
   From your perspective? _____
   From your audience's perspective? _____
4. Is there sufficient material available?
   Material exists. _____
   Material can be obtained in time. _____
5. Have you narrowed your topic to fit the situation? _____
6. What are your overall feelings at this stage? _____

                                                                       Your score _____

The more you shave off, the narrower the topic becomes. Like the carver, you decide what shape to give your topic and when to stop shaving. For example, let's assume that you wanted to speak on the welfare system. One way to narrow your topic would be for you to focus on how the welfare system helps women. Your topic could be focused even further. You might explore how the welfare system helps women in California or, more specifically, women in Los Angeles. Or, to take another possibility, if you wanted to talk on the computer revolution, you might choose to focus on how the computer has revolutionized education or, even more specifically, on the use of computers to teach writing skills.

You can use the selection manageability chart in the overall assessment of your preparation for each speaking assignment you undertake.

Formulating a Purpose Statement

Once you have identified your topic and narrowed its scope, reexamine exactly *why* you are speaking. What is your purpose? What do you hope to accomplish?[4] Most speakers have one of two general objectives when they prepare to deliver a speech: They aim either to inform listeners (to share new information or insights with the audience) or to persuade listeners (to persuade audience members to believe in or do something). However, in actual speaking situations, purposes are not always as clear as we have described here. Thus persuasion speeches usually contain informative material, and information speeches may sometimes contain elements of persuasion. (Informative and persuasive speaking are discussed in more detail in Chapters 18 and 19.)

The Informative Speech.   If your purpose is to inform, your primary responsibility is to relay information to your audience in an interesting, organized, and professional manner. You hope to provide a learning experience for listeners and perhaps share with them information they did not possess prior to your talk. In other words, if your main goal is to inform an audience, you must be certain the data you provide enhance listener understanding, and you must find ways to help the audience remember what you say. In keeping with their primary purpose, informative speakers may explain something, demonstrate how something functions, or describe how something is structured. To ensure that your purpose is clear—initially to yourself and ultimately to your listeners—it helps to develop a *purpose statement*. What this means is that you commit to writing a summary of what you want to accomplish; you describe what you hope to do with your speech. The purpose statement of an informative speech often contains such words as *show*, *explain*, *report*, *instruct*, *describe*, and even *inform*. The following are some purpose statements for particular informative speeches:

To explain how selected Chinese character letters evolved

To describe how a recession affects college students

To inform class members about current IRS regulations that affect them

To instruct class members in how to give an insulin injection

To report on the Rastafarian cult of Jamaica

Notice that each example is stated in infinitive-phrase form and begins with "To." Notice also that each statement contains one and only one idea and that it is written from the speaker's perspective.

Sometimes, in addition to isolating a purpose statement, we also find it helpful to view the speech from the perspective of its listeners. To facilitate this process, you can formulate speaking objectives. Speaking objectives identify what you want audience members to take away after hearing your presentation; that is, speaking objectives describe the behavior or response you want audience members to exhibit as a result of listening to you talk. For instance, you may want your listeners to be able to list,

Purpose Statement Practice

1. Working individually or with a group, compile a list of five potential informative speech topics for eventual in-class delivery (approximate speaking time, 7 minutes).

2. Formulate a purpose statement for each topic and evaluate it according to these criteria: Is it clearly stated? Does it contain a single idea? Can the material be covered in the time available?

3. Develop an appropriate behavioral objective for each purpose statement.

explain, summarize, state, and/or apply certain information, as in the following:

> After listening to this presentation, the audience will be able to explain the process of photographic development.
>
> After listening to this speech, the audience will be able to name three kinds of unlawful employment interview questions.

The Persuasive Speech.   The same principles used for the informative speech may be applied when formulating specific audience purpose statements or objectives for the persuasive speech. During a persuasive speech your main goal is to reinforce or change an audience's beliefs. Or you may be interested in making the students in your class think or behave in a particular way. The words *convince, persuade, motivate,* and *act* commonly turn up in persuasive speech purpose statements:

> To persuade audience members to purchase investment real estate.
>
> To motivate listeners to contribute money to the American Cancer Society.
>
> To persuade class members to become actively involved in the anti-nuclear-weapons movement.
>
> To convince class members to ask their dentists to apply a newly developed plastic coating to their teeth to prevent tooth decay.

In like fashion, from a behavioral objective perspective you might desire that audience members support a plan or take some overt action:

> After listening to my presentation, audience members will purchase savings bonds.
>
> After listening to my presentation, students will sign up to will their eyes to an eye bank.

To sum up, from a presentation development perspective, formulating both precise speech purpose statements and speech behavioral objectives makes good sense. Each device can help you focus your efforts and clarify your goals.

In recent years public-speaking theorists have begun to look more closely at writing instructions. Many speakers now are encouraged to develop theses for their speeches as well. A statement of the speech thesis simply divides the topic into its major components. For example:

> Speech Thesis: A recession affects college students by increasing tuition costs, reducing course availability, and limiting career opportunities after graduation.
>
> Speech Thesis: Investment real estate can provide you with income, security, increasing equity, and some tax benefits.

As you can see from these examples, the thesis brings you a step closer to the structure of the speech itself.

HOW TO MEET THE SPEECHMAKER'S CHALLENGE

Effective speechmakers do not approach their task haphazardly. As we have seen, careful thought precedes the actual speaking event. Every speaker, from novice to professional, can benefit from following these suggestions:

1. Focus your attention on the characteristics displayed by those whom you perceive to be good speakers. Consider the extent to which you measure up to the standards they set. Begin to identify ways of improving your speaking skills.

2. Since a systematic self-analysis is a prerequisite to effective speechmaking, conduct one. Take the time you need to survey your likes, dislikes, and concerns. Effective speakers know themselves well. They know what they care about, and they know the ideas they would like to share with others.

3. Analyze your audience. Effective speakers work to adapt their ideas to reflect the needs and interests of audience members. Presentations are not meant to be delivered in personal echo chambers or vacuums. Rather, they are delivered with the specific purpose of informing or persuading others—of affecting others in particular ways. The degree to which you succeed is directly related to how well you know and are able to predict the reactions of your listeners.

4. Analyze the occasion. It is essential that you learn why, when, where, and for how long you are expected to speak. Without this information your preparation will be incomplete and insufficient.

5. Determine if your topic is supported by your interests, your audience's interests, and the demands of the occasion. Be certain to evaluate the selected subject of your speech according to these criteria: Is the topic worthwhile? Is the topic appropriate? Is the topic interesting? Is there sufficient research material available? Have I sufficiently narrowed my focus?

SUMMARY

Determining the occasion and your role in it is an essential step in the speech-preparation process. Once you have identified the date, time limit, and location of the speech as well as the nature of the occasion and the audience, you can start thinking about a suitable topic. Choosing a topic usually involves two steps: selecting a subject area and narrowing it down to a manageable topic. You can evaluate your topic by answering these questions: Is the topic worthwhile? Is it appropriate for the intended audience? Is it interesting? Is there sufficient research material available? Will there be enough time to cover the topic adequately?

After you have chosen your topic, you need to reexamine your purpose for speaking. Most speakers have one of two general objectives when they prepare to deliver a speech: They aim either to inform listeners (to share new information or insights) or to persuade them (to convince them to believe in or do something). To ensure that your purpose is clearly expressed, you should formulate a purpose statement, which is a summary of what you want to accomplish expressed in an infinitive phrase.

SUGGESTIONS FOR FURTHER READING

Devito, Joseph A. *The Elements of Public Speaking.* New York: Harper & Row, 1981. Helpful for speakers having topic selection difficulties.

Ehninger, Douglas, Bruce E. Gronbeck, Ray E. McKerrow, and Alan H. Monroe. *Principles and Types of Speech Communication.* Glenview, Ill.: Scott, Foresman, 1981. Includes useful material on speech subjects and public-speaking occasions.

Fletcher, L. *How to Design and Deliver a Speech* 2d ed. New York: Chandler, 1979. Offers the reader a step-by-step strategy for formulating speech purpose statements.

Ilardo, Joseph A. *Speaking Persuasively.* New York: Macmillan, 1981. Provides detailed theory about topic selection.

NOTES

1. Art Linkletter, *Public Speaking for Private People* (Indianapolis, Ind.: Bobbs-Merrill, 1980), pp. 106–107.

2. For a study of the topics treated in public speeches by the leaders of the largest corporations in the United States, see Robert J. Myers and Martha Stout Kessler, "Business Speaks: A Study of the Themes in Speeches by America's Corporate Leaders," *The Journal of Business Communication*, 17: Vol. 3 (1980), pp. 5–17.

3. Thomas Leech, *How to Prepare, Stage, and Deliver Winning Presentations* (New York: Amacom: 1982), p. 11.

4. For a step-by-step explanation of how to establish your speech purpose, see Leon Fletcher, *How to Design and Deliver a Speech*, 2d ed. (New York: Harper & Row, 1979), chap. 6.

15

Developing Your Speech: Gathering Support for Your Ideas

Research is the process of going up alleys to see if they are blind.

Marston Bates

The world is already full of speakers who are too busy to prepare their speeches properly; the world would be better off if they were also too busy to give them.

William Norwood Brigance

Basic research is what I am doing when I don't know what I am doing.

Wernher von Braun

CHAPTER PREVIEW

After finishing this chapter, you should be able to:

Identify and use the various research resources available to you
Provide examples of how personal observations can be integrated into a presentation

Conduct an informal survey

Conduct a personal interview

Identify the various types of supporting material, including definitions, statistics, examples and illustrations, and testimonials; use comparison and contrast, repetition and restatement

Explain how visual and audio aids can enhance a presentation's effectiveness

---

Your first step in the topic development stage of the speech preparation process is to gather material, such as illustrations, statistical evidence, expert opinions, and quotations, to integrate into your speech.

HOW TO CONDUCT RESEARCH

During the speech preparation process, one of your chief tasks is gathering information. Some potential sources available to you are published works, other people, and, of course, yourself. Most of the time you will have some personal knowledge of the topic. If you are discussing some aspect of sports medicine, you may have had a football, baseball, track, tennis, or swimming injury. You may have played the piano as a child or work in an industry which relates directly to your topic. Far too often speakers fail to realize that their personal experiences with a topic can be used to establish credibility and add interesting and pertinent examples to a speech.

Library Research

Libraries contain information storage and retrieval systems, resources that are invaluable to every type of research. Whatever your topic, the odds are that some library contains information relevant to that subject. The library is one of the few real bargains left in our society. A huge array of material is available free; other materials and services (those available through a variety of photo and electronic systems) are yours for only a minimal cost. In addition, every academic and public library has on its staff knowledgeable individuals who have been trained to aid you with your investigatory work.

When you begin your library research, you will need to consult several reference sources—sources you may have already encountered during your educational career. Your goal during this phase of research is to compile a preliminary bibliography. Thus, your first stop may well be the library's card catalog. After examining this aid, you will move on to a variety of newspaper, magazine, and journal indexes. Depending upon your subject, you may also consult bibliographical information sources, encyclopedias, and almanacs. The reference librarian may also be able to point you toward a number of promising vertical files.

Card catalogs are traditionally organized according to the Dewey decimal system, which was developed during the nineteenth century, the more recently developed Library of Congress system, or a combination of both. The Dewey decimal system classifies human knowledge into nine areas, with a separate category for encyclopedias and works of general information. Here are the major categories:

000	General works		500	Pure science
100	Philosophy		600	Technology
200	Religion		620	Engineering
300	Social sciences		640	Home economics
	310	Statistics	650	Business
	330	Economics	670	Manufactures
	340	Law	680	Other manufactures
	350	Public administration	700	The arts
	380	Public services and	800	Literature
		utilities	900	History
400	Language			

Each major class is divided into sections, as you can see for social sciences and for technology. Although found in libraries all over the country, the method of division used in the Dewey decimal system is too restricted to accommodate the collections of large libraries.

Larger libraries use the Library of Congress (LC) system, which combines the Dewey numbering system with an alphabetical system. This permits a much larger number of categories. There are 20 major sections in the Library of Congress system:

A	General works		J	Political science
B	Philosophy-religion		K	Law
C	History-auxiliary sciences		L	Education
D	History and topography (except America)		M	Music
			N	Fine arts
E–F	America		P	Language and literature
G	Geography-anthropology		Q	Science
H	Social sciences		R	Medicine

S Agriculture	V Naval science
T Technology	Z Bibliography and library science
U Military science	

Whatever the system, when using the card catalog, your task is to use the author, title, or subject cards contained within it to help you locate relevant books. Figure 15-1 is a sample title card. In addition, if your library has an "open stack" policy, browse through titles near those you identified, because they too may contain information you can use.

Since magazines, newspapers, and scholarly periodicals may contain information valuable to you, indexes are critical resources. One of the first indexes you will consult will probably be *The Reader's Guide to Periodical Literature*. It can lead you to a variety of popular and mass-distribution magazines, including *Time, Newsweek,* and *U.S. News & World Report*, all of which may contain information relevant to your subject. Likewise, *The New York Times Index* and *The Wall Street Journal Index* head the list of indexes that you should consider. If your topic warrants it, you may also need to explore issues of *Education Index, Psychological Abstracts,* and *Sociological Abstracts*. These sources will offer you leads to articles that have appeared in a number of scholarly journals.

The *World Almanac, Statistical Abstract of the United States,* and *Information Please Almanac* are only three of many such reference works

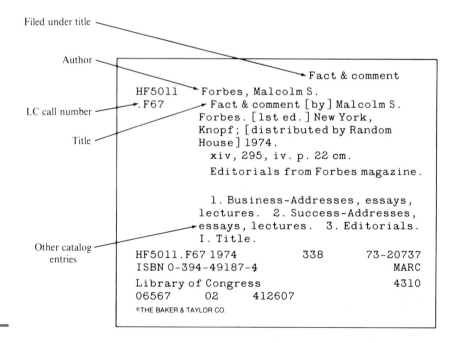

FIGURE 15-1
Title Card

The Criminal Investigation

1. Working individually (but in groups), select a well-known crime to investigate. Potential topics might include the Sam Shepherd case, the Jean Harris–Herman Tarnower ("Diet Doctor") case, the Sacco-Vanzetti case, the Charles Manson case, the Lee Harvey Oswald case, and the Bruno Hauptmann case.
2. Using the resources available in your library, compile a bibliography of materials relevant to such an investigation.
3. Finally, rank your list of entries by placing a 1 next to what seems to be your most promising source, a 2 by the next most promising source, and so on.
4. Compare your list with the lists developed by fellow group members. Discuss the number of sources cited by each individual in your group, the most unusual material located, and the decisions you made when rank ordering your references.

that can provide the speechmaker with interesting factual and statistical evidence. In like fashion, multivolume encyclopedias, such as the *Britannica* and the *Americana*, and one-volume versions, such as the *Random House Encyclopedia* and the *Columbia Encyclopedia*, may also be consulted. Specialized encyclopedias such as the *McGraw-Hill Encyclopedia of Science and Technology* may be of service to a speechmaker whose topic is technologically oriented.

Biographical materials can be located in the *Dictionary of National Biography*, the *Dictionary of American Biography*, and even *The New York Times Obituary Index*. Similarly, *Current Biography* can help you research the lives of public figures prominent today.

Many libraries now house records, films, tapes, photographs, and other nonprint resources you may want to examine in carrying out your speech research. They may provide you with material to integrate into your presentation, possibly as an audio or visual aid. An increasing number of libraries also make use of on-line data bases. These are computerized collections of information which users have access to via telephone links.

Speaker-Generated Materials

You may also wish to generate information that can be used to help you support or "flesh out" your presentation. You have three primary techniques at your disposal to accomplish this: (1) personal observation, (2) the survey, and (3) the interview.

Personal Observation and Experience. One of the best ways to research a topic is to examine what you know about it. Search your own background and experiences for materials you might want to integrate into your presentation. If your topic is one that merits direct observation of an event, person, or stimulus, then by all means go out and observe. Such observational excursions might take you to a biology laboratory, an airport, a supermarket, or a construction site, for example.

Direct observation can provide you with a better understanding of your topic and enable you to incorporate your new personal experiences into your presentation in the form of examples, illustrations, or quotations. When conducting a direct observation, be sure to take careful notes. If feasible, arrive at the location with tape recorder or video recorder in hand. Sit down immediately after the experience and record your thoughts and feelings. All your firsthand notes should be filed with the materials gathered during your library research.

Informal Surveys. Developing a scientific, reliable survey instrument is complicated. However, informal surveys can be used to provide the speechmaker with useful and, at times, entertaining information. For example, if you are investigating the possibility of adding cable television courses to your curriculum, a survey of your school may produce data you can use. (For instance, you might be able to discover the percentage of students interested in enrolling for such courses.)

Informal surveys normally consist of no more than 5 to 10 questions. Before attempting to conduct an informal survey with a prospect, you need to identify yourself and state the purpose of your survey: "Hello, I'm ——. I'm investigating the feasibility of incorporating cable televised courses into the regular curriculum of the college." You would then be free to conduct the survey either orally or in writing.

A sample of 25 to 50 people and some simple mathematical calculations should provide adequate statistical information to integrate into your presentation. In addition, you may gain more than expected. While running the survey or examining the results, you may also find yourself privy to some interesting off-the-cuff remarks offered by the prospect—remarks you may also be able to incorporate into your speech.

Interviews. An interview is similar to a survey except that it is usually more detailed and assumes that the person being interviewed is in some way an expert on the topic under consideration. On your campus or in your community you will probably find knowledgeable people to interview about current issues or a variety of other topics. Political leaders, for instance, can often be persuaded to talk to student speakers, as can business and religious leaders. And of course the faculty members of a college are often most eager to cooperate. Be advised, however, that to obtain useful

The Survey

1. Divide into groups. Each group should select a controversial topic to work with.

2. Working together, develop a list of 5 to 10 questions about your chosen topic.

3. Each individual in the group should proceed to a particular campus location. Once there, each survey taker should seek the cooperation of 5 to 10 people; he or she should request that they answer the questionnaire devised in step 2.

4. Group members are then to come together and pool the information they have collected. Work out percentage responses for questions, if possible. (For example: "Thirty percent of those persons surveyed noted that they would not attend a televised course if given the choice.")

5. Present your results to the class.

6. How useful is this type of research? Of what value can it be to a speaker?

information, you must carefully analyze beforehand what it is that you want to know. You must then present your respondents with specific questions that, when answered, will provide you with the information you need to develop your speech. However, remember to allow your interviewee to talk freely when answering a question. Many interesting responses give rise to new and exciting lines of questioning.

Be sure you record the information gathered during the interview accurately. Take careful notes and repeat or verify the correctness of any direct quotations you intend to use in your presentation. Also be certain to credit the interviewee as the source of your information during the speech unless your respondent specifically requests not to be mentioned by name. By the way, interviews conducted by professionals either on the radio or on television can also provide you with much-needed expert information. Remember to scan the local listings for potentially interesting programs.

It is important to organize the information you collect so that it is easily retrievable and eminently usable. We suggest that you buy a pack of 5 by 7 note cards and record the information gathered on them. For example, you might note the source of your data at the top of the card and follow it below with a direct quotation or summary of the information gathered. This procedure can be used for material derived from print, nonprint, survey, and interview sources alike. Also be advised that since it's impossible to "make appointments" with ideas, you should be prepared

Direct observation is an effective research method and can add a personal touch to your speech. (Jull Cannefax/EKM-Nepenthe)

to record any of your own thoughts in this fashion as well. For instance, an idea about a possible organizational format to use for your speech may occur to you. If so, write it down. Don't count on your memory. Ideas not committed to paper are easily lost and not often easily found. During the information and idea development process, your stack of reference cards should continue to grow.

INTEGRATING YOUR RESEARCH: TYPES OF SUPPORTING MATERIAL

Taken together, the research you have conducted and the experiences you have had should yield a wealth of information—information you will want to integrate into your presentation. Making your research and experiences "live" for an audience is not an easy task, however; in fact, it is one of the key challenges facing the speechmaker. Below are some of the major ways that research and experience can be made understandable and believable for an audience.[1]

Definitions

Definitions can be used to help explain what a stimulus is or what a word or concept means. It becomes especially important to use definitions when your listeners are unfamiliar with the terms you are using or when they might have associations for words or concepts that are different from the ones you are using. Only if you explain *how you are defining a term* can you hope to share your meanings with your listeners. Thus, the purpose of a definition is to add to the understanding of your audience.

For example, in his speech "Leadership Challenges in the Private Sector" Earl G. Graves defined leaders as "people who move others." Similarly, in her speech "On Woman's Right to Suffrage," Susan B. Anthony took pains to define what she believed was meant by the phrase "we, the people": "It was we, the people, not we, the white male citizens; nor yet we, the male citizens; but we, the whole people who formed the union."

Statistics

Select a word for which people have different associations, for example, abstract concepts like honesty, jealousy, freedom, justice, and love. Write your own definition and share it with the class.

Statistics are simply facts expressed in numerical form. They may be employed to explain how things are related to each other or to indicate trends. In order for statistics to be effective as support they must be honest and credible. If used appropriately, they can make the ideas you are presenting memorable and significant. For example, on the program "Teenage Suicide: Don't Try It!" (aired on December 10, 1981, over Channel 5, WNEW TV), a speaker noted: "The reason that we're talking about adolescent suicide is because it has grown 250 percent in the last 5 years in our country. It's a very, very serious problem. Today when we're together in the next hour 57 of your peers will attempt to take their own life—will attempt to kill themselves. Fifty-seven in an hour. That's a lot. Eighteen of those kids your age will make it today. They'll die, and they'll die at their own hand."

In the excerpt on page 366, Russell Baker explains his view of how statistics are used in Washington.

Examples and Illustrations

Examples are representative cases; as such, they serve to specify particular instances.[2] *Illustrations*, on the other hand, tell stories and thus create more detailed narrative pictures. (See p. 453 for an effective use of an illustration.) Both examples and illustrations may be factual or hypothetical.

Jacqueline D. St. John, in a speech entitled "Reflections and Perspectives on the Woman's Movement in 1976," used examples effectively to show that history—or the people who write history—had passed over women:

FROM POOR RUSSELL'S ALMANAC

Russell Baker

Numbers in Washington are much easier to understand than in most places because there are only five. There are (1) the million, (2) the hundred million, (3) the billion, (4) the trillion and (5) the megaton.

In counting, strangers are often confused by the Washington system of modifying numbers with the phrases "give or take," "estimated at" and "on the order of magnitude of." Each of these phrases significantly alters the number's value.

For example, "twenty billion give or take a billion" means that the final cost of, say a new exca-vation will probably not exceed the contractor's quoted price by more than three or four billion dollars.

By contrast, the expression "on the order of magnitude of twenty billion dollars" means that the excavation will cost approximately thirty billion dollars, while "estimated at twenty billion dollars" means the hole will probably cost between forty and fifty billion dollars.

In general, "on the order of magnitude of" increases the value of the number by 50 percent, and "estimated at" increases it on the order of magnitude of 100 percent.

How could such women as these be left out of revolutionary history? Margaret Cochran Corbin, "Captain Molly," who was buried with military honors at West Point; Deborah Sampson Gannet who fought under the assumed name of Robert Shurtleff and served with the Fourth Massachusetts Regiment fighting against British, Tories and Indians; and Mary Hays, "Molly Pitcher," who fired artillery cannons against Hessian and British troops.

Testimonials

Whenever you cite the opinions or conclusions of others, you are using *testimony* or a *testimonial*. The use of testimony offers you the opportunity to connect the ideas contained in your speech with the thoughts and attitudes of respected and competent individuals. The testimony you include in your presentation need not be derived exclusively from present-day sources. The words of persons who lived in times past may also be used to tie together today and yesterday. When using testimonials, be certain to consider whether the individuals you choose to cite as authorities are deemed credible sources, if their ideas are understandable, and if their comments are relevant to your purpose.

In a speech on book censorship in the United States, one student eloquently explained her stand by quoting the words of Nobel Prize–winning author Aleksandr Solzhenitsyn:

> Woe to that nation whose literature is disturbed by the intervention of power. Because that is not just a violation against "freedom of print," it is the closing down of the heart of the nation, a slashing to pieces of its memory.

In a speech delivered before the House Judiciary Committee, Representative Barbara Jordan explained her stand on the impeachment of Richard Nixon by quoting the words of James Madison: "If the President be connected in any suspicious manner with any person and there be grounds to believe that he will shelter him, he may be impeached."

Comparisons and Contrasts

Whereas *comparisons* stress the similarities possessed by two entities, *contrasts* stress the differences. Both are employed by speakers to help make the unknown, the unfamiliar, or the unclear understandable. William L. Laurence combined comparison and contrast when he described the atomic bombing of Nagasaki:

> As the first mushroom floated off into the blue, it changed its shape into a flower-like form, its grand petals curving downward, creamy white outside, rose-colored inside. . . . Much living substance had gone into those rainbows. The quivering top of the pillar was protruding to a great height through the white clouds, giving the appearance of a monstrous prehistoric creature with a ruff around its neck, a fleecy ruff extending in all directions, as far as the eye could see.

Similarly, a Rockwell International spokesperson used an analogy to explain the amount of energy needed to launch a rocket into space:

> If you ran all the rivers and streams of America through steam turbines at the same time—you'd get only half of the 160 million horse-power that all five of the Saturn's F-1 engines generate.

In like fashion, President Ronald Reagan used comparison and contrast to eulogize the crew of the ill-fated shuttle *Challenger* when he delivered these words to the nation on January 28, 1986:

> There's a coincidence today. On this day 390 years ago, the great explorer Sir Francis Drake died aboard ship off the coast of Panama. In his lifetime the great frontiers were the oceans, and a historian later said, "He lived by the sea, died on it and was buried in it." Well, today we can say of the Challenger crew, their dedication was, like Drake's, complete. The crew of the space shuttle Challenger honored us by the manner in which they lived

their lives. We will never forget them nor the last time we saw them this morning as they prepared for their journey and waved goodbye and "slipped the surly bonds of earth to touch the face of God."

Repetition and Restatement

When a speaker uses *repetition*, the same words are repeated verbatim. When a speaker uses *restatement*, an idea is reiterated using different words. If used sparingly, these devices can add impact to a speechmaker's remarks and thereby increase memorability.[3]

One of the most famous examples of the successful use of repetition was in a speech delivered by Martin Luther King, Jr., in 1963 at the Lincoln Memorial:

> I say to you today, my friends, so even though we face the difficulties of today and tomorrow, I still have a dream. It is a dream deeply rooted in the American dream. I have a dream that one day this nation will rise up . . . live out the true meaning of its creed—we hold these truths to be self-evident, that all men are created equal. . . .
>
> I have a dream that my four little children will one day live in a nation where they will not be judged by the color of their skin but by the content of their character. I have a dream today. . . .
>
> I have a dream that one day every valley shall be exalted, and every hill and mountain shall be made low, the rough places shall be made plain, and the crooked places shall be made straight and the glory of the Lord will be revealed and all flesh shall see it together.

PRESENTATION AIDS: AUDIO AND VISUAL SUPPORT FOR IDEAS

The first question you need to ask yourself about audio and visual presentation aids is, "Do I need them?" Many speakers make the mistake of not using such aids when the content they wish to share with an audience really demands them. Other speakers use too many audio and visual aids; they so clutter the speech's content that the presentation becomes confusing and loses momentum. In this section we will consider (1) how you can determine whether your presentation would be improved by the use of audio and visual aids and (2) how you can select and prepare such aids when they are needed.

Why Use Presentation Aids?

Presentation aids serve numerous functions. Ideally, they make it easier for the audience to follow, understand, respond to, and retain the content

Types of Support

Identify specific ways in which each of the following types of support could be integrated into your forthcoming class presentation(s).

1. Definition
2. Statistics
3. Examples and illustrations
4. Testimonial
5. Comparison and contrast
6. Repetition and restatement

of your speech. Thus when deciding whether to use an audio or visual feature, begin by asking yourself if it will help clarify your message. For example, if your presentation contains highly technical information, the use of an appropriate aid may help reduce listener confusion. If the presentation needs additional impact, the use of an aid can help increase listener motivation. If you want to emphasize an important point, an audio or visual implement can add emphasis. A three-dimensional model of the molecular structure of a virus might, for instance, precipitate more interest in audience members than would the use of words alone. In like fashion, the damage smoking does to a human lung can be depicted with the aid of visuals in such a way as to capture the attention of smokers and nonsmokers alike. Aids can also help an audience remember what you have said. A chart, for example, can help dramatize statistical data, perhaps indicating the number of infants who fall prey to sudden-death syndrome each year or symbolizing the decline in real income. By providing your audience with an alternative channel, audio and visual aids give needed reinforcement to key points and ideas.[4]

Selecting and creating materials to help accomplish your speechmaking goals is not an easy task.[5] In fact, once you decide to use audio or visual aids, there are a number of serious decisions to be made. Initially, you will need to identify those precise points in your presentation at which aids will be effective. One way to prepare yourself to make such a judgment is to examine how producers of newscasts select audio and visual aids to facilitate the jobs of on-camera newscasters. After all, in many ways you are the producer of your own speech presentation.

Another strategy you can employ to help determine your presentation aid needs is to conduct a material brainstorming session. Simply examine the information you have and ask yourself the following question repeatedly: Which pieces of information can be improved with audio or visual aids?

Visual aids often enhance a presentation. They should be clear and simple, and visible to the entire audience. (John Blaustein/ Woodfin Camp & Associates)

Keep a record of each idea that comes to mind. Be sure to indicate how the audio or visual support would be used. Once you have analyzed your needs for audio and visual reinforcement, it is time to reconsider your identified possibilities. At this point, let's examine a sampling of the types of visual aids at your disposal.

Objects or Models

In your brainstorming session you may have determined that you would like to use an object to illustrate a particular concept. The object you choose can be the "real thing," for example, a set of earphones, a food processor, or a computer. However, unfortunately there are many objects that are impractical to bring with you to class or to other speechmaking locations. Objects like automobiles are too large to use, and objects the size of microelectronic chips may be too small. In many cases it may become necessary to substitute a model for your selected object. A model can be built by creatively using clay, papier-mâché, wood scraps, or other inexpensive materials. Your aim is simply to create a reasonable facsimile of

Mediaids

1. Select a 30-minute newscast to view alone or with a group.
2. As you watch the program, complete a chart like this one:

Date:
Newscast:

Time:

Audio/visual aid   Purpose   Effect achieved

You might determine, for example, that a film clip of a woman shopping in a supermarket was utilized to aid the viewer's understanding of inflation. If you felt this image was overused and trite, you would indicate this on your chart in the Effect achieved column. On the other hand, you might determine that a graph demonstrating a sharp increase in urban crime in the past 5 years added impact to the discussion; this too would be entered under Effect achieved.

3. Compare your observations with those of others in your class or group. Which aids used on television would have been equally effective if integrated into a speech? Were some audio or visual aids more appropriate to the television medium than to a live presentation? Why?

the desired object—one that will enable you to share your information with listeners in a more meaningful fashion.

Graphs

You can use *graphs* to help you turn an already effective presentation into an even more successful one. The most commonly used graphs are circle or pie graphs, bar graphs, line graphs, and pictographs. The general rule to follow in graph making is that a single graph should be used to communicate only one concept or idea. Consider the graph in Figure 15-2. Such a graph is far too "busy" or cluttered for an audience to read easily and quickly. Your goal in devising a graph is to eliminate extraneous information and to focus audience attention, not diffuse it. Emphasize the essentials.

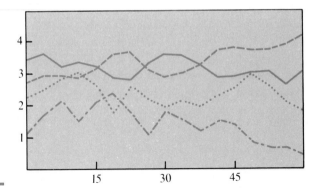

FIGURE 15-2
Line graph

A *pie graph* is simply a circle with the various percentages of the whole indicated by "wedges." In a speech on local systems of taxation one student used a pie graph to stress the large percentage of the municipal budget allocated to schools (see Figure 15-3).

If your goal is to compare the performance of one variable over time, a bar graph might be your choice (see Figure 15-4). Bar graphs can also be used to contrast various events at a particular point in time. In Figure 15-5, a student compared the number of burglaries in four different police precincts on a single day. The bar graph clearly showed the wide discrepancy among the precincts, from over 30 burglaries in precinct 2 to fewer than 5 in precinct 4.

Like bar graphs, line graphs can illustrate trends over a particular time span (see Figure 15-6). Such a graph can establish if a perceptible trend is visible. The line graph is one of the easiest types of graphs for audience members to follow.

Pictographs utilize sketches of figures to represent the concept under discussion (see Figure 15-7). During your research you may discover sketches or pictures that could be integrated into a pictograph to help vitalize your content.

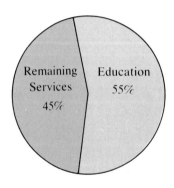

FIGURE 15-3
Pie graph

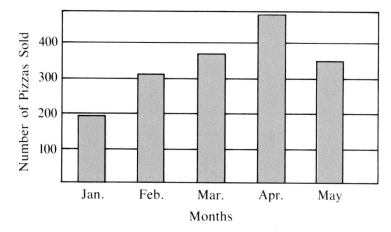

FIGURE 15-4
Bar graph

Photographs and Drawings

Finally, you may find photographs or sketches that can add interest or impact to your presentation and provide a reality dimension as well. For example, one student juxtaposed a photograph of the deceased singer Karen Carpenter (taken from the cover of a national weekly magazine) with a photo of her own sister to illustrate that anorexia nervosa is a disease that afflicts the famous as well as the ordinary person.

Drawings, like photographs, can help generate a mood, clarify, or identify. In explaining the sequence of plays that led to a success for his team, one speaker used a sketch like the drawing in Figure 15-8. Would you recommend that he simplify the sketch?

If possible, use a variety of dark, rich colors like red, black, blue, and green in the drawing to add contrast. But remember, unless the drawing

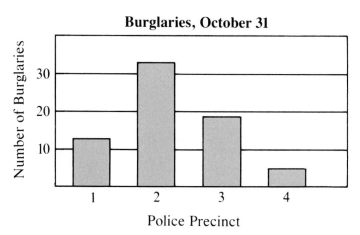

FIGURE 15-5
Bar graph

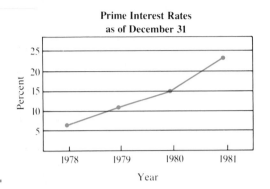

FIGURE 15-6
Line graph

is large enough to be seen, it will not increase your audience's attention or strengthen your presentation.

Guidelines for Using Visual Aids

When judging visuals, remember that they must be appropriate to the audience, the occasion and location, the content of your speech, and you.

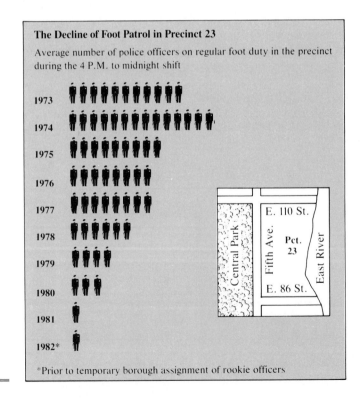

FIGURE 15-7
Pictograph
Source: New York City Police Department. © 1982 by The New York Times Company. Reprinted by permission.

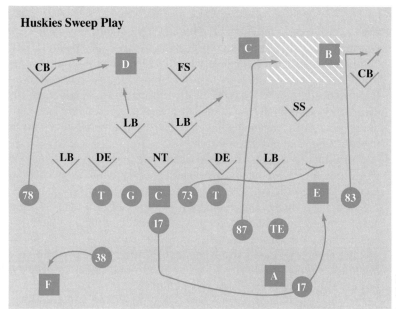

FIGURE 15-8
Drawing

In addition, when developing your visual materials, keep in mind three key guidelines: (1) simplicity, (2) clarity, and (3) visibility. By *simplicity* we mean that the visuals should be as transportable as possible (so that you can easily bring them with you to the presentation) and as easy to use as possible. Give careful consideration to the size and weight of large items. Ask yourself if the visual can be displayed without disrupting the environment. Ask yourself if it can be set up and taken down in a minimum amount of time. With regard to the criterion of *clarity*, you'll recall that the purpose of a visual aid is to enhance understanding, not to increase confusion. Ideally each visual should depict only one idea or concept, or at least be able to be displayed so that only relevant portions are visible at the corresponding speech juncture. *Visibility* is the third factor you need to attend to. Since a visual serves no purpose if it cannot be seen and read, you must determine if your audience will be able to see and read the aid with relative ease. Make sure that lettering is tall enough (three-quarters of an inch high or larger) and that photographs or pictures are large enough.

The most popular method used to present all but three-dimensional visuals is to display them on a chartboard or on oaktag. Given a number of variously colored felt markers, a yardstick, and a little time, you should be able to create visuals that will enhance your speech. If you are willing to invest a bit more in terms of time, energy, and expense, the "press-on" letters that are widely available in stationery stores can provide your work with a "professional" appearance. You may, if desired, use more sophisticated equipment to present your visuals. Overhead projectors, film, video-tape, and 35-mm slides are frequently employed. Overhead projectors are commonly used by training professionals and salespeople. Transparencies can be created from almost any 8½ by 11 original of a photograph, illustration, or graph. In this case the image can be projected onto a screen or a light-colored wall (if a screen is unavailable). The room need not be completely darkened to use the overhead projector, but be sure to rehearse using your transparencies in order to test their visibility and their clarity. (Setup time is about 10 minutes.)

Film clips can also be used to add life and motion to your presentation. For film, a screen or light-colored wall is used in a room that can be darkened. In addition, you should realize that it will take about 15 minutes for you to prepare the room and equipment for use. Without adequate setup time a film clip can become more of a hindrance than a help. Slides can be used with less difficulty than film. However, we suggest that unless you have been trained in multimedia or multi-image production, the number of slides you use should be kept to a minimum. (Also be prepared to handle jammed slide trays and burned-out bulbs.)

Videotape recorders have greatly improved and simplified the use of video and film clips by speakers. Video stores have many tapes that can be used to increase audience interest. One speaker used a clip from Abbott and Costello's "Who's on First?" routine to introduce the topic of language. A speaker on real estate used examples from a local real estate program on cable television. A company president regularly uses clips from the various *Rocky* films to help motivate her sales force. The channel C-Span has greatly enhanced our ability to incorporate current events into speeches. If your topic is current, check the C-Span listings—if they are available in your area—to determine when the topic will be covered. Thus, in addition to quoting the public official in question, you can bring that person as a "video guest" to briefly illustrate a point.

When using video, carefully edit the segment to 30 seconds or less and cue up the tape before you begin the speech. Far too many speakers press the "play" button only to find that they have no picture or sound on the monitor. One speaker we observed recently began his presentation only to have to go almost immediately to a coffee break while repairs were done on the video equipment. Audiences today are simply not prepared to sit while you and others tinker with the electronic gadgetry. Prepare it carefully in advance and rehearse!

A Look at Audio Aids

Audiotape is readily available and easy to use as an accompaniment to your speech presentation. Cassette players come in a variety of forms and easy-to-carry sizes. Since speechmakers often find it advantageous to integrate a brief song excerpt or a segment from an interview or newscast into their presentations, audiotape has become a popular support medium. One student, for example, reinforced an informative presentation entitled "The Speech Capabilities of Dolphins" with a few moments of dolphin sounds that she had recorded during a visit to an aquarium. Another chose to add impact to a speech called "Teenage Runaways" by using a segment of the Beatles' song "She's Leaving Home."

If you decide to use audiotape to enhance your speechmaking performance, cue the tape to the precise point at which you wish to begin. Do this before you arrive at the front of the room to prevent the process of "finding the right spot" on the tape from bringing your presentation to an untimely halt.

To conclude, once you have decided on your topic and have conducted your research, it's time to begin to think actively about integrating presentation aids into your speech. There is little doubt that a well-chosen, well-designed visual or audio aid can add interest and impact to your message.

HOW TO IMPROVE YOUR ABILITY TO SUPPORT YOUR IDEAS

A speech devoid of support is like a skeleton devoid of skin; the structure is there, but the flesh is missing. By developing an understanding of the way support functions to amplify a speech's ideas, you increase your chances of becoming a proficient speaker. The speaker who is adept at finding and using support realizes the following:

1. Support rarely if ever surfaces on its own. You need to search yourself, other people, and published materials to find it.
2. In order for ideas to affect listeners, the imagination of audience members must be stirred. Supportive devices can help serve this function. Definitions, statistics, examples and illustrations, testimonials, comparison and contrast, and repetition and restatement can all be used to increase the understandability, believability, and impact of spoken words.
3. Audio and visual aids can also be used to enhance a presentation's effectiveness. If appropriately designed and integrated, they will help increase listener comprehension, retention, and motivation.

SUMMARY

The first step in the topic development stage of the speech-preparation process is to gather a variety of effective research materials to integrate into your presentation. You may consult published works, including books, journals, magazines, and newspapers available in the library. You may be able to draw on your own personal observations and experiences. Or you can interview other people or conduct a survey.

Depending on the nature of your topic, you can make your research interesting and understandable to your audience by using various kinds of verbal support: definitions, statistics, examples and illustrations, testimonials (quotations from others), or comparisons and contrasts. You can often increase the impact and memorability of your speech by using repetition and restatement.

Many speeches can be enhanced with visual and audio support. Objects, models, graphs, photographs, drawings, slides, videotapes, and audiotapes can be incorporated into the presentation to reinforce, clarify, and dramatize concepts.

SUGGESTIONS FOR FURTHER READING

Ehninger, Douglas, Bruce E. Gronbeck, Ray E. McKerrow, and Alan H. Monroe. *Principles and Types of Speech Communication*, 9th ed. Glenview, Ill.: Scott, Foresman, 1982. Provides an excellent overview of the speech-support process.

McCormick, Mona. *The New York Times Guide to Reference Materials*. New York: Popular Library, 1971. A fine guide to library research and reference materials.

Minor, Edward O., and Harold R. Frye. *Techniques for Producing Visual Instructional Media*. New York: McGraw-Hill, 1970. Provides specific information for producing professional-quality visuals.

Morrisey, George L. *Effective Business and Technical Communication*. Reading, Mass.: Addison-Wesley, 1975. Contains useful information on how to develop presentation aids.

O'Sullivan, Kevin. "Audio Visuals and the Training Process." In *Training and Development Handbook*, edited by Robert L. Craig. New York: McGraw-Hill, 1976. Contains a rather complete survey of presentation aids. Can easily be adapted to meet the needs of public speakers.

Todd, Alden. *Finding Facts Fast*. Berkeley, Calif.: Ten Speed Press, 1979. A readable and usable tool; guaranteed to save you time.

NOTES

1. For a more comprehensive treatment of supporting materials, see Douglas Ehninger, Alan Monroe, and Bruce Gronbeck, *Principles and Types of Speech Communication*, 8th ed. (Glenview, Ill.: Scott, Foresman, 1978), chap. 7.

2. For a discussion of the power of the example in public speaking, see Scott Consigny, "The Rhetorical Example," *Southern Speech Communication Journal*, Vol. 41 (1976), pp. 121–134.

3. The power of restatement is explained in a study by R. Ehrensberger, "An Experimental Study of the Relative Effects of Certain Forms of Emphasis in Public Speaking," *Speech Monographs*, Vol. 12 (1945), pp. 94–111.

4. For a discussion of research that reveals how visual aids help increase recall, see W. Linkugel and D. Berg, *A Time to Speak* (Belmont, Calif.: Wadsworth, 1970).

5. For a work on how to prepare and use visual aids, see James W. Brown, Richard B. Lewis, and Fred F. Harcleroad, *AV Instruction: Techniques, Media and Methods* (New York: McGraw-Hill, 1973).

16

Designing Your Presentation: The Organizer in You

Every speech ought to be put together like a living creature, with a
body of its own, so as to be neither without head nor without feet,
but to have both a middle and extremities, described proportionately
to each other and to the whole.

Plato

CHAPTER PREVIEW

After finishing this chapter, you should be able to:

Explain how the *principle of redundancy* affects speech organization
Describe the framework that is basic to any speech presentation
Identify main and subordinate ideas
Create a complete sentence outline
Identify five methods of ordering your ideas
Use internal summaries and transitions effectively
Develop an effective speech introduction
Develop an effective speech conclusion
Use the *tryout* to refine speech design

Y̲ou can have the best ideas in the world and the most interesting and eye-opening support for those ideas, but if you are unable to organize your ideas and integrate your support so that audience members can follow what you're trying to communicate, you might as well not speak at all. In your role as speechmaker, organization is one of the main challenges you will have to face. It is the second step in the topic development stage of the systematic speaking process (see page 321).

What is your goal when organizing your ideas? Primarily, you want to order your materials in such a way that communication between you and your audience will be facilitated rather than hampered. How can you accomplish this? You must plan. Just as an architect develops a plan for a building, so you must develop a plan for your speech. Your plan reveals the structure you will adhere to, the developmental sequence you think will work best to communicate the contents of your talk. Of course, just as an architect considers numerous design possibilities before selecting one to use, so you should also test potential patterns to determine which helps clarify and amplify your ideas the most. Fortunately, you will not have to chart your way blindly through an array of myriad organizational possibilities. Instead, communication theorists have developed guidelines to help with this phase.

THE SPEECH OUTLINE: BUILDING THE FRAMEWORK

Because of the nature of a speechmaking occasion, it is impossible for the speechmaker's audience to go back over presented material and reexamine it. Your listeners need to be able to comprehend your message the first time they hear it, because they will probably never hear it again. There is no rewind button for audience members to push if they become distracted or confused. Speakers must therefore structure their messages so that listener confusion is kept to a minimum.[1]

We discovered earlier that communicators are not necessarily adept listeners. For this reason we advise you to base your speech's organization on the *principle of redundancy*. In other words, to ensure audience comprehension, you will need to build a certain amount of repetition into your presentation. Only if this is done will listeners be able to follow your ideas easily. This basic developmental principle is often expressed this way: Tell them what you are going to tell them, then tell them, and finally, tell them what you have told them.

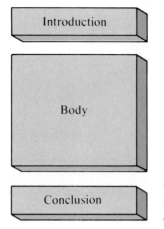

FIGURE 16-1
The speech
framework

One of the best ways to organize your speech is to use an *introduction-body-conclusion format* (see Figure 16-1). We refer to this structure as your "speech framework," because it provides a frame or skeleton on which any speech or formal presentation can be built.

The speech you develop should be organized to fit the preceding framework description. Your introductory remarks and your concluding statements should each occupy approximately 10 to 15 percent of your total presentation. This leaves 70 to 80 percent of your time for you to develop the ideas contained in the body of your speech. Since the body will function as the main portion of your presentation, it is often advisable to begin by preparing this part of the speech; once this is set, you can move on to develop the introduction and the conclusion. Let's consider the three key parts of a speech in that order.

THE BODY OF YOUR PRESENTATION: CHOOSING THE RIGHT APPROACH

As you begin to organize the body of your speech, you must think in terms of a logical structure for your ideas. Recognize that your audience members will be unlikely to recall a long, wandering, unstructured collection of data. In examining the evidence you have gathered, you will need to attempt to determine which of your materials support your main ideas and which support subordinate ideas. (By "subordinate" we mean those ideas which function as amplification for more important ones.) In many ways, subordinate ideas can be viewed as the base or the foundation on which larger ideas are constructed (see Figure 16-2). Consequently, you should begin the organizational process by arranging your materials into "clusters" of main and subordinate ideas.

A good speech is built on a solid framework. Review your outline and preliminary drafts carefully and get the reactions of a respected and knowledgeable colleague. (Ulrike Welsch)

Your main ideas will be the two to five major points you want the audience to remember after the presentation is completed. If, for example, you want listeners to recall the three major outcomes of World War II, those outcomes should be the major points in the speech. One way to begin to structure your research material is to put the ideas into boxes:

Specific Purpose: _____

I   II   III

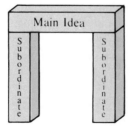

FIGURE 16-2
Idea construction

Place your main ideas into boxes, as shown on page 382. For example, if you are going to develop a speech on computer viruses, you might begin with the following major points

Purpose: To inform the audience about computer viruses.

Thesis: The audience will understand what a computer virus is, how it is spread, and how it can be prevented.

I	II	III
Definition of Computer Virus	Spread of Computer Viruses	Preventive Measures

The speaker is off to a good start. He or she now needs to develop these major points into complete sentences using parallel structure.

I. Computer viruses can be defined in two ways.

II. Computer viruses are spread by people and machines.

III. Computer viruses can be prevented.

Many people report that they are helped by developing the material in a system like the one shown in Figure 16-3. Here we see the entire process with a place to plug in information that is contained in the main idea and the supporting ideas. Once you have completed such a structure, you are ready to create a more traditional outline.

As you continue pulling these clusters together, arrange them in this fashion:

Main idea
    Subordinate idea
        Subordinate idea
    Subordinate idea
        Subordinate idea
        Subordinate idea

If you have taken notes on cards, it is possible to begin to "lay out" or pattern the body of your speech in the following way.

Purpose statement
    I. Main idea
        A. (Supports I)
            1. (Supports A)

Presentation Planning Worksheet

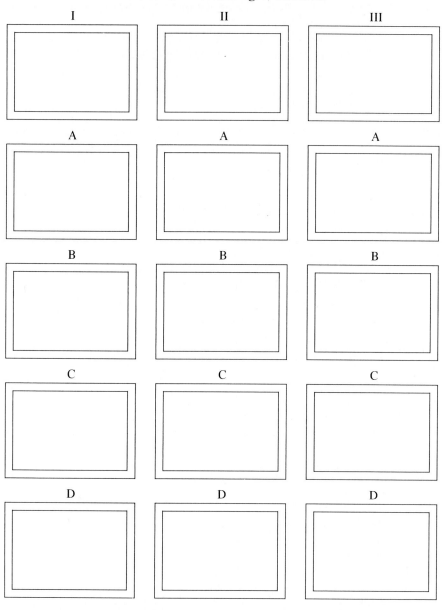

FIGURE 16-3
Presentation
Planning
Worksheet

    2. (Supports A)
    3. (Supports A)
  B. (Supports I)
    1. (Supports B)
    2. (Supports B)
II. Main idea
  A. (Supports II)
  B. (Supports II)

As the preceding example reveals, the outline you develop indicates the relative importance of each item included within it. The main points, symbolized with Roman numerals I, II, III, and so on, are the most important items you wish your audience to remember. Your subpoints, symbolized with capital letters A, B, C, etc., are supportive of but less important than main points. Likewise, sub-subpoints, symbolized by Arabic numbers 1, 2, 3, etc., are supportive of but less important than subpoints. Thus, a correct outline, using appropriate symbols and margins would look like this:

Purpose: To inform audience members about myths and realities concerning acquired immune deficiency syndrome (AIDS).

I. Several myths about the disease AIDS are prevalent in society today.
  A. Many people believe they can contract AIDS by touching objects that a person infected with the disease touched recently.
    1. They use handkerchiefs to open doorknobs.
    2. They wear gloves to handle money.
    3. They will not sit on toilet seats.
  B. Others are frightened of touching people they suspect could have the disease.
    1. They avoid shaking hands.
    2. Kissing is out of the question.
    3. They avoid coming into contact with someone who is crying.
II. Much is known about how AIDS is spread.
  A. When the virus is dry it is dead.
  B. It doesn't live long when exposed to the air.
  C. The disease is transmitted by exposure to the semen or blood of an infected partner through a break in the skin.

Ordering Your Ideas

Obviously, the ideas contained in your speech should be organized in a way that will make sense to your audience. To help accomplish this, there are

Lay It All Out

1. For practice, record the following information on 3- by 5-inch cards.

   Barry W. Keenan and Joseph Amsler kidnapped Frank Sinatra, Jr., from his Lake Tahoe hotel room on December 8, 1963.

   C. Burke Elbrick, U.S. ambassador to Brazil, was kidnapped by revolutionaries on September 4, 1969.

   The children of the wealthy are easy prey for kidnappers.

   Lt. Colonel Donald J. Crowley, U.S. air attaché in the Dominican Republic, was kidnapped by terrorists.

   J. Paul Getty, 3d, grandson of the U.S. oil mogul, was kidnapped by persons demanding $2.8 million in exchange for his life.

   Kidnapping victimizes the rich.

   Kidnapping victimizes the famous.

   Patricia Hearst was kidnapped by members of the Symbionese Liberation Army, who demanded that her father, Randolph Hearst, donate $2 million in food to the poor.

   Daniel A. Mitrione, U.S. diplomat to Uruguay, was abducted by terrorists who demanded the release of political prisoners.

   An Exxon executive living in Campana, Argentina, was kidnapped by Marxist guerrillas.

   Terrorist organizations have used kidnapping as a key means to publicize their varied causes.

   Kidnappers prey upon the rich, the famous, and those they perceive to be in a position to help further their political ends.

   Charles A. Lindbergh, Jr., son of the famed aviator, was abducted and eventually killed by kidnappers who demanded a $50,000 ransom.

2. Lay the cards on a large table or other open area. After examining your various options, arrange the items into main and subordinate ideas. Note: You need not use all the cards. Select only those which support your purpose statement and main idea.

3. Compare the layout you devised with those devised by others. Eventually it will become necessary for you to place the provided information into the standard outline form given in the text.

five generally accepted organizational formats: (1) chronological, or time, order, (2) spatial order, (3) cause-effect order, (4) problem-solution order, and (5) topical order. We will examine each in turn.

Chronological, or time, ordering is the technique used to discuss the development of an idea or a problem in the order in which it occurs or occurred in time. For example, one student chose to explore the events that resulted in a successful politician's popularity among his city's residents.

Purpose statement: To explain the reasons behind the erosion of Mayor Edward Koch's power base in New York City.

I. Edward Koch's downfall began when major associates were charged with corruption.
II. Mayor Koch then lost the support of a number of minority groups.
III. Mayor Koch next found that even mainstream members of his own party were prepared to oppose his reelection.

Think of three topics you could develop using a chronological pattern of organization. Why do they lend themselves to such an arrangement?

As you can see, the student considered the steps in the decline of Edward Koch in the order in which they occurred. Another student used a time format for the following speechmaking project:

Purpose statement: To examine the history of the insanity defense in criminal jurisprudence.

I. In the seventeenth and eighteenth centuries, belief in the practice of witchcraft influenced popular legal conceptions of mental disorder.
II. The nineteenth-century showcase for the insanity defense was the trial of Daniel M'Naghten, a would-be political assassin.
III. It was not until 1954 that the courts began to acknowledge that a wide variety of diseases or defects may impair the mind.
IV. In 1982, the John Hinckley case and the public's reactions to it again raised questions regarding our attitude toward crime, punishment, and personal responsibility.

Any event that has occurred in time can be examined chronologically. When preparing a time-ordered presentation, it is up to you to decide the point at which to begin and end your chronology and to choose the events you wish to include within the sequence. As you can probably tell, time ordering is most often used in informative speeches.

A *spatial pattern* of organization describes an object, person, or phenomenon as it exists in space. An object, for example, might be described from

Top to bottom
Bottom to top

Left to right
Right to left
Inside to outside
Outside to inside

How could you use a spatial pattern of organization to describe yourself? For practice, try it.

The point is that you must select a particular orientation and carry it through. One student selected a spatial pattern to explain the appearance and functioning of a beehive:

I.   The outside of the hive
II. The inside of the hive

Another student used spatial organization to describe the interior design of the White House.

I.   The entrance is a study in perspective.
II.   The first floor is a study in contrasts.
III. The second floor containing the living quarters is a study in the personality of the occupant.

Like the time order, the spatial order is used most frequently by speakers who are delivering informative speeches.

Visuals can be used effectively to help reinforce the information contained in a spatially organized presentation, whether you intend to discuss the components of a computer, the terrain of a national park, the design of a new car, or the floor plan for a new style of home. The use of a spatial pattern involves organizing your ideas according to an area concept, and that area concept should be reflected in the main points of the outline.

SKILL BUILDER

Speaker's Choice

1. Select a rock, shell, piece of driftwood, or some other such object from nature.
2. Describe the object to a partner, a group of students, or the entire class, using a spatial pattern of organization.
3. Explain the reasons for your particular type of spatial approach.
4. Would approaching the object from a different angle have altered your audience's understanding and appreciation of it? How?

The *cause-effect* pattern of organization requires you to compartmentalize your materials into those related to the causes of a problem and those related to its effects. It is then up to you to decide which aspect you will explore first. Thus, in a speech designed to examine the issue of drunk driving, you might begin by discussing the percentage of drivers during a certain period who were drunk when involved in car accidents (cause). You might then discuss the number of deaths that occur each year that are attributed directly to driver intoxication (effect). Following this approach, one student first discussed the physiological and psychological causes of obesity and then considered the health-related effects that could result from being overweight.

You can vary the approach by discussing the effect prior to considering the cause. In the following example, a student used an effect to cause pattern to reveal the causes of excessive student stress:

I.   The number of students suffering from stress-related ailments is increasing at an alarming rate.
II. Experts have identified four major explanations for this increase.

As we see, the cause-effect and effect-cause order is quite a versatile one and is used in both informative and persuasive speeches.

A *problem solution* type of organization requires that you (1) determine what the problems inherent in a particular situation are and (2) present a solution to remedy them. Thus you might discuss the problems that develop when large numbers of students entering college are deficient in writing skills. The second portion of your speech could then suggest a number of ways in which the identified problem could be alleviated (perhaps, for example, by expanding tutoring programs or adding noncredit remedial courses to the curriculum). Accordingly, if you were concerned about the increased crime in your community and chose to speak about it from a problem solution perspective, your first task might be to establish in the minds of your listeners that a problem does indeed exist. From there you could proceed to propose various solutions to your identified problem.

One student used a problem solution order to persuade her listeners that their state should raise the legal drinking age to 21:

I.   The problems caused by intoxicated teenagers are increasing.
II. Raising the legal drinking age to 21 will do much to allieviate the situation.

The problem-solution format is most frequently employed in persuasive speaking.

At times your speech may not fit neatly into any of the preceding patterns. When this happens, you may choose to develop or cluster your

How could you use a cause-effect pattern of organization to explain a recent disagreement you had with a professor, employer, friend, or family member?

material by dividing it into a series of appropriate topics. Thus you would use a *topical pattern* of organization. In doing this you could, for example, consider using any of the following categorical arrangements: the advantages and disadvantages of a particular proposal, the social, political, and economic factors that contribute to a problem, or the perceptions that upper-class, middle-class, and lower-class people might have on the issue in question. When using a topical pattern, you may find that you integrate or intermingle cause and effect, time, problem and solution, or spatial organizational formats with it.

One student used a topical format to explain to his listeners the various factors that help shape attitudes toward the abortion issue:

I. The family is a prime attitude influencer.
II. Religious groups play a role.
III. Economic pressures also exert force.

Another student used a topical format to persuade her listeners that shield laws (laws that protect journalists from having to reveal their sources) should exist:

I. Shield laws do protect the public's right to know.
II. Shield laws do protect the reporter from having to serve as government informant.

Because of their wide applicability, topical formats are used very frequently.

Selecting an appropriate organizational format is an important factor in determining whether your speech will be successful. Just as fashion designers must create an exciting pattern or design in the clothes they wish you to buy, so you must select an appealing pattern for your presentation.

Internal Summaries and Transitions: Connecting Devices

In order for you to transmit your ideas to an audience with clarity and fluidity, it will be necessary for you to discover ways to move from one idea to the next. To do this, you must become acquainted with internal summaries and transitions.

The body of the presentation should contain brief, internal summaries; these are designed to help listeners remember the speech's content. Examples: "Thus far we have examined two key housing problems. Let us now consider a third," or "The four characteristics we have discussed thus far are. . . ." Besides aiding audience recall, transitional words or phrases serve to facilitate the speaker's movement from one idea to another; in effect, they bridge the gap between ideas, eliminating abrupt switches.[2] Thus, to indicate that additional information is forthcoming you might use such transitional words and phrases as "equally important," "next," "second," "furthermore," "in addition," and "finally." To signal that you will be discussing a cause-effect relationship, you could use expressions like "as a result," "consequently," and "in short." To indicate that there is a contrasting view to the one being elaborated, you would use such phrases as "after all," "in spite of," "on the other hand," and "and yet." In practice, the use of expressions such as "likewise" and "similarly" signals that a comparison will be made, and phrases like "for example" and "for instance" let the listener know that a point will be illustrated.

BEGINNINGS AND ENDINGS

Once you've outlined the body of your speech and considered the need for transitional devices, you are ready to add the "tell them what you are going to tell them" and the "tell them what you have told them" components. In other words, it's time to develop your introduction and conclusion.[3]

The Introduction

The function of your speech's introduction is to gain the attention of audience members, make them want to listen to your speech, and provide them with an overview of the subject you will be discussing. Mastering the art of designing an introduction is much like mastering any art form; that is, it requires creative-thinking energy. You will need to examine your purpose, the speech itself as developed, your analysis of the audience, and your own abilities. All too frequently, the introduction is overlooked or neglected because speakers are in too much of a hurry to get to "the heart of the matter." However, in speaking, just as in interpersonal communication, first impressions do count. Thus, the opening moments of contact with one person or with a multitude can affect the developing relationship between speaker and listeners either positively or negatively.

Unquestionably the first few moments of your speech—the introduction—will affect your audience's willingness to process the remainder of your presentation. It is at this point that people will decide whether what you have to say is interesting and important or foolish and inconsequential. In case of the latter verdict, your audience may elect to "tune you out" for the remainder of your speech. On the other hand, a well-designed introduction can help you develop a solid rapport with audience members, one that will make it easier for you to share your thoughts and ideas with them.

The material you include in your introduction must be selected with care. Since in all likelihood your listeners have not been waiting in line for

> Use brainstorming techniques to devise a number of ways you could introduce yourself to a group of people you don't know.

several days just to hear you speak, you will need to work to spark their interest; you will need to motivate them to listen to you. Some student speakers have been known to go a bit overboard in attempting to fulfill this objective. A number have been known to yell, throw books across the room, and, in one recent case, fire a blank from a starter pistol. Such devices, while startling, can backfire and turn audiences against you. (After all, it is difficult to listen to ideas or evaluate content if you fear for your own physical well-being.) Other speakers look for a joke—*any* joke—to use as an attention-getting device. Unfortunately, a joke chosen at random is seldom related to the speaker's topic and thus serves to confuse and possibly alienate listeners rather than interest and involve them the way a well-selected anecdote might. Still other speakers insist on beginning their presentations with statements like "My purpose here today is . . ." or "Today I hope to convince you. . . ." Such openings only suggest that the speechmaker has forgotten to consider the motivation and attention aspects of the introduction.

What types of materials serve as the best interest-arousing devices? What are some effective examples for us to examine? Consider this. Years ago television shows began by merely flashing the title of the program onto the screen. Today, however, it is common practice to use a "teaser" to open a show. The teaser usually reveals segments of the show designed to arouse the interest of potential viewers—designed to encourage them to "stay tuned." Without this device, many audience members would probably switch channels to explore the offerings of competing networks. Even though your audience cannot easily "switch" speakers, they can decide not to listen *actively* to what you have to say. Therefore, you too must design a teaser to include in your introduction—material that will interest and appeal to your listeners.

Effective speechmakers begin their talks in a number of different ways. They may relate an unusual fact, make a surprising statement, or cite a shocking statistic. Or they might ask a question, compliment the audience, or refer to the occasion. Sometimes they will use a humorous story or illustration to promote interest and provide a lead-in to the topic. At still other times they will rely on a suspense-filled tale or a human interest story to capture the attention of their listeners. People enjoy listening to stories about other people. For this reason, the described plight of a family left homeless by a fire might be used effectively to open a speech on fire prevention, and a description of people severely injured in an automobile accident might introduce a speech supporting the use of air bags. Equally, if you have selected a certain topic because you have a personal interest in it, it would be acceptable for you to use a personal anecdote to begin your presentation.

Let us examine a few examples of these various approaches. Some of the most effective introductions use *humor*, as in the following examples from speeches by President Ronald Reagan and Commissioner Barbara Franklin.

> The story is that there was an agent overseas who happened to be in Ireland and there was an emergency and it was necessary to contact him immediately. So they called in another agent and they said, "Now, you'll go there. His name is Murphy and your recognition will be to say, " 'Tis a fair day but it'll be lovelier this evening.' "
>
> So he went to Ireland and—a little town in Ireland, into the pub, elbowed himself up to the bar, ordered a drink and then said to the bartender, "How would I get in touch with Murphy?"
>
> And the bartender says, "Well, if it's Murphy the farmer you want, it's two miles down the road and it's the farm on the left." He said, "If it's Murphy the bootmaker, he's on the second floor of the building across the street. And," he says, "my name is Murphy."
>
> So he picked up the drink and he said, "Well, 'tis a fair day, but it'll be lovelier this evening."
>
> "Oh," he said, "it's Murphy the spy you want."
>
> *From a speech by President Reagan at a bill-signing ceremony at the Central Intelligence Agency, Langley, Virginia. White House transcript, June 23, 1982. © 1982 by The New York Times Company. Reprinted by permission.*

> As a federal regulator, I accept speaking engagements these days with more and more trepidation. The trepidation turns to outright fear as the day of the speech arrives and the experience of Winston Churchill comes to mind.
>
> On one of his trans-Atlantic tours, a student asked, "Mr. Churchill, doesn't it thrill you to know that every time you make a speech the hall is packed to overflowing?"
>
> Churchill pondered the question for a moment. Then he replied, "Of course, it is flattering. But always remember that if I were being hanged, the crowd would be twice as big."
>
> Churchill's point is not lost today. In view of predictions that government regulation is an idea whose time is passing, the prospect of a public lynching is very intimidating—especially to a potential "lynchee."
>
> I'll take my chances this evening. In fact, I welcome this opportunity to discuss the issue of regulation with those of you who ultimately will decide where it goes—consumers, the business community, and government officials.
>
> *From a speech by Barbara Hackman Franklin, commissioner of the Consumer Product Safety Commission, delivered at a conference on "The Conspicuous Consumer," Boston College, Boston, Massachusetts, November 29, 1978.*

Another kind of effective introduction is an *illustration*—which can also add drama to a presentation, as in the following remarks by William Stanmeyer:

On July 2, 1972, four-year-old Joyce Ann Huff, a beautiful little girl to judge by the newspaper photo, happily went out to play in the yard of her home in Los Angeles County. She played awhile, her mother occasionally glancing at her from a kitchen a few feet away. . . .

Neither Joyce Ann nor her mother noticed a yellow 1966 Chevrolet carrying three men roll up the street and pause while a man in the back seat took aim with a shotgun at the little girl. But they heard a thunderous explosion as the shotgun drove forty-two pellets into Joyce Ann's body and drove her soul forever from the face of the earth. Splattered with blood, Joyce Ann died within five minutes in the arms of her sobbing mother. . . .

What, if anything, under our present system of criminal justice, will happen to the murderers?

From a speech by Dr. William Stanmeyer, reprinted in Vital Speeches of the Day, *January, 1973, pp. 182–186.*

For a third kind of effective introduction, see how Representative Paul Findley combined a *question* and a *surprising statement* in order to make his point:

Have you ever considered this question: What was America's greatest invention? Was it Alexander Graham Bell's telephone? . . .

Was it the Wright brothers' airplane, which gave men wings, for good or ill? . . .

Was it atomic energy, which ushered in an age that is only now beginning to unfold?

Each has a claim to greatness. Each is uniquely American. Each has contributed immensely to progress. Which would you choose?

My choice may surprise you. It is none of these. My choice is nothing more tangible than a manuscript, and yet it has become the most vital force for freedom and progress history has known. It is uniquely an American invention. It is the federal union plan for government as embodied in the United States Constitution.

From a speech by Congressman Paul Findley, reprinted in Vital Speeches of the Day, *October 15, 1962, p. 26.*

One student began a speech in similar fashion:

Do you know who you voted for in the last presidential election? I bet you don't. I bet you think you voted for the Democratic, Republican, or Independent candidate. But you didn't. You voted to elect the members of the electoral college. In the course of my speech, I will explain why this practice is undemocratic, un-American, and unacceptable.

Finally, many speakers use a few startling statistics in the introduction to capture the audience's interest. Here are two examples:

Why exercise? There are some 50 million adult Americans who do not engage in physical activity for the purpose of exercise. That's equivalent to the entire population of France—and it was once said that 50 million Frenchmen can't be wrong. Can 50 million Americans be wrong? We think they are, and that's why we are here.

From a speech by Theodore G. Klumpp, consultant to the President's Council on Physical Fitness and Sports. Reprinted in Vital Speeches of the Day, *December 15, 1974, pp. 135–138.*

According to figures published by the U.S. Department of Justice, 192,000 women will be raped this year. The majority of these women will be young—in fact most will be between the ages of 16 and 34. Will you, your sister, your wife or your girlfriend be one of them? Research shows many of these attacks can be avoided. I'd like to tell you how.

From a student speech, "How to Protect Yourself from Being Raped."

After you have used your introduction to spark interest and motivate your listeners to continue attending to your presentation, it then is necessary for you to *preview* your speech for them; that is, you need to let your listeners know the information you will be discussing, as students did in the following examples. Consider

There are three weight classes of people in our society: the overweight, the underweight, and those who are the right weight. Unfortunately, many people fail to understand the role weight plays in their lives. Your weight affects how your body functions. Let's explore how.

and

People have traditionally relied on oil or gas to heat their homes. Today, solar energy is gaining favor as an alternate home heating source. However, I believe there are four good reasons why it is inappropriate to consider installing a solar energy system in your home at this time.

Your preview should correspond to your purpose statement. As such, it should help audience members know what to listen for. Additionally, by placing it subsequent to the attention and motivation step, you ensure that your purpose statement will get a fair hearing.

The Conclusion

Whereas the introduction functions to gain attention and preview the speech, the conclusion summarizes the presentation and leaves your audience thinking about what they have just heard. The conclusion provides a sense of completion.

The conclusion's summary function may be considered almost a preview in reverse. In other words, during your preview you revealed to audience members the subject of your efforts; during the summary stage you will review for them the material you have covered. For example, your summary might begin, "We have examined three benefits you will derive from a new town library." During the remainder of your summation the three benefits alluded to might then be restated, thus helping to cement them in the minds of the listeners. Many inexperienced speechmakers counter that the summary appears to be superfluous. ("After all, I've just said all of that not more than two minutes ago.") However, it is important to remember that you're speaking for listeners, not for yourself. The summary provides some of the built-in redundancy mentioned earlier; it enables audience members to leave the occasion with your ideas freshly impressed on their minds. In effect, the conclusion serves a memory-refreshing function and helps clarify many of the issues or ideas you just discussed.

Besides summarizing what has been discussed, your ending should also be used to heighten the impact of your presentation. You can realize this objective in a number of different ways. One commonly employed technique is to refer again to your introductory remarks. This practice helps give your speech a sense of closure. If, for example, you are speaking about child abuse and you began your presentation by showing pictures of abused children, you might paraphrase your opening remarks and show the pictures again as a means of arousing the sympathy and support of your audience. Quotations and illustrations also make effective conclusions. For example, if you were speaking about the problems faced by veterans of the Vietnam war, you could provide a moving conclusion by quoting a number of former GIs or retelling some of the challenges they faced. Of course, you are also free to draw upon your own experiences when designing a conclusion. Keep in mind that just as with introductions, audiences respond to endings that contain personal references, surprising statements, startling statistics, or relevant humor.

Let's examine how some of these techniques work in practice. One student, for example, used this illustration to end his speech on "The Nature of AIDS":

> "I take their hand and talk to them. I tell them I was happy I could make things easier. Then I say, 'Thank you for letting me work for you.'" But every night before Jerry Cirasulolo goes to sleep, he also recites a little prayer: "Please God, give me the strength to keep on caring. And please don't let me get AIDS."

In his speech on physical fitness referred to earlier, Theodore Klumpp concluded with a *surprising statement* to keep his audience thinking about his remarks:

Unfortunately, nature does not appear to favor mind over matter, and the full utilization of only our mental capacities does not appear to be enough. I believe that we must do everything we can, as we grow older, to resist the inclination to slow down the tempo of our living. I am convinced that if you will just sit and wait for death to come along, you will not have to wait long.

From a speech by Theodore G. Klumpp, Vital Speeches of the Day, *December 15, 1974.*

Knowing that quotations can add impact to a speech's conclusion, Robert Kennedy often ended his speeches with these words by the poet Robert Browning:

Some men see things as they are, and ask, "Why?" I dare to dream of things that never were, and ask—"Why not?"

And humor, when used appropriately, can help keep people on your side. One student began a speech on healthy living by saying:

Medical experts tell us that even laughter is healthy. In fact it is bad to suppress laughter. It goes back down and spreads your hips!

Another student began a speech directed at entering freshman students with the following letter:

Dear Mom and Dad:
Just thought I'd drop you a note to clue you in on my plans.
    I've fallen in love with a guy named Buck. He quit high school between his sophomore and junior years to travel with his motorcycle gang. He was married at 18 and has two sons. About a year ago he got a divorce.
    We plan to get married in the fall. He thinks he will be able to get a job by then. I've decided to move into his apartment. At any rate, I dropped out of school last week. Maybe I will finish college sometime in the future.
    Mom and Dad, I just want you to know that everything in this letter so far is false. NONE OF IT IS TRUE.
    But, it is true that I got a C in French and a D in math. And I am in need of money for tuition and miscellaneous.

                                                                Love,

In a speech on auto insurance, one speaker used quotations from accident reports.

ACCIDENT REPORTS

Coming home, I drove into the wrong house and collided with a tree I don't have.

The other car collided with mine without giving warning of its intention.

I thought my window was down, but found it was up when I put my head through it.

I pulled away from the side of the road, glanced at my mother-in-law, and headed over the embankment.

I had been driving for 40 years when I fell asleep at the wheel and had an accident.

I had been shopping for plants and was on my way home. As I reached an intersection, a hedge sprang up, obscuring my vision.

To increase the effectiveness of your introductions and conclusions, then, use some of these techniques:

1. Humor, when appropriate
2. Interesting illustrations or quotations
3. Rhetorical questions
4. Surprising statements or unusual facts
5. Startling statistics

HOW TO TELL HOW YOU ARE DOING: THE TRYOUT

Never would the playwright, producers, director, and performers of any theatrical production of importance "open" a show without first conducting a series of tryouts, or preview performances. These performances, often staged before groups of invited guests or audiences who pay reduced ticket prices, provide the cast and backers with the opportunity to experience audience reaction and, if necessary, to make needed alterations. As a speechmaker, you would be wise to afford yourself the same advantage.

Once you've researched your topic, identified your supporting materials, and outlined your presentation, it's time to become your own audience, as you explore the "sound" and "feel" of your speech. Two essential ingredients in your first tryout are your speech notes and a watch. If possible, also bring along a tape recorder so you can review the precise language you used to express your ideas. Before starting, check the time and turn on the recorder. You can then begin speaking. In effect, what you are doing is preparing an oral rough draft of your presentation. What should you be seeking to determine? First, you will want to know if your presentation consumes too much or too little time. If a run-through takes 25 minutes and your time limit is 5 minutes, you have serious revision work ahead of you. If, on the other hand, you have designed a "60-second wonder," you may find you need to go back to the library for more material. Second, as you examine the sound of your speech you may find that some of your ideas are not expressed as clearly as you would like. You may also discover

One essential step in preparing a speech is revision, and an oral run-through will often show you where you need to make changes. (Steven Baratz/The Picture Cube)

that some thoughts are reiterated again and again and again. Or perhaps your speech's structure is confusing because of missing or inappropriately placed transitions. Likewise, you may have failed to develop an effective attention-getting step, or the information contained in the body of your presentation may be too detailed or too technical for your target audience. Similarly, your conclusion may fail to satisfy the psychological requirements you demand from it.

An oral run-through of a speech often shows where revision is needed. The speech may run too long or too short, or its ideas may need clearer expression.

Use a copy of the following checklist to analyze your first tryout:

Topic
Date
Specific purpose
Length of presentation
Introduction
    Attention step
    Preview step
    Most effective components
    Needed changes

Body
  Main points
  Support
  Most effective components
  Changes needed
Conclusion
  Summation function
  Psychological appeal function
  Most effective components
  Changes needed

When it's time to make your revisions, we suggest you employ the modular revision method. Just as electronic equipment is designed with modules that can be removed for repair or replacement, so you can extract selected modules from your outline in order to revise them, replace them, or completely delete them according to need. For example, if you find that your main attention-getting component is not as effective as it could be—improve it. If the supporting material under, say the second main point in the body of your speech is confusing—rewrite it. If an illustration is too long and drawn out—shorten it. In other words, your goal during the tryout phase of preparation is to refine your speech until it is as close as possible to the one you will actually present. Once you reach that point, it is time to think about your delivery.

SUMMARY

Organization is one of the main challenges facing the speechmaker. One of the best ways to organize your speech is to use an introduction-body conclusion format. Since the body of the speech is the main part of your presentation, it should be prepared first. There are five generally accepted ways to organize the ideas in your speech: (1) You present the ideas in *chronological order*, (2) use a *spatial pattern* to describe your subject, (3) examine the issue in terms of its *causes and effects*, (4) look at the situation from a *problem solution perspective*, or (5) use a *topical pattern*, dividing your material into a series of appropriate topics. The body of your presentation must also include internal summaries and tran-

sitions to help listeners recall your speech's content.

After the body of the speech has been completed you are ready to prepare the introduction and conclusion. The introduction should gain the attention of the audience members, make them want to listen to your speech, and provide them with an overview of the subject to be discussed.

Among the devices used to enhance introductions are humor, illustrations, questions, surprising statements, and statistics. The purpose of the conclusion is to summarize the material covered, heighten the impact of the presentation, and enable the audience to leave the occasion with your ideas freshly impressed on their minds. Among the devices found to increase the effectiveness of conclusions are a surprising statement, quotation, and humor.

When you have completed the outline for the entire speech, you should become your own audience: try it out and analyze the results.

SUGGESTIONS FOR FURTHER READING

Connolly, James E. *Public Speaking as Communication*. Minneapolis: Burgess Publishing, 1974, pp. 35–47. Offers an audience-centered rationale for speech organization. Discusses a number of different organizational patterns, including chronological, spatial, cause and effect, and problem solution.

Cronkhite, Gary. *Public Speaking and Critical Listening*. Menlo Park, Calif.: Benjamin/Cummings, 1978. Offers advice on how to structure and sequence ideas for presentation.

Gibson, James. *Speech Organization: A Programmed Approach*. San Francisco: Rinehart Press, 1971. Self-taught speech organization.

Reid, Loren. *Speaking Well*. New York: McGraw-Hill, 1977. Chapter 11 provides a comprehensive treatment of introductions and conclusions.

Taylor, Anita. *Speaking in Public*. Englewood Cliffs, N.J.: Prentice-Hall, 1979. Contains a plethora of sample introductions and conclusions for study.

Van Ekeren, Glenn. *The Speaker's Sourcebook*. Englewood Cliffs, N.J.: Prentice-Hall, 1988. A fine source of humorous stories for many topics.

Whitman, Richard F., and John H. Timmis, "The Influence of Verbal Organizational Structure and Verbal Organizing Skills on Select Measures of Learning," *Human Communication Research*, Vol. 1 (1975), pp. 293–301. This article considers the ways in which speech organization affects audience response.

NOTES

1. A number of studies reveal how organization affects reception. For example, see Christopher Spicer and Ronald E. Bassett, "The Effect of Organization on Learning from an Informative Message," *Southern States Communication Journal*, Vol. 41 (1976), pp. 290–299, and John E. Baird, Jr., "The Effects of Speech Summaries upon Audience Comprehension of Expository Speeches of Varying Quality and Complexity," *Central States Speech Journal*, Vol. 25 (1974), pp. 119–127.

2. D. L. Thistlethwaite, H. deHaan, and J. Kamenetsky suggest that a message is more easily understood and accepted if transitions are employed. See "The Effect of 'Directive' and 'Non-Directive' Communication Procedures on Attitudes," *Journal of Abnormal and Social Psychology*, Vol. 51 (1955), pp. 107–118. Also of value on this aspect of speech organization is E. Thompson, "Some Effects of Message Structure on Listeners' Comprehension," *Speech Monographs*, Vol. 34 (1967), pp. 51–57.

3. For a more comprehensive treatment of introductions and conclusions, see Chapter 11 in Loren Reid, *Speaking Well* (New York: McGraw-Hill, 1977).

17

Meeting Your Public: The Speechmaker Speaks

The human brain is a wonderful thing. It operates from the moment
you're born until the first time you get up to make a speech.

Howard Goshorn

CHAPTER PREVIEW

After finishing this chapter, you should be able to:

Identify your personal level of speech anxiety

Use deep muscle relaxation and thought-stopping techniques
to reduce speech anxiety

Discuss four types of speech delivery: manuscript, memorization,
impromptu, and extemporaneous

Demonstrate how the use of appropriate nonverbal behaviors can
enhance presentation effectiveness

Develop an effective rehearsal schedule

Analyze a speechmaker's performance (including your own) by referring to content, organization, language, and delivery dimensions

Your research is done. Your speech is prepared. The date for your presentation is set. What happens next? If you're like most speakers, your mind turns to delivery. You wonder if you will ever gather the courage to stand and speak before an audience. The answer is "Of course!" You've come this far, and it's now time to complete the journey. Actually, there are only two more hurdles: your own anxiety and your need to rehearse.

A GUIDE TO HANDLING ANXIETY AND CONQUERING SPEECH FRIGHT

Fear, or anxiety, is something that affects *all* public speakers.[1] Thus if you experience a certain amount of apprehension before, during, or after presenting your speech, rest assured that you are not alone. Despite knowing this, students sometimes allow their fears to get the better of them. Instead of using anxiety as a positive force, they allow it to overwhelm them. To combat this, we suggest you work to discover how you can make whatever "speech fright" you may be feeling work for you.

Your Speech Fright Quotient

How anxious are you about delivering the speech you have prepared? Use this inventory to find out. For each of the following statements, choose the number that you believe best represents your response and record it on a separate sheet of paper:

1. I am afraid I will forget what I have to say.
   Not afraid   1   2   3   4   5   Extremely afraid
2. I am afraid my ideas will sound confused and jumbled.
   Not afraid   1   2   3   4   5   Extremely afraid
3. I am afraid my appearance will not be appropriate.
   Not afraid   1   2   3   4   5   Extremely afraid
4. I am afraid the audience will find my speech boring.
   Not afraid   1   2   3   4   5   Extremely afraid
5. I am afraid people in the audience will laugh at me.
   Not afraid   1   2   3   4   5   Extremely afraid
6. I am afraid I will not know what to do with my hands.
   Not afraid   1   2   3   4   5   Extremely afraid

7. I am afraid my instructor will embarrass me.
    Not afraid   1   2   3   4   5   Extremely afraid

8. I am afraid audience members will think my ideas are simplistic.
    Not afraid   1   2   3   4   5   Extremely afraid

9. I am afraid I will make grammatical mistakes.
    Not afraid   1   2   3   4   5   Extremely afraid

10. I am afraid everyone will stare at me.
    Not afraid   1   2   3   4   5   Extremely afraid

Next, add the numbers you chose and score yourself as follows:

41–50   Very apprehensive
31–40   Apprehensive
21–30   Normally concerned
11–20   Overconfident
10   Are you alive?

Although the quiz you just completed is not a scientific instrument, it should give you some indication of your fear level. Notice that you must display some level of anxiety to fall into the normal category. If you were not at all nervous about speaking in public, not only would you not be normal, you also would probably not be a very effective speechmaker.

Before we can cope with these fears, we need to develop a clearer understanding of some of the more common causes of speech fright.

Fear of Being Inadequate. If feeling adequate is a state in which an individual feels confident and capable, feeling inadequate is just the opposite, that is, feeling inferior and incapable. Feeling inadequate may cause us to assume that we will be unable to cope with the writing or speaking situations that present themselves to us. Do you fear to take risks because you imagine your performance will not be good enough, will be judged inadequate or not up to par? When you disagree with something you have read or heard, do you feel more comfortable swallowing hard and sitting quietly than you do speaking up for or writing about what you think is right? Is it easier for you to go along with the group than to write or speak your objections to the actions or words of others? If you feel inadequate, you probably prefer to play it safe; you do not want to risk further alienation.

Fear of the Unknown. A new job may cause us to feel fearful because co-workers, the situation, and our responsibilities are unfamiliar, unknown, or sketchy. Likewise, we may fear writing a paper or delivering a speech for the same reasons. Each event has a threatening, unknown quality to it, a quality that many people prefer not to deal with. We do not know how people will react to what we say and write. We simply are more comfortable with what is familiar—with the true and the tried. Although we have a cognitive understanding of what will or will not happen before an audience or in the mind of a reader, we let our emotions take charge, causing us to react emotionally and behave irrationally.

Fear of Being Judged.   How sensitive are you to the judgment of others? Are you concerned about your friend's opinion and/or judgment of you? Your instructor's? Do you believe that what an audience, reader, or teacher says about you is necessarily true? Sometimes we become so sensitive to the judgment(s) of others that we want to avoid judgment on any account. Public speaking is one such situation.

Inability to Face Consequences

In the extreme, two things may result from giving a speech: The audience may like it or dislike it. It may be a success or a failure. In the classroom, an unsatisfactory speech may earn a failing grade. In a business situation, it can result in the loss of an important account. Whatever the result, the speaker must be prepared to deal with the consequences.

Learning to Cope with Your Fears

We are largely the playthings of our fears.

Horace Walpole

One of the best ways to cope with the fear of speechmaking is to carefully design and rehearse your presentation. If you follow the system of preparation that we suggest, you will meet both of these requirements. Preparation notwithstanding, you may still find that you experience some anxiety about the speaking event.

Let us now explain how such anxiety may be controlled. The first thing you need to do is recognize the actual bodily sensations and thoughts that accompany and support your feelings of nervousness. Try the Skill Builder "What Does Anxiety Mean to You?"

SKILL BUILDER

What Does Anxiety Mean to You?

1. Describe the bodily sensations you experience whenever you are nervous or afraid.
2. Compile a list of thoughts that pass through your mind whenever you are nervous or anxious.

Examine the symptoms that you and others in your class identified during the preceding exercise. Did your lists contain any of the following common complaints?

A rapid or palpitating heartbeat
Stomach "knots"
Shaking hands, arms, or legs
A dry mouth
A stiff neck
A lump in the throat
Nausea
Diarrhea
Dizziness

In like fashion, when people are queried as to their fear-related thoughts, statements like the following emerge:

"I just can't cope."
"I'm irritable."
"I'm under such pressure."
"This is a nightmare."
"I know something terrible is going to happen."
"Why does the world have to crumble around me?"

Having identified the physical and mental sensations that accompany a fear response, your next step is to learn how to control such reactions.[2] The next section describes two behavior-modification techniques that can help you accomplish this.

Deep Muscle Relaxation: The Physical Side of Fear

It has been scientifically established that muscle tension commonly accompanies fear and anxiety. However, we also know that a muscle will relax after being tensed. Deep muscle relaxation is based on this fact. Now try the following. Tense your arm. Count to 10. Relax your arm. What feelings did you experience? Did your arm become heavier? Did it then become warmer? Try tensing and relaxing one or both of your legs. It is reasonable to expect that you can calm yourself by systematically tensing and relaxing each section of your body in turn.

Tense/Relax

1. Imagine that your body is divided into four basic sections:
   a. Hands and arms
   b. Face and neck
   c. Torso
   d. Legs and feet
2. Sit comfortably. In turn, practice tensing and relaxing each section of your body.
   a. *Hands and arms.* Clench your fists. Tense each arm from shoulder to fingertips. Notice the warm feeling that develops in your hands, forearm, and upper arms. Count to 10. Relax.
   b. *Face and neck.* Wrinkle your face as tightly as you can. Press your head back as far as it will go. Count to 10. Relax. Roll your head slowly to the front, side, back, and side in a circular movement. Relax.
   c. *Torso.* Shrug your shoulders. Count to 10 in this position. Relax. Tighten your stomach. Hold it. Relax.
   d. *Legs and feet.* Tighten your hips and thighs. Relax. Tense your calves and feet. Relax.

You will want to try using the "Tense/Relax" exercise several times prior to your actual speech presentation. Many students report that their "butterflies" or tensions tend to settle in particular bodily sections. Thus, check the bodily sensations you listed in the "What Does Anxiety Mean to You" Skill Builder and, if desired, personalize the "Tense/Relax" exercise to treat your individual symptoms.

The Mental Side of Fear: Thought Stopping

Anxiety is not simply a physical phenomenon; it manifests itself in cognitive, or thought-connected, ways also. Thus it is equally important for you to work to eliminate anxiety- or fear-producing thoughts as well. Many people use the word *relax* to try to calm themselves. Unfortunately, *relax* doesn't sound very relaxing. We advise you to substitute the word *calm* in its place. Try the exercise below.

A variation on the "calm technique" is to precede the word *calm* with the word *stop.* In other words, when you begin to think upsetting thoughts, say to yourself, "Stop!" Then follow that command with, "Calm." For example:

Calm

1. Work through the tension release procedure described in the previous section.
2. Once you experience that warm feeling throughout your body, say to yourself: "Calm." Try this several times, each time working to associate the "detensed" feeling with the word *calm*.
3. The next time you find yourself in a stress-producing situation, say "Calm" to yourself and attempt to achieve the desired state.

"I just can't get up in front of all those people. Look at their cold stares and mean smirks."

"Stop!"

"Calm."

You may find that you want to adapt this thought-stopping technique to help you handle anxiety-related symptoms in interpersonal situations as well.

Remember, no matter how you choose to deal with it, fear is a natural response to the public-speaking situation and should probably never be eliminated completely. But you do need to learn to *cope* with fear; only in this way can you increase your chances of delivering a successful, well-received presentation.

Speakers report that other techniques can help reduce speech fright as well. Some try to put a bit of humor early in the speech in order to obtain a favorable response from the audience. They say that such a reaction helps them calm their nerves for the remainder of the presentation. Others look for a friendly face and talk to that person for a moment or two early in the speech. Others use charts, graphs, and other visuals to help them organize the material. In this technique the visual shows the next major point to be covered, thus eliminating the necessity for the speaker to remember it or to refer to his or her notes. Still others report that they rehearse the speech aloud by standing up in front of an imaginary audience and talking through the material again and again and again. What other techniques have you and your classmates found helpful?

Think you can or think you can't, either way you will be right.

Henry Ford

DELIVERY OPTIONS

At this point we should note that all speakers need to rehearse their presentations. It is common knowledge that presidents practice by videotaping and reviewing their performances prior to delivering a public address. Likewise, corporate leaders often spend hours rehearsing and refining the presentations they will deliver at sales meetings, stockholder meetings, and other business-related functions. Actors and performers of course also rehearse before opening in a new play or production. It stands to reason that only the most foolhardy and unconcerned souls would undertake to deliver a speech that they had not adequately prepared.

By now you have tried out your presentation in oral form at least once. During the tryout stage your purpose was to analyze your speech in order to identify any changes that needed to be made. This done, you are now ready to begin rehearsing the speech *as you will deliver it.*

There are four general types of delivery available to you as a speechmaker: (1) manuscript, (2) memorization, (3) impromptu, and (4) extemporaneous. Although we recommend the extemporaneous style of delivery, we will briefly examine all four options.

Manuscript

A *manuscript speech* is written out word for word and then read aloud by the speechmaker. Such presentations are delivered in situations where it is imperative that precise language be used. Since presidential addresses are often held up for close scrutiny not only in this country but throughout the world, they will often be read from a typed page or a teleprompter. Similarly, corporate speakers, whose task it is to discuss matters that may have sensitive legal and commercial ramifications, may also choose to deliver a manuscript speech. Unfortunately, the use of a manuscript tends to reduce the amount of eye contact between the speaker and his or her audience. Furthermore, speakers reading aloud often sound as if they are reading to rather than talking to the audience, and thus it is difficult if not impossible to establish the much-needed conversational quality.

Memorization

A *memorized speech* is a manuscript speech that the speaker has committed to memory. This delivery style helps perpetuate—and frequently even accentuates—a "canned" speech quality. Speakers who have memorized their lines are simply less able to respond to audience feedback, or "vibes," than they would be if they were working from notes. And then of course there is the problem of retention. Speechmakers who insist on memorizing their presentations word for word often find themselves plagued by long, awkward silences during which they may valiantly attempt to recall forgotten material. You may indeed wish to memorize certain key words, phrases, or segments of your speech, but at this point in your career there is little reason for you to commit the entire presentation to memory.

Impromptu

A presentation that is delivered as an *impromptu* speech is in many ways the antithesis of one delivered from memory. While the memorized style requires extensive preparation, the individual who delivers an impromptu speech often has no more than a few seconds or minutes to gather his or her thoughts. Impromptu speaking situations may be precipitated by a boss who without prior warning asks an employee to discuss the status of a project that is still in its developmental stages. If you are faced with such a request, you will need to rely on what you have learned about patterning your ideas; that is, using an introduction-body-conclusion structure will facilitate your task.

Extemporaneous

The *extemporaneous speech* is researched, outlined, and then delivered after careful rehearsal. Extemporaneous speaking is more audience-centered than are any of the previously considered styles. Since it is prepared in advance and rehearsed, the speaker is free to establish eye contact with the members of the audience and is also free to respond to feedback. In addition, as the extemporaneous speaker may utilize notes, he or she is not plagued by the need to commit the entire presentation to memory. Nor is the speechmaker handicapped by the use of a manuscript that must be read word for word, thus inhibiting needed adaptations.

Unfortunately, many speakers confuse the manuscript, memorized, and impromptu styles of speaking with extemporaneous delivery. Although asked to give an extemporaneous speech, some individuals insist on writing their speeches out word for word and then either memorize or read them. Others spend too little time preparing their addresses and deliver what is essentially a poorly developed impromptu presentation. Either approach defeats their purposes, and both approaches decrease speechmaking effectiveness. Since the extemporaneous mode has been found to be the most effective style for most public speakers, we suggest you use it. But above all, don't turn extemporaneous speaking into what it is not.

VOCAL AND VISUAL CONSIDERATIONS

When we speak in public, we have three basic tools at our disposal: (1) verbal, (2) visual, and (3) vocal. By this time, you have exerted a considerable effort to develop the verbal aspects of your presentation. We now need to devote some time and attention to the vocal and visual dimensions.

In addition to your ideas, what aspects of yourself do you wish to communicate to an audience? If you're like most speakers, you want your audience to accept you as a credible source. As we will see in Chapter 19, this means you want your listeners to believe you are

Competent
Trustworthy
Dynamic

How are these characteristics communicated? Obviously, when conveying these attributes we do utilize our verbal resources, including language and its structure. However, far too frequently speakers forget that vocal and visual cues also help convey credibility. As we noted in an earlier chapter, the nonverbal components of a message account for at least 65 percent of the total meaning transmitted to listeners. Thus the visual and vocal dimensions of your speech will merit your careful attention.

Visual Cues

How do you think a speechmaker should *look* when going before an audience? Close your eyes and picture the individual's attire, posture, gestures, movements, and eye contact. Let's briefly explore each of these visual components.

Attire. The topic, the audience, and the occasion are all factors you should consider when deciding what to wear to deliver your speech. Sometimes speakers make thoughtless errors in dress. For example, one student delivered a very serious tribute to a well-known leader while wearing a shirt emblazoned with a huge Mickey Mouse emblem. (When asked why he wore that particular outfit, he responded, "I didn't think anyone would notice.") One woman chose to address a group of executives on the need for conservatism in office attire while outfitted in a bright red suit, polka-dot silver blouse, and floppy red and silver hat. (Audience members later commented on the dichotomy between her topic and her personal clothing.)

SKILL BUILDER

A Picture of Success

1. Bring in a picture of someone you think looks like an effective speaker.
2. Describe the attributes that contribute to this person's "speaker credibility."

Recognize that it's up to you to choose what you will wear; your clothing does not choose you.

Posture. As a public speaker, naturally you are expected to stand up when addressing your audience. Thus, unless you are physically disabled—in which case your audience will of course understand—you will want to be on your feet. The problem is that standing is something that many of us do not do very well. The posture you display communicates; it sends potent messages to the audience. Although this may seem obvious, speakers often insist on assuming stances or positions that work against rather than for them during their presentations. For example, some speakers lounge on or drape themselves over the lectern as if unable to stand without its assistance. Others perch on one foot like a homing pigeon. Some prop themselves against the wall behind them, giving the impression of wanting to disappear into it. In order to prepare yourself to stand properly in public, we suggest that you assume your natural posture and ask others to critique it. Are you too stiff? Do you slouch? Do you appear too relaxed? Feedback can help ensure that you put "your best posture forward" when you rise to speak.

Gestures. As we noted in our chapter on nonverbal communication, the movements of a speaker's hands and arms are referred to as *gestures*. The gestures you employ when speaking in public may be purposeful, helping to reinforce the content of your speech, or purposeless, detracting from your message. The problem most of us encounter is that we exhibit certain favorite gestures which are habitual. Furthermore, we often fail to recognize that we do things like scratch our neck, put our hands in and out of our pockets, jingle our keys or bracelets, or smooth our hair. Our use of such meaningless mannerisms often increases when we find ourselves faced with a stressful situation such as speaking in public. In fact, when people are nervous, it is not unusual for them to add to their repertoire of annoying gestures. Thus speakers will sometimes tap their pencils or rings on the lectern or even crack their knuckles—things they would never do in normal circumstances.

Gestures can serve a number of useful purposes. They can help you emphasize important points, enumerate your ideas, or transmit the relative shape or size of an object to an audience. Thus your job as a speechmaker is really twofold: First, you need to work to eliminate *annoying* gestural habits; second, you need to incorporate *appropriate* gestures that can be used to enhance the ideas contained in your speech.

Movements. It needs to be understood that your presentation really begins when you are introduced or called upon to speak—that is, before you have uttered even your first syllable. The manner in which you rise and approach

Stand before your class. As you recite the alphabet, perform as many annoying gestures as you can. Recite the alphabet a second time. During this recitation, gesture in as appropriate a manner as possible.

Moving To and From

1. Your instructor will introduce you to the class as if it were actually your turn to speak.
2. When called upon, rise and approach the lectern while displaying one of the following attitudes:
   a. A speaker who is extremely fearful
   b. A speaker who is angry at having to make a speech
   c. A speaker who is tired and exhausted
   d. A speaker who is hung over
   e. A speaker who is frantically trying to organize his or her ideas
   f. A speaker who is totally unprepared
   g. Your choice
3. Repeat the exercise, this time approaching the podium confidently.
4. Finally, begin at the podium and return to your seat while displaying one of the following attitudes:
   a. Disappointed
   b. The buffoon
   c. "Lost"
   d. Still shuffling papers
   e. Timid
   f. Exhilarated
5. Repeat this last phase, this time moving to your chair confidently.

the speaker's stand communicates a first impression of you to your listeners. Similarly, the gait you use and the facial expressions you display as you complete your speech and return to your seat also send important signals to the listeners. Far too many speechmakers approach the lectern in an inappropriate way. For example, they may walk in a way that "broadcasts" a lack of preparation. Some even verbalize this by mumbling something like "I'm really not ready. This will be terrible." Others apologize for a poor showing all the way back to their seats. Carefully consider your manner of moving to and away from the speaker's stand.

The way you move communicates whether you are in control. You may have noticed that confident persons walk with their heads erect, adopt a straight rather than circuitous path, exhibit an assured rather than a hesitant or frenetic pace, and display open rather than closed arm movement.

Eye Contact. Like movement, *eye contact* also communicates. Unfortunately, some speakers "talk" to walls, chalkboards, windows, trees, and the floor rather than to their listeners. Establishing eye contact with audience members demonstrates to them that you feel they are important and that you want to share your message with them. It is not uncommon for some speakers to appear embarrassed to look at any audience members and for others to seek out the attention of one individual, avoiding looking at anyone else. Similarly, while some student speakers avoid meeting the eyes of the instructor during a speech, others choose to focus on him or her exclusively. Be sure that your gaze includes all the members of the audience. Look at each individual as you deliver your speech. Such contact will draw even the most reluctant listeners into your presentation.

Vocal Cues

The voice is one of our main speechmaking tools. Your voice is to your speech as the artist's brush is to a painting. The brush carries the colors to the canvas just as your voice transmits your ideas to the listeners. In this text's nonverbal chapter we considered four basic vocal dimensions: volume, rate, pitch, and quality. We suggest that you review that material during your rehearsals.

Keep in mind that your goal as a public communicator is to use your voice to reinforce the content of your speech. Obviously, in order to respond to your ideas your audience must first hear them. Maintaining your voice at an appropriate *volume* is your responsibility. If you are to address a group in a large auditorium, a public address system will probably be provided. The system should be of good quality and have sufficient power for the space. If you are addressing a group in a smaller room, you will probably be expected to speak without such amplification. By observing the people in the rear of your space, you should be able to determine if you are speaking loudly enough for them to hear you easily. If you observe confused, upset looks, speak up. On the other hand, if your voice is normally loud and you notice those seated nearest to you cringing, "turn down" your speaking volume a bit.

As to *pitch*, work against falling into the "monotone trap." If you maintain one predominant tone throughout your presentation, you will only create a sense of boredom in the audience. Use pitch to reflect the emotional content of your material; use it to create interest.

Like volume and pitch, *rate* also communicates. Speaking too quickly or too slowly can impede audience understanding. Thus, respond to audience feedback and speed up or slow down your pace as appropriate.

Nonfluencies are another problem every public speaker needs to consider. While simple "uhs" or "ums" are normal during interpersonal communication encounters, they are not routinely expected during speech-making. In other words, during person-to-person conversations we realize

The Top Ten

1. Write the following top-10 presentation errors on the chalkboard:
   a. the inappropriate dresser
   b. the slumper
   c. the hyperactive
   d. the "hare"
   e. the "tortoise"
   f. the pacer
   g. the blaster
   h. the eye avoider
   i. the mad gesturer
   j. the "scaredy cat"
2. In turn, students are to select one role each to work with. Reading from the front page of the newspaper or a telephone directory, their task is to "act out" the roles they chose.
3. Observers are to identify the type of presentation error being exhibited. Also discuss the factors that cause speakers to fall into each of the top-10 traps.

that individuals are thinking about or planning what they are going to say next. In contrast, we expect public speakers to have prepared their remarks carefully, and thus we permit them fewer nonfluencies. We suggest that you attempt to eliminate as many of the latter from your delivery as possible.

Synthesize your understanding of the visual and verbal dimensions of public communication by trying the Skill Builder "The Top Ten." An awareness of common speechmaking errors should help you avoid them. So will adequate rehearsal of your presentation.

COMMUNICATING CONFIDENCE AS A SPEECHMAKER: PRACTICE PROCEDURES AND FINAL TIPS

Careful practice or rehearsal of your presentation can help you attain the level of confidence you need in order to deliver an effective speech. At this point you have prepared an outline and appropriate visuals. Your task is to synthesize these ingredients into a polished presentation. Although rehearsal is a highly individualized matter, we can provide you with some basic guidelines.

This teacher's delivery is enhanced by eye contact with audience, natural gestures, and appropriate dress. (Susan Lapides/Design Conceptions)

Begin the rehearsal process by reading through your outline several times. As you proceed, develop a list of key words and main points to be covered. These may become the basis of your delivery notes.

Second, *learn* your first and last sentences. Many speakers find it helpful to commit the first and last sentences of an address to memory, or at the very least to become very familiar with them. (As one student put it, "That way I know that I'll be able to start and stop the speech.")

Third, conduct a preliminary auditory rehearsal. Stand up and face an imaginary audience. Present the entire speech. Time yourself. This will give you an idea of how the final address will sound.

Fourth, conduct additional rehearsals. Rehearse for several days, sometimes alone, at other times before a small group of friends or relatives. If desired, use audio or videocassette recorders to gather feedback.

When rehearsing, be sure to incorporate all your audio and visual aids into the presentation. Also be certain to practice delivering the speech in a number of different locations. This will help reduce the "foreign" feel of the actual presentation room. Your goal is to develop a flexible delivery—one that will enable you to meet the unique demands posed by the live audience.

If you follow the developmental presentation plan we have outlined, you will find yourself ready and eager to deliver your speech. Not only will you have carefully prepared your address and rehearsed it, you will also have at your disposal tested techniques to help you control your nerves. At this juncture we can offer only a few additional presentation pointers.

Keep a log of your progress during rehearsals. Each time you rehearse, note the location of your rehearsal, problems encountered, changes made, and progress observed.

MICROPHONES

Erma Bombeck

If there is anything in this world as fiercely independent as a microphone, I don't know what it is.

I mean, imagine the year is 1775. At the Provincial Convention in Virginia, statesman Patrick Henry rises to his feet to make an impassioned plea for liberty or death. He approaches the microphone and as the entire assembly awaits his first words he asks, "Can everyone in the back hear me?"

Those seven words have preceded more speeches than the proverbial cocktail hour.

In ten years of lecturing, I have seen microphones go from an occasional passive screech to real screaming militancy. To begin with, microphones do not like to be touched by a union or otherwise. Because I am short, I tried to adjust one the other week. I gave it just a simple tweak, mind you, and it went as limp as a two-dollar permanent in a sauna. I gave the entire speech from a squatting sprinter's position.

Some microphones work great as long as you blow into them. So you stand there like an idiot blowing and saying, "Are we on? Can you hear me?" Everyone admits they can hear you blowing. It's only when you speak the microphone goes dead.

Others have a weird sense of humor. They're punchline poopers. You'll be sailing along with a three-minute story, building to a big pitch and just as you say, "So why isn't the dog drinking his daiquiri?" the microphone goes silent and you're left muttering, "Gee, I guess you had to have been there."

Some speakers spend half their lives looking for the on/off switch of microphones. There aren't any. I've looked for them under the light, on the shelf, on the side, the goose-neck, offstage. I suspect most of them are triggered by a remote control in a 1936 pickup truck in a garage across from the auditorium.

I have been warned that microphones are supersensitive and you have to talk right into them to be heard. These are usually the ones that cross you up by picking up your entire luncheon conversation including, "My God, do you mean the management is charging you ten dollars for this lunch! Has he never heard of the Geneva Convention?"

Some speakers, more secure than I, have dared to make fun of microphones. Recently, book columnist and reviewer Bob Cromie spoke in our town and opened with the traditional, "Can everyone in the back hear me?"

When someone yelled, "No" he said, "Then how did you know what I asked?"

All night long that microphone floated toward the door. Didn't surprise me a bit.

1. Arrive at your speaking location with ample time to spare. Be sure that you have prepared equipment to house your notes and presentation aids.

2. If you are going to use a public address system or other electronic equipment, test it so you do not have to adjust sound levels or replace bulbs or batteries unnecessarily during your presentation.

3. Give ample consideration to your clothing and appearance. Your confidence and believability will increase if you look the part of a speaker. (But don't distract yourself with appearance worries *while* you are speaking.)

4. Let your audience know that you are prepared by the manner in which you rise when introduced and then walk confidently to the podium.

5. While speaking, work to transmit a sense of enthusiasm and commitment to your listeners. Some speechmakers actually find it useful to write the word *enthusiasm, commitment,* or *confidence* on a 3 by 5 card that they take with them to the speaker's stand. The card helps them remember to communicate that particular quality during the presentation.

6. Complete your speech before returning to your seat. You've worked hard to communicate your speechmaking credibility to audience members, so don't blow it in the last few seconds. Last impressions, like first impressions, count.

At this point there is little more we can advise except to say, "Have fun!" Public speaking should be a rewarding and enjoyable experience, not just for the members of your audience but for you as well.

HOW TO ANALYZE YOUR SPEECHMAKING EFFECTIVENESS

As soon as you have completed your presentation, the first question you will ask yourself is, "How did I do?" No doubt you will also want to know what your peers and your instructor thought of your performance.[3] You and your listeners can evaluate your speechmaking abilities by analyzing how effectively you were able to handle each of the following: content, organization, language, and delivery.

Content

Was the subject of your speech appropriate? Was it worthwhile? Was your purpose communicated clearly? Did you research the topic carefully? Were audiovisual aids helpful? Were a variety of supports used? Were each of your main points adequately developed? Were the main divisions of your speech effectively bridged by transitional words and phrases?

Organization

How effective was your organizational approach? Did you begin with material that gained the attention of the audience? Did you preview each of the main points covered? Were your main points arranged in a logical sequence? Was the number of main points appropriate for your time limitation? Was the organizational design of your speech easily discernible? Did your conclusion provide your speech with a sense of closure? Did it motivate listeners to continue thinking about your presentation?

Language

Was the language you used to explain your ideas clear? Was it vivid? Did your speech sound as if it should be listened to rather than read? Were any of the words or phrases you used offensive to certain audience members?

Delivery

Did you maintain effective eye contact with the members of the audience? Did you approach the speaking situation confidently? Were you able to use an extemporaneous style of delivery? Could you be heard easily? Was your speaking rate appropriate? Did you articulate clearly? Were you able to convey a sense of enthusiasm as you spoke? Did your gestures help reinforce your content?

The Skill Builder "Personal Debriefing" can help you conduct a personal performance inventory.

When it is time for the audience to comment on your presentation, we suggest that, like you, they consider the positive dimensions of your performance before making recommendations for improvement. Speaker and audience alike should remember that a postpresentation analysis is designed to serve a constructive rather than a destructive function. Such an analysis should help build confidence, not destroy the speaker's desire to try again.

Your instructor will probably wish to provide you with a more formal analysis of your work. In doing so, he or she may use an evaluation form similar to this one. At any rate, the following can be used as a personal guide.

Personal Debriefing

Before joining in a discussion of your speechmaking effectiveness, make
a list of the following:

1. What I believe I did well
2. What areas need improvement

EVALUATION FORM

NAME _____   SPEECH _____

Specific Purpose: _____

_____.

1. Content

_____ Based on accurate analysis of speaking situation
_____ Specific goal of speech was apparent
_____ Subject appropriate, relevant, and interesting to intended audience
_____ All material clearly contributed to purpose
_____ Had specific facts and opinions to support and explain statements
_____ Support was logical
_____ Handled material ethically
_____ Used visual and/or audio aids when appropriate
_____ Included a variety of data—statistics, quotations, etc.
_____ Moved from point to point with smooth transition

2. Organization

_____ Began with effective attention getter
_____ Main points were clear statements that proved or explained specific goals
_____ Points were arranged in logical order
_____ Each point was adequately supported
_____ Concluded with memorable statement that tied speech together

3. Language

_____ Ideas were clear
_____ Ideas were presented vividly
_____ Ideas were presented emphatically
_____ Language was appropriate for intended audience

4. Delivery

_____ Got set before speaking
_____ Stepped up to speak with confidence
_____ Maintained contact with audience
_____ Sounded extemporaneous, not read or memorized
_____ Referred to notes only occasionally
_____ Sounded enthusiastic
_____ Maintained good posture
_____ Used vocal variety, pitch, emphasis, and rate effectively
_____ Gestured effectively
_____ Used face to add interest
_____ Articulation was satisfactory
_____ On finishing, moved out with confidence
_____ Fit time allotted

Additional Comments:

SUMMARY

Anxiety or fear of speaking affects all speechmakers. One of the best ways to cope with your fear is to design and rehearse your presentation carefully. In addition, you should learn to recognize the causes of fear, and the physical and mental sensations that accompany a fear response so that you can learn how to control them with appropriate behavior-modification techniques.

There are four general types of delivery options: (1) manuscript (a speech that is written out word for word and then read aloud), (2) memorization (a manuscript speech committed to memory), (3) impromptu (a speech delivered on the spur of the moment), and (4) extemporaneous (a speech that is researched, outlined, and delivered after careful rehearsal).

In delivering the speech you have three basic tools at your disposal: verbal, visual, and vocal. Far too frequently the verbal component is overemphasized at the expense of the nonverbal aspects. But effective speechmaking requires that you pay attention to the visual aspects of your delivery, such as your clothes, posture, gestures, movements, and eye contact, and that your vocal cues reinforce—rather than sabotage—your content.

Careful rehearsal of your presentation can help you attain the level of confidence and competence required to deliver an outstanding speech. To ensure continued improvement, you should conduct postpresentation analyses, which will enable you to profit from each speaking experience.

SUGGESTIONS FOR FURTHER READING

Cohen, Edwin. *Speaking the Speech.* New York: Holt, Rinehart and Winston, 1980. Professional speakers tell how they handle anxiety.

DeVito, Joseph, Jill Giattino, and T. D. Schon. *Articulation and Voice: Effective Communication.* Indianapolis: Bobbs–Merrill, 1975. A fine discussion of the voice and its relationship to speaking.

Jeffrey, Robert C., and Owen Peterson. *Speech: A Text with Adapted Readings.* New York: Harper & Row, 1980. Presents a comprehensive overview of delivery methods.

Hegstrom, Timothy G. "Message Impact: What Percentage Is Nonverbal?" *Western Journal of Speech Communication.* Vol. 43 (1979), pp. 134–142. Discusses how nonverbal messages affect a public speaker's performance.

. Sarnoff, Dorothy. *Speech Can Change Your Life.* New York: Doubleday, 1970. This popular book offers a variety of presentation tips.

NOTES

1. See James C. McCroskey, "Oral Communication Apprehension: A Summary of Recent Theory and Research," *Human Communication Research*, Vol. 4 (Fall 1977), pp. 78–96. Also note that volume 29, number 3 (1980), of *Communication Education* is devoted exclusively to communication apprehension, theory and practice.

2. For a more detailed guide to fear-control training, see Herbert Fensterheim and Jean Baer, *Stop Running Scared!* (New York: Dell, 1977).

3. For a listing of behavioral objectives for representative A, B, and C speeches, see Valgene Littlefield, "Behavioral Criteria for Evaluating Performance in Public Speaking," *The Speech Teacher (Communication Education)*, Vol. 24 (1975), pp. 143–145.

18

Informative Speaking

**There are things that are known and things that are unknown;
in between are doors.**

Anonymous

CHAPTER PREVIEW

After finishing this chapter, you should be able to:

Define informative speaking

Explain why developing the ability to send and receive informative
messages is important

Distinguish between three types of informative discourse

Explain how to create *information hunger* and increase
listener comprehension

Develop and present an informative speech

In Chapter 14 we introduced you to two categories of speechmaking—
informative and persuasive—and gave you an opportunity to formulate sample purpose statements for each type of address. At this
point we want to increase your ability to prepare and deliver effective
informative speeches by showing you how you can apply your speechmaking knowledge and skills to this particular presentation.

SPEAKING INFORMATIVELY

What's happening? How does it work? What's going on? What is it? What does it mean? These are some of the questions that the speaker who delivers an informative speech may attempt to answer. Whenever you prepare a speech to inform, your goal is to offer your audience more information about something than they already have. Your objective is to update and add to their knowledge, refine their understanding, or provide needed background material.[1]

How does the informative speech relate to your life? What informative messages have you received recently? Have you listened to a television news report? A radio commentary? Instructions or directions from a friend, employer, coworker, or instructor? Our world is filled with informative messages that we depend on. Although a large portion of such messages are informal, others have been carefully planned, structured, and rehearsed in order to achieve maximum audience impact. The simple fact is that in today's world it has become increasingly important for you to develop the ability to share information with other people.

Unless you are adept at sending and receiving informative messages, you will be unable to establish common understandings. We once worked with an executive who had ascended through the corporate structure to the position of vice president. Although this individual possessed a fine mind and excellent analytical abilities, he considered the process of passing information on to individuals situated both above and below him in the organizational hierarchy "a deadly bore." In other words, he saw little need to inform others of his activities or his accomplishments. Not surprisingly, this individual no longer holds his former position of power and influence. When his company merged with another organization he lost his job, primarily because he was unable to explain his responsibilities and achievements to the corporation's new owners. Thus, knowing how to design and deliver effective informative messages has important career and life implications.[2]

How many people do you know whose job requires them to deliver speeches? What percentage of their time is devoted to speech preparation and delivery?

INFORMATIVE PRESENTATION TYPES

Let's continue by considering three types of informative speeches: (1) messages of explanation, (2) messages of description, and (3) messages of definition.

Messages of Process Explanation

If your purpose is to explain how to do something (for example, how to motivate employees), how something is made (for example, how to make

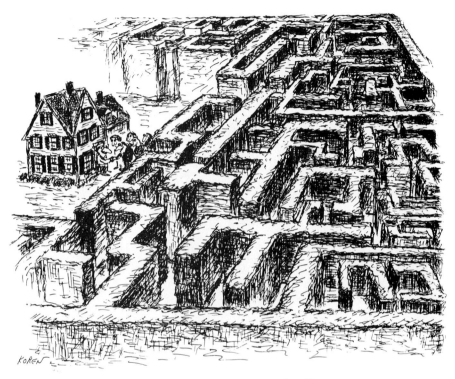

"Your instructions were perfect."

Drawing by Koren; © 1982 The New Yorker Magazine, Inc.

glass), or how something works (for example, how a slot machine works), then you are preparing to deliver a message of process explanation. Your primary goal is to share your understanding of a particular process or procedure with listeners and in some instances to equip audience members with the skills they need to replicate the process.

When organizing a speech of process you must be especially careful to avoid overcondensing the data. It is not uncommon for inexperienced speakers to recite long lists of facts that merely enumerate the myriad steps involved in a particular process. Instead of delivering a hard-to-follow, perfunctory outline, you would be wise to substitute *meaningful information groups.* For example, grouping your information under such headings as Gathering Ingredients, Blending Ingredients, and Adding the Garnish would be considerably more effective than simply relaying the 15 steps involved in preparing a chocolate mousse. Besides facilitating audience understanding, the grouping system also aids audience retention.

When developing a speech of process explanation, it is also important for you to consider the length of time it actually takes to accomplish your

"Be prepared" could well be Julia Child's motto in her role as TV chef. Some processes are best explained by preparing samples of the various steps in advance. (AP/Wide World Photos)

objectives. To combat the time factor, take a tip from televised cooking shows. Notice how an "on-the-air" chef always demonstrates part of the process "live" but has also already prepared other parts of the dish in advance in order to save time. This technique can be of great value to you too.

What processes are you equipped to speak about?

Messages of Description

One of your responsibilities as a speaker is to be able to *describe* a person, place, or thing for listeners. For instance, if you were a "site-location specialist" for a fast-food chain it might be your charge to describe potential store locations to the firm's management. Or if you were a spokesperson for a nuclear plant that had experienced a radiation leak it might be your obligation to deliver a presentation to the media in which you describe the location and extent of the mishap. Whatever the nature of your descriptive message, your aim will be to help your listeners develop mental "close-ups" of places, people, or things. To do this you will need to find ways to describe

A Demonstration

Design and present a 3- to 5-minute speech in which it is your purpose to demonstrate how to do something or explain how something works. An outline is required.

the condition, size, shape, color, and age of your particular subject in order to make it "live" for your audience.

Of course, visual aids of the type discussed earlier will be particularly relevant to such a presentation. For example, photographs, maps, and drawings can make it easier for you to describe the findings of a significant archeological dig, the pathos of a "bag lady," the appearance of "the Elephant Man," or the blight of an inner-city slum. Messages of description call on you to "paint" with words. Whatever your topic, you will want to ensure that the words and phrases you select will evoke the appropriate sensory responses in your listeners. To do this you will need to communicate how your subject looks, tastes, smells, feels, and sounds.

Process Probers

1. Accompanied by two to three others, proceed to a location of your choice. Once there, observe the environment and compile a list of possible process speech topics. Formulate topics suggested by the stimuli around you.
2. Compare your list with those made by others in your group. (Feel free to brainstorm additional topic possibilities.)
3. In order to determine whether the topics generated will be suitable for delivery, consider these questions:
   a. Is the process of interest to me?
   b. Do I know or want to learn about it?
   c. Can I accomplish my objectives in the time allotted?
   d. Will my presentation provide the audience with new, useful information?
4. Develop a 5- to 6-minute presentation during which you demonstrate how to do something or make something or explain how something works. Be sure to prepare an outline and use accompanying visuals.

A Description

Design and present a 3- to 5-minute speech in which you describe an object, a place, a structure, or a person. Use space in order to organize the speech. An outline is required.

Messages of Definition

The question, "What do you mean?" is commonly asked by us and of us. In most cases when it is used, the questioner seeks a clarification or elaboration of ideas from the speaker. Sometimes a satisfactory answer can be supplied in a sentence or two. At other times, however, it takes a speech or even a book to define a concept adequately. For example, books with titles like *Theory Z*, *Leader Effectiveness Training*, *The Preppy Handbook*, and *Happiness Is . . .* are actually works of definition in which the authors attempt to discuss their meaning for a particular concept or idea with us. From this perspective it stands to reason that an informative *speech of definition* likewise serves to provide an audience with the explanation of a term's meaning. "Dancercise," "aerobics," "ESP," and "muscular dystrophy" are among the topics that are appropriate to a definitional presentation. Can you think of others?

Many students find that topics such as "The Meaning of Obscenity," "Prejudice," "Friendship," or "Shyness" give them the freedom they need to develop effective speeches of definition. Since many of the concepts you may choose to define will have connotative or subjective meanings not traditionally found in dictionaries, not all members of your audience will

"Image, Image on the Wall . . ."

1. Select a natural object—a piece of driftwood, a large shell, or a photograph of a rare bird.
2. Place the object at the front of the classroom.
3. Divide into pairs of partners. Each pair is to use as many sensory images as possible to describe the object.
4. Compare the images developed by the pairs of individuals.
5. Repeat the experience, substituting a new object.

Which would be more effective in depicting the ancient ruins of Stonehenge: a verbal description or a photograph? Sometimes a picture truly is worth a thousand words. (Ellis Herwig/Stock Boston)

agree with the meaning you put forth. In one television talk show, for example, two experts on shyness were unable to agree on what it means to be shy. How would you define shyness? In order to explain your meaning for the term you might offer examples of what it feels like to be shy, describe how a shy person behaves, and then go on to discuss the consequences of shyness. Perhaps you would explain shyness by comparing and contrasting the shy person with the extrovert. Or you might choose to discuss the causes of shyness and then focus on different types or categories of shyness. No matter how you choose to order your ideas, your organization should be suggested by and grow out of the topic.

SKILL BUILDER

"And the Meaning Is . . ."

1. For practice, working either individually or in groups, compile a list of potential topics for a speech of definition.
2. Select five of the topics on your list and develop purpose statements for them.
3. Design and present a 3- to 5-minute speech in which you define a concept or idea. Organize it carefully and submit an outline.

Visual aids make it easier to describe the material in your speech. (McGraw-Hill photo by Stacey Pleasant)

HOW TO CREATE "INFORMATION HUNGER" AND INCREASE LISTENER COMPREHENSION

In order to be effective a speaker needs to accomplish four tasks: (1) make the listeners want to learn more about the topic, (2) communicate the information clearly and understandably, (3) stress the key points, and (4) find ways to involve the members of the audience in the presentation.

Work to Arouse Listener Interest

Which speakers have succeeded in increasing your hunger for knowledge about a topic? What did they do to accomplish this?

Your primary goal during an informative speech may be to deliver a message of explanation, description, or definition, but making your presentation interesting and relevant (significant) for your listeners must be equally important. In other words, you want to work to increase each listener's "hunger" to receive your message. You will be more adept at creating information hunger in your listeners if you have analyzed your audience carefully (see Chapters 13 and 14) and you are convinced that by using the proper vehicles you will be able to generate the interest that will motivate them to listen to the information you have to share with them. To accomplish your objective, remember to use a number of the interest-arousing devices we discussed in Chapter 15. For example, you can relate stories detailing your own experiences or the experiences of others; you can pose rhetorical questions for audience members to answer; you can draw analogies for listeners to consider. You can work to arouse the curiosity of your receivers; you can incorporate humor or use eye-catching visual aids. Obviously, your effectiveness as a speaker will increase to the extent that you are successful in creating a desire and a need to know among audience members.

Watch for Information Overload

Listeners will become informed only if they are capable of processing the information you deliver in your speech. A key danger of informative speaking is that your audience will begin to suffer from a malady called "information overload." Two actions trigger this condition: (1) The speechmaker delivers far more data than the audience ever desired to find out about the topic, thereby confusing listeners and causing them to "tune out" and "turn off" to what is being communicated. (2) The speechmaker "dresses" the ideas of the presentation in words the listeners do not understand. Thus, instead of using clear language and speaking at a level receivers can comprehend, the speaker frustrates listeners by using unfamiliar jargon or words that soar beyond the reach of their vocabularies. Forgetting that an informative speech fails if the ideas contained in it are superfluous or not clear to listeners, some speakers end up talking to themselves rather than to the members of the audience. Remember, your speech does not have to be encyclopedic in length or sound incomprehensibly complicated to merit audience attention. However, it must by all means be understandable.

Avoid Conveying Too Little Information

In an effort to avoid information overload, speakers often overcompensate by underestimating the intelligence of the audience members and telling them little that they did not already know. As a speechmaker you need to achieve a balance between providing too little information and providing too much. As a rule, effective speechmakers neither underestimate nor overestimate the capabilities of those listening to them. Instead, they motivate their listeners to want to fill in any information gaps they may be experiencing. Doing this requires that you not "overkill" your subject by saturating the listeners with so much material that they lose interest; instead, you carefully choose the supporting materials to achieve your objectives with ease, using an appropriate mix of new information and supporting materials. Once one point is made, be ready to move on to the next one.

An effective speaker presents just the right amount of information for the level of the audience. (McGraw-Hill photo by Mary Schoenthaler, courtesy of Pace University)

Emphasize the Key Points of Your Speech

As we have seen, emphasis can be added through repetition (saying the same thing over again) and restatement (saying the same thing in another way). As long as you do not become *overly* repetitious and redundant, these devices will help your listeners process and retain the main points of your speech.

The organization you employ can also reinforce your presentation's main ideas. Remember, you can use your introduction to preview ideas, and you can use your conclusion to help make those ideas memorable. Transitions and internal summaries also help create a sense of idea cohesiveness.

Find Ways to Involve Your Listeners

People learn more if they become involved with the material presented to them. Effective speechmakers do not view audience members as passive

To Define or to Describe, That Is the Question

1. Prepare a 5-minute speech of definition or description. Be sure to use whatever speaking aids you believe will help bring your presentation "to life" for the audience.
2. Prepare an outline and a listing of the bibliographic sources you consulted.

receptacles; rather, they work to find ways to have them take an active part in the presentation. Thus receivers may be called on to perform an activity during the presentation itself. For example, if you were giving a speech on how to reduce stress, you might have your listeners actually try one or two stress-reducing exercises. Or if the title of your speech were "How to Read an EKG," you might pass out sample EKG reports for audience members to decipher.

Become an Effective Information Provider

Remember that people want to understand and remember information that they perceive as relevant to their lives. Few of us would have an interest in the development of bees. If, however, we found that the bee we were learning about was a new variety of "killer" bee which is extremely resistant to common insecticides and that droves of these bees were on the way to our community within the next 2 weeks, we might develop an intense interest very quickly!

Audiences want to listen to "new" information. In this case the term *new* means "new to them." A historical blunder may be new and have relevance to today's college or business audience. The cable television industry has found that the weather is worthy of its own channel. The weather forecast is constantly being updated and therefore is considered "new."

Audiences also respond well to information that is given emphasis. You may use your organization of main ideas to help you emphasize the material you want people to retain. Repetition can help as well. Martin Luther King understood the value of repetition in his "I Have a Dream" speech. The Reverend Jesse Jackson uses repetition to help foster retention as well as emotional involvement in his presentations. As you prepare your informative speech, look for ways to let repetition augment your message.

Take your mind out every now and then and dance on it. It is getting all caked up.

Mark Twain

Novelty or Creativity. As an effective speaker you must constantly look for ways to approach information from an unusual direction. If you are the

Brain Game

1. How many uses can you find for a block of wood?
2. How many uses can you find for an old tire?
3. How might you approach a speech entitled "Pins and Needles"?

fifth speaker your audience will hear on the homeless, you must have a different slant or approach to the topic or the audience may well be bored from the outset. You may wish to take a different point-of-view—through the eyes of a child, for example. Look for analogies that bring topics home to an audience. "The number of people entering teaching today is diminishing. It is like _____ (a stream drying up?)" Try others.

As you prepare your presentation, remember that you are looking for creative ways of bringing your topic to life for the audience.

Visual Aids. You will want to include visual aids in your informative presentations. Remember that you are your primary visual aid. The way you stand, walk, talk, and gesture is extremely important to the effectiveness of your presentation. Avoid hiding behind a lectern reading notes. Move to the side. Use gestures to show the size and shape of objects. If a particular article of clothing is important to your topic, you may wish to wear it. Foreign students, for example, sometimes wear clothing from their homelands when they give informative speeches about their cultures.

Bring objects or make simple models if you cannot bring the objects to class. Use charts and graphs when appropriate. If you have access to computer software and can manipulate a spreadsheet, do not be afraid to create computer-generated bar, line, and pie graphs. You can easily have the graph transferred to a transparency at a local copy shop so that it can be used with an overhead projector.

You can also consider using video and audio clips to create interest. Students are able to use camcorders to conduct interviews or show processes at work. For example, one student interviewed fellow students about campus parking problems. Another showed a brief tape of a chemical reaction which could not have been accomplished in the classroom without endangering the audience.

The more visuals you use, the more planning you will need. As we mentioned in Chapter 15, audiences today are not willing to wait while you activate and cue up a VCR or audiotape recorder. Make sure that the equipment is in place and ready before you begin the speech.

SAMPLE INFORMATIVE SPEECH OUTLINE

The Unthinkable

Purpose: To inform the audience about the potential results of a nuclear war.

Introduction

I.   Are you familiar with these lyrics by songwriter-satirist Tom Lehrer?

> We will all go together when we go,
> All suffused with an incandescent glow.
> No one will have the endurance
> To collect on his insurance
> Lloyd's of London will be loaded when we go!

II. Today I would like to explain what the results of a nuclear war would be.

Body

I.   Nuclear war has been proposed as a way to solve a number of the world's problems.
   A.   Some feel it will solve the population problem.
   B.   It has also been discussed by officials as a way to solve the oil problems in the Middle East.

II. Our government has taken steps to ensure that we will survive as a nation.
   A.   The U.S. Postal Service plans to distribute special change-of-address cards to survivors of a nuclear blast.
   B.   The Federal Preparedness Agency has stockpiled 71,000 pounds of opium near Washington, D.C.
   C.   The Department of Housing and Urban Development has made plans to rent the homes of owners who cannot be located.
   D.   The Constitution, Bill of Rights, and Declaration of Independence will be safe.
      1.   When war breaks out, a National Archives Guard will push a button causing these documents to descend into a 50-ton vault.
      2.   They will remain there until the war is over.
   E.   A command post for top-echelon leaders has been built at Mount Weather, 80 miles west of Washington, D.C.
   F.   The president will be safe.
      1.   She or he will be aboard a $250 million 747.
      2.   The plane is designed to fly far above the nuclear fallout.

The purpose statement guides the speaker in developing the outline.

A rhetorical question gets the audience involved.

Lines from a protest song—to the tune of "She'll Be Coming Round the Mountain"—set the ironic tone of the speech.

Tells the audience the purpose of the speech.

The body is organized into three main points, each with a number of subpoints. Note that every entry is a complete sentence and contains only a single idea.

Gives dramatic examples of the government's hopelessly inadequate plans in case of a nuclear attack.

The third main point stands in contrast to the second main point, showing what a nuclear bombing is really like.

Vivid descriptions and startling statistics convey the horrors of a nuclear attack.

A surprising statement makes Hiroshima relevant to today.

States the conclusion. Repeating the first two lines of the protest song provides a sense of unity.

III.   To discover what would happen to the general population if the "unthinkable" occurred, we need only look at the results of the bomb that leveled Hiroshima.
   A.   Parents and children were separated.
      1.   When found, some children looked like boiled octopuses.
      2.   Others were never seen again.
   B.   People suffered greatly.
      1.   Some ran screaming back into the fire that was consuming the city.
      2.   Others developed an abnormal thirst and spent their last agonizing hours screaming for water.
   C.   In Hiroshima destruction ruled.
      1.   The death toll was 130,000.
      2.   Sixty-eight percent of all buildings were destroyed.
      3.   Thousands who survived the initial blast eventually succumbed to radiation sickness and cancer.
   D.   The bomb that leveled Hiroshima in 1945 was only one-millionth as powerful as today's nuclear weapons.

Conclusion

   I.   Nuclear war is truly the "unthinkable" force on earth today.
   II.   "We will all go together when we go, All suffused with an incandescent glow. . . ."

Sources

Lists the sources used in preparing the speech.

Glasstone, Samuel, and Philip Dolan, eds. *The Effects of Nuclear Weapons.* Department of Defense and Energy Research and Development Administration, 1977.
National Academy of Sciences. *Long Term World Wide Effects of Multiple Nuclear Weapons Detonations.* National Academy of Sciences, 1975.
O'Brien, Ellen. "Memoirs of Preparing for a Nuclear War," *The Record,* March 5, 1982.
Schell, Jonathan. "Reflections: The Fate of the Earth," *The New Yorker,* February 1, 1982.
Zuckerman, Ed. "How Would the U.S. Survive a Nuclear War?" *Esquire,* March 1982.

Developed as part of a class exercise by students in the course "Basic Speech Communication" at New York Institute of Technology.

SAMPLE INFORMATIVE SPEECH

The speaker gains attention by establishing common ground with the listeners.

Computer Viruses: A Growing Menace

As human beings, we all suffer from a variety of illnesses ranging from the common cold to more serious maladies such as pneumonia. Perhaps the most annoying illness for most of us is the virus. A virus leaves us with many unanswered questions, such as, Where did it come from? How do I get rid of it? What if I cannot get over it?

Computers are susceptible to viruses as well. These viruses, like their human counterparts, also are contagious and leave many unanswered questions. The idea of a computer having a virus may sound like something out of science fiction. It is very real and extremely frightening. I would like to take the next few minutes to explore computer viruses—what they are, where they have occurred, and what we are doing to eliminate them.

A virus, whether biological or electronic, is basically an information disorder. Biological viruses are tiny scraps of genetic code—DNA or RNA— that can take over the machinery of a living cell and trick it into making thousands of flawless replicas of the original virus. Like its biological counterpart, a computer virus carries in its instructional code the recipe for making copies of itself. Placed in a host computer, the typical virus takes temporary control of the computer's disk operating system. Then, whenever the infected computer comes in contact with an uninfected piece of software, a fresh copy of the virus passes into the new program. Thus, the infection can be spread from computer to computer by unsuspecting users who either swap disks or send programs to one another over telephone lines. A single strategically placed computer with an infected memory— say, an electronic bulletin board—can rapidly infect thousands of other systems.

Where have these viruses hit? The most serious outbreaks so far have occurred in personal computers. But security experts say the greatest risk would come from infected large mainframe computers, such as those governing the IRS and air traffic control. Forty years after the dawn of the computer era, when we are dependent on high-speed information processing, the computer world is being threatened by an enemy from within. Some 250,000 computers may have been hit with viruses in the very recent past.

Computer experts began warning of the possibility of viruses as early as 1984, but the viruses did not begin to surface until 1988, when IBM, Hewlett-Packard, and Apple all began to report incidents of viruses. The University of Delaware and Lehigh University both reported that faculty and student personal computers were experiencing the malady. How did this happen? In one case, Drew Davidson, a 23-year-old programmer, had a message called "Universal Message of Peace" flash across thousands of Macintosh screens. It did no harm since it erased its own instructions and thus disappeared without a trace. How did Davidson accomplish this task? Apparently he inserted it into some game software that was distributed to a Macintosh users group. The game was subsequently published with the virus in it.

In a more serious incident, a Christmas greeting appeared mysteriously

---

Marginal annotations:

The use of personal pronouns involves the audience.

The speaker personifies computers. An effective analogy is used.

The speaker forecasts the speech's development.

The speaker begins to consider the first main point of the speech.

A definition is used to clarify the subject under discussion.

Comparison and contrast are used.

An analogy is carried through the discussion.

A question is used to raise the second main point of the speech.

Statistics enhance the credibility of the data.

Evidence is used to summarize known information.

Specific instances add support.

Questions are raised for us to ponder together with the speaker.

The speaker continues with more examples as support.

on terminals connected to a worldwide network owned by IBM. Users who followed the instructions inadvertently triggered a viruslike self-replicating mechanism, sending an identical copy of the original program to every name on their electronic mailing lists. In a matter of days, the virus clogged the 350,000-terminal network!

The virus is personified.

Some viruses have been playful. In one instance the screen featured the likeness of the Cookie Monster from *Sesame Street*. It would not disappear until the user typed in the letters "COOKIE." Many viruses are not playful. One example was called GOTCHA. It featured a likeness of Madonna and then proceeded to erase all the files on the user's disk.

Again, evidence and highly credible individuals are used to increase the importance of the information provided.

The speaker gives us the facts, using parallel structure for emphasis.

To date, real disaster has been avoided. Most states have laws which prohibit computer tampering, and a federal law spells out harsh penalties for tampering with government computer data. For example, Texas is just one of 48 states that have passed laws against computer mischief, but the states are not alone—the federal government is involved too. Former President Reagan signed a law that established harsh penalties for unauthorized tampering with government computers. Recently, the Software Development Council led by Michael Odawa launched a movement to plug any loopholes in that law. Said Odawa, "I say, release a virus, go to jail!" So far, real disaster has been avoided. No insurance company rolls have been wiped out. No air traffic systems have been jammed. No military data have been erased. But the possibility of tragedy still is real.

A question introduces the third main point of the speech.

What are we doing to eliminate viruses? Many vaccinations have been and are being created to protect our computer software from these viruses. Like a biological vaccination, a vaccine program is a preventive measure—an attempt to protect an uninfected disk from invasion by an uninvited program. Vaccines surround memory locations in computers and sound alarms when tampering occurs. However, there are many strains of viruses. Thus, vaccines are often ineffective.

Once more, an analogy is used. A definition also adds clarity.

The audience is involved as an argument parallel to the one used in the war on drugs is offered here. This adds impact to the conclusion.

As an individual computer operator, however, you can practice safe computing. Remember, if you get a floppy disk from someone, it has been in everybody else's computer, too. So don't share disks. Don't copy software. Don't let anyone touch your machine. Just say no! A computer virus is truly a menace to be avoided by individuals, corporations, and governments alike. Hopefully, a disaster can be avoided.

Sources

"A Virus Carries Fatal Complications," *The New York Times*, June 26, 1988.
"Computer Systems under Siege," *The New York Times*, January 31, 1988.
"Invasion of the Data Snatchers," *Time*, September 26, 1988.
Interview with Robert Hoffer, programmer and manager of The Computer Center, Montvale, New Jersey, January 18, 1989.

Developed by students as part of a class project at the College of New Rochelle.

SUMMARY

An informative speech gives an audience more information about something than they already have. It can update and add to their knowledge, refine their understanding, or provide background material. There are three basic types of informative presentations: speeches that *explain* a process; *describe* a person, place, or thing; or *define* a term. In order to be effective, an informational speaker needs to accomplish four tasks: (1) make the listeners want to learn more about the topic, (2) communicate the material clearly and understandably and not overload listeners with information, (3) stress the key points, and (4) find ways to involve the members of the audience in the presentation.

SUGGESTIONS FOR FURTHER READING

Rodman, George. *Public Speaking: An Introduction to Message Preparation.* New York: Holt, Rinehart and Winston, 1978. Presents a readable discussion of definition and description as they relate to the informative speech.

Timm, Paul R. *Functional Business Presentations: Getting Across.* Englewood Cliffs, N.J.: Pren-tice-Hall, 1981. Discusses the informative speech in the instructional setting.

Wilcox, P. *Oral Reporting in Business and Industry.* Englewood Cliffs, N.J.: Prentice-Hall, 1967. Focuses on informative speaking in the business setting.

NOTES

1. Although compiled years ago, a valuable source to consult is Charles Petrie, "Informative Speaking: A Summary and Bibliography of Related Research," *Speech Monographs,* Vol. 30 (1963), pp. 79–91.
2. For a fine chapter on the informative speech, see Douglas Ehninger, Alan H. Monroe, and Bruce E. Gronbeck, *Principles and Types of Speech Communication,* 8th ed. (Glenview, Ill.: Scott, Foresman, 1978), chap. 7.

19

Persuasive Speaking

Man is the only animal that laughs and weeps; for he is the only
animal that is struck with the difference between what things are,
and what they ought to be.

William Hazlitt

CHAPTER PREVIEW

After finishing this chapter, you should be able to:

Define *persuasive speaking*

Identify how your perceptions of your persuasive goal and your
audience influence your ability to be an effective persuader

Define and distinguish between attitudes and beliefs

Explain the concept *source credibility*

Develop and present a speech to persuade

O ur aim in this chapter is to increase your ability to prepare and
present persuasive speeches by showing you how to apply your
speechmaking knowledge and skills to this particular type of discourse.

SPEAKING PERSUASIVELY

Whenever you deliver a *persuasive speech*, your goal is to modify the thoughts, feelings, and/or actions of your audience. You hope your listeners will eliminate attitudes or behaviors you do not approve of and adopt those which are compatible with your interests and the way you see the world. Persuasive discourse is becoming increasingly important; more than ever, in fact, we are concerned with being able to influence others.[1]

Today's business environment demands effective persuasion skills. If you are negotiating a piece of property for your new corporate headquarters, trying to persuade a town planning board to change zoning laws, speaking to a jury to persuade them to rule in favor of your client, attempting to convince a Fortune 500 company to use your services, running for public office, or working in thousands of other situations, you will have the opportunity to practice and refine the presentation skills you are learning in this class.

THE PERSUADER'S PURPOSE

We can analyze the goals of persuasive speakers by examining what they want their speeches to accomplish. For example, a speaker may believe that flying saucers exist even though most of the audience may not. A speaker may oppose bilingual education while others support it. A speaker may want audience members to sign up to become organ donors in case of their own deaths, and the audience members may feel some real reticence about committing themselves to such an action. The objective of the speaker, sometimes referred to as the *proposition* of the speech, indicates the type of changes the speaker would like to create in audience members through their experience of the speech. Typically, speakers desire two general outcomes: They want to convince listeners that something is so (they want to change the way audience members *think*), or they want to cause audience members to take action (they want to change the way they *behave*). Whatever the general nature of the proposition, however, it most likely will reflect at least one of these persuasive goals: adoption, discontinuance, deterrence, or continuance.[2]

Many theorists contend that to persuade audience members to act differently you must first persuade them to think differently. What do you believe? Why?

When your goal is adoption, you hope to convince audience members to accept a new idea, attitude, or belief (for example, that saccharin is hazardous to their health) with the hope that in time that belief will also be supported by action (they will totally eliminate saccharin from their diets). When your goal is discontinuance, you hope to convince audience members to stop doing something that they are now doing (drinking while pregnant, for example). When your goal is deterrence, you want to encourage audience members to avoid some activity or way of thinking (for example, if you don't smoke now, don't begin; if you believe that every woman has the right to exercise control over her own body, don't vote for candidates who would make abortions illegal). Finally, if your goal is continuance of a way of believing or acting, you want to encourage people to continue to think or behave as they now do (for instance, do not falter in your support of economic sanctions against South Africa, or keep purchasing U.S.-made products).

What is noteworthy is that adoption and discontinuance goals ask listeners to alter their way of thinking and/or behaving, whereas deterrence and continuance goals ask them not to alter the way they think or behave but rather to reinforce or sustain it. In general, persuaders find the latter two objectives easier to accomplish. That doesn't mean, however, that accomplishing the first two is impossible. Although they may be more difficult to achieve, if the speaker uses a variety of appeals and a sound organizational scheme and has credibility, the goals can be realized.

HOW TO BECOME A MORE EFFECTIVE PUBLIC PERSUADER

Whenever we try to cause others to change their beliefs, attitudes, or behaviors, or whenever others try to influence us, we are participating in the *persuasive process*.[3] Let's examine a number of the procedures you can use to increase your persuasiveness as a speaker.

To what extent do you think job effectiveness is related to the ability to influence others? Explain your answer.

Identify Your Persuasive Goal

To be a successful persuader, you must have a clearly defined purpose. You must in fact be able to answer these questions:

What response do I want from audience members?
Would I like them to think differently, act differently, or both?
Which of their attitudes or beliefs am I trying to alter? Why?

Acting on a good idea is better than just having a good idea.

Robert Half

Unless you know what you want your listeners to think, feel, or do, you will not be able to realize your objective.

Know Who You Are Trying to Reach

The nature of your persuasive task is partly related to the extent and type of change you hope to bring about in people. Your task will be simplified if you have some idea of how the audience members feel about your proposed change. For example, to what extent do they favor the change? How important is it to them? What is at stake? The more ego-involved the

"I found the old format much more exciting."

Drawing by Levin; © 1982 The New Yorker Magazine, Inc.

members of your audience are, the more committed they will be to their current positions and hence the harder it will be for you to affect them.[4]

Understand Listener Attitudes

In order to be able to influence others, you need to understand the favorable and unfavorable mental sets or predispositions that audiences bring to a speech event; that is, you need to understand *attitudes*—including how they are formed, how they are sustained, and how they may be changed by you. The following forces or factors are among the most important shapers of our attitudes.

Family. Few of us escape the strong influence exerted by our families.

The Attitude Dig

Prepare a 3- to 4-minute presentation that explains an attitude you hold on a controversial issue such as busing, abortion, or gun control. Discuss the forces and factors that led you to form your attitude, and explain what would have to happen for you to change your attitude.

Many of our parents' attitudes are communicated to us and eventually are acquired by us. As communication theorists Scott Cutlip and Alan Center write, "It is the family that bends the tender twig in the direction it is likely to grow."

Religion.   Believers and nonbelievers alike are affected by religion. In fact, the impact of religion is becoming ever more widespread as churches strive to generate and guide attitudes on such social issues as abortion, civil rights, the death penalty, child abuse, and divorce.

Schools.   More people than ever are attending school; they start young (sometimes before the age of 5), and many attend until they are in or beyond their twenties. Moreover, the traditional role of the school has expanded since large numbers of adults are now returning to complete their educations. The courses taught, the instructors who teach them, the books assigned, and the films shown all help shape attitudes.

Economic and Social Class.   Economic and social status also shape our attitudes. Our economic status helps determine the social arena we frequent. Our view of the world is likewise affected by the company we keep and the amount of money we have.

Culture.   As the seventeenth-century poet John Donne wrote, "No man is an island, entire of itself. . . ." From the crib to the coffin we are influenced by others—in person and through the media. The groups we belong to, our friends, and the fabric of the society in which we find ourselves all help form and mold us. Our social environment contains the ingredients that help determine our mental sets and in turn our attitudes. We shape our social institutions and are reciprocally shaped by them.

In this excerpt from *The Female Eunuch*, Germaine Greer describes how society has traditionally defined and shaped what a woman is—and she rejects the stereotype.

I'm sick of pretending eternal youth. I'm sick of belying my own intelligence, my own will, my own sex. I'm sick of peering at the world through false eyelashes, so everything I see is mixed with a shadow of bought hairs; I'm sick of weighting my head with a dead mane, unable to move my neck freely, terrified of rain, of wind, of dancing too vigorously in case I sweat into my lacquered curls. I'm sick of the Powder Room. I'm sick of pretending that some male's self-important pronouncements are the objects of my undivided attention. I'm sick of going to films and plays when someone else wants to, and sick of having no opinions of my own about either. I'm sick of being a transvestite. I refuse to be a female impersonator. I am a woman. . . .

Understand Listener Beliefs

Besides understanding your listeners' attitudes, it will also facilitate your persuasive efforts if you understand their beliefs and how they might respond when important beliefs are challenged.[5] Although *attitude* is sometimes used interchangeably with the term *belief*, the two are distinguishable.

Beliefs and attitudes are related to each other as buildings are related to the bricks used to construct them. In many ways, beliefs are the "building blocks" of attitudes. Whereas attitudes are measured on a favorable-unfavorable scale, beliefs are measured on a probable-improbable scale. Thus, if you say you think something is true, you are really saying you believe it. According to the psychologist Milton Rokeach, your belief system is made up of everything which you agree is true. This includes all the information and biases you have accumulated from birth. Forming along with this system is your disbelief system, which is composed of all the things you do not think are true. Together, the two significantly affect the way you process information.

How do you react when someone questions your position on what you feel is a critical issue? Why?

SKILL BUILDER

The Believer and the Disbeliever

1. Think of 10 different completions of this sentence:
   I believe . . .
2. Next, think of 10 different completions to this sentence:
   I do not believe . . .
3. Attempt to identify how what you *believe* and what you *do not believe* influence you by describing how each belief and nonbelief listed above affected what you did or said in a particular situation.
4. Finally, attempt to describe how your behavior would change if you *did not believe* what you said you believed and if you *believed* what you said you did not believe.

It is necessary to recognize that some beliefs will be more important than others to members of your audience. The more central or important a belief, the harder we will work to defend it. Thus the more significant a belief is, the less willing the audience members will be to change it and the more resistant they will be to your persuasive efforts.

Prepare to Use These Two Principles of Influence

First, we have a desire to be consistent with what we have already done. In other words, once we take a stand, our tendency is to behave consistently with that commitment.[6] Therefore, it is important for you, the would-be persuader, to determine how your speech can engage that force. If you can find a way to get your audience members to make a commitment (to take a stand or go on record), you will have set the stage for them to behave in ways consistent with that stand.

Second, we respond to social proof. That is, one method we use to determine what is right is to find out what other people think is right.[7] Consequently, as an aspiring persuader, you can use the actions of others to convince your listeners that what you're advocating is right. As motivation consultant Cavett Robert notes: "Since 95 percent of the people are imitators and only 5 percent initiators, people are persuaded more by the action of others than by any proof we can offer."[8]

Prepare to Use Effective Reasoning Techniques

You will be more apt to achieve your persuasive goal if you can explain to audience members the logical *reasons* why they should support what you advocate. The most common forms of logical reasoning are deduction, induction, reasoning from causes and effects, and reasoning from analogy.

When we reason deductively, we move from the general to the specific. In other words, we offer general evidence that leads to a specific conclusion. In contrast, when we reason inductively, we move from specific evidence to a general conclusion. The following example moves from the general to the specific.

> Major premise: People who study regularly instead of cramming usually get better grades.
> Minor premise: You want to get better grades.
> Conclusion: Therefore, you should study regularly instead of cramming.

This is deduction in action. You can evaluate deductive reasoning by asking two questions:

The audience responds best to a speaker whose presentation is logical, well-organized, and sincere. (McGraw-Hill photo by Mary Schoenthaler, courtesy of Pace University)

1. Are both the major and the minor premises true?
2. Does the conclusion follow logically from the premises?

When needed, be sure to give evidence to buttress your major and minor premises.

In the next example, we move from the specific to the general, progressing from a series of specific facts to a general conclusion.

1. After growing up on a diet of television violence, Ronnie Zamora committed a murder.
2. After watching a television show, *Born Innocent*, a group of teenagers emulated the rape scene shown on the program.
3. After the movie the *Deerhunter* was aired on television, 28 people died imitating the Russian roulette scene contained in it.
4. The violence depicted on television is copied in real life.

Whenever speakers use what is true in particular cases to draw a general conclusion, they are reasoning by induction. For instance, the speaker who concludes that the sexualized violence against women shown on MTV videos leads to acts of sexualized violence against women in society because in a number of cases men have enacted in real life the situations they saw depicted on the videos is reasoning inductively. You can evaluate the effectiveness of inductive reasoning by asking two questions:

1. Is the sample of specific instances large enough to justify the conclusion drawn?
2. Are the instances cited representative or typical ones?

When we reason from causes and effects, we either cite observed causes and hypothesize effects or cite observed effects and hypothesize causes. We use causal reasoning every day. Something happens, and we ask ourselves, "Why?" In like fashion we speculate about the consequences of certain acts; that is, we wonder about an act's effects. The following statements illustrate causal reasoning:

Smoking cigarettes causes cancer.
Smoking cigarettes causes heart disease.
Smoking cigarettes can cause problems during pregnancy.
Cigarette smoking is hazardous to your health and should be eliminated.

To evaluate the soundness of causal reasoning ask these questions:

1. Is the cause cited a real one or a false one?
2. Is the cause cited an oversimplification?

When we reason from analogy, we compare like things and conclude that since they are alike in a number of respects, they are also alike in some, until this point, unexamined respect. If, for example, you argued that the methods used to decrease the high school dropout rate in a nearby city would also work in your city, you would first have to establish that your city is similar to that other city in a number of important ways— number of youths, number of schools, skilled personnel, financial resources. If you could persuade audience members that the two cities were alike except for the fact that your city had not instituted such a program and that your dropout rate was therefore significantly higher, you would be arguing by analogy.

To check the validity of the analogy you draw, ask these questions:

1. Are the two things being compared alike in essential respects? That is, do the points of similarity outweigh the points of difference?
2. Do the differences that do exist matter?

SKILL BUILDER

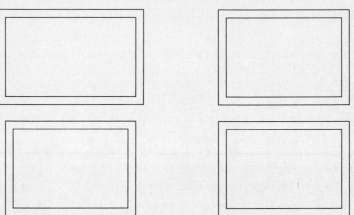

Reasons

Individually or with a partner, select one persuasive topic. Write three to five basic reasons why people should believe or take action on the topic. Use the boxes we discussed earlier.

What seem to be the best reasons? Are you incorporating logical as well as emotional appeals or reasons into your plan? Share your ideas with the class members.

What is important to keep in mind is that persuasion is more likely to occur as a result of effective reasoning than it is without it.

Gain the Attention of Your Receivers

Before you can persuade or convince other persons about something, you must first get their attention. In his book *The Art of Persuasion*, Wayne Minnick relates how one 9-year-old girl succeeded in getting the undivided attention of a male guest at her party. It seems that all the boys had gathered at one end of the room, talking to each other and ignoring the girls. "But I got one of them to pay attention to me, all right," the little girl assured her mother. "How?" inquired the mother. "I knocked him down!" came the undaunted reply.

We are not suggesting that you knock down your listeners to get their attention, but indisputably you will need to find ways to encourage your audience to listen to you. It is your responsibility to put them into a receptive frame of mind. You can do this in several different ways: You can compliment your listeners or you can question them. You can relate

To what extent do friends, co-workers, politicians, and advertisers have to compete to get your attention? Which strategies are the most effective? Why?

your message directly to listener interests or you can surprise your audience by relating to them in a way they would not expect. Once you get the attention of your receivers, you must then work to hold it.

Make Audience Members Feel, Not Just Think Logically

Why is the following excerpt from a student speech effective?

> My father had lung cancer and cancer of the spinal column. He was ill for only 5 weeks. The last weeks of his life were spent in a hospital. He was operated on, given radiation treatments, and placed in a medical contraption that was supposed to increase his limited mobility. It didn't. The bill for his 5-week stay in the hospital amounted to $20,000. My father was by no means a wealthy man. However, neither was he eligible for Medicare. Thus, his illness consumed my parents' entire savings. There is something terribly wrong with a health care system that is permitted to inflict such a terrible blow on patients and their families. National health care has become a necessity.

Many changes in human behavior result from messages that mix emotional appeals with rational reasons. Since few people will change their attitudes or take action if they are unmoved or bored, effective speakers develop emotional appeals that are designed to make listeners feel.[9] Whether that feeling is sadness, anger, fear, sympathy, happiness, greed, nostalgia, jealousy, pride, or guilt depends on the speaker's topic and the type of audience response desired.

Here is how Edward R. Murrow, a reknowned radio broadcaster, used emotional appeal to heighten one of his World War II reports:

> April 15, 1945
> . . . Permit me to tell you what you would have seen, and heard, had you been with me on Thursday. It will not be pleasant listening. If you are at lunch, or if you have no appetite to hear what Germans have done, now is a good time to switch off the radio, for I propose to tell you of Buchenwald. It is on a small hill about four miles outside Weimar, and it was one of the largest concentration camps in Germany, and it was built to last. As we approached it, we saw about a hundred men in civilian clothes with rifles advancing in open order across the fields. There were a few shops; we stopped to inquire. We were told that some of the prisoners had a couple of SS men cornered in there. We drove on, reached the main gate. The prisoners crowded up behind the wire. We entered.
> And now, let me tell this in the first person, for I was the least important person there, as you shall hear. There surged around me an evil-smelling horde. Men and boys reached out to touch me; they were in rags and the remnants of uniform. Death had already marked many of them, but they were

smiling with their eyes. I looked out over that mass of men to the green fields beyond where well-fed Germans were ploughing.

A German, Fritz Kersheimer, came up and said, "May I show you round the camp? I've been here ten years." An Englishman stood to attention, saying, "May I introduce myself, delighted to see you, and can you tell me when some of our blokes will be along?" I told him soon and asked to see one of the barracks. It happened to be occupied by Czechoslovakians. When I entered, men crowded around, tried to lift me to their shoulders. They were too weak. Many of them could not get out of bed. I was told that this building had once stabled eighty horses. There were twelve hundred men in it, five to a bunk. The stink was beyond all description.

When I reached the center of the barracks, a man came up and said, "You remember me. I'm Peter Zenkl, one-time mayor of Prague." I remembered him, but did not recognize him. . . .

As I walked down to the end of the barracks, there was applause from the men too weak to get out of bed. It sounded like the hand clapping of babies; they were so weak. The doctor's name was Paul Heller. He had been there since 1938.

As we walked out into the courtyard, a man fell dead. Two others—they must have been over sixty—were crawling toward the latrine. I saw it but will not describe it.

In another part of the camp they showed me the children, hundreds of them. Some were only six. One rolled up his sleeve, showed me his number. It was tattooed on his arm. D-6030, it was. The others showed me their numbers; they will carry them till they die.

An elderly man standing beside me said, "The children, enemies of the state." I could see their ribs through their thin shirts. The old man said, "I am Professor Charles Richer of the Sorbonne." The children clung to my hands and stared. We crossed to the courtyard. Men kept coming up to speak to me and touch me, professors from Poland, doctors from Vienna, men from all Europe. Men from the countries that made America.

We went to the hospital; it was full. The doctor told me that two hundred had died the day before. . . . Dr. Heller pulled back the blankets from a man's feet to show me how swollen they were. The man was dead. Most of the patients could not move. . . .

I asked to see the kitchen; it was clean. The German in charge had been a communist, had been at Buchenwald for nine years, had a picture of his daughter in Hamburg. He hadn't seen her for almost twelve years, and if I got to Hamburg, would I look her up? He showed me the daily ration—one piece of brown bread about as thick as your thumb, on top of it a piece of margarine as big as three sticks of chewing gum. That, and a little stew, was what they received every twenty-four hours. . . .

Dr. Heller, the Czech, asked if I would care to see the crematorium. He said it wouldn't be very interesting because the Germans had run out of coke some days ago and had taken to dumping the bodies into a great hole nearby. Professor Richer said perhaps I would care to see the small courtyard. I said yes. . . . The wall was about eight-feet high; it adjoined what had been a stable or garage. We entered. It was floored with concrete. There were two rows of bodies stacked up like cordwood. They were thin and very white. Some of the bodies were terribly bruised, though there seemed to be little flesh to bruise. . . . I tried to count them as best I could and arrived at the conclusion that all that was mortal of more than five hundred men and boys lay there in two neat piles.

There was a German trailer which must have contained another fifty, but it wasn't possible to count them. . . . It appeared that most of the men and boys had died of starvation. . . . But the manner of death seemed unimportant. Murder had been done at Buchenwald. God alone knows how many men and boys have died there during the last twelve years. . . .

As I left that camp, a Frenchman who used to work for Havas in Paris came up to me and said, "You will write something about this, perhaps?" And he added, "To write about this you must have been here at least two years, and after that—you don't want to write any more."

I pray you to believe what I have said about Buchenwald; I have reported what I saw and heard, but only part of it. For most of it I have no words. . . .[10]

The people who listened to Murrow's broadcasts did not soon forget them. President Reagan understood the need for emotion as well. He chose a poem to close his tribute to the astronauts lost in the *Challenger* disaster.

Let us close with these lines written by a 19-year-old World War II fighter pilot, John Gillespie Magee, Jr., shortly before his own death in the air:

HIGH FLIGHT

Oh, I have slipped the surly bonds of Earth.
And danced the skies on laughter-silvered wings:
Sunward I've climbed and joined the tumbling mirth
Of sun-split cloud—and done a hundred things
You have not dreamed of—wheeled and soared and swung
High in the sunlit silence. Hov'ring there.
I've chased the shouting wind along and flung
My eager craft through footless halls of air.
Up, up, the long delirious burning blue
I've topped the wind-swept heights easy grace
Where never lark or even eagle flew—
And, while with silent lifting wing I've trod
The high untrespassed sanctity of space.
Put out my hand and touched the face of God.

In like fashion your goal should be to compel your listeners to remember your ideas and proposals, and a key to this is to arouse their feelings. As a speaker, you must appeal not just to the heads of your audience members but also to their hearts. Thus, although your speech should be grounded in a firm foundation of logic and fact, it should also be dressed in feeling.

Arouse Needs and Issues Relevant to Your Purpose

Balance is a state of psychological health or comfort in which our actions, feelings, and beliefs are related to each other as we would like them to be. When we are in a balanced state, we are content or satisfied. Thus we engage in a perennial struggle to keep ourselves "in balance."

What message does this carry for you as a persuasive speaker? If you wish to convince your listeners to change their attitudes or beliefs, you must first demonstrate to them that the current situation or state of affairs has created an *imbalance* in their lives and that you can help alleviate that problem. Remember, human behavior depends on motivation. If you are to convince your receivers to believe and do what you would like them to do, you must make your persuasive messages appeal to their needs and goals.

A popular device used to analyze human motivation is the schematic framework devised by the famous psychologist Abraham Maslow.[11] According to Maslow's Hierarchy of Needs, motivation is seen as a pyramid with our most basic needs at its base and our most sophisticated needs at its apex (see Figure 19-1). Maslow defined *survival needs* as the basic necessities of life: shelter, food, water, and procreation. *Safety needs* include the need for security and the need to know that our survival requirements will be satisfied. At the third level are *love* and *belonging needs*. It is Maslow's belief that once these are met, our esteem goals can be addressed. Our *esteem needs* include the need for self-respect and for the respect of others. Our efforts to obtain particular goals are often attempts at satisfying esteem needs because success tends to attract respect and attention. Finally,

FIGURE 19-1
Maslow's Hierarchy
of Needs

Climbing the Motivation Pyramid

For each of the following situations, identify the types of appeals you could use to persuade listeners to believe or behave as you would like them to. First, imagine a particular type of audience. Second, gear some part of your persuasive effort to *each level* of Maslow's pyramid. Which level/appeal do you think would be most effective? Explain your reasons.

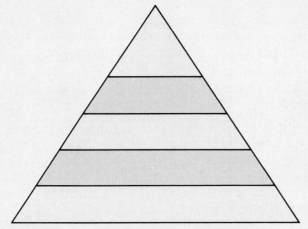

1. You want to persuade someone to stop smoking.
2. You want to persuade someone to donate blood.
3. You want to persuade someone to support capital punishment.
4. You want to persuade someone to protest using domestic animals for experimental research.

at the peak of Maslow's hierarchy is the need for *self-actualization*. When we satisfy this, we realize our potential; that is, we become everything we are capable of becoming.

How does Maslow's hierarchy relate to you as a public persuader? Find out by trying the exercise above. Remember, salient needs make salient motives. Your goal is to make your receivers identify their needs with your proposal. Whenever you attempt to do this, you will probably have to zero in on personal feelings.

Promise a Reward

Demonstrate how personal needs can be satisfied by your proposal. You should stress how your ideas can personally benefit the persons you are trying to persuade. Make the individuals believe that your proposal will

What are your own most important needs? How might someone use this information to persuade you to buy one of the items listed here?

supply a reward. (Remember that different audiences value different types of rewards.)

For practice, think of three different audience groups and identify the most important needs of each. Imagine that you are a salesperson trying to persuade each of these groups to purchase one of the following items: (1) a guitar, (2) a plant, (3) a dog, (4) a hat, (5) an attaché case. Describe the strategies you would use in getting each group to make the purchase. What types of adaptations would you make? To what extent would you display your awareness of individual differences?

It is important to remember that people are usually preoccupied with how something will benefit them personally. Your listeners, whoever they are, will want something in return for behaving as you would like them to behave.

HOW TO BECOME A MORE CREDIBLE PERSUADER

Consider this.

"THE BEST IN THE WEST"

ED BRADLEY: In the Old West, when a man wanted to settle a score, he went out and found himself a hired gun. Today, when he wants to settle a score, he goes out and finds himself a lawyer. And if he's lucky, he finds Gerry Spence, who dresses more like a hired gun than a hired lawyer. Spence sees himself as a Marshall Dillon, a good guy fighting the bad guys for causes he believes in and for causes he feels are just and significant. . . .

You're on the stand; you're under oath. How good are you as a lawyer?

GERRY SPENCE: I'm the best lawyer I ever knew. . . .

ED BRADLEY: Gerry Spence isn't modest, but he probably isn't wrong. He just may be the best trial lawyer in America. He hasn't lost a trial since 1969.

GERRY SPENCE: . . . Gerry Spence walks up to a jury, and he gives that jury everything that he is. He gives—he says, "Here I am. Here is all of me. Here is my heart and my guts and my soul, and the truth, and my belief, and everything that I am. Here it is, and I—and I—and I ask you to take it."

Reprinted by permission from *60 Minutes* telecast, January 24, 1982.

In part, your success as a persuader will be determined by what the "targets" of your efforts think of you—in other words, by your credibility.[12]

When we use the term *source credibility* we are talking about how an audience perceives you, not what you are "really" like. If your receivers accept you as a credible source, they probably believe you are a person of good character (trustworthy and fair), *knowledgeable* (trained, competent to discuss your topic, and a reliable source of information), and *personable* (dynamic and/or charismatic, active, and energetic). As a result your ideas are more likely to get a fair hearing. However, if your receivers believe you are a liar (untrustworthy), incompetent (not knowledgeable enough about your topic), and passive (lacking in dynamism), they are less apt to respond as you desire.

It is entirely possible—and even probable—that you may be judged by listeners to be more credible about some topics than others. For example, here are two pairs of imaginary statements. Which statement in each pair would you be more apt to accept?

> The United States must never negotiate with terrorists. Strength is the only language they will understand.
>
> Ronald Reagan

□

> The United States must never negotiate with terrorists. Strength is the only language they will understand.
>
> Boy George

□

> The world of contemporary music has room in it for everyone. The message music sends is tolerance.
>
> Boy George

□

> The world of contemporary music has room in it for everyone. The message music sends is tolerance.
>
> Ronald Reagan

If you're like most people, you find the first statement in each pair the most credible. Why? Because we regard the source to be knowledgeable about that subject. Similarly, you may be judged to be more credible by certain types of audiences than by others. Regardless of the circumstances, however, it will be up to you to help build your credibility by giving your listeners reasons for viewing you as competent, trustworthy, and dynamic.[13] To help listeners perceive you as competent, you can reveal your own experiences with the subject to them and can suggest why you feel you've earned the right to share your ideas with them. You can help your listeners perceive you as trustworthy by demonstrating a respect for different points of view and communicating a sense of sincerity about the issue being

The audience's perception of the speaker's credibility is the key to success in persuasion. (Frank Siteman/The Picture Cube)

considered. Of course, you can also help audience members perceive you as a dynamic source if you speak with energy, use assured and forceful gestures, and exhibit vocal variety.[14]

Note that the audience's assessment of your credibility can change during or as a result of your presentation. Thus, we can identify three types of credibility:

Initial credibility—your credibility before you actually start to speak
Derived credibility—your credibility during your speech
Terminal credibility—your credibility at the end of your speech.

Of course, if you have high initial credibility, your task should be easier. But keep in mind that your actual speech can destroy high initial credibility just as easily as it can enhance an initial judgment of low credibility. Thus what you say and how you deliver that message are important credibility determiners. For instance, do you consider Art Buchwald's character Randolph Habermeyer, chief lobbyist for the American Hot and Cold Steel Company, a credible source (see page 461)?

As Ralph Waldo Emerson wrote:

The reason why anyone refuses his assent to your opinion, or his aid to your benevolent design, is in you. He refuses to accept you as a bringer of truth, because, though you think you have it, he feels that you have it not. You have not given him the authentic sign.

THE LOBBYIST AGAINST IMPORTS

Art Buchwald

Randolph Habermeyer, chief lobbyist for the American Hot and Cold Steel Company, was awakened by his Swiss-made Computer Alarm Clock. He got up and turned on his Sony television set to hear the news.

Then he showered and shaved with the new electric razor his wife had bought which said Made in Germany.

He then started dressing. Since he was going to testify in front of a congressional committee he selected his suit carefully, deciding on an imported Pierre Cardin pin stripe. He also chose a conservative silk tie that came from Thailand. Finally he put on his Italian-made Gucci shoes. He filled his Paris-made Hermes briefcase with all the papers he would need for his testimony.

It was raining out so he grabbed his trench coat. It was his favorite coat, and he was amazed that the Spanish, of all people, could manufacture trench coats at a third the price of the American ones.

Habermeyer kissed his wife good-bye and got into his Mercedes-Benz to drive from Potomac to the Capitol. In the Mercedes he had a phone, which had been made in Taiwan, and he called his office to dictate several messages to his secretary on a German-made Grundig machine.

He also had a pocket-size Dutch-made Philips recorder in the car to remind him of things he wanted to do the next day.

Suddenly he looked at his gas gauge and realized he was short of gas.

He stopped at a BP (British Petroleum) station and filled up the tank.

Habermeyer was listening to his radio as he drove along. They were advertising a new "Star Wars" rocket ship from Hong Kong. He made a note to buy one for his son for Christmas.

The next commercial had to do with a French Cuisinart blender. Habermeyer decided to get one for his wife because she had said they were still the best on the market.

As he was driving along he realized he had time to buy some cigars. Since Cuban ones were still not on the market, he favored the ones made in the Canary Islands.

The clerk was pushing a new cigar that had been manufactured in the Philippines, but Habermeyer said he'd stick with his Flamencos.

He also bought a throwaway lighter made in South Korea.

Then he got back into his Mercedes and drove up to the Hill.

Before going to the committee room to testify, he dropped off to see a congressman friend and gave him a box of Swiss chocolates that one of the people from the company had brought back on a recent trip. The lobbyist knew the congressman had a sweet tooth, and he couldn't think of a better gift to give him.

Finally Habermeyer went to the committee room to testify. He was the second witness. He sat at the table, took out his prepared statement and began to read.

"On behalf of the American Hot and Cold Steel Company, as well as all American steel companies, I am raising my voice in angry protest over the flagrant dumping of foreign steel in this country. Mr. Chairman, this committee must decide whether we will permit the importation of foreign steel at the price of sacrificing American jobs and doing mortal damage to the American economy.

"The time has come for us to say, 'Enough is enough.' We cannot survive when we have to compete with the labor costs of other nations. It is your patriotic duty to see that the United States is protected from the flooding of foreign imports which I, as an American citizen, find despicable . . ."

Habermeyer took 30 minutes to read his statement and then looked at his Japanese Seiko watch and realized his time was up.

Reprinted by permission of G. P. Putnam's Sons from THE BUCHWALD STOPS HERE by Art Buchwald. Copyright © 1976, 1977, 1978 by Art Buchwald.

You should now realize that public persuasion involves more than simply communicating with others in a public setting. It is your responsibility to familiarize yourself with the beliefs, attitudes, and needs of those you hope to persuade. Only by doing so will you be in a position to influence others and understand how they try to influence you.

Presenting a Persuasive Speech

As a persuasive speaker you must show a great deal of interest in and enthusiasm for the topic at hand. At the moment of presentation it must become the most important issue in the world for both you and your listeners. The audience members must feel that you have a real sense of conviction about the topic and the solution you suggest.

Be aware that audience members may object to what you say. As a persuader it is important for you to be able to handle the objections in an effective manner. First, be prepared for opposing points of view. Rehearse possible answers to the concerns expressed. Second, consider the source of the objections. Audience members may refute your facts. If you make a statement about the number of millionaires in your state and a class member has just completed a study on wealth in the United States and has up-to-date statistics, you will need to agree, restate your findings, or suggest that it is a good point that you both should explore. Another way to handle opposing views is to agree with them as much as possible. "I agree that life insurance may not be the best investment . . ." is a disarming technique often used by life insurance persuaders to counter objections to purchasing insurance.

Refute the argument in a professional manner. Do not become angry

Meeting the Challenge

1. Using whatever speaking aids and strategies you believe will increase your ability to influence your listeners, prepare a 5- to 7-minute persuasive speech.

2. Provide an outline and a listing of bibliographic sources consulted.

3. Develop a purpose or goal statement and several valid, well-supported reasons for accepting the argument. Use facts and the well-documented opinions of experts to build as effective a case as you can. Be sure to have an effective beginning and ending. The ending should reemphasize what you want the audience to do or believe.

4. If time allows, audience members may ask questions. Be prepared to respond to them in an appropriate manner that increases your credibility.

that anyone would dare refute your reasoning. Instead, remember that your credibility is at stake while you are in front of others. Respond to the question or objection in an authoritative manner and move on to other questions. Maintain control.

SAMPLE PERSUASIVE SPEECH OUTLINE

Would You Die for a Drink?

Purpose: To persuade the audience to act to keep the drunken driver off the road.

The purpose statement clearly identifies the persuasive nature of the speech.

Introduction

I. Johnny Carson and F. Lee Bailey have something in common.
   A. On a recent weekend they were both arrested and charged with drunken driving.
      1. Many people chuckled to themselves over this.
      2. Is drunken driving really a laughing matter?
   B. Driving while intoxicated is a very serious problem in this country.
      1. Over 35 percent of all automobile accidents are alcohol-related.
      2. Drunken driving is responsible for more than 25,000 deaths each year.

Using well-known personalities as examples gets the audience's attention and interest.

Statistics support the argument of the introduction that the problem is a serious one.

3. Drunken driving is responsible for more than 750,000 injuries each year.

II. Today, I will examine how our society treats the drunken driver, and I will suggest what we can do to ensure that drunken drivers stay off the roads.

The introduction concludes with a preview.

Body

I. First, let's look at the societal attitudes which permit drunken drivers to remain on the road.

Announces the first main point of the speech.

    A. People seem to empathize or identify with the drunken driver's plight.

        1. Since 80 percent of all adult Americans drink, there is an "it could have been me" attitude about drunken driving.

        2. The arrests of Carson, Bailey, and other personalities are a source of gossip, not outrage.

Involves the audience by using as examples experiences they're likely to be familiar with.

    B. Peer pressure causes many people—including college students—to drink to excess.

    C. Few people act to protect the intoxicated person.

        1. Few offer to call a cab so that the intoxicated individual won't drive.

        2. Few encourage the intoxicated person to sleep before getting behind the wheel.

Explains how and why previous efforts to solve the problem have failed.

    D. To date, legislative efforts to curb drunk driving have been ineffective.

        1. The National Highway Safety Council estimates that $1 billion is spent annually to reduce drunk driving.

        2. Legislators have tried harsher punishments only to find that although the number of arrests decreases, the number of drunken drivers does not.

        3. Judges regularly hand out suspended sentences to drunken drivers.

        4. In New Jersey alone, thousands of drivers simply refuse to take the mandatory informational training seminars on drunk driving.

II. Now, let's look at what you can do to help curb drunk driving.

The second main point is an appeal for the audience to take action.

    A. Avoid drinking and driving yourself.

    B. Since as a host you may be sued in civil court if your guest is involved in an accident, encourage those who are drunk to stay out of the driver's seat.

Subpoints A–D give examples of specific things the audience can do to help.

    C. Support the efforts of MADD (Mothers Against Drunk Drivers) and RID (Remove Intoxicated Drivers).

    D. Finally, support mandatory usage of the PBT (Preliminary Breath Test).

1. Today, drivers can refuse to take a breath test.
2. Mandatory breath tests would provide more accurate information for enforcement officials.
3. In Norway, for example, the PBT is coupled with random roadblocks and a mandatory 21-day sentence in a labor camp.

Conclusion

I. We have seen that societal attitudes contribute to the prevalence of drunk driving and that legislative and personal action need to be taken to correct this problem.

Summarizes the two main points of the speech.

II. The next time you find yourself chuckling over the arrest of some prominent public figure for reportedly driving while intoxicated—think again!

Makes a final appeal to the audience to change their attitudes.

Sources

Bradel, P. "Preliminary Breath Test in Traffic Enforcement," *Journal of Police Science and Administration*, March 1981, pp. 23–27.

"Drinking and Driving Don't Mix," *Newsday*, December 9, 1981.

Faulkner, S. "Consultation Report on Drinking and Driving," *Journal of Studies on Alcohol*, Vol. 42, March 1980, pp. 151–153.

Mookherjee, H., and H. W. Hogan. "Attitudes and Driving Behavior among Americans," *Journal of Social Psychology*, Vol. 112, December 1980, pp. 315–317.

Muscarella, Leni. "Dying for a Drink," *The Record*, March 7, 1982.

"The War against Drunk Drivers," *Newsweek*, September 13, 1982, pp. 34–39.

Developed as part of a class exercise by students in the course "Basic Public Speaking" at the College of New Rochelle, New York.

SAMPLE PERSUASIVE SPEECH

Book Censorship: A Problem for Our Time

Do you believe you can go to the library and borrow any book you want? According to Czechoslavakian dissident Milan Simecka, there are countries in the world where you can do this. But what I ask you is, "Is the United States one of those countries?" Though this may surprise you, unfortunately the answer is not a resounding yes. Book censorship is a problem that must be alleviated.

The speaker uses a rhetorical question to spark audience interest.

Testimony and a question are used to promote curiosity.

USA Today reports that in the 1980s censorship complaints increased in our country from 300 per year to almost 1,000 per year. Even more sadly, in just one 2-year period alone—between 1982 and 1983—there were 22 book burnings in 17 of our United States; book burnings—where are

The speaker's goal is stated clearly and succinctly. The organizational format—problem solution—is also previewed here.

you living? Nazi Germany? *Freedom of Information*, a publication of the Society of Professional Journalists, reports that our "censors are building a Library of Condemned Books that may soon become the world's fastest-growing but unused collection." As a case in point, efforts to censor books occur in one-fifth of our nation's schools every year—and, surprisingly, half succeed. What is happening to one of our most sacred rights—freedom of expression?

What are the censors hoping to accomplish? For what reasons are they banning books? In 1984 the Associated Press reported that the Lindenwald, New Jersey, school board voted to limit access to three books it considered inappropriate for some children—one was about an overweight youngster, and another dealt with divorce and family relations. Are these topics we should not be free to read about? Are children not experiencing these problems themselves, and can't reading about such situations actually increase their ability to cope with and understand them? I would think so. Yet our list of book casualties is increasing, not decreasing, and it is growing at an alarming rate. Who are the victims? The victims are books we probably grew up with.

For example, journalist Christine Moore notes that in Fairfax County, Virginia, one school administrator is revising *Huckleberry Finn* by deleting "offensive racist" remarks. In a Baton Rouge suburb, the books *Cinderella* and *Snow White* were burned because they contained "satanic" material. And ERA opponent Phyllis Schlafly has announced that she will devote her energies to purifying school textbooks of feminist influences. Reports are that she is meeting with success. And in St. David, Arizona, one group succeeded in removing books by Conrad, Hawthorne, Hemingway, Homer, Poe, and Steinbeck from required reading lists. Even more recently, in Panama City, Florida, in 1988, the following books were banned by the school board because it was felt they contained either the curse "god-damn" or "a lot of vulgarity": Shakespeare's plays *Twelfth Night* and *The Merchant of Venice* and the novels *Mr. Roberts*, *The Great Gatsby*, and *The Red Badge of Courage*. Why are events like these problems?

You forfeit your cultural heritage when you destroy books. You forfeit the stuff that feeds our minds. As President John F. Kennedy noted: "Our young people constitute the greatest resource our country has—and books are essential to their intellectual growth into thoughtful and informed citizens." To be sure, as educator Gilbert Highet observed, it is through books that we "can call into range the voice of a man far distant in time and space, and hear him speaking to us mind-to-mind, heart-to-heart." We must not take our books for granted. I do not want to read censored thoughts, censored fears, and censored dreams. I do not want to look for a volume to find that its use has been restricted. Our strength as a nation lies in our ability to have access to ideas. Censors may have a right to

The speaker's position is enhanced by an abundance of statistical evidence.

The speaker tells us that one of our most basic rights is in danger; fear is used to stimulate support.

The speaker clarifies for us the possible motivations of censors and then works to combat these stances.

Books are personified as victims.

The speaker supplies a number of examples of the censors' work. The extent and nature of the censorship problem are clarified for us.

The speaker explains the dangers inherent in book censorship. Both emotional and logical appeals are used.

decide what their own children may read, but they should not have a right to decide what I will read.

If you feel the same way as I do, then you will join with me in organizing a school chapter of People for the American Way, a group founded to fight censorship. After all, the book, as our Librarian of Congress Daniel Boorstin likes to put it, is our "TV of the mind." The number of titles we have access to should be increasing, not diminishing. I firmly believe that the world of books is the most wonderful creation of man. Nothing should be permitted to destroy them. If we are to live on in freedom, our books must live on too.

The speaker proposes a solution that could help alleviate the problem.

Sources

Bernstein, Richard. "Opening the Books on Censorship," *The New York Times Magazine*, May 13, 1984.

"If Books Are Gutted Education Will Bleed," *USA Today*, August 9, 1983.

Hentoff, Nat. "Selling the American Heritage for Big Texas Bucks," *The Village Voice*, October 4, 1983, p. 6.

Moore, Christine. "Textbook Censorship Multiplying," *FOI '82*, 1982.

Palmer, Barbara. "Censorship: The Battle Is Heating Up," *USA Today*, June 21, 1984.

Developed as a class exercise by students enrolled in the basic communication course at the College of New Rochelle.

SUMMARY

The goal of a persuasive speech is to modify the thoughts, feelings, and/or actions of an audience. To be an effective persuasive speaker you need first to identify your persuasive goal and learn as much as you can about the general attitudes and beliefs of your audience as well as what their opinion of your specific proposal is likely to be. You should then tailor your presentation accordingly to get their atten-

tion, appeal to their needs and goals, and promise them a meaningful reward for accepting your proposal.

Source credibility—what the audience thinks of you—will also help determine whether your persuasive efforts will be successful. A credible speaker is one perceived by audience members as a person of good character who is knowledgeable and personable.

SUGGESTIONS FOR FURTHER READING

Cialdini, Robert B. *Influence*. New York: Quill, 1984. A fascinating analysis of the persuasion process; understandable and readable.

Ilardo, Joseph A. *Speaking Persuasively*. New

York: Macmillan, 1981. A comprehensive examination of the process of persuasion in public speaking.

O'Donnell, Victoria, and June Kabel. *Persuasion:*

An Interactive-Dependency Approach. New York: Random House, 1982. An in-depth treatment of behavior and behavior change.

Triandes, Harry C. *Attitude and Attitude Change.* New York: Wiley, 1971. A scholarly examination of attitudes and beliefs.

Zimbardo, Philip G., Ebbe B. Ebbesen, and Christina Maslach. *Influencing Attitudes and Changing Behavior*, 2d ed. Reading, Mass.: Addison-Wesley, 1977. A good overview of research and theory.

NOTES

1. For an excellent explanation of why we study persuasion, see chap. 1 in Joseph Ilardo, *Speaking Persuasively* (New York: Macmillan, 1981).
2. See Wallace Folderingham, *Perspectives on Persuasion* (Boston: Allyn & Bacon, 1966), p. 33.
3. For a chapter defining persuasion, see chap. 1 in Gary Cronkhite, *Persuasion: Speech and Behavioral Change* (Indianapolis: Bobbs-Merrill, 1969).
4. See M. Herif and C. Hovland, *Social Judgment* (New Haven: Yale University Press, 1961), and C. Herif, M. Sherif, and R. Nebergall, *Attitude and Attitude Change* (Philadelphia: Saunders, 1965).
5. A framework for understanding the importance of beliefs is provided by Martin Fishbein and Icek Ajzen in *Belief, Attitude, Intention and Behavior: An Introduction to Theory and Research* (Reading, Mass.: Addison-Wesley, 1975). See especially chaps. 1 and 8.
6. Prominent theorists such as Leon Festinger, Fritz Hieder, and Theodore Newcomb view the desire for consistency as a central motivator of behavior. For a more contemporary discussion of the topic, see Robert B. Cialdini, *Influence* (New York: Quill, 1984), pp. 66–114.
7. Cialdini, p. 117.
8. Ibid.
9. For a discussion of the role of affect, see, for example, Mary John Smith, *Persuasion and Human Action* (Belmont, Calif.: Wadsworth, 1982).
10. From *In Search of Light: The Broadcasts of Edward R. Murrow 1938–1961*, edited by Edward Bliss, Jr. (New York: Alfred A. Knopf, 1967).
11. Abraham Maslow, *Motivation and Personality* (New York: Harper & Row, 1954), pp. 80–92.
12. The variable of *source credibility* has received much attention from researchers. For sample studies, see R. Applebaum and K. Anatol, "The Factor Structure of Source Credibility as a Function of the Speaking Situation," *Speech Monographs*, Vol. 39 (1972), pp. 216–222. A valuable and still worthwhile summary of experimental research on source credibility is provided in Kenneth Andersen and Theodore Clevenger, Jr., "A Summary of Experimental Research of Ethos," *Speech Monographs*, Vol. 30 (1963), pp. 59–78.
13. Speakers can enhance their credibility early in a speech. For example, see R. Brooks and T. Scheidel, "Speech as Process: A Case Study," *Speech Monographs*, Vol. 35 (1968), pp. 1–7.
14. The nonverbal aspects of source credibility are discussed in more detail in Chapter 17.

Epilogue

Beyond the Book: Where Do You Go from Here?

No one knows the story of tomorrow's dawn.

African proverb

They told me to write about life.
To discover new insights,
To probe my inner soul,
To meditate on my faith,
To reflect on ideals,
And to have it in by Friday.

Anonymous

CHAPTER PREVIEW

After finishing this epilogue, you should be able to:

Explain why developing your communication skills is a lifelong task

Demonstrate an ability to use a number of strategies to help make your present and future communication contacts more effective

Explain why we need to acknowledge change

Provide examples of important *life passages* you have made or expect to make

Explain what is meant by changing *communication chairs*

Define and discuss the dangers inherent in "frozen" evaluations

Identify typical *nonchange* excuses

Assess your ability to apply the principles discussed in this and previous chapters to the arenas of your life

Use checkbacks to help maintain and improve your communication skills

Continue your communication skill development on your own

As we mentioned at the beginning, we wrote this book for you. What we wrote at the outset is even more relevant now. The topics you have studied should serve you well as you enter into personal and professional relationships. The skills you have mastered should help you fulfill your needs, reach your goals, and improve the quality of your life. But, as we indicated in Chapter 1, your assignment to develop your interpersonal, small-group, and public communication abilities has no "due date"; it is a lifelong process. You have completed this term's work, but your lifelong learning program has just begun. As Aldous Huxley wrote, "There's only one corner of the universe you can be certain of improving and that's your own self." Let us examine a number of strategies you can use to help make your present and future communication experiences as rewarding as you would like them to be. Remember, you can surpass *yourself!*

HOW TO CONTINUE IMPROVING YOUR COMMUNICATION EFFECTIVENESS

> Actually, the process of birth continues. The child begins to recognize outside objects, to react affectively, to grasp things and to co-ordinate his movements, to walk. But birth continues. The child learns to speak, it learns to know the use and function of things, it learns to relate itself to others, to avoid punishment and gain praise and liking. Slowly, the growing person learns to love, to develop reason, to look at the world objectively. He begins to develop his powers; to acquire a sense of identity, to overcome the seduction of his senses for the sake of an integrated life. . . . The whole life of the individual is nothing but the process of giving birth to himself; indeed, we should be fully born, when we die—although it is the tragic fate of most individuals to die before they are born.
>
> *Erich Fromm*

Today is not exactly like yesterday, the day before yesterday, or the day before that. Thus the one thing you can count on is change. We

As a person changes throughout life, communication skills must also change and adapt. (Laimute E. Druskis, Taurus)

ourselves change with time, the people with whom we interact and relate change with time, and the situations in which we are involved change with time. To deal with change, we must acknowledge it. Only by doing so can we keep our communicating selves fresh and effective. In her book *Passages*, Gail Sheehy puts it this way:

> We are not unlike a particularly hardy crustacean. The lobster grows by developing and shedding a series of hard, protective shells. Each time it expands from within, the confining shell must be sloughed off. It is left exposed and vulnerable until, in time, a new covering grows to replace the old.

It can be said that like the lobster, we develop from within. As we move through the various stages or passages of our lives, we too shed the protections in which we have encased ourselves.

Let us explore the types of shells you have shed in your own life. Experiences such as graduation, an engagement, moving away from home, marriage, childbirth, death, a broken relationship, divorce, entering the job market, and being fired can cause us to feel vulnerable because all such transitions require adaptation and change. However, as Sheehy writes, "we must be willing to change chairs if we want to grow. There is no permanent compatibility between a chair and a person. And there is no one right chair. What is right at one stage may be restricting at another, or too soft." The message for us is that we must be prepared to change "communication chairs" also. The communication strategies we employed successfully at one point in our lives may be inadequate or inappropriate to the situations and individuals we interact with today. Just as the physician's practice of medicine changes as new drugs are discovered and marketed and as the attorney's practice of law changes as laws are revised or removed from the books, so your practice of communication should change as you leave one life experience and enter another. As this happens, you may notice subtle or dramatic alterations in your sense of self, in your feelings about others, or in your values and attitudes. This is normal because each change asks you to develop and react in some particular way. Thus everyone is expected to play the "change game," but only those who take the time to understand it have an advantage.

Guard against Frozen Evaluations

Think of a situation when someone's frozen evaluation of you—or your frozen evaluation of him or her—caused difficulties. How did the frozen evaluation cause the problem? What could have prevented it?

Have you ever stopped to realize that while others can stop you temporarily, you are the only one who can do it permanently?

Consider this. A mature elephant has no difficulty lifting a 2-ton load with its trunk. Why is it, then, that when employed by a circus these huge animals stand quietly for hours tied to a very small, light wooden stake?

When the elephant is still a "young child" and not very strong, it is restrained by a heavy chain to an immovable stake in the ground. The small elephant tries to break the chain but realizes that no matter how hard it tries, it cannot break loose. As the elephant matures and gains weight and strength, it does not try to break loose because it *thinks* it can't. Don't we sometimes behave like these elephants? We limit ourselves in thought and behavior because of earlier experiences. What is sad is that sometimes we do not let ourselves move beyond the imaginary boundaries we have established.

Whenever you consciously or unconsciously apply your evaluation of a person (yourself or another), a situation, or an idea to the future and the past, ignoring the changes in the objects of your assessment, you are making what William Haney calls a "frozen evaluation." He notes that some of our most immutable evaluations are those we make about ourselves, although evaluations we make about others can be equally harmful.

Worn-out evaluations can do us and others a great disservice. People, situations, and ideas are all in constant flux. Try to prevent your judgments from becoming "set" or fixed. Effective communicators have the courage to acknowledge past and future changes in the people, situations, and objects they evaluate. Effective communicators can substitute the premise of change for the assumption of nonchange.

Since change is inevitable, remember to take it into consideration whenever you render evaluations. People, situations, and things alter with

Changes

1. Compile a list of self-evaluations that have remained relatively unchanged over the years. (For example, "I am shy.")
2. Identify specific examples that could be used to invalidate each of these self-evaluations.
3. Compile a list of evaluations you have made about others that have remained relatively unchanged over a period of time. (For example, "Haynes is a poor teacher.")
4. As before, identify data that could be used to expose the fallacies in these evaluations.

time, and if you refuse to deal with the change itself, you are actually refusing to deal with that person, situation, or thing.

Avoid "Nonchange" Excuses

You can also do damage to yourself and your relationships with others if you convince yourself you are unable to change. Such an excuse prevents you from trying out new behaviors, assuming new roles, or interacting successfully in new situations. Change may be difficult, but it can be accomplished.

To be sure, at times our environment constricts and limits the possibilities for change open to us. However, at other times our environment "stretches," and we find ourselves operating within a somewhat different context. The environment we were born into is not the same one we are interacting in now. Although your past certainly influences who you are

"Excuses, Excuses—"

1. Compile a list of excuses that you or others you know use to avoid dealing with change. (For example, "I can't unlearn poverty," "I was spoiled as a child, so I always have to get my way," or "I was taught that men don't do dishes and that women belong in the home.")
2. Explain why the concept of change makes the validity of each of these excuses doubtful.

today, the way you plan and prepare for your future can also influence you. You will permit yourself to grow if you recognize that you are constantly reorganizing and constantly changing. For this reason, the attitudes and values you bring with you from the past into the present may not apply to the current "you" or the present situation. Remember Alice's answer when the Caterpillar inquired who she was:

> I hardly know, sir, just at present—at least I know who I was when I got up this morning, but I think I must have changed several times since then.

Openness, curiosity, and the willingness to take risks and experiment can all be assets. You will be wise not to let habits, rigid attitudes, or unyielding opinions hinder your growth by reducing your receptiveness to alternative ways of thinking and behaving.

A LOOK AT THE MAJOR ARENAS OF YOUR LIFE: FAMILY, FRIENDS, EDUCATION, AND WORK

The extent to which you develop the skills to help you communicate with others will influence whether you will be able to make your way through your "people environment" successfully. Your *people environment* is composed of at least four different arenas: family, friends, education, and work. One reason we wrote this book was to help equip you with the interpersonal, small-group, and public communication competencies that would enable you to relate effectively in any of these contexts—that is, wherever you happen to find yourself. It is time for you to assess your ability to function in each of these different environments. Doing so will permit you to identify your needs and the demands placed on you when you communicate with others in the vital areas of your life.

Your reactions should indicate to you how communication influences your relationships with others in each of these sectors. After all, as Virginia Satir notes in *Peoplemaking*, "communication is a huge umbrella that covers and affects all that goes on between human beings." Let us be certain to examine the umbrella's spokes. Use the following exercises to recognize, reaffirm, and set communication skill priorities. Once you understand your priorities in each of your major arenas, you will be able to act more consistently to achieve them.

Whether we are interacting interpersonally, participating in a small group, or delivering a speech, we sometimes communicate in ways that are hurtful to ourselves or others. Being able to identify the behaviors that impede our functioning and being able to recognize behaviors that can be substituted are important steps in improving our communication abilities.

Graduation is a time of fresh opportunities, when we are ready to explore new environments. Change brings with it a chance to grow, and commencement speakers often use this theme to urge graduates to take risks and accept challenges. (Jim Anderson/Stock Boston)

What happens to us in one arena may be quite different from what happens to us in another, and our perception of ourselves can also change from one arena to another. Accounting for such differences is part of the growth process. By now it should be apparent that one key to communication effectiveness is *behavioral flexibility*.

The goal of the exercise on page 476 is to identify the ways in which your evaluation of your communication assets and liabilities affects your ability to function in each communication arena.

Realize that you can choose to ignore your weaker behaviors and drift through an encounter, or you can choose to deal with your problem behaviors

Where Am I Now?

1. On a separate sheet, for each category, identify specific behaviors that you would like to *avoid* exhibiting during communication with particular individuals.

Family

Person 1
Person 2

Friends

Person 1
Person 2

Education

Person 1
Person 2

Work

Person 1
Person 2

2. On a separate sheet, for each category, identify specific behaviors you would *prefer* using during communication with particular individuals.

Family

Person 1
Person 2

Friends

Person 1
Person 2

Education

Person 1
Person 2

Work

Person 1
Person 2

Where Are You Now?

1. Use the following set of scales to measure your ability to apply the skills discussed in this book to each of the communication arenas indicated. The number 1 on the scale represents little or no confidence in your ability, whereas the number 5 indicates total confidence in your ability. Select the number that best reflects your assets.

	Family	Friends	Education	Work
Your self-concept	1 2 3 4 5	1 2 3 4 5	1 2 3 4 5	1 2 3 4 5
Your perceptual skills	1 2 3 4 5	1 2 3 4 5	1 2 3 4 5	1 2 3 4 5
Your listening skills	1 2 3 4 5	1 2 3 4 5	1 2 3 4 5	1 2 3 4 5
Your ability to send and receive nonverbal cues	1 2 3 4 5	1 2 3 4 5	1 2 3 4 5	1 2 3 4 5
Your ability to communicate verbally	1 2 3 4 5	1 2 3 4 5	1 2 3 4 5	1 2 3 4 5
Your ability to be assertive	1 2 3 4 5	1 2 3 4 5	1 2 3 4 5	1 2 3 4 5
Your ability to interact with others to solve problems	1 2 3 4 5	1 2 3 4 5	1 2 3 4 5	1 2 3 4 5
Your leadership ability	1 2 3 4 5	1 2 3 4 5	1 2 3 4 5	1 2 3 4 5
Your conflict-management skills	1 2 3 4 5	1 2 3 4 5	1 2 3 4 5	1 2 3 4 5
Your ability to meet the speechmaker's challenge	1 2 3 4 5	1 2 3 4 5	1 2 3 4 5	1 2 3 4 5
Your ability to adapt to a specific audience	1 2 3 4 5	1 2 3 4 5	1 2 3 4 5	1 2 3 4 5

2. What do your ratings tell you about your level of skill mastery? Which skills consistently pose problems for you? Which pose problems for you in only one context? In which arena do you experience the most problems? The fewest problems? Why?

and face your communication challenges. In order to develop a skill fully, however, you must want to improve yourself. You must be willing to work, and you must be personally committed. You must believe the goal you seek is desirable—a target worth striving for. You will probably want to enhance your abilities to communicate in all arenas. Your chances of succeeding will be increased if you contract to practice all the interpersonal, small-group, and public communication skills we have considered. After all, these skills are vital to your success in each area of your life.

CHECKBACKS: EXERCISES YOU CAN USE AGAIN AND AGAIN

MOTHER TO SON

Langston Hughes

Well, Son, I'll tell you
Life for me ain't been no crystal stair.
It's had tacks in it.
And splinters.
And boards torn up.
And places with no carpets on the floor.
Bare.
But all the time
I'se been climbin' on
And reachin' landin's
And turning corners
And sometimes goin' on in the dark
Where there ain't been no light.
So, Boy, don't you turn back.
Don't you set down on the steps
'Cause you find it's kinder hard.
Don't you fall now—
For I'se still goin', Honey,
I'se still climbin'
And life for me ain't been no crystal stair.

Lloyd Jones tells us, "The men (or women) who try to do something and fail are infinitely better than those who try to do nothing and succeed." Why?

We wrote this text hoping that you would find it a practical manual for developing communication skills—and one you could use again and again. Thus, each of the Skill Builders can be repeated at various points throughout your life. Your responses will trace your growth and development as a communicator. We have also included a number of key Checkback exercises that you can repeat through the years to help ensure that you are continually working to maintain, nourish, and improve your communication skills.

Up To Date

Describe yourself 10 years ago, 5 years ago, and today in terms of physical appearance, personality characteristics, intellectual ability, and communication skills. Use the following chart to guide your observations. Be sure to repeat this exercise every 5 years.

1. TEN YEARS AGO

    a. Physical appearance:
    b. Personality characteristics:
    c. Intellectual ability:
    d. Communication skills:
       Interpersonal:
       Small-group:
       Public:

2. FIVE YEARS AGO

    a. Physical appearance:
    b. Personality characteristics:
    c. Intellectual ability:
    d. Communication skills:
       Interpersonal:
       Small-group:
       Public:

3. TODAY

    a. Physical appearance:
    b. Personality characteristics:
    c. Intellectual ability:
    d. Communication skills:
       Interpersonal:
       Small-group:
       Public:

Which aspects of yourself have undergone the most revision? Why?

THE SEARCH

Shel Silverstein

I went to find the pot of gold
That's waiting where the rainbow ends.
I searched and searched and searched and searched
And searched and searched, and then—
There it was, deep in the grass,

Life Time

1. Describe your self-concept. In your analysis, include a description of the roles you believe you have performed effectively this year, the roles you feel you need to work on, and new discoveries you have made about yourself.
2. Discuss the types of relationships you've shared with significant others during the year. Include a description of relationships that have ended, relationships that have been maintained, and relationships that have just begun.
3. Discuss your ability to communicate on the job. What are your strengths? Your problem areas?
4. Identify your communication goals for the coming year.
5. Repeat this exercise annually.

"Same Time Next Year"

1. This exercise should be conducted on the same day of every year. It will give you an opportunity to plot your communication-skills development in the main arenas of your life.
2. On a photocopy of the chart that follows, use a pen or pencil of one color to plot your personal communication abilities and another color to plot your professional communication abilities. Label each line with this year's date. Redraw the lines each year as necessary, or reproduce the graph for each year's self-examination.
3. What do your "life lines" reveal about your ability to communicate effectively in each of these arenas?
4. Identify factors that might account for the stability and/or the change in your arena life lines.

Under an old and twisty bough.
It's mine, it's mine, it's mine at last. . . .
What do I search for now?

We hope we have provided you with the impetus to continue to develop your communication skills. You now have a body of knowledge and

"SAME TIME NEXT YEAR" EVALUATION CHART

Year: _____

Color Code:

Professional Life _____

Personal Life _____

	Self-concept	Per-ception	Listening	Non-verbal	Verbal	Assertion	Inter-viewing	Group problem solving	Public speaking
High skill 5 mastery									
4									
3									
2									
Low skill 1 mastery									

a series of exercises you can use to gain a better understanding of yourself, of others, and of the relationships you share. Certainly, we have not covered everything there is to say about communication. However, we think the materials in this text will help make each of you a more effective communicator.

Since communication occupies most of your time, it makes sense to try to do it well. Good luck!

SUMMARY

Developing your ability to communicate is a lifelong task. For that reason, it is important that you make a commitment to continue improving your communication abilities even though this particular course is ending.

A number of strategies can help you: (1) Be prepared to adapt your communication strategies to changes in your life. (2) Guard against frozen evaluations. (3) Avoid "non-change" excuses. (4) Analyze how your "people environment" affects the nature of your interactions. (5) Use the Checkbacks we provide to monitor your progress.

SUGGESTIONS FOR FURTHER READING

Bolles, Richard Nelson. *The Three Boxes of Life*. Berkeley, Calif.: Ten Speed Press, 1979. A valuable resource for job hunters and job changers.

Bolles, Richard Nelson. *What Color Is Your Parachute?* Berkeley, Calif.: Ten Speed Press, 1978. A best-selling career and self-development guide.

Gillies, Jerry. *Friends: The Power and Potential of the Company You Keep*. New York: Barnes & Noble, 1976. A thorough discussion of the various aspects of friendship. Contains useful suggestions on how to assess the nature of your own friendships and relationships.

Heller, Robert. *Super Self: The Art and Science of Self-Management*. New York: Atheneum/SMI, 1979. A practical guide to self-control and self-development.

Moore, Charles Guy. *The Career Game*. New York: Ballantine Books, 1976. A career development handbook. Describes strategies that can be used to analyze career alternatives and market yourself.

O'Neill, Nena, and George O'Neill. *Open Marriage: A New Life Style for Couples*. New York: Avon Books, 1972. A provocative and insightful discussion about how couples communicate.

O'Neill, Nena, and George O'Neill. *Shifting Gears*. New York: Avon Books, 1974. Describes strategies for achieving personal potential.

Satir, Virginia. *Peoplemaking*. Palo Alto, Calif.: Science and Behavior Books, 1972. A book on how to develop a healthy, supportive family communication system. Contains good exercises.

Sheehy, Gail. *Passages: Predictable Crises of Adult Life*. New York: Dutton, 1976. A best-seller; identifies changes and strains in person-to-person relationships that occur during life stages.

Viscott, David. *How to Live with Another Person*. New York: Arbor House, 1974. A useful, practical work.

Wahlroos, Sven. *Family Communication: A Guide to Emotional Health*. New York: New American Library, 1974. A useful guide. Emphasizes the role communication plays in relationships; offers 20 rules to help improve the quality of interpersonal contacts.

Answer Key

Blindering Problem (p. 71)

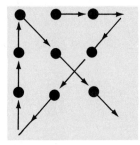

The Detective (p. 74)

1.	?	7.	?
2.	?	8.	?
3.	F	9.	?
4.	?	10.	?
5.	?	11.	?
6.	T		

The States (p. 255)

1.	Maine	8.	Illinois	15.	Colorado
2.	New York	9.	Mississippi	16.	New Mexico
3.	New Jersey	10.	Wisconsin	17.	Wyoming
4.	Delaware	11.	Arkansas	18.	Utah
5.	Ohio	12.	Minnesota	19.	Idaho
6.	Georgia	13.	Oklahoma	20.	Washington
7.	Alabama	14.	North Dakota		

Lost on the Moon (p. 264)

1. Two 100-pound tanks of oxygen (necessary for breathing)
2. Five gallons of water (necessary to replace fluid lost due to perspiration, etc.)
3. Stellar map of Moon's constellations (necessary to find directions)
4. Food concentrate (supplies daily food requirements)
5. Solar-powered FM receiver-transmitter (can transmit a distress signal)
6. Nylon rope (50 feet) (good for tying injured; also helps in climbing)
7. First-aid kit with injection needles (medicine and bandages may be needed)
8. Parachute silk (can be used for shelter from the sun's rays)
9. Life raft (could function as a self-propulsion device)
10. Signal flares (could be used as a distress signal)
11. Two .45-caliber pistols (could make self-propulsion devices from them)
12. One case of dehydrated milk (provides food; can be mixed with water for drinking)
13. Portable heating unit (useful only if the party landed on the dark side of the Moon)
14. Magnetic compass (almost useless, since the Moon probably has no magnetic poles)
15. One box of matches (useless on the Moon)

Adapted from a release of the National Aeronautic and Space Administration (NASA).

Index